KU-607-371

contents

 introduction

We hope that you find this book a useful resource for you in your current care practice, and in your development as a care worker. Whatever area of care or support that you are involved in, this book aims to provide you with ideas based on theories and research, models of good practice, and information about policy that will enable you to work more effectively with people. The book is organised into chapters which can either be read in order or you may like to start with a chapter that particularly interests you. The glossary at the back will assist you if you come across new words or phrases that you are unfamiliar with; many of these are explored in depth in the chapters.

Chapter 1 Context of care focuses on the organisation of social care services and explores some of the political issues that effect change in the way care is delivered. It looks at the historical background to community care and some of the factors that influence the current provision of social care. We investigate the legislative framework of care and look at funding arrangements.

Chapter 2 Reflective practice. Recent years have seen more attention paid to standards in care practice; in order for us all to address this we need to think about our own care practice and identify how we can improve. The chapter provides some models of reflection and looks at theories of learning.

Chapter 3 Values in care practice covers important themes such as the principles that should guide our care practice. The chapter explores aspects of individuality that we need to consider if we are going to respond to individual care needs. It looks at some ideas relating to how care workers should understand their role in promoting the rights of individuals. The chapter presents policy and legislation that shapes current ideas about the values that should inform care work.

Chapter 4 Working with service users also investigates different aspects of the relationship between carers and users. The relationship you have with service users and the activities that you carry out with them will depend on the support needs of individuals and what your care worker role is.

Chapter 5 Collaborative working. Whatever service you work for it is unlikely that you work in isolation. There is an increasing expectation that organisations work in partnership with each other in order to secure continuity in care delivery. The chapter looks at partnership working in relation to organisations, and also effective collaboration between individual professionals.

Chapter 6 Assessment investigates good practice in the assessment of individuals. In order to respond well to people's care or support needs we need to identify what their needs are. The chapter considers current policy relating to assessment, introduces models of assessment and discusses some of the key issues that arise when assessing people. It identifies what skills you require in order to assess people effectively.

Chapter 7 Adult protection. The chapter explores some of the reasons why people who use care services can be particularly vulnerable to abuse. It discusses theories of why people do abuse those that they are providing care or support for. The chapter also looks at the responsibilities of all care workers to ensure that good care practice prevents situations of abuse from arising.

Chapter 8 Planning and reviewing services. Responding to assessed need is usually carried out through a care plan and this chapter explores stages in this planning process. The chapter informs you of the policies and guidance that indicate how care planning should take place. It also provides guidance in order to develop your skills in planning and reviewing care with the people that you are responsible for.

Features of the book

Each chapter has the following features that are designed to help you in your reading.

- ⤴ *Case studies*   The case studies in the book cover many care settings and service user groups. They are designed to illustrate a point made in the main text, or to help explain a particular issue. If the case study does not seem particularly relevant to your own area of care practice then you might want to reflect on a real work situation to help you develop your understanding of the chapter.
- ⤴ *Think it over*   These are a useful tool to help you explore some of the themes discussed in the chapter. They encourage you to focus on a topic and think about it in more depth.
- ⤴ *Check your understanding*   These questions should assist you in reflecting on what you have just read in order to consolidate your understanding before moving on to a new topic.

Glossary

If you come across a word or phrase in a chapter and you are not sure what it means then you can see if it is explained in the glossary. If it is not in the glossary it may be useful to look it up in any ordinary dictionary.

Terminology

The language used in social care dialogue changes regularly. The phrase 'service user/s' is used to refer to individuals or groups of people who use social care services.

Relationship of the book to care qualifications

This book can be useful for a number of care qualifications. At the back of the book is a grid detailing the relationship of this book to the Care Level 4 NVQ award. If you are studying for the Learning Disability Awards Framework, Certificate in Mental Health Care, you will find this book a useful resource. As the book is an HE level text it will also be a useful resource if you are studying for a degree in social work or any care-based foundation degree.

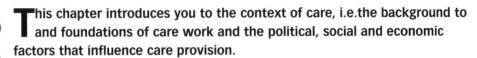

context of care

1

This chapter introduces you to the context of care, i.e.the background to and foundations of care work and the political, social and economic factors that influence care provision.

Care work is affected by many aspects of society and so takes place in a context. If we were discussing care in a particular time period or in a particular country, there would be a different focus on the way that care is provided. The meaning of the word 'care' is also influential. Do we mean doing things for people, providing support and services to them or promoting their rights so they feel enabled themselves?

It is important to acknowledge that the political and legislative context of care is very fluid; this changes all the time and creates an environment in the care sector in which change is a constant feature. As care workers we should make sure we are aware of current issues and debates about care provision so that we are up to date.

The legislation and policies referred to in this chapter relate to England, but sometimes legislation specifies that there are specific differences for Wales and Scotland. In Wales the Welsh Assembly promotes policies within the boundaries of legislation passed at Westminster. In Scotland devolution has facilitated the creation of law-making processes through the Scottish Parliament. Devolution has led to interesting debates within the field of care, for example the Scottish Parliament made a statement providing free personal care for people, which fuelled the debate south of the border.

This chapter addresses the following areas:

- ⮑ Brief history of the development of care services
- ⮑ Factors influencing the provision of care
- ⮑ The current provision of care
- ⮑ Informal care
- ⮑ Respite care
- ⮑ The policy framework
- ⮑ Health and social care services
- ⮑ Implementing policy
- ⮑ Identifying what people need from care services
- ⮑ Primary care trusts
- ⮑ Funding
- ⮑ Current issues in the provision of care
- ⮑ Regulation and inspection

After reading this chapter it is hoped you will be able to:

1 understand the current organisation of care services
2 consider issues relating to the provision of care services
3 know key legislation that informs the current provision of care
4 understand the range of factors that impact on care.

Brief history of the development of care services

That care is a changing environment is illustrated by looking back at the development of care services over the last century and more.

Nineteenth century

In the early part of the 19th century people were encouraged to support their families due to lack of structured provision outside of family life. Older people who were unable to look after themselves were cared for by their families, particularly their children. Those without appropriate family support were looked after in workhouses. These institutions provided assistance to live and health care on the basis that the residents were still able to work – an early form of occupational welfare! There were also charitable organisations established by philanthropists, who had the social position and wealth to help support the welfare of local people. Learning disabled people and those with mental ill health were housed in large institutions known as asylums. Older people were gradually living longer during this period and many older women were placed in the asylums because there was nowhere else appropriate. However the rising infant mortality rate was an issue, so public health gradually became a key issue in terms of housing, sanitation, etc.

The following are statistics on the numbers of people being cared for in asylums in mid-nineteenth century.

	Patients in asylum (in year)		
Year	1844	1860	1870
Total numbers of people in institutions	11,272	23,717	35,163

The notion of the care that should be provided can be ascertained from the following quote about an institution for those with mental illness:

> It is a vast and straggling building ... The gates are kept by an official who is attired in a garb as nearly as possible like that of a gaoler. All the male attendants are made to display the same forbidding uniform. [Mortimer Granville on Hanwell Asylum, London 1877, in Scull (1979), page 195]

Twentieth century

There was a growth in the development of hospitals at the end of the 19th century. In the 20th century, after World War One, there was a policy potential for extending National Health Insurance and increasing the use of local authority services, but this was not taken up. In 1929 local authorities could take over the Poor Law infirmaries as municipal hospitals, however this only happened in practice in London.

The demography of a population affects how people perceive the need to care for people. We are often told of the age time bomb, as our population gets older. It is viewed in a negative rather than a positive way.

1900–1920

This period saw the beginning of the development of a structure to comprehensive social policies that covered a wide range of areas in people's lives. There had been an economic recession, which meant there was limited public provision of care, however this did not meet the demands of society.

1920–late 1940s

This period ended with the development of the welfare state in Britain, the National Health Service and the local authority structure for social care. World War Two had a huge impact on this country and how succeeding governments approached welfare. The emergency medical services had been set up to respond to the casualties of war. Before this only hospital services had been discussed. However in 1942 the Beveridge Report *Social Insurance and Allied Services* set out the aims of tackling the 'five giants' or 'social evils' of welfare. This was a comprehensive and holistic approach to developing the well-being of individuals.

The five giants were:
1 Want   (Poverty)
2 Ignorance (Education)
3 Squalor   (Housing)
4 Idleness   (Employment)
5 Disease   (Health)

Think it over

When you consider the modern equivalents of the above terms, how do they link together in relation to health and social care, and the lives of the people that you support?

A White Paper in 1944, *A National Health Service,* led to the 1946 National Health Service Act. Hospitals were nationalised under the control of the government, and a tripartite system of care was launched with hospitals, local authorities and general practitioners. The system focused on regional planning and diversity. Interestingly it had been envisaged that local authorities would play a leading role in co-ordinating the delivery of this structure, and that this would involve having responsibility for health centres; but for various reasons this did not happen. The focus of the government remained on the acute hospital sector, which was aided by a rise in medical specialities and medicine. The NHS was also responsible for the chronic hospital sector where people with learning disabilities and mental ill-health were housed, separated from the rest of society, often since childhood. In these institutions there was a very different understanding of what was needed in terms of support, and individuals were managed rather than cared for; there was no notion of these individuals having rights.

1950s–1960s

Government spending on welfare increased during this period. This was encouraged by support from the public and by the need to care for those who had fought or participated in the war.

1970s–1980s

The cost of delivering welfare under the NHS far exceeded the various estimates that were made between 1948 and 1974. After this time different governments sought to control these costs. During the 1980s the Conservative government aimed to privatise welfare provision by introducing the idea of a market approach to developing and delivering services. They identified that there were too many costs involved in local authorities directly providing care to people through the current system.

1990s

The Conservative Party in the 1990s changed the balance between the state monopoly of welfare, with the majority of services being provided by the National Health Service, and the local authority social services departments. They developed a market style approach to welfare, by encouraging private businesses to develop their capacity for providing care. This has been continued by the Labour Party since 1997, and remains a strong theme.

The development of community care

Community care or residential care?

Community care usually refers to the provision of care and support to people in the community (rather than in hospitals or large institutions). The phrase 'in the community' can mean a number of things, from people being cared for in their own homes and accessing usual community-based care services to being cared for in homes housing groups of people who live together with support. As long ago as 1971, the Commission on Mental Illness recommended community care for 'people diagnosed as mentally ill and mentally handicapped'. The structure of health and social care services at the time could have supported a substantial change from people living in asylums, as domiciliary teams did exist with home nurses, home helps and meals services (a limited provision by voluntary organisations). However, this change never materialised and discussions about community care continued.

Domiciliary care is central to community care if community-based care means individuals living in their own homes. The policy in 1971, *Better Services for the Mentally Handicapped,* called for an expansion of residential homes, rather than discussing the planning of these home-based services.

What community care means has been regularly contested. The original idea may have involved only own home-based care, however the concept of community care was redefined to include residential care. The effect of this was that 39,000 new local authority homes were opened between 1948 and1960, predominantly for older people. This indicated a lack of a clear policy as to what community care was going to mean for individual service users. Discussions on community care ignored the existence of informal carers and their role, there was no policy relating to carers and how to support them in their role in providing community-based care.

However, with an increasing number of well-publicised scandals regarding treatment of individuals in institutions, such as the exposure of bad practices at Ely Hospital in 1968, there were calls for a review of policy.

Think it over

Individual own home or group care in the community?

Each person is an individual and should have their individual circumstances looked at when establishing whether they should be provided with support in their own home, or move to a care home. Think generally about the advantages and disadvantages of each care setting for

- ⊃ the individual in need of support
- ⊃ the organisation responsible for providing care
- ⊃ relatives of the individual.

The closure of institutions may indicate problems in implementing policy. There was a time when the NHS was reluctant to close long-stay mental health and learning disabled hospitals. The policy of closing them down only gathered momentum in the 1980s when health authorities were given a financial incentive by the Conservative government to close their large institutions and sell the land. However, today there are still people being cared for in these larger institutions. The *Valuing People* White Paper specified that those remaining in such institutions should be found alternative appropriate homes by April 2004.

The following table illustrates the changes in the provision of accommodation in care homes by the NHS and local authorities, as private and voluntary organisations assumed more responsibility for opening up care homes.

Number of beds	1985	1995
	(in thousands)	
NHS elderly care beds	55	37
NHS mental health care beds	97	50
NHS learning disabled care beds	50	18
Local authority residential home beds	116	64
Subtotal	*318*	*169*
Private/voluntary residential home beds	117	213
Private/voluntary nursing home beds	27	115
Subtotal	*144*	*328*
Total	462	497

[Webster in Webster (2001), page 221]

Case Study

Living together in the community

Freddie was born in 1942. At the time the doctors told his parents that he would not be able to do anything in his life; he was mentally retarded.

Freddie was placed in Willow Grange Hospital, a very large hospital in the countryside. He lived with other children and was cared for by nurses.

In 1992 Freddie moved from Willow Grange Hospital to a hostel, where he lived with 11 others; some of the people he had lived with moved with him, and there were also others there. Freddie attended a local day centre, he had a key worker and reviews, and this led him to identify that he wanted to move when an opportunity arose.

Freddie has now moved to a new home. He calls it his home as he helped to choose it. He lives just with two other men whom he gets on with. Although Freddie will always need support in his life, he has a very different experience to what he had in his early life.

Although the idea of people living in the community is valued, there has been extensive criticism of the manner in which community care was introduced.

Taken overall, the policy of care in the community failed because it left some people vulnerable, others a threat to themselves or a nuisance to others, with a small minority a danger to the public. With the dedication of staff it did, though, bring many beneficial changes to the care and treatment of people with mental illness. Sheltered employment and rehabilitation programmes were developed, and new drugs were discovered. During the past thirty years, many people left the Victorian asylums for a better quality of life in their own neighbourhoods with support from community-based staff. [Department of Health (1999), page 24]

Factors influencing the provision of care

Here we explore what influences the lives of individuals who use care services. Care relates to individual people, who, just like you and I, are affected by the place we live and how long we live there. Many factors affect people's lives. For those who need care these include

⊃ social exclusion

⊃ resources

⊃ structure of care organisations and services

⊃ the relationships between care services and other organisations.

Social exclusion

Many people who require care or support in their lives, experience social exclusion. 'The poorest in society seem often not to have benefited greatly from government intervention in social and economic matters.' [Malin *et al* (2002), page 44]

The low benefit take up has compounded the problems of social exclusion. 'If carers don't get the right support then their health suffers and it leads to poverty and isolation.' [Redmond (2003)]

The Joseph Rowntree Foundation undertakes research into the welfare of people in the UK. Its report, *Being and Becoming: Social Exclusion and the Onset of Disability* [Burchardt (2003)] identified the following statistics relating to poverty and need:

⊃ The poorest 20% of the population, based on income, are two and a half times more likely to become disabled than the wealthiest 20%.

⊃ People with lower educational qualifications are more likely to become disabled.

⊃ Risk of disability is higher for those not in work or in lower status jobs.

Governments have a responsibility to make sure that people are provided with an environment that addresses these problems; the challenge for policy makers is in ensuring that the ideas and strategies that they come up with address what are known as the determinants of ill-health and disability.

In the past health and social care have been seen as quite separate areas of activity. A recent White Paper, *Modern Local Government: In Touch With The People*, revisited the notion that social care is a very separate area of activity in people's lives. It made it clear that local authorities need to stop thinking in this way if they are to 'promote the economic, environmental and social well-being of all their citizens'. This reflects that a person's well-being cannot be secured through either housing or social services, but needs a more comprehensive and holistic approach.

Political ideas

The Labour government has taken a 'third way' approach to care, balancing social provision for those in need with private enterprise. Traditional socialist views promote the provision of support for those in need based on the redistribution of resources. These ideas are now contested. Political ideas may be based on the values of a political party but recent years have seen a changing emphasis.

When policy is being determined, values will influence both the overall idea of the policy and the detail. Questions may arise which will inform the development of policy such as:

⊃ What responsibility should family members have for supporting their relatives?

⊃ Do professionals know best or should patients/service users have a say in the care they receive?

⊃ Who should pay for this service?

⊃ Should this service be provided to everyone or just a few?

Structure of care organisations and services

There is often a tension between central and local government. Central government sets the agenda for local governments and establishes mechanisms for them to obtain funds, either through local council taxes or through central grants.

The Labour government (1997–) says that they want to promote a 'philosophy of devolution and earned autonomy' [Crown (2002), page 32]. They state that they plan for more local decision-making through local government, but there has also been accusation of more centralised presidential type control.

Resources

Budgets

On a national scale governments are bound by the constraints placed on spending by the Treasury. The money committed to public services is always hotly contested at election time. Governments have to balance what they say they can spend on certain things against what the public expects or wants them to do.

Facilities

The availability of facilities influences the provision of appropriate services. Sometimes services are provided using existing resources. We mentioned earlier that the White Paper *Valuing People* set a deadline of April 2004 for the last remaining learning disabled individuals to leave long-stay institutions. However, this date has been amended as there is not appropriate provision available in the community to address the needs of these people. Facilities have an impact on care. Some of the failings of the general policy of community care have been ascribed to the lack of facilities that were available to respond to this policy. Resources were not sufficient to compensate for the lack of established facilities.

Professional skills

The skills of professionals also have an impact on the type of care that can be provided. The current need for nursing type care in the community has put pressure on district nursing services, and is an issue for domiciliary care services. This chapter later looks at what is required of the care worker in terms of their skills and knowledge, and what policies have been developed to influence what we do as care workers.

Relationship of care services to other organisations

It is worth considering how care services link to other services that aim to support people in need. You may work for an organisation that supports people as to any of the following.

Alcohol and substance use

People who use care or support services sometimes find it difficult to manage areas of their lives, and this can develop into abuse or addiction to substances that are harmful to them. Addictions can cause people to behave in ways that harms themselves or others. It can also have a negative impact on their physical or mental health, or lead them into illegal behaviour.

Criminal justice system

The criminal justice system has to provide a balance between care and control, punishment and rehabilitation. The feeling at the moment is that there is a stronger emphasis on control, which has moved the criminal justice system away from other care services.

The 2003 Mental Health Bill regarding mentally disordered offenders states

- ⊃ the need for the courts to be able to make an order for treatment in the community instead of a criminal justice disposal
- ⊃ the difficulty in balancing the safety of the individual from harming themselves and/or others
- ⊃ the need for protection of the individual from harm by others, including discrimination
- ⊃ the need for therapeutic treatment and rehabilitation
- ⊃ the need to recognise that some people may not be able to benefit from treatment but still require support in a secure environment.

Housing

The relationship between housing and care provision is one of two things. Firstly, people's circumstances are strongly influenced by their home situation. Secondly, care services are being provided through the Supported Living agenda to promote appropriate housing solutions for people with mental health needs, or those who are learning disabled.

The benefits system

Benefits sometimes provide a means for individuals accessing particular support. There is a strong association between disability, older age and poverty. Many people do not claim the benefits that they are entitled to. This may be due to

- ⊃ the stigma

⊃ inability to understand the application process

⊃ inability to complete forms due to language and sight

⊃ inability to access information

⊃ social isolation, which can mean that people do not see adverts in libraries.

Health care

The origins of the welfare state saw locally based family services as the cornerstone of welfare provision. The alignment between health services and social care is affected by the structures and funding of care services. There is more recognition now that a holistic approach is being taken of the need to incorporate the health care and social care needs of individuals. The introduction of the single assessment process was an attempt to address this. A strong theme in this chapter and throughout the book is the overlap of social care with health.

Children and young people's services

The Special Educational Needs and Disability Act 2001 is the most recent legislation requiring children and adults to have their individual needs met in the education sector. This will have an impact on the status and role of disabled people in the future as they are not routinely segregated. This is supported by the *Valuing People* White Paper, which states that one aim is to 'help integrate disabled children into mainstream leisure and out of school services' [Department of Health (2001), page 33].

Transitions from children services to adult services can be problematic. The Child and Adolescent Mental Health Services (CAMHS) was developed in response to gaps in the service for some adolescents.

Connexions is the service created for 13–19-year-olds who will be provided with a personal adviser to support them. The *Valuing People* White Paper discusses the issue of transition to adult life in relation to learning disabled people.

Connexions partnerships will need to be responsible for liaising with the Learning and Skills Council and the Employment Service to review appropriate transition and ensure continuity. Arrangements can stay in place if appropriate until the person's 25th birthday. Adult social services departments are responsible. [Department of Health (2001), page 42]

The current provision of care

Structure of care services

Figure 1.1 *Department of Health responsibilities*

Figure 1.2 *Relationship between central government and organisations and authorities engaged in care*

Organisations involved in the provision of care

Statutory provision

This is usually considered to incorporate providers of care services who have a statutory duty to provide services because of their relationship to central government. Two key players in this arena have always been

⊃ local authority managed social services departments

⊃ the National Health Service.

In the past the NHS has been responsible for health care, and social services have been responsible for social care. They have interacted where professionals have needed to work together in relation to particular service users.

The Health Act 1999 and the Health and Social Care Act 2001 have challenged the responsibilities of these organisations in relation to each other. In some areas the local health trust takes on the work that has been carried out by the local authority through its social services departments. Where organisations commission other organisations to perform certain functions they may still retain the statutory responsibility for ensuring their suitability.

In other areas the local authority has merged its departments to form social care and housing departments. This area is still developing, and localities are restructuring based on local need and experience.

Think it over

In your own locality investigate the established or proposed changes to social services departments and think about the following:

1 What plans do the local NHS trusts have for the area?
2 How will these changes affect the individuals that you work with?

Independent providers

Whilst there have always been independent providers in the form of charities these types of providers are no longer on the periphery of care service delivery. Since the NHS and Community Care Act 1990, the creation of the internal market has allowed and encouraged independent organisations to establish a niche in the care market. Some of these providers were established voluntary organisations, others were private businesses. These organisations might remain as small concerns with perhaps one home, or they may develop into large established businesses.

Whilst independent organisations are now mainstream providers of social care services there have been tensions about the provision of care by non-public agencies; some people would prefer services to people to remain funded by and provided by publicly managed and delivered organisations.

Not-for-profit organisations

These are companies established to provide a particular service. They act as independent businesses but all their profits are invested in the organisation to benefit the service they provide.

Private organisations

The care industry is big business and some organisations have developed their capacity to operate within the care sector by expanding the services that they provide, or the region that they provide to. These organisations assume responsibility for the delivery of care on the basis of contracts, either with local authorities, or directly with individuals who need care services.

Voluntary

A definition of the voluntary sector is that it 'covers formally constituted organisations, managed by unpaid committees, that are not part of the state or the market or the informal world of spontaneous or unstructured action. The term includes organisations with paid staff; they can trade, but not distribute profits. Their objectives are generally taken as being to enhance public benefit.' [Alcock (1998), page 162]

Charities

Charities are voluntary organisations that have been formally registered by The Charity Commission, which then regulates them. Some charities, but not all, operate to provide a service to the public; some of these provide care-related activities.

Some charities operate as large businesses with a pressure group remit, that 'in modern times have played an increasingly influential and continuous role in the political process... they are not democratically accountable to the general public. It is the political parties which have to accept that form of responsibility and which are vulnerable to the verdict of the electorate at every General Election, and at other elections to a lesser extent as well.' [Forman and Baldwin (1996)]

Charities play a key role in the development of services for people. Some registered charities are service user groups managed by disabled people or those with mental health issues. They may respond to policy discussion documents – this activity has been made more accessible with new technology. Any individual can access recent documents via the internet and can usually submit comments to the Minister about them.

Community groups

In recent years there has been an emphasis on community groups who may or may not work in a formal manner to provide some form of support to local people. Community organisations have a valuable role to play in meeting the people who need services. Sometimes statutory services have been found lacking in their ability to engage with some people in their locality, due to cultural perceptions, language or lack of appropriate access to the community communication network.

Volunteers

This covers much support activity that takes place both informally and in a structured way managed carefully by organisations. There are many assumptions made about volunteers. They may work for voluntary organisations, statutory services or private businesses. An individual may be formally contracted as a volunteer and be expected to undertake a certain number of hours or activities within that contract. Alternatively, a volunteer may provide support in a more flexible manner with no obligation to turn up at a particular time or perform any required tasks.

Some volunteers will receive expenses or 'pocket money' payment to carry out a certain role. Other volunteers do not access any funds for the work that they carry out.

Recent National Minimum Wage and Working Time Directives have required some organisations to review their approach to having volunteers.

Informal care

This type of care refers to the care that is delivered to individuals by relatives, neighbours, or friends. The word informal is misleading, as this type of care is very often substantial in terms of both time and type of activity, and may be permanent and ongoing. A carer is someone who 'provides or intends to provide a substantial amount of care on a regular basis' [Carers (Recognition and Services) Act 1995].

Carers do not always recognise that they are entitled to support; the charity Carers UK estimate that £660 million of carers allowance is not claimed each year [Community Care (11 Dec 2003)]. For years many people have been providing care to relatives without recognising themselves as carers. 'A crucial step in addressing the needs of carers is recognition.' [Seddon and Robinson (2001), page 157]

The census in 2000 recognised the need for the government to identify the extent of informal caring that was taking place in individuals' homes. As care workers we are employed (either paid or unpaid) to perform a certain role with individuals who need care or support. Many people live with family members who need support; they do not even identify themselves as carers as they see the role that they are carrying out as an extension of the family relationship.

The nature of work undertaken by informal carers includes:

- ⊃ *Personal care* – washing, bathing, dressing, and general attention to physical needs and comforts
- ⊃ *Domestic care* – cooking, cleaning and laundering
- ⊃ *Auxiliary care* – baby-sitting, child-minding, shopping, transport, odd-jobbing, gardening, borrowing and lending
- ⊃ *Social support* – visiting and companionship
- ⊃ *Surveillance* – 'keeping an eye on' vulnerable people

[Abbotts and Ackers (1996), page 167]

Case Study

Informal carers

Grace

Grace is 23 years old. She moved here from Trinidad five years ago to live with her 83-year-old grandmother. Grace helps her grandmother to get up in the morning and makes sure that she has something for her lunch whilst Grace goes to work. Grace was grateful that her grandmother wanted her to come and live with her so she does not mind helping her at home.

Mr and Mrs MacDonald

Mr and Mrs MacDonald are in their 60s. They have three children, one of whom, Nicholas, lives at home with them. He is learning disabled and needs support with many of his usual home and personal care activities.

Holly

Holly is 20 years old. She has been caring for her mum who has had multiple sclerosis for two years. Her mother has not coped well with the deterioration in her capabilities and she is a regular drinker, which affects her mood; she gets cross with Holly if Holly refuses to buy her any alcohol. Holly has lost contact with many of her friends as they have gone to university. Holly works part-time at a local baker's so that she can spend a lot of time with her mum.

Questions

1 With each of the above families, identify what the needs of the following people might be:
    ⊃ The person with care/support needs.
    ⊃ The carer/s.
2 What services are available to support these families?
3 What professionals could work with these families to enable them to manage their situations better?

Further Research

Investigate the work of the Carers National Association and the website for Carers UK to explore the extent of caring that occurs in this country and the types of support that are available.

The government's carers strategy

The government has attempted to address the needs of carers through the carers strategy. However there are reservations about the success of this policy and its implementation.

> The modest rights conferred upon carers are compromised by a lack of funding and there appears to be a divergence between policy and practice in crucial areas, for instance informing carers of their rights to assessment.
> [Arksey and Hepworth (1999) in Seddon and Robinson (2001)]

The Labour government's approach to supporting carers includes:

Information
    ⊃ Charter outlining expectations and standards of long-term care
    ⊃ Consistency in charging of services
    ⊃ Health information
    ⊃ NHS direct helpline
    ⊃ Internet information.

Support
    ⊃ Carers' involvement in planning and providing services
    ⊃ Consultation with carers' organisations.

Care
    ⊃ Right to have health needs met
    ⊃ Local authority powers to provide services to carers

⊃ Emphasis on carers' breaks, £140 million targeted funds

⊃ Financial support for working carers.

Legislation to support carers

The legislation to support carers includes the Carers (Recognition and Services) Act 1995 and the Carers and Disabled Children Act 2000.

The carers grant that is provided centrally has been used in different ways by local authorities. The following is an example of this.

The Kirkby Carers Resource Centre provides

⊃ focus of support for carers in the borough

⊃ two three-hourly evening sessions each week

⊃ carers voucher scheme

⊃ carers support worker to the most vulnerable.

[Social Services Inspectorate (2002), page 12]

The Labour government produced the carers national strategy document *Caring About Carers* in February 1999. This has been supported by legislation such as the Carers and Disabled Children Act 2000:

> Great Britain has an estimated 5.7 million carers and one in six households (17%) contains a carer. Of the estimated 5.7 million carers, 1.7million devote at least 20 hours a week to caring. Of those, 855,000 care for 50 hours or more. [Crown (1999), 'Explanatory Notes to Carers and Disabled Children Act 2000', page 80]

> The Act makes four principal changes to the law with the objective of enabling local authorities to offer new support to carers to help them to maintain their own health and well-being.

Carers are entitled to an assessment independently of the person that they provide care for. As a result of this assessment they may be provided with the carers allowance.

Respite care

Respite care is care provided on a temporary, although very often regular, basis. Direct Payments has enabled individuals to target care as required. For example, a care user can employ short-term support to cover for their carer who needs to have a break, or they may move into a care home where they can have appropriate support. Many care homes have beds for respite care. The advantages are that the family carer is able to have a break knowing that their relative is in a supportive care environment and they do not need to worry about them.

Respite care can be arranged through a local authority care manager or may be arranged directly with a respite care provider.

A study by Nicoll *et al* identified the following:

Social support during respite care may have given the carer a sense of returning to normal life.

Support during caring may have been a means to share the emotional or physical burdens, leaving the carer more able to enjoy the respite period. [(2002), page 482]

The policy framework

What is policy?

In order for care services to be delivered the way the government intends, the Department of Health has to devise written statements about what should happen. These statements are written as policy documents, guidelines or pieces of legislation, depending on whether the law needs to change to accommodate the new ideas. An example of a policy statement from the government outlining their plans for the future is the NHS Plan. This document provides a comprehensive framework for the development of smaller policies. Policies relating to health and well-being have since referred to the Plan.

Legislation

For a policy document to become law it has to progress through the Houses of Parliament, the Commons and the Lords, and receive Royal Assent. An Act is a legal document that provides

Permissive powers

'An organisation may…' This allows an organisation or person to carry out certain functions with the support of legislation.

Statutory duties

'An organisation shall…' This specifies what individuals or organisations are required to do.

The Care Standards Act was a piece of legislation setting out the formal arrangements for the inspection of standards within care services. The legislation allows the government to make changes to the current organisation of regulation and inspection. It gives new organisations both duties and powers to undertake particular work activity.

Policy statements

A White Paper is a policy statement relating to a particular aspect of government. The objectives contained within a White Paper do not always require legislation; it may be possible to carry out their contents within the current framework of the law and so no further legislation is required. Whilst they are not legally binding documents, there is a strong expectation that the contents of a White Paper are taken on board by individual authorities. There is sometimes disappointment that a White Paper is not continued in development to become an Act of Parliament. This was true of the *Valuing People* White Paper:

This very broad ranging document on learning disability set out guidelines for how services should be organised, and what people with a learning disability should expect from care services.

Policies sometimes have a variety of agendas that they aim to address. They link in with each other. For example, all current policies should aim to

⊃ promote the involvement of service users in planning

⊃ respond to human rights and equality legislation

⊃ acknowledge the health and social services agenda

⊃ develop partnership with the independent sector.

The context of care is influenced by legislation that applies to the following areas:

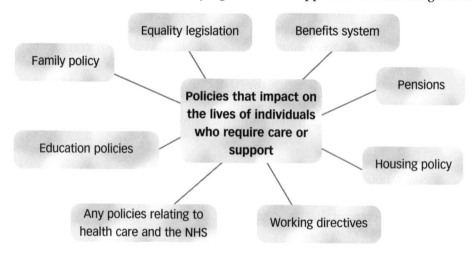

Figure 1.3 *Areas of care influenced by legislation*

Since the Labour Party came to power in 1997 they have introduced a range of legislation that has enabled changes to the organisation and delivery of care. The NHS Plan was 'a plan for investment, a plan for reform' and it set out the expectations of change in the provision of care services. It is not specific to the acute health care sector and is therefore relevant to the social care sector as well.

The NHS Plan

This 10-year policy proposal established the following principles:

⊃ The NHS will provide a universal service for all based on clinical need, not ability to pay.

⊃ The NHS will provide a comprehensive range of services.

⊃ The NHS will shape its services around the needs and preferences of individual patients, their families and carers.

⊃ The NHS will respond to different needs of different populations.

⊃ The NHS will work continuously to improve quality services and to minimise errors.

⊃ The NHS will support and value its staff.

⊃ Public funds for health care will be devoted solely to NHS patients.

○ The NHS will work together with others to ensure a seamless service for patients.

○ The NHS will keep people healthy and work to reduce health inequalities.

○ The NHS will respect the confidentiality of individual patients and provide open access to information about services, treatments and performance.

National service frameworks

The National Service Framework for Older People is the key vehicle for ensuring that the needs of older people are at the heart of the reform programme for health and social services. [Department of Health (2001), page 5]

The principles of the National Service Framework for Older People are to

○ assure standards of care

○ extend access to services

○ ensure fairer funding

○ develop services which promote independence

○ help older people to stay healthy

○ develop more effective links between health and social services and other services such as housing, and partners in the voluntary and private sectors.

[Department of Health (2001), page 5]

An example of strategies to implement policy is provided with the National Service Framework for Older People. There are five underpinning programmes that will support local and national implementation:

○ Finance

○ Workforce development

○ Research and development

○ Clinical and practice decision support services

○ Information.

The National Service Framework for Mental Health sets out priorities for this service users group, illustrating the importance of joint working with health services and social care services, and also significantly acknowledging the importance of support for carers.

National Service Framework for Mental Health

Mental health promotion

Standard One:

Health and social services should

○ promote mental health for all, working with individuals and communities

○ combat discrimination against individuals and groups with mental health problems, and promote their social inclusion.   →

Primary care and access to services

Standard Two:

Any service user who contacts their primary health care team with a common mental health problem should

- ⊃ have their mental health needs identified and assessed
- ⊃ be offered effective treatments, including referral to specialist services for further assessment, treatment and care if they require it.

Standard Three:

Any individual with a common mental health problem should

- ⊃ be able to make contact round the clock with the local services necessary to meet their needs and receive adequate care
- ⊃ be able to use NHS Direct as it develops for first level advice and referral on to specialist helplines or to local services.

Effective services for people with severe mental illness

Standard Four:

All mental health service users of CPA should

- ⊃ receive care which optimises engagement, anticipates or prevents a crisis, and reduces risk
- ⊃ have a copy of a written care plan which includes the action to be taken in a crisis by the service user, their carer and their care co-ordinator; advises their GP how they should respond if the service user needs additional help; is regularly reviewed by their care co-ordinator
- ⊃ be able to access services 24 hours a day, 365 days a year.

Standard Five:

Each service user who is assessed as requiring a period of care away from their home should have

- ⊃ timely access to an appropriate hospital bed or alternative bed or place, which is in the least restrictive environment consistent with the need to protect them and the public; as close to home as possible
- ⊃ a copy of a written after-care plan agreed on discharge, which sets out the care to be provided, identifies the care co-ordinator, and specifies the action to be taken in a crisis.

Caring about carers

Standard Six:

All individuals who provide regular and substantial care for a person on CPA should have

- ⊃ an assessment of their caring, physical and mental health needs, repeated on at least an annual basis
- ⊃ their own written care plan which is given to them and implemented in discussion with them. →

Preventing suicide

Standard Seven:

Local health and social care communities should prevent suicides by

➲ promoting mental health for all, working with individuals and communities

➲ delivering high quality primary mental health care

➲ ensuring that anyone with a mental health problem can contact local services via the primary care team, a helpline or an A&E department

➲ ensuring that individuals with severe and enduring mental illness have a care plan which meets their specific needs, including access to services around the clock

➲ providing safe hospital accommodation for individuals who need it

➲ enabling individuals caring for someone with severe mental illness to receive the support which they need to continue to care.

In addition they should

➲ support local prison staff in preventing suicides among prisoners

➲ ensure that staff are competent to assess the risk of suicide among individuals at greatest risk

➲ develop local systems for suicide audit to learn lessons and take any necessary action.

Health and social care services

The NHS Plan identified that 'if patients are to receive the best care, then the old divisions between health and social care need to be overcome' (Section 7.1).

This section explores the legislation that has had a significant impact on the organisation of the care sector, especially in relation to the changing boundaries of health and social care. At a strategic level there was the creation of four new regional directors of health and social care posts. They are responsible for

➲ overseeing the development of the NHS and social care

➲ assessing performance

➲ managing the appointment, development and succession planning of senior management staff, and supporting ministers and troubleshooting.

Key legislation relating to the merging of health care and social care includes the Health Act 1999 and the Health and Social Care Act 2001.

Health Act 1999

Partnership in Action proposed a new way of working together for health organisations and social care organisations. The Health Act provided the legislation to enable these more flexible ways of working together, especially in relation to the funding of services to people. Previously, funding has been an obstacle to joint working as it provides a complex dimension to organising projects. More opportunities for pooled funding and targeted resources for joint projects provides not only an incentive, but also the mechanism for the merging of health and social care services. The Act facilitates a more proactive approach to joint working and the taking on of responsibilities by one organisation that have previously been delivered by another.

Care Standards Act 2000

> The main purpose of the Act is to reform the regulatory system for care services in England and Wales. [Crown (2000), 'Explanatory Notes to the Care Standards Act', page 34]

This legislation provided a framework for the regulation of care services across a number of care settings and service user groups.

The main points relevant to adult social care are that the Act

1 established the new regulatory body for care services (National Care Standards Commission). It should be noted that this body would become the Commission for Social Care Inspection with the Social Services Inspectorate and the social care responsibilities of the Audit Commission).

2 established the General Social Care Council for

⊃ registration of social care workers

⊃ setting standards in care work

⊃ regulating the education and training of social workers.

3 requires the Secretary of State to maintain a list of individuals considered unsuitable for work with vulnerable adults

⊃ Care organisations must obtain clearance from the Criminal Records Bureau for new employees.

Health and Social Care Act 2001

This legislation established care trusts. Care trusts are the new organisations that assume responsibility for a particular geographical area in relation to a particular area of care.

They may operate with a particular remit for one group, as with mental health trusts, or they may assume more general responsibility across service user groups.

Benefits of care trusts

The benefits of care trusts are

⊃ the development of new approaches to the provision of services by a single body

⊃ a consistent approach to quality improvement by bringing together existing systems to work more effectively

⊃ a single strategic approach, with a single set of aims and targets

⊃ the potential for financial flexibility and efficiency

- better and clearer working arrangements for staff, with more varied career opportunities
- a single management structure, multi-disciplinary teams managed from one point, co-location of staff, as well as single or streamlined cross-disciplinary assessments
- better communication between staff about packages of care. Care Trusts will be in an excellent position to develop a single information system.

The Health and Social Care Joint Unit was established in August 1998 to develop policy on joint working between health and social services. It has focused on issues relating to:

- Continuing care
- NHS funded care
- Delayed discharges.

Modernising Social Services [Department of Health (1998)] specified the use of pooled budgets to promote the potential for integration. Integrated provision was also a feature of the document *Delivering the NHS Plan: Next Steps on Investment, Next Steps on Reform* [Crown (2002)].

The Health and Social Care Change Agent Team was set up in January 2002 to

- help in reducing delayed transfers of care
- support aspects of the NSF that relate to transfers of care
- assist in developing a more integrated service, using the Health Act 1999.

It aims to support the issues arising through what are known as

- *Winter pressures* – the additional numbers of people who experience vulnerability over the winter period, and require care and support services at this time.
- *Bed blocking* – the rather derogatory term given to the group of individuals who are in hospital but who no longer have medical needs and are therefore deemed fit for discharge. The reason for delay in their discharge is sometimes associated with the complexities of arranging care packages in the community where there are constraints on resources, or a lack of, or delay in, services that are available.

The Delayed Discharge Act 2003 which came into full effect in 2004, provided a financial penalty to local authorities for delaying the discharge of a person from hospital. 'If they cannot meet the agreed time limit they will be charged by the local hospital for the costs it incurs in keeping older people in hospital unnecessarily.'

- Costs of readmission.
- Lack of available carers in areas, especially rural areas.
- Lack of resources to supply equipment in preparation for a move home.

The London Borough of Bromley has in the past used additional winter pressures money to provide intensive medical, nursing and therapy care for patients in their own home to 135 people; half of these would have needed admission to hospital without this service, see *Modernising Social Services* [Department of Health (1998)].

One direction in which all this could be leading is the shift of adult services out of local government into the NHS. While official statements deny this intention there is a distinct shift in this direction, perhaps enhanced by the development… of separation of adult social care from child care in some local authorities. [Hill (2003), page 194]

There has also been recognition that the role of professionals within both social care settings and health care needs to be explored to consider any parallel activity. Approved mental health professionals have been identified in the Mental Health Bill 2002. This is in recognition that some roles performed by a named social worker could be taken on by other mental health nurses, psychologists, occupational therapists [Department of Health (2002), page 22].

The relationship of values to policy

In your reading you will find that authors have different perspectives on policy and that this may influence their discussion on issues relating to care. In this section we will be looking at groups of ideas – ideologies.

The following is a summary of some ideas about welfare, as discussed by Deacon (2002):

Each of these perspectives offers a different formulation of what should be the role and purpose of welfare. They are not mutually exclusive, but each draws upon and articulates a different understanding of human nature and of the relationship between welfare and human behaviour and motivation.

Welfare as an expression of altruism. This perspective assumes that the creation of a more equal and cohesive society will foster a sense of mutual obligation and help to realise the moral potentialities of its citizens. The task of welfare is to redistribute resources and opportunities, and thereby provide a framework for the encouragement and expression of altruism.

Welfare as a channel for the pursuit of self-interest. This perspective assumes that the overwhelming majority of people who claim welfare will act rationally to better the conditions of themselves and their dependents. The task of welfare is to provide a framework of incentives that channels this desire for self-improvement in ways conducive to the common good.

Welfare as the exercise of authority. This perspective starts from the premise that a significant proportion of claimants lack the capacity to pursue their own self-interest. In consequence they do not respond to changes in the framework of incentives in the way that the previous perspective assumes. The task of welfare is to compel such people to act in ways that are conducive to their long-term betterment, and hence to the common good.

Welfare as a transition to work. This perspective has developed in response to the previous two. It starts from the premise that cash benefits alone can never alleviate the problem of poverty. The more generous such benefits become, the more they undermine work incentives and threaten the stability of the family. The task of welfare should be to serve as a transition to paid employment.

Welfare as a mechanism for moral regeneration. This perspective starts from the assumption that people are also motivated by a sense of commitment, and by an acceptance that they have obligations to the communities in which they live. The task of welfare is to foster and enhance this sense of duty, and it should look to do so through persuasion and moral argument.

The government is advised on ideas about policy by organisations who represent care services, as well as other departments. The new Commission for Social Care Inspection will advise ministers and policy makers on

⊃ the impact of policies on the ground

⊃ how best to assess performance

⊃ appropriate intervention when a council fails to provide an adequate service.

There are many factors that influence the development of policy – not just values that underpin the sector. Sometimes it is difficult to identify the principles that policy developers say they have when you consider the policies that they develop.

Think it over

1 Find out in your place of work what policies have had an influence on how the service is provided and consider what the effects have been.

2 Did the values of the policy match with the values of the organisation?

You may already have strong views on care and how it should be provided. During your reading you will develop an understanding of the contemporary issues that inform the current development of policy; it is important that you are able to participate in any debates about this.

Think it over

Find a recent policy that has an impact on your place of work, think about what the impact has meant and make notes on

⊃ who the policy was written by

⊃ when was it written or introduced

⊃ what events or situations preceded the policy – in other words, why do you think this policy originated

⊃ what the stated aims of the policy are – give a summary of these

⊃ how you think this policy has had an effect on the service or service users, staff, finances etc.

We have so far looked at the ideas that influence policy, what policies are, and how to recognise the values that are inherent in policy. We will now look at the policy-making process.

The policy-making process

Policy has to take into account current legislation. If existing legislation does not enable new policy to be implemented then new legislation must be proposed.

All new policy needs to respond to and facilitate the spirit and letter of the Human Rights Act 1998. This marked 'a change in the constitutional relationship between citizens and the state' [Home Office Communication Directive 2000), page 1]. 'One of the reasons for changing our mental health laws, which date largely from 1959, is to bring them more fully in line with the European Convention on Human Rights.' [(2002), page 19] Governments sometimes look abroad for inspiration about new policies. For example, the system of reimbursement is based on a policy that has had an impact in Scandinavia.

The document *Facing the Facts* identified that

1 policy guidance at national level is needed to confirm the direction of strategic change within the framework of the government's modernising agenda for health and social care services

2 national objectives for health and social care services for people with learning disabilities are needed, together with targets for achievement in the medium term. (Department of Health (1999), page 5]

In the report on *Better Government for Older People*, the vision is 'to improve public services for older people by better meeting their needs, listening to their views, and encouraging and recognising their contribution.' [University of Warwick (2001)]

Case Study

London Borough of Hammersmith and Fulham

'A good approach that has promising prospects for improvement.'

It is important for government, local authorities, the NHS, and care organisations to consider how policies relate to each other in different environments. An illustration of this is the Human Rights Act 1998. This legislation has had a major impact on the implementation of other policies that were already established and has influenced the development of new policies.

Human rights legislation needs to be considered because

⊃ it is the law

⊃ it can bring benefits to service users.

'Human rights legislation has been used innovatively as a framework to improve the equality and dignity of people with learning disabilities in their relationships with carers.' [Audit Commission (2003), discussing the Doughty Street HR Unit and LSE HR Centre Research (2002)]

Implementing policy

> But once the policy framework is in place, then it is the planning, commissioning and management of social services that the foundations of good service delivery are laid. [Social Services Inspectorate (2002), page 34]

One of the functions of the Social Services Inspectorate was to 'monitor the implementation of government policy for the personal social service. The Act thus promotes the independence of older people and means that more people will be cared for in the most appropriate setting for their needs.' [HSC (2003/2009), LAC (2003), page 21: 3]

In order to promote the discharge of hospital patients back to their own homes or into care homes, the government has determined that from 5 January councils will pay £100 each day for care (£120 in London and some parts of the South East).

The requirements for smooth transfer of a person from hospital to home once their medical needs have been met and they are fit for discharge need to be worked out. The following are the questions that need to be asked in this regard.

Assessment of social care needs	
Identification of resources to meet that need	Are there enough carers working for domiciliary care agencies? Is there a vacancy at a suitable care home of the person's choice?
Obtaining equipment to enable successful transition home	Is specialist assessment (physiotherapist/occupational therapist) available? Is equipment available?

The stick approach to this might mitigate against collaborative working.

In the White Paper *Modernising Mental Health Services* ideas were prised out through the NSF Mental Health. An amount of £700 million was provided over three years from 1999 to 2001 to support the implementation of new services to address the standards.

National action focused on five key areas:
- Finance: revenue, capital and estates
- Workforce planning and education and training
- Research and development
- Clinical decision support systems
- Information

Community care

When studying the development of community care, policies have not always demonstrated an understanding of the issues relating to service user needs. Walker [(1982) in Community Care] discussed community care policies of the time with the opinion that '… the problem of mental handicap has been wrongly conceived and therefore that community care policies have been restricted and inadequate.'

A theme throughout the development of community care is that it is an example of repeated delay in the implementation of a policy.

A very important requirement with policy is that different aspects link up for the benefit of the individual. Government departments do not always show cohesion when it comes to organising policy shaped around the individual.

Examples of where this fails to happen is in supported employment systems. Any payment that a disabled person receives for any work that they have undertaken can affect their benefits.

Identifying what people need from care services

Since the 1990 NHS and Community Care Act the process of care management has been developed to ensure that individuals are provided with an assessment of their needs prior to the delivery of care. The chapter on assessment (Chapter 6) explores all the issues relating to the assessment process and the current organisation of assessment. In mental health services the care programme approach has provided a comparable assessment framework.

Section 46. (1) Each local authority
(a) Shall … prepare and publish a plan for the provision of community care services in their area

Section 47. (1) …the authority
(d) shall carry out an assessment of his needs for those services
(e) having regard to the results of that assessment, shall then decide whether his needs call for the provision by them of any such services.

This legislation also required that local authorities understand what the care needs are in their locality and plan for meeting these needs.

Care services

This section looks at the range of services that are provided to individuals and groups who need care or support.

Accommodation

In the section on the history of care we saw that some people who needed support used to be placed in large institutions. This gradually changed to more locally based residential provision in communities.

Care homes

Care homes vary in size and some have more than 50 older people living in them. There is a preference, especially in learning disabled accommodation, for smaller homes as this reflects ideas of normal living.

The Care Standards Act 2000 specifies the term of care home but still attributes status of residential or nursing care through the registration process. Registered for residential or nursing provision, they are also provided with registration specific to a number of service users and service user groups category.

The aims of a care home are to meet the identified needs of individuals who live in that home. This is achieved through regular assessment of needs and the care planning process. Each care home has to produce a statement of purpose that specifies what it provides for people. The initial assessment of need can serve as a contract for the provision of care. An older person may live in a care home for years; for many it is their last home. Care homes may be able to provide for people until they die if the home is equipped with appropriate skilled care workers.

The Centre for Policy on Ageing discusses the inference that independence can only be maintained for older people if they stay in their own homes [CPA (2001)].

The Care Standards Act 2000 provides a structured framework for the regulation of care homes as explained later in the chapter.

Supported living

Care homes are not the only type of accommodation services available to people. Housing associations have been providing supported tenancies for people in need of care or support, and there has been a growth in this in the latter part of 2003 with the supported living agenda of national government being applied locally.

Tenancy arrangements are provided where a housing association or other organisation manages the accommodation and obtains or delivers the support services for people who are learning disabled or with mental health needs. The idea of tenancy arrangements is that the support allocated can be more specific to individuals.

Individuals are benefiting financially from these living and support arrangements which can increase their independence.

Sheltered housing

Within older people's services sheltered housing, either in the form of purpose-built complexes or apartment blocks, have been providing a good balance between independent living and security and well-being (including peace of mind that someone is available to talk and to help).

Very sheltered housing is a more recent solution to the care needs of people who want to retain their independence but who have a range of complex care needs. They may live in a sheltered housing scheme and receive additional support provided externally.

Care at home

People can receive services in their own home. Some learning disabled adults and people with mental health problems have continued to live with their parents, who may themselves be in need of support due to their age. For many people the transition through adulthood requires that they have support in their home lives. Ideas about what form this support should take are under constant review.

Domiciliary care

Statistics say that 400,000 households receive a domiciliary care service each week [Department of Health, Community Care Statistics (2001)]. Domiciliary care refers to services that are provided to people in their own home, described by the Social Services Inspectorate as 'the mainstay for many older people living at home' (2002). Community-based care incorporates the idea that individuals may be best placed in their own homes. In order for some people to remain in the home that they live they may need one of the following:

- ⊃ adaptations to their accommodation
- ⊃ aids to daily living tasks
- ⊃ support with getting washed and dressed in the morning and at night
- ⊃ assistance with using the toilet.

As early as 1958 the then government stated that: 'The underlying principle of our services for the old should be this: that the best place for old people is in their own homes, with help from the home services if need be.' [Townsend (1962), page 196]

Care support workers who support individuals in their own home provide a range of personal care and physical support services to enable people to function in their own homes.

> Physical functioning was consistently associated with greater use of both statutory and private home care services, suggesting that efforts should continue to be made to improve older people's physical functioning, such as preventive home visits. [Stoddart *et al* (2002), pages 348–360, 358]

Intermediate care

This was introduced through the National Service Framework for Older People. The aim was to provide support to individuals to reduce the need to enter hospital for acute health care services. It also would provide support to people when they left hospital to reduce the need for re-admission. The principle behind it was prevention which, whilst being a valued concept in health care, has been missing from dialogue on social care. Some of the strategies for delivering intermediate care are

- rapid response teams
- intensive rehabilitation services
- recuperation facilities
- one-stop older people's service
- integrated home care teams.

Primary care trusts have developed initiatives based around their district nursing services, with home care staff focusing on rehabilitation. Local authority home care teams are being provided with specific training on rehabilitation so that they can increase their role in developing the ability of older people in their own homes. 'They will have the freedom to decide the precise organisational arrangements for their area.' (Section 7.5)

Any services which form part of a package of intermediate care as defined in the regulations must be provided free of charge for six weeks.

The aim of intermediate care was to

1 provide services that would prevent a person needing hospital admission
2 ensure people did not need re-admission to hospital when they had left.

Day services

Older people may attend day centres or lunch clubs. At these centres activities may be provided in-house by the staff, or sometimes they are brought in from outside. The activities include

- therapeutic activities, which may include aromatherapy, music and art activities
- physical activity in the form of gentle exercise
- day trips
- the provision of lunch at these centres, which gives some people the chance to have a hot meal.

Some centres are able to respond to the particular social needs of a cultural or religious group in a local area.

Learning disability

Historically, learning disabled adults have attended adult training centres where they take part in a range of activities including

- sports
- crafts
- domestic skills
- personal hygiene
- relationships
- health care.

With care planning and reviews there has been a move away from group activity at the centre so that activities have been more focused around the needs of the individual. This prompted the name change to social education centres.

The purpose of day centres for adults with learning disabilities is partly affected by the level of discrimination against people in usual everyday activity and partly by the level of resourcing required to enable disabled people to access usual community facilities and activities.

A primary activity in usual life for many people is that of paid employment. Learning disabled people may need a different approach in terms of the support required to undertake work activity; they may need assistance in terms of appropriate work relations, pace and level of work. There is an emphasis on day services being a focal point for accessing supported employment.

Facing the Facts Services for People with Learning Disabilities: A Policy Impact Study of Social Care and Health Services [Department of Health (1999)] identified that there would be the development of alternatives to the ATCs and SECs for people, including a rise in

- ⊃ supported employment
- ⊃ outreach groups
- ⊃ continuing education.

It also identified that there would also be less use of NHS managed day services [Department of Health (1999), page 15].

The White Paper *Valuing People* stated that individuals should engage in more locally based community activities in small groups rather than minibus groups of people travelling to an allocated slot for disabled people at the sports centre.

Care Direct

There have been some projects to try to support individuals out of hours. The NHS Direct Service, which provided 24-hour telephone support, was piloted in terms of social care in some areas.

Care Direct provides information and help for older people.

Care Direct was awarded £2 million of Department of Health grants in the first year – 2002. The results of the pilot were that 40% of all callers to Care Direct are 70 years and over, which is a significant support to a potentially isolated group of people.

An example of a Care Direct scheme is Gloucestershire Care Direct. When this was set up it worked closely with

- ⊃ social services
- ⊃ rapid response teams

and established links with Age Concern to ensure that it was able to provide comprehensive support to older people in the area.

The commissioning of care services

We mentioned earlier the development of private businesses in the delivery of care. Since the 1990 NHS and Community Care Act the role of the local

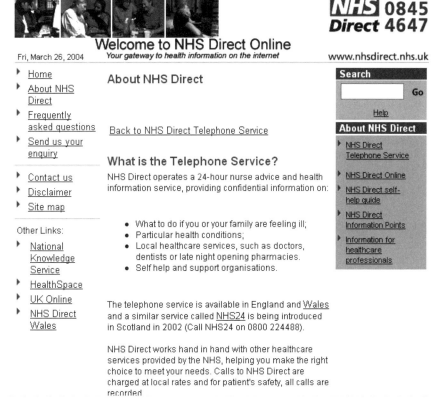

Figure 1.4 *Care Direct*

authority in providing services has changed. Social services departments now have a responsibility to secure care services, but not to provide them directly. This has enabled other care providers to become key providers in some localities.

Commissioning is the process of securing care services for a region or in a particular activity.

Key elements of commissioning care

The key elements in commissioning care are

- ➲ *Analysis* It is important to identify what services are needed in a local area. The devolved nature of this planning means that local initiatives can be developed to creatively respond to the specific requirements of a population.

- ➲ *Strategic planning* This involves having a broad overview of a range of issues and being able to apply these to the short and long term.

- ➲ *Contract setting* Contracts are legal agreements as to what services an organisation is going to provide and at what cost. A contract might be small for one service to a small group of people in one geographical area, or it could be a larger contract dealing with a whole range of services across a wide locality.

- ➲ *Market management* Authorities have needed to ensure that there are sufficient providers to meet the needs of individuals in a region. An example of where this is problematic is in home care services. In some geographical areas, domiciliary care agencies have had difficulty meeting the obligations of a number of care packages.

ADVERT

Expressions of interest are sought to provide:

Out of Hours Community Mental Health Support Services

A contract for 3 years commencing 1 October 2004 will be awarded

Providers must be able to demonstrate:

- An ability to provide quality mental health services
- Be financially viable
- Cost effective service

For a Tender Information Pack please contact:

Jake at Heather County Council

Figure 1.5 *Advertisement for care organisation*

- *Contract monitoring* Organisations who take up contracts will have different levels of experience regarding managing the contract and meeting the needs of the purchasing authority.

'There was much to be done to develop a quality dimension to commissioning, including robust systems of quality assurance and assistance to providers with issues such as training and retention.' [Social Services Inspectorate (2002), page 2] This statement in relation to older people's services explains that commissioning is complex and requires structured systems in order that local authorities manage the process well.

A further dimension to tendering has been the introduction of *best value*, as organisations have to demonstrate that they are securing the best services by investigating comparable alternatives.

Think it over

Does your organisation have a relationship with a local authority or the National Health Service? If it does, what are the features of the relationship?

Primary care trusts

Led by clinicians and local people, primary care trusts are the cornerstone of the local NHS, and are responsible for

- assessing the health needs of their local community
- preparing plans for health improvement
- being the leading NHS organisation for partnership working with local authorities and other partners.

Primary care trusts are reviewing their remit for the social care needs of people and some trusts are employing more care workers as they co-ordinate the delivery of care to people in their localities.

Think about the services your own organisation provides.

1 Who is the service managed by?

2 What is the relationship of your own organisation to others?

Funding

In this section we explore how money influences the provision of care. The organisation of finances are national. At central government level the finances have to be allocated by the Treasury to different departments.

The following are the main themes of government policy and the privatisation of welfare:

Main themes	Characteristics
Privatisation	Privatisation of state monopolies
Delegation	Delegation of budgeting authority
Competition	Competitive tendering
Enterprise	Encouragement of social markets

[Adapted from Thompson (1992), page 24, in Abbott and Ackers (1996), page 113]

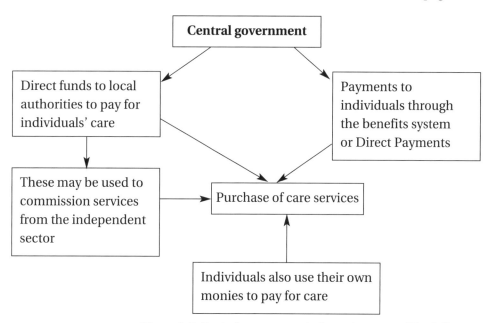

Figure 1.6 *Central government is the main source of funds for care*

New policies relating to particular service user groups may have associated grants with them. This can be advantageous to particular groups, but may also discriminate against other groups or individuals. 'Rationing can be defined as the allocation of scarce resources in such a way that they are withheld from some of those who could benefit from those resources.' [Malin *et al* (2002), page 139]

Case Study

Paying for care

Mr Peck is 92 years old and has finally decided to move into a care home. Whilst he is still very able mentally his physical mobility has reduced over the recent months and he knows he cannot really manage. He owns his house, which he bought with his wife in 1963 for £2600. He has been paying National Insurance through his salary all his working life and feels that he has worked hard to provide for his wife when she was alive and their family. Mr Peck is surprised that the care manager talks to him about his finances when he discusses moving to a care home, as he thought he would be looked after in his old age.

Think it over

Should individuals pay for their own care if they can afford to? Having read through the case study make two lists:

1 Give the reasons why Mr Peck should be able to keep his house and any financial assets he has, and pass them to his children for them to benefit from.

2 Give the reasons why the sale of Mr Peck's house should be used to pay for his care in the foreseeable future, along with other assets that he has.

Paying for care is likely to remain a debatable issue for some time. It is connected with the issue of pensions and working age, which is currently being discussed as being raised to 70 years.

Case Study

The Home Care Budget for Leicestershire County Council

Population	606,800 (estimate 1999)
Social services budget 2001/2	£100.6 million
Domiciliary services	
Home care hours:	1.42 million to 4000 households at a cost of £12.89million
Mobile meals:	£570,000
Lunch clubs:	£45,000 meals and transport
Household and incontinence laundry service:	1134 users (183 using the incontinence service) £418,000

Further Research

Investigate the resources of the organisation that you work for. Establish what their main items of expenditure are and also how they obtain their income.

Gloucestershire County Council high court judgement in 1995; LAs cannot cut services indiscriminately, but are able to and should take resources into account both in the assessment of need and the provision of resources. [Blakemore (2003), page 211]

This means that the public must both want such welfare services and be willing to pay for them. [Hirst (1998), page 3, in Kleinman (2002), page 74]

The Audit Commission has recommended giving councils more freedoms to raise a larger portion of their overall budgets from local taxation, reducing the amount coming from central government and allowing councils to set more local priorities [CC11(2003)].

Think it over

Think about the advantages and disadvantages of monies being allocated and services distributed locally, compared to centrally.

There are some current debates in relation to funding.

The reasons for the growth over time in health spending have been examined in some detail in the OECD countries, and the following factors have been identified:

➲ Inflation in the health sector has tended to be slightly higher than in the economy as a whole.

➲ Demographic changes have created extra demands on the health system, particularly from a growing proportion of older people who make more use of health care.

➲ Intensity of use of health services has been increasing constantly, with each individual on average making more use of them: more consultations, more hospital admissions, more operations, and more prescriptions. In turn these are more expensive because of the advanced equipment, more and better paid registered nursing and medical staff, higher standards and so on. [Webster (ed) (2001), page 308]

Think it over

In the organisation where you work think about the following.

➲ Do the patients/service users pay for the care that they receive?

and

➲ Write a list of the key expenses in your work setting.

The table below is local authority personal social services gross expenditure (in £000s) by client group for the period 1999–2000.

	Older people	Children	Learning disability	Physical disability	Mental health	Total
HQ costs						161
Area officers/ senior managers	102	188	28	29	33	380
Care management/ assessment	369	567	78	107	145	1265
Residential care	3453	792	922	242	242	5651
Non-residential care	1719	1259	605	454	213	4252
Total	5644	2807	1633	832	633	11 887

[Department of Health (2002) in Hill (2003), page 181]

The government has taken several approaches to introduce private finance into the care sector through first the private finance initiative and then the public private partnerships. Media attention has been on the use of private monies to build new hospitals, but there are contentious ideas about how to develop the role of private finances in the provision of care.

At organisational level of care

Organisations obtain funding from local authorities to pay for the care services that they are providing. This payment is sometimes made directly to the individual, who then makes a payment to the service provider. The monies may also be paid directly to the organisation where a long-term contract has been negotiated. The independent sector has been more focused on the relationship of individual service users to the exchange of monies, but this model is now applied to local authority managed services as well.

In a care home the registered manager or accountant will obtain monies from the people who live in the home and this may be made by direct transfer from their own account.

Traditionally, nursing care, as with most NHS services, has been provided free of charge. There appears to be continued dispute over who has responsibility for paying for the care needs of people, whether they have nursing or personal care needs. The NHS has a responsibility for financing the continuation of care following transition to alternative accommodation after leaving hospital.

The Coughlan judgement of July 1999 ascertained the following:

> The nursing service must be provided by the NHS where the primary need of the person for nursing home accommodation is a health need.

> If the secondary need for accommodation is nursing then this can be provided by either the NHS or social services department.

Organisational care

Maisie is moving into Sherwood Lodge Care Home. She has assets of £73,000 as she sold her house when she moved. Maisie does not have any children and has been given advice from Age Concern about her finances. She will be paying for her care each week through a standing order that she has arranged. When the money that she has reduces to under £11,500 she can have a financial assessment with a local authority care manager who will arrange a contract for the continuation of care, usually in the same home. Age Concern has also given Maisie some advice about having an advocate and the legal arrangements for managing her money in the future if she needs additional support.

Organisations are accountable for the monies that they spend. Maisie has an individual accounts book in the home and her money is not used to finance the care of other people. If Maisie has any particular items that she wants or particular activities that she wants to get involved in then she can finance this.

Individuals

Before the 1990s individuals were very removed from discussions about finances and who would pay for their care. The relationship between individuals and finances was not so tightly monitored. Groups were provided with care and monies were often pooled to accommodate the group needs rather than being attached to meet individual need. Currently, care services are provided to individuals on the basis of need. Once a person's needs are established there are then services that an individual may be entitled to free, or services that they will need to have a financial assessment for to establish any level of contribution. There are also care services available to individuals who wish to purchase these separately.

There are some services that an individual is entitled to as a statutory entitlement, and they will be provided free of charge. These are

- an assessment of need
- provision of accommodation and day services for learning disabled individuals
- accommodation for some individuals with mental health needs.

Some services are also an entitlement but the individual may need to undergo a financial assessment in order to establish whether they need to make a contribution. These are

- moving into a care home
- home care (domiciliary) services.

There are also some care or support services that people can access which they may not have been assessed for, or may have been assessed for, but not found to be entitled to. Some of these services individuals can access independently by making their own arrangements and paying directly themselves.

The changing relationship of individuals to the care that they receive in terms of money has meant that some people are able to be more assertive about the care that they receive, as evidenced in a social services report. 'Why am I charged for two half-hour visits per day when the carer is in such a hurry and stays for less than fifteen minutes each time?' [Social Services Inspectorate (2002), Section 3.21]

Resource allocation is a tighter science than it used to be. Budgets have to be justified and then accounted for. The White Paper *Valuing People* stated that 'decisions about resource allocation need to be evidence-based and take account of the likely increase in demand for services from people with learning disabilities'. [Department of Health (2001), page 95]. It also identified that quality assurance needed to be a feature of the budget. 'The application of best value principles will achieve better value for money.'

Legislation since the 1990s has progressed a change in the relationship of individuals to the state with respect to money. Disabled people and older people are no longer viewed as having state handouts and are viewed as claiming what is rightfully theirs. The Direct Payments policy, discussed in the chapter on assessment (Chapter 6) is an example of this change, as are the changes associated with carers legislation.

One of the first discussions in this chapter explored the relationship between poverty and individuals who have care or support needs that have been identified through research. Appropriate financial support can facilitate the participation of individuals in society and prevent them from developing additional needs associated with poverty. The Labour government has been developing its strategy for enabling disabled people to engage in employment whilst also obtaining support through additional income. Some people who require support of care services are financially self-sufficient due to either current income or past ability to earn and save. In recent years more attention has been paid to the potential for providing support to individuals in need through the allocation of more funds directly to them. Benefits are one means of providing additional income to people in order for them to make decisions about the level and type of support that they want.

The following are examples of benefits.

Carer's allowance	Paid to full-time carers, 35 hours + pw of people receiving other benefits Aged 16 years +	
Disability living allowance	For people who need help looking after themselves (even if no one is actually providing help) Aged 3–65 years (allowance continues beyond 65 if a claim is made before)	*Care component* Higher rate: £56.25 Middle rate: £37.65 Lower rate: £14.90 *Mobility component*: Higher rate: £39.30 Lower rate: £14.90

The benefit system provides an example of how complex individual's lives can be where they have to obtain income from different sources. Many authorities have care managers who have developed a level of expertise in this area in order to support individuals in maximising their incomes.

Case Study

Financial support

Sean is 38 years old and lives with his mother who is 72 . He receives the highest rate care component of Disability Living Allowance. He has £3200 savings and the services he gets from social services total more than £200 per week.

Sean is able to access funds from the Independent Living Fund (1993). This provides him with additional funds to support his living at home.

His mother provides him with support and has recently had a carers assessment in order for her to access support.

Think it over

Think about the current circumstances of Sean and look up the relevant benefits that would suit this individual at this time.

Current issues in the provision of care

Ideas and values have an influence on care policy. Ideology refers to groups of ideas which inform the understanding of how care should be provided, and what values should underpin it, for example the rights-based approach to providing care. Having outlined the current organisation and structure of care services we now turn to some of the ideas that shape the services that are provided.

We can glean the ideas that inform care services from policies that are put into place.

Individual responsibility

The provision of care to individuals is also tied up in the notions of the family, and responsibilities that families have. If a person has the money to pay for their own care or health should they pay for it, or should this be an essential provided by the state? The Conservative government of the 1980s famously stated that there was no such thing as the idea of community, their leader, Margaret Thatcher, believing in individuals taking responsibility for themselves and their families, so that there was no need for any supporting framework called the community. The development of community-based care meant additional family responsibilities to people. It was only in the mid-1990s that this has been addressed through the National Carers Strategy.

Independent living

The idea of community-based care has been developed into one of independent living, so that there is a move away from (large) group care. This is reflected in strategies associated with day services, and in learning disabled and mental health residential services. It is having less of an impact in older people's services.

There are 7 million people who are disabled, of whom 4 million use equipment from NHS or social services. The NHS Plan identified the need to integrate health and social care community equipment providers to improve this service and increase use by 50%. It will be supported by a National Service Framework for Long Term Health Conditions [Department of Health (2004)].

Eligibility

Fair Access to Care Services [Department of Health (2003)] revisited the issue of eligibility criteria in relation to local authorities providing care services to people. As a means of entitling some people to services, eligibility also necessarily excludes people from services. The idea that a person may have needs but is not actually eligible for services can be difficult to understand, but it is a reality of current service provision.

> Assessment and provision of services should always be needs-led and outcome-focused. [Department of Health (2003), page 14, Section 3.3]

Partnership with service users

Other chapters in this book focus on the relationship that care workers and organisations should have both with services users and other care providers. Working in partnership with service users and other care organisations empowers people and gives service users control through facilitating their input in the policy-making process.

Examples of this happening include:

⊃ The new Commission for Social Care Inspection (CSCI) want to know from service users if the services
  – promote their independence
  – provide the opportunities they seek
  – offer them protection when they need it
  – support their rights and choices.

○ User Focus and Citizen Engagement Audit Commission 17 June 2003 states 'Strong user focus is underpinned by core values, such as honesty, inclusiveness, fairness and realism. Those councils that are succeeding in engaging users are committed to these and similar values and demonstrate them in their organisational behaviours and priorities.'

○ The People's Parliament aims to provide a framework for the organisation of disabled people to have input into the way that services are organised and policies that are introduced.

○ The Learning Disability Partnership Boards should ensure that

– people with learning disabilities and carers contribute to the board

– local cultural diversity is reflected in its membership

– local independent sector and voluntary sector are fully engaged.

They are responsible for

– developing and implementing the joint investment plan for delivering the government's objectives

– overseeing inter-agency planning and commissioning of comprehensive, integrated and inclusive services that provide a genuine choice of service options to people in their local community

– ensuring that people are not denied their right to a local service because of a lack of competence or capacity amongst service providers

– using Health Act flexibilities

– ensuring arrangements are in place to achieve a smooth transition to adult life for learning disabled young people.

Think it over

Identify and think about the key policies that have an impact on the work that you do. Make a list of how the policies affect

○ the lives of the individuals that you support

○ the organisation that you work for

○ the role that you have.

Responding to individual need

Services should be developed focusing on the needs of different community groups. Ethnic minority groups should inform services so that they are provided in an appropriate way and do actually meet needs.

Agencies and organisations which commission or provide community care services have a responsibility to address the needs of ethnic minority older people with them. [Department of Health (1998), page 7]

Service user control

The main advantage of direct payments is that the person can decide who will best meet their needs and when. Direct payments give the user a far greater amount of freedom and control than they would if receiving services directly from the local authority or other service provider. [Luckhurst (2002), page 19]

Traditional methods of consultation using public meetings are not recommended in the literature. Baxter *et al* (1990) noted that consultation should be carried out at local level with community organisations rather than through public meetings. Such links improve understanding of the experiences that are common to different minority ethnic communities, any differences from majority needs, and provide an opportunity to develop proposals for specific action.

Staff from minority communities are often treated as experts and trouble-makers. [Ethnic Minorities and Learning Disability (2001), page 54]

A lack of consultation means that services remain inappropriate and inflexible, service staff do not develop a sensitivity to the circumstances of minority ethnic groups or to the support needs which they themselves identify, and users feel under-valued. [Butt and Mirza (1996) in Department of Health (2001), page 15]

An example would be withholding correspondence in the interests of the patient with, or sometimes without, their consent.

In the Mental Health Bill 2003:

Decisions to apply compulsion will be made subject to overriding principles. The code of practice must set out the general principles and the circumstances in which they will apply.

The principles will require:

➲ patients to be involved when decisions are made about them;
➲ the decision maker to demonstrate that the proposed treatment imposes the minimum level of intrusion consistent with the ability to address the person's disorder and its effects;
➲ decisions to be taken in a fair and open way, so that the patient knows what is happening.

In the document *Nothing About Us Without Us: The Report from the Service Users Advisory Group* it was explained that the involvement of learning disabled people has helped government to understand what needs to change [Department of Health (2001), page 11].

A SSI report in 2002 [Social Services Inspectorate (2002), page 17] relating to older people identified the concerns of older people themselves as being

➲ high staff turnover
➲ unreliability
➲ unpunctuality

➲ poor training

➲ failure to stay for the full time.

The 2003 Mental Health Bill recognises that:

> Patients may challenge decisions to treat them compulsorily including during the initial 28 day period, by making an application to the Mental Health Tribunal. [Department of Health (2002), page 8]

Regulation and inspection

Statutory organisations

Any work sector can require systems to ensure that quality is being maintained and that standards are observed; this is no less true in the care sector. In a sector where people's rights are being given more respect it is important that the users of care services are provided with appropriate mechanisms for telling service providers what they think of the services that they are getting.

There are several strategies for applying standards to the provision of care to ensure that the quality of care services is appropriate and these operate on a national level managed through organisations established by central government. The origins of current regulations were established in the Care Standards Act 2000.

Local authorities have to publish an Annual Best Value Performance Plan. This provides a results oriented approach to monitoring services [Department of Health (1998)]. This relates to both the quality and costs measured through how economic, efficient and effective services are.

The Audit Commission monitors whether the authority is applying the following criteria of continual improvement:

➲ Challenging

➲ Comparing

➲ Competing

➲ Consulting.

Best value will be a duty to deliver services to clear standards – covering both cost and quality – by the most effective, economic and efficient means available. [Department of Health (1998)]

Local authorities are required to establish the following for all their services:

➲ specific objectives and performance

➲ a programme of fundamental performance reviews

➲ local performance plans.

[Hill (2003), page 64]

Best value inspections ascertain two dimensions to the quality of services:

1 What is the standard of quality in current services?

2 What are the prospects for improvement?

It portrays the results of these inspections with star ratings that are published and publicly available. You may have seen them in your local or a national paper before. These 'provide an objective starting point for reviewing and planning improvements to services' [Social Services Inspectorate (2003), page 2].

Council	Adults' services		Children's services		Performance rating
	Serving people well?	Capacity for improvement?	Serving people well?	Capacity for improvement?	
Cornwall	Most	Promising	Yes	Excellent	☆☆☆
Newcastle upon Tyne	Most	Excellent	Most	Excellent	☆☆☆

Organisations

The Care Standards Act 2000 introduced a new body for the regulation of care services, the National Care Standards Commission. From April 2004 the Commission for Social Care Inspection (CSCI) took over this role. This is a new independent body, created from the Health and Social Care (Community Health and Standards) Act 2003. It takes responsibility for the role that has previously been carried out by the National Care Standards Commission, the Social Services Inspectorate and the SSI/Audit Commission Joint Review team.

It has responsibility to

⊃ promote improvement in social care

⊃ inspect all social care – public, private and voluntary

⊃ register services that meet national standards

⊃ inspect council social services

⊃ publish an annual report to Parliament on social care

⊃ hold performance statistics on social care

⊃ publish the star ratings for council social services.

The CSCI aims are to

⊃ put the people who use social care first

⊃ improve services and stamp out bad practice

⊃ be an expert voice on social care

⊃ practice what we preach in our own organisation.

The Commission will be able to track the service provided for a person from the point at which their needs are met, through to the planning and delivery of the services they receive.

They will work closely with other inspectorates, especially the Commission for Healthcare Audit and Inspection, which has a similar responsibility in health care services. Reports are provided from these regulatory bodies that are in the public domain. These include specific inspection reports based on individual visits.

General information about the quality of services provided nationally, for example the following information was provided from the Social Services Inspectorate:

(1) Independence at home

  ⊃ Home care services still expect users to be passive

  ⊃ Home care services provided by some parts of the independent sector are not reliable enough

  ⊃ Many councils have difficulty finding skilled workers to support disabled people

  ⊃ Too many people still have to wait too long for special equipment and for adaptations to their homes

(2) Identity and belonging

  ⊃ Some good local services with respect for different cultures

  ⊃ Disabled parents need more support

  ⊃ Range of projects for people with brain injury, but more local appropriate support and homes needed

  ⊃ Carers need support

(3) Active citizens

  ⊃ Day services are improving, but more community-based activities are needed

  ⊃ Only a third of councils provide the advocacy services which are valued

  ⊃ Social services need to work with other departments to promote job opportunities of people

(4) The way councils work

  ⊃ Direct payments are benefiting people and should be promoted more

  ⊃ Assessment should focus on need

  ⊃ Information to people needs to improve

  ⊃ Councils should involve local people to check that they are using the social model of disability

  ⊃ Improvement should continue in services at the difficult time when children transfer to adulthood

  ⊃ The best councils actively involve disabled people in planning, developing and evaluating

[Department of Health/Social Services Inspectorate (2003)]

Just as there are standards to which care workers should aspire, there are also standards that specify the quality of the care to be provided to individuals in a particular service setting. Checking on organisations that provide services involves requiring organisations to audit themselves and this has been facilitated through the creation of National Minimum Standards. National Minimum Standards originate from the Care Standards Act. They are the statements that are to be referred to in the inspection of particular care organisations.

National Service Frameworks are policy statements that establish the priorities that need to be worked to, and the standards which need to be addressed generally, usually across a range of organisations. The National Service Framework for Older People is introduced by the Department of Health as '... this ambitious programme of change ....' [Department of Health (2001), page 14]

The themes are:

Respecting the individual:
Standard 1: Rooting out age discrimination
Standard 2: Person centred care

Intermediate care
Standard 3: Intermediate care

Providing evidenced based specialist care
Standard 4: General hospital care
Standard 5: Stroke
Standard 6: Falls
Standard 7: Mental health in older people

Promoting an active, healthy life
Standard 8: The promotion of health and active life in older age

Case Study

Organisation of care services

Portsmouth Social Services
Reviewed by team: Audit Commission and Department of Health
January to March 2003

'The Council has an impressive record in tackling regeneration and has achieved beacon status for neighbourhood renewal.'

Some of the main findings are:

- 'Users and carers are very positive about the services they receive in Portsmouth.'
- 'Assessment and care planning is generally good.'
- 'Support for carers is good but more priority now needs to be given to carers' assessments.'
- 'Adult mental health services are of an exceptionally high standard.'
- 'Reviews and carers' assessments need to be prioritised and planning for people with physical disabilities needs to improve.'

Care workers

The Care Standards Act also established the General Social Care Council. It has a specific role in regulating the care workforce. It is undertaking a process of registering care workers, and has started this process with social workers. In the future there will be a requirement for all care workers to be registered as a means of tracking poor practice and ensuring that people who are not deemed fit to work in the care sector are appropriately excluded from it.

A further means of ensuring the appropriateness of care workers is through the checks undertaken by the Criminal Records Bureau when people first gain employment with an organisation.

The Training Organisation for the Personal Social Services is responsible for the development of the care workforce. They have developed induction and foundation standards that provide standards to which newly employed care workers need to demonstrate they can work to.

Within different areas of the care sector there are other qualifications that are enabling a more professional approach to care work. Raising standards in care practice is also about promoting good practice through the development of the workforce. The following are ways in which this is being done.

- ➲ The Certificate in Community Mental Health Care (Pavillion/City and Guilds).
- ➲ The Learning Disability Awards Framework links in with NVQs and is focused on learning disability.
- ➲ The government has introduced Foundation degrees as a Level 4 Higher Education award that focuses on the knowledge and skills needs of the work sector.
- ➲ National Vocational Qualifications are occupational standards that employees should work to. They are written around general work roles and provide statements indicating the quality of the work that should be performed.

    – NVQ Levels 2, 3 and 4.

    – Registered Manager Award NVQ 4.

Other resources that have been set up to support the development of standards are

- ➲ Social Care Institute for Excellence

    This reviews information to establish a foundation of knowledge about what works in social care. They also produce good practice guidelines.
    www.scie.org.uk

- ➲ Electronic Library for Social Care
    www.elsc.org.uk

- ➲ National electronic Library for Health
    www.nelh.org.uk

In this section we have looked at the regulatory context of care and how organisations have to respond to the requirements of the Care Standards Act 2000. We now look at how the legislation impacts on the individual care worker.

As care workers we need to adhere to the following code of practice produced by the GSCC as part of their remit under the Care Standards Act 2000.

General Social Care Council: Code of Practice for Social Care Workers

The purpose of this code is to set out the conduct that is expected of social care workers and to inform service users and the public about the standards of conduct they can expect from social care workers. It forms part of the wider package of legislation, practice standards and employers' policies and procedures that social care workers must meet. Social care workers are responsible for making sure that their conduct does not fall below the standards set out in this code and that no action or omission on their part harms the well-being of service users.

Status

The General Social Care Council expects social care workers to meet this code and may take action if registered workers fail to do so.

Employers of social care workers are required to take account of this code in making any decisions about the conduct of their staff.

Social care workers must:

- protect the rights and promote the interests of service users and carers;
- strive to establish and maintain the trust and confidence of service users and carers;
- promote the independence of service users while protecting them as far as possible from danger or harm;
- respect the rights of service users whilst seeking to ensure that their behaviour does not harm themselves or other people;
- uphold public trust and confidence in social care services; and
- be accountable for the quality of their work and take responsibility for maintaining and improving their knowledge and skills.

1 **As a social care worker, you must protect the rights and promote the interests of service users and carers**

   This includes:

   1.1   treating each person as an individual;   →

1.2 respecting and, where appropriate, promoting the individual views and wishes of both service users and carers;

1.3 supporting service users' rights to control their lives and make informed choices about the services they receive;

1.4 respecting and maintaining the dignity and privacy of service users;

1.5 promoting equal opportunities for service users and carers; and

1.6 respecting diversity and different cultures and values.

2 **As a social care worker, you must strive to establish and maintain the trust and confidence of service users and carers**
This includes:

2.1 being honest and trustworthy;

2.2 communicating in an appropriate, open, accurate and straightforward way;

2.3 respecting confidential information and clearly explaining agency policies about confidentiality to service users and carers;

2.4 being reliable and dependable;

2.5 honouring work commitments, agreements and arrangements and, when it is not possible to do so, explaining why to service users and carers;

2.6 declaring issues that might create conflicts of interest and making sure that they do not influence your judgement or practice; and

2.7 adhering to policies and procedures about accepting gifts and money from service users and carers.

3 **As a social care worker, you must promote the independence of service users while protecting them as far as possible from danger or harm**
This includes:

3.1 promoting the independence of service users and assisting them to understand and exercise their rights;

3.2 using established processes and procedures to challenge and report dangerous, abusive, discriminatory or exploitative behaviour and practice;

3.3 following practice and procedures designed to keep you and other people safe from violent and abusive behaviour at work;

3.4 bringing to the attention of your employer or the appropriate authority resource or operational difficulties that might get in the way of the delivery of safe care;

3.5 informing your employer or an appropriate authority where the practice of colleagues may be unsafe or adversely affecting standards of care;

3.6 complying with employers' health and safety policies, including those relating to substance abuse; →

3.7 helping service users and carers to make complaints, taking complaints seriously and responding to them or passing them to the appropriate person; and

3.8 recognising and using responsibly the power that comes from your work with service users and carers.

4 As a social care worker, you must respect the rights of service users while seeking to ensure that their behaviour does not harm themselves or other people

This includes:

4.1 recognising that service users have the right to take risks and helping them to identify and manage potential and actual risks to themselves and others;

4.2 following risk assessment policies and procedures to assess whether the behaviour of service users presents a risk of harm to themselves or others;

4.3 taking necessary steps to minimise the risks of service users from doing actual or potential harm to themselves or other people; and

4.4 ensuring that relevant colleagues and agencies are informed about the outcomes and implications of risk assessments.

5 As a social care worker, you must uphold public trust and confidence in social care services

In particular you must not:

5.1 abuse, neglect or harm service users, carers or colleagues;

5.2 exploit service users, carers or colleagues in any way;

5.3 abuse the trust of service users and carers or the access you have to personal information about them or to their property, home or workplace;

5.4 form inappropriate personal relationships with service users;

5.5 discriminate unlawfully or unjustifiably against service users, carers or colleagues;

5.6 condone any unlawful or unjustifiable discrimination by service users, carers or colleagues;

5.7 put yourself or other people at unnecessary risk; or

5.8 behave in a way, in work or outside work, which would call into question your suitability to work in social care services.

6 As a social care worker, you must be accountable for the quality of your work and take responsibility for maintaining and improving your knowledge and skills

This includes:

6.1 meeting relevant standards of practice and working in a lawful, safe and effective way;

$\longrightarrow$

6.2 maintaining clear and accurate records as required by procedures established for your work;

6.3 informing your employer or the appropriate authority about any personal difficulties that might affect your ability to do your job competently and safely;

6.4 seeking assistance from your employer or the appropriate authority if you do not feel able or adequately prepared to carry out any aspect of your work, or you are not sure about how to proceed in a work matter;

6.5 working openly and co-operatively with colleagues and treating them with respect;

6.6 recognising that you remain responsible for the work that you have delegated to other workers;

6.7 recognising and respecting the roles and expertise of workers from other agencies and working in partnership with them; and

6.8 undertaking relevant training to maintain and improve your knowledge and skills and contributing to the learning and development of others.

These standards influence the role of the care worker and also the approach that the care worker should take in carrying out their responsibilities. They are evident in all the chapters in this book and there is a grid at the back of the book referring to sections that relate to these.

One of the aims of this chapter has been to give you a good foundation of knowledge relating to the current organisation of care and how your role as care workers fits into this framework. A theme throughout has been one of change, that the context of care is dynamic and subject to a range of influences.

Further Research

Think about the way that your own organisation has changed in the time that you have been there and make a list of what these changes have been. For each of these changes explore the reasons behind them, and the effects that these changes have had on

➲ the organisation as a whole

➲ the service users

➲ yourself and other care workers.

It is good practice to become very aware of changes that take place as this helps us to be more adaptable to change, and more professional in the way that we manage this with service users.

The subjects covered in this chapter are constantly changing so you need to find ways of finding out what is new. The internet provides a very useful means of keeping up to date with new legislation as well as providing guidelines relating to your role as a care worker. This form of communication has enabled the government to go some way in meeting its aim to be more open. Keeping up with the news is also a means of making sure that you know what changes are proposed, or taking place. At the end of 2003 the Prime Minister commenced a major initiative aimed at involving the public, including you and I, in political debates.

The following websites are useful to keep you up to date with legislation, official guidelines and news on care issues.

⊃ www.official-documents.org.uk
Government website for accessing all legislation

⊃ www.doh.gov.uk
Department of Health

⊃ www.dwp.gov.uk
Department for Work and Pensions

References and further reading

Alcock P (ed) (1998) *The Students Companion to Social Policy*, Oxford, Blackwell

Abbot P and Ackers L (1996) *Social Policy for Nurses and the Caring Profession*, Buckingham, Open University Press

Blackmore K (2003) *Social Policy: An Introduction*, Buckingham, Open University Press

Burchardt T (2003) *Being and Becoming: Social Exclusion and the Onset of Disability*, London, Joseph Rowntree Foundation

Crown (2000) *Explanatory Notes to the Care Standards Act*, London, HMSO

Crown (2002) *Delivering the NHS Plan: Next Steps on Investment, Next Steps on Reform*, London, HMSO

Deacon R (2002) *Perspectives on Welfare*, Buckingham, Open University Press

Department of Health (1998) *Modernising Social Services*, London, HMSO

Department of Health (1998) *They Look After Their Own Don't They?*, London, HMSO

Department of Health (1998) *Best Value*, London, HMSO

Department of Health (1999) *Modernising Mental Health: Safe, Sound and Supportive*, London, HMSO

Department of Health (1999) *Facing the Facts Services for People with hearing Difficulties: A Policy Impact Study of Social Care and Health Services*, London, HMSO

Department of Health (2001) *Valuing People*, London, HMSO

Department of Health (2001) *National Service Framework for Older People*, London, HMSO

Department of Health (2001) *Nothing About Us Without Us: Report form the Service Users Advisory Group*, London, HMSO

Hill M (2003) *Understanding Social Policy*, Oxford, Blackwell

Department of Health (2002) *Mental Health Bill: Consultation Document*, London, HMSO

Department of Health (2003) *Fair Access to Care Services*, London, HMSO

Department of Health (2003) *Independence Matters: An Overview of the Performance of Social Care Services for Physically and Sensory Disabled People*, London, HMSO

Department of Health (2004) *National Framework for Long-Term Health Conditions*, London, HMSO

Department of Health, *Modern Local Government: In Touch with the People*, London, HMSO

Forman F N (1999) *Mastering British Politics*, Basingstoke, Macmillan

Kleinman M (2002) *TA European Welfare State: European Social Policy in Context*, Basingstoke, Macmillan

Luckhurst L (2002) 'Direct cash in the hand', *Mental Health Today*, June

Malin N, Wilmot S and Manthorpe J *Key Concepts and Debates in Health and Social Policy*, Buckingham, Open University Press

Mir G, Nocon A, Ahmad W and Jones L (2001) *Report to the Department of Health, Learning Difficulties and Ethnicity*, London, HMSO

Nicoll, M, Ashworth M, McNally, L, Newman, S (2002) 'Satisfaction with respite care: a pilot study', *Health and Social Care in the Community* 10(6), 479–84

Personal Social Services Research Unit (2003) CAREdirect Evaluation Newsletter 3

Scull (1979) in Webster C (ed) *Caring for Health: Ethnicity and Diversity*, Buckingham, Open University Press

Seddon D and Robinson C (2001) 'Carers of older people with dementia; assessment and the Carers Act', *Health and Social Care in the Community* 9(3), 151–158:152

Stoddart H, Whitley, E, Harvey I, Sharp, D (2002) 'What determines the use of home care services by elderly people?' *Health and Social Care in the Community* 10(5), 348–60:358

Townsend (1962) in Webster C (ed) *Caring for Health: Ethnicity and Diversity*, Buckingham, Open University Press

Walker A (1982) in *Community Care*, Oxford, Blackwell

Webster C (ed) (2001) *Caring For Health: Ethnicity and Diversity,* Buckingham, Open University Press

University Of Warwick (2001) *Making a Difference: The Better Government of Older People,* National Evaluation Report

reflective practice

2

Whether you are at the beginning of your career in care or well established in your experience, it is always healthy to approach your work with the attitude that there is room for improvement. This chapter aims to support you in developing your ability to improve your care work by enabling you to become a reflective practitioner. A reflective practitioner is someone who thinks about their work, learns from this and then develops. The chapter starts by looking at what reflective practice is and why we should be interested in this. It will then introduce you to some theories about learning and give you an opportunity to explore the way that you learn as an individual. We then look at some models of reflection that you could use in order for you to explore and improve your own care practice.

Have you ever thought about something that happened at work, maybe thinking over the events of a day whilst you were on your way home or later on that day or evening? If you have then reflective practice will not be new to you, as you have already thought back over your work, and so, 'reflected on your practice'. What might however be new to you may be the idea of having a structure to this thinking, developing the ability to think about your own care practice in a way that encourages further learning and development.

What do we mean by the phrase 'reflective practice'? Quinn describes reflection as involving the following three stages [Quinn in Davies *et al* (2000), page 81]:

1 Looking back over what has happened – *retrospection*.

2 Making a judgement about the way you responded to a situation – *self-evaluation*.

3 Thinking about this in an enlightened way – *reorientation*.

It is this process that we are going to be looking at in this chapter, the aim being that as care workers we do not get stuck in a rut in our work.

This chapter addresses the following areas:

- ⊃ What is reflective practice?
- ⊃ The aims of reflective practice
- ⊃ Policy context
- ⊃ Knowledge
- ⊃ Skills
- ⊃ Understanding
- ⊃ Theories of learning
- ⊃ Models of reflection

⊃ Connecting learning with our care practice

⊃ Objectives

⊃ What to reflect on

⊃ Frameworks for evaluation

⊃ Evidence-based practice

⊃ Integration of theory and practice

⊃ SWOT analysis

⊃ Use of research

⊃ Who to reflect with

⊃ Why reflect?

⊃ Ethical issues in reflection

⊃ When should I reflect?

⊃ Supporting your peers and developing others

After reading this chapter it is hoped that you will be able to

1 understand why reflective practice is important in care work

2 understand theories of learning

3 know how to use models of reflection

4 know the range of resources that can be used to facilitate reflection.

What is reflective practice?

> Reflection is a process of reviewing an experience of practice in order to describe, analyse, evaluate and so inform learning about practice. [Reid (1993) in Ghaye and Lillyman (1997), page 6)]

Reflection is a process of reviewing (describing, analysing and evaluating) and therefore learning about practice.

If you said you had thought about your work when you have finished at the end of a shift then we could say that you have reviewed it, that you have looked over it again. This may have been a very useful exercise for you and it may have led you to work differently in the future. If so then you have probably analysed or evaluated your work. We shall look at what these words mean in this section, but before we look in depth at what reflective practice is, it would be useful to think about what it is that we do as care workers, and why we do it.

Let us look at what care work entails. Thinking about your job as a whole, you could separate out your work role into what you know and what you do.

You could do this when you start a job, or you could do it by looking at your job description . When you start a job the description of it will sometimes specify what experience you have, what knowledge you have, and also other factors to do with your approach to working with people. We can call these areas knowledge, skills and understanding. The relationship between them is set out in the diagram below.

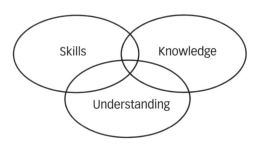

Skills Knowledge

Understanding

Figure 2.1 *Dimensions of your care role*

Think it over

Read through the following task that is being carried out and identify the following:

1 What the care worker needs to *know* in order to carry out that task.

2 What the care worker needs to *be able to do* in order to carry out that task.

3 What *attitude* to their work would enable the care worker to perform the task appropriately.

This task involves assisting a person with their personal care first thing in the morning. Carrying out the task is described in the following way.

'I knock on the person's door and ask them if they would like to get up. I assist them in getting out of the bed, being careful to not take any of the weight of the person.'

The following table sets out these dimensions in more detail.

What I do	The **Knowledge** I have in order to do this	The **Skills** I use	The **Attitude** I have that affects my approach
1 I knock on the bedroom door	I *know* that this individual action shows respect		I *respect* the person. I *value* the person's privacy
2 I ask the person if they want to get up	I *know* how to communicate with a person who has a hearing impairment I *know* how to communicate with someone when they are in bed	I can communicate with a person whose hearing is impaired	I *value* the person's sense of control I *understand* the importance of empowerment
3 I physically assist the person to get out of bed	I *know how to* provide appropriate physical assistance I *know* the guidelines for moving and handling	I *can* assist the person without putting them or myself at risk of physical injury	I *am sensitive to* how the individual may experience this action

What we have done here is break this care task down into the knowledge, skills and the attitude or understanding that I would need in order to carry this task out well. By doing this we can explore what role these play in developing our ability to carry out this task effectively. Some aspects of my knowledge, skills or attitude may be a feature of general knowledge and not something restricted to care work, e.g. it is unlikely a manager would have to give you a long induction showing you how to knock on the door; it may, however, be necessary to explain to you the reasons for, and importance of, knocking on the door. Depending on the particular task, there is sometimes more of an emphasis on knowledge, sometimes on skills, and sometimes on attitude.

To illustrate this I will go over the same task as if I do not have any of the knowledge, skills or attitudes that we have identified as being important in the table above.

> 'I walk into the person's room and prop the door open, as it is then easier for me later to assist her to the bathroom. I don't ask her what she wants to do, as it is the same routine everyday, so it is pointless to me to have a dialogue about it. I then assist the person out of bed; it hurts my back supporting them, but it is quicker than waiting for her to move herself.'

As you can see, the way that I carry out this task now does not make use of any of the knowledge about communication or moving and handling. Also, I am not using my practical skills to support the person appropriately, and I do not have a good understanding of the need to respect the person's privacy or their independence, and this affects my attitude. The way I carry out this task has a direct influence on the person that I am supporting. Their experience of this task would be completely different if I carried it out in the way it was described earlier. This is just a very small task to illustrate the point. Imagine the impact that lack of knowledge, skills and a poor attitude would have on the lives of individuals across the whole of their day.

Of course your role as a care worker is not just a grouping of tasks. You may wonder how appropriate it is to divide the work you do into such tasks, as care work is not a production line activity. In care work it is important to understand the actual purpose of the work activity, and how the individual tasks fit together to provide a purpose for the person being supported. For example, a 'task' may be to support Andrew, who is learning disabled, travelling from his home to the local college for a course. The easiest way to do this would be to drive him there – it's only 10 minutes in the car. If this task is explored in more depth we may see that there are some important elements to it which would not be addressed if we drove Andrew there.

The aims of the task should be

- ↪ that Andrew takes responsibility for attending the college
- ↪ that he develops his ability to make his own way to the college by public transport so that he develops his independence.

These aims will influence the way that the original task is carried out. Instead of just driving Andrew to the college, his support workers would need to devise a plan with him for developing his ability to gradually undertake this journey independently. The purpose of the task is therefore very significant; it can be described as its 'function'.

Think it over

Identify a care task that you carry out in a routine way regularly at work. Think about what the function of it is for the person you are assessing, how it supports their overall care needs, and the development of their independence or general well-being. In what ways could you improve how you carry out this task in order to enhance the role you are playing in the overall care/support needs of the person you are caring for?

How we develop our care practice involves developing all areas, i.e. our knowledge, skills and our understanding or attitude.

Bloom in Maslin-Prosthero [(1997), page 185] separates out learning into three 'domains':

1 The *cognitive* domain concerns our thinking and memory, and our capacity for understanding new knowledge.

2 The *psychomotor* domain deals with our abilities, the skills that we have, what we can physically do.

3 Our *affective* domain relates to our understanding, i.e. our approach, our attitude to what we do.

We do not always think about our work in relation to these three areas; we tend to just get on with our work. Hopefully, reading through this chapter will give you an opportunity to stop and think, to take stock of the kind of work that you are in and what contribution you are making to it.

If we return to the case of Andrew (page 60) and think about the support workers working with him, we can see that they need to make use of all three of these domains if they are going to promote his independence. All care work requires us to make good use of all of these domains. Whilst we may sometimes be very conscious of our use of one domain, our best practice comes together when we know, understand and can actually perform a task.

The support workers may need to develop their knowledge of supporting Andrew in his learning about the journey, perhaps the different strategies that they could use. They may need to develop their skills in assisting him in a way that doesn't limit the development of his independence. They may need to apply their understanding of Andrew's rights and the importance of developing his independence in the long term, so that they do not choose the easy option in the short term.

Andrew's support workers may not actually be conscious of using all three domains in this activity; sometimes we are more aware of this than at other times. I may be very aware of my use of the *cognitive* domain if I have read about how to do something and then I try to remember what I read as I am doing the task, such as giving medication. I may be very aware of my *psychomotor* domain if I am trying out something new, that I have watched somebody else do, such as using a new hoist for the first time. I may be very aware of using my *affective* domain if I am talking to relatives and I am aware of observing the confidentiality of the individual that I support.

Reflection is not just about looking back, it is about moving forward. Reflective practice is about developing knowledge, skills and understanding so as to maximise these for the benefit of the people that you work with.

The aims of reflective practice

Care work is very pressurised; time is limited so we need to value the impact that reflective practice can make on us in the long term. Who is responsible for making sure that we provide the best care at all times to the people that we support? Is it

⊃ our colleagues?

⊃ our managers?

⊃ the Commission for Social Care Inspection?

Although these do have a role, which we will explore in a later section, you have a key responsibility in both developing and then monitoring your own ability. Reflective practice can play an important role in this.

Reflective practice can

⊃ expose poor practice

⊃ identify issues that arise in care work

⊃ assist in understanding what you do in work

⊃ justify particular types of intervention

⊃ increase accountability

⊃ highlight good practice

⊃ promote good practice

⊃ enhance good practice, and further improve what you do at work

⊃ promote quality in your provision of care

⊃ help manage stress.

Of course there are other ways of achieving these desired outcomes; you could attend a training course, be supervised more closely or follow instructions whenever you undertake a task. Reflective practice does not replace these methods of learning and developing, it provides an additional tool for addressing all of the above, and also for enhancing your ability to maximise these other methods of improving your practice. It can help by

⊃ bridging the gaps between what you learn on a course or in training and what actually happens when you are at work

⊃ providing a framework for you to discuss your work with yourself. This is known as 'counter discourse' and is particularly useful if you work alone and do not have many opportunities to talk about your work with others.

Figure 2.2 *Which approach is the reflective one?*

Policy context

Later in the chapter we are going to explore the role that policy plays in the reflection process. Policy is discussed in every chapter in this book because it informs our responsibilities in different aspects of care work. The idea of reflective practice has been developed in response to a number of developments in care work. As discussed in the chapter on the context of care (Chapter 1), the relationship of professionals to individuals who need care/support has changed; they are no longer expected to be grateful recipients of a paternalistic approach to care provision; the focus is more on rights and the empowerment of individuals. There is an increased emphasis on justifying why a certain course of action was taken, or why a particular type of intervention has been adopted. It relates to the 'why?' of care practice. There is more regulation in care work with the introduction of the Care Standards Act 2000, and from this the development of accountability. There now needs to be evidence that forms the basis of decision-making.

That evidence can come from your own experience, 'I did it before and it worked', or from others' experience, 'Someone else did it before and it worked.'

Certain key words in the Care Standards Act need to be looked at here: *accountability, responsibility* and *autonomy.*

➲ *Accountability*

This is defined as being 'responsible, required to account for one's own conduct.' [Concise Oxford Dictionary (1991)] As a care worker there will be people who you feel you have to 'report to' about your work. This may not mean checking in with them all the time, but it may be a line manager or supervisor who is responsible for the service as a whole.

➲ *Responsibility*

This is having the 'authority, the ability to act independently and make decisions.' [Concise Oxford Dictionary (1991)] These are the responsibilities that you have in the role that you perform and the function of that role.

➲ *Autonomy*

This is 'the right of self-government'. This relates both to accountability and responsibility. The autonomy that you have includes the decisions about your work that you are allowed to make, self-management, and the way you set priorities.

Case Study

Accountability, responsibility and autonomy

In order to explore accountability and responsibility we shall look at the role of Nadia, a care support worker (night duty) in a care home for older people.

Responsibility Nadia is responsible for ensuring the safety and well-being of individuals during the night, and responding to care/support needs as they arise.

Accountability In a direct way Nadia is accountable to

➲ the older people who live in the care home – the residents

➲ the care home manager

➲ the other night staff

➲ the day care support workers.

She is also accountable to

➲ the Commission for Social Care Inspection

➲ the Company Management Committee and the Director

➲ the relatives of the residents

➲ the public in their expectation of what support is provided in care homes.

Autonomy Nadia has control over making decisions about what time to undertake certain tasks. She has to respond in the best way to issues that arise in the night, as in the case of someone who is unwell. She needs to use her initiative in responding to phone calls from people who are phoning in sick.

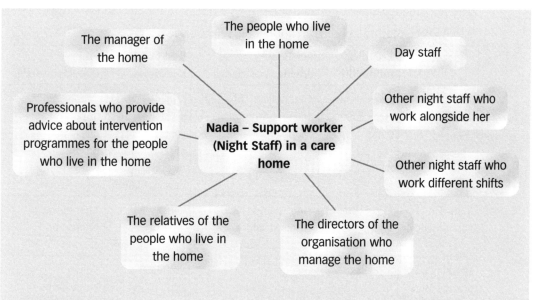

The manager of the home

The people who live in the home

Day staff

Professionals who provide advice about intervention programmes for the people who live in the home

Nadia – Support worker (Night Staff) in a care home

Other night staff who work alongside her

Other night staff who work different shifts

The relatives of the people who live in the home

The directors of the organisation who manage the home

Task

Look at the chart identifying the different people who benefit from the work of Nadia, and then identify who are the people or other agencies who benefit from your own work.

Think about what relationship you have to these other people or agencies in terms of your

⊃ responsibilities

⊃ accountability

⊃ autonomy.

The idea of reflective practice must take account of the context of your care practice. This means that you need to consider not only who benefits from your work, but who is responsible for you knowing about what you need to do.

Let us return to the three domains of learning that we looked at earlier and explore these in more detail.

Knowledge

What we know about anything is built up over time – i.e. it is cumulative. So, what is knowledge?

There are different types of knowledge, sometimes divided into the following four areas:

1 *Technical rationality* – knowledge of the facts.

2 *Personal/practice knowledge* – life experience and knowledge acquired through general work activity.

3 *Experiential knowledge* – acquired through your care work.

4 *Ethical/moral knowledge* – intuitive judgements.

We can consider these different types of knowledge in relation to the subject areas of this book, as in the table below.

	Technical rationality	Personal/ practice knowledge	Experiential knowledge	Ethical/ moral knowledge
The context of care	Facts about government policy	That policies, funding and organisations change with time	Knowledge about how to ensure the organisation responds to new legislation	Valuing the important role I have in promoting the values of the organisation
Values in care practice	Legislation relating to discrimination	Some people have different values	Dilemmas arise in providing care	That these are important
Working with service users	Models of intervention with different service user groups	General communication skills	Strategies to support people that can be most effective	Valuing empowerment
Assessment	What assessment tools to use	Importance of first contact when meeting people	Different expectations of the assessment from service users	Knowledge of the importance of the individual owning their assessment
Planning care	Organisational policy and the care planning process	Knowledge that change can be difficult for people	Knowledge about the availability of services in the local area	Importance of service user control over the planning process
Collaborative working	Organisational expectations. Theories of collaborative working	General awareness of the complex nature of communicating with different people	Knowledge of how best to work with a particular agency	Knowledge of the importance of collaborative working, even if at times there are tensions to overcome
Adult protection	No Secrets Knowing my responsibility for protecting adults	Awareness of abuse as an issue in society	Knowledge of the difficulties in maintaining confidentiality	Knowing how important protection is

The way we acquire knowledge may be different for these subject areas. For example, you may not have read about collaborative working before, but feel you have quite a bit of knowledge about it based on working with a range of professionals from other agencies. You may feel that your knowledge of values developed before you started working in care work, as you have always had an awareness of issues to do with discrimination and confidentiality.

Using our knowledge

Bloom's cognitive hierarchy provides a way of exploring what we can do with our knowledge.

Stage in the processing of knowledge	Definition
Knowledge	Information, facts
Interpretation, understanding	Making sense of this knowledge
Application	Using this knowledge by connecting it to the work situation
Analysis	Thinking about the knowledge from different angles, asking yourself questions about it
Synthesis	Bringing together different areas of knowledge in order to understand a situation, or use a skill
Evaluation	Looking back on a situation using this knowledge and making a judgement about it

To identify valuable information you can draw on to inform your reflection, you need to be able to distinguish between different types of information, for example is the information fact or an opinion?

Think it over

Lisa is thinking about how effective her care practice is in relation to ascertaining what service users think of the Supported Living scheme that she manages.

'I know exactly what people think of the scheme because I get staff to support the tenants in completing a questionnaire. The tenants know that they can complain about anything that they are not happy with. Staff inform me of any issues in supervision, and the tenants have regular meetings, at which they can say anything.'

From Lisa's account distinguish between what is fact and what is opinion.

The following table shows responses to the above exercise.

I know exactly what people think of the scheme	*Fact?* Lisa may only know part of what people think
I get staff to support the tenants in completing a questionnaire	*Fact?* Evidenced by signed questionnaires
The tenants know that they can complain about anything	*Fact?* Some tenants may not feel comfortable complaining
Staff inform me of any issues in supervision	*Fact?* Evidenced by supervision notes
The tenants have regular meetings	*Fact?* Evidenced by dates of meetings and minutes
The tenants can say anything at these meetings	*Fact?* Tenants may feel uncomfortable speaking up

Lisa's impression of what she knows is influenced by her expectations of what should be happening.

When we focus on evidence we may emphasise what we saw as 'hard' data the paperwork and statistics that support statements (see page 87). This may mean that we miss the point when it comes to valuing the opinions of individuals within the service. Initially we may think that facts are more important than opinions, but is this true? If a service user *feels* that they do not go out as much as another service user, this may be untrue, however it doesn't mean we can dismiss it as being of no significance. The service user's experience is valuable and important. The fact that they FEEL like that is the significant point, whether or not there is any truth underlying that feeling. It then becomes important to understand why the service user feels like that and to address this feeling. If we had ignored this comment and just looked at statistics that showed us it wasn't true, then we would have been missing the point.

It is important to know how to interpret information and how to understand the value of a piece of information, and how to piece them together so that they make sense as a whole. It is much more common now for research to make explicit reference to anecdotes as a valuable contribution to the results of research. This represents a shift towards accepting qualitative knowledge as well as quantitative information.

Knowledge becomes a resource for us to use in our work. It can inform our understanding of how to perform certain tasks. It can help us to understand why a person might behave in a certain way. It can prevent us from intervening in a way that could be harmful. In order for us to utilise the knowledge that we have, we need to become more conscious of it.

What do you know you know?

The table below [Pedler *et al* (2001), page 56] separates out four types of knowledge. These depend on being very aware of our knowledge (Box A), having knowledge that we do not realise we have (Box C), being aware that there are areas of knowledge we do not know about (Box B), or areas of knowledge that we do not even know exist (Box D).

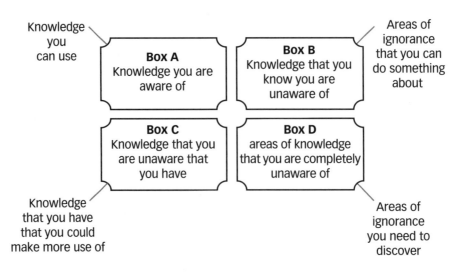

Figure 2.3 *Types of knowledge*

What do we know?

Serena is a home support worker for a home care agency. She has been doing the job for six months. She mainly supports older people, but also has provided care in homes of people with physical mobility needs. The following is the knowledge that Serena has acquired.

Box A Knowledge you are aware that you have.
Serena knows what the care needs are of older people and how to support them in their homes effectively. She is conscious of this knowledge and uses it all the time.

Box B Knowledge that you know you are unaware of.
Serena knows that she needs to find out more information about how to communicate with older people with sensory impairments.

Box C Knowledge that you are unaware you have.
Serena has developed a lot of knowledge about supporting people in rehabilitation through the work that she does with people in their own homes.

Box D Knowledge that you don't know exists.
Serena doesn't know that she has a whole are of knowledge missing – knowledge relating to the mental health needs of older people. She does not realise that older people can have specific health needs.

The following illustrates what we should aim to do with these different areas of knowledge.

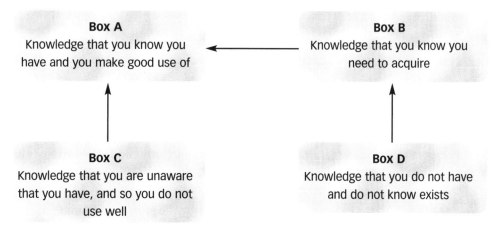

Box A
Knowledge that you know you have and you make good use of

Box B
Knowledge that you know you need to acquire

Box C
Knowledge that you are unaware that you have, and so you do not use well

Box D
Knowledge that you do not have and do not know exists

How does this process apply to Serena's situation? Her aim is to develop more of a command of the knowledge that she already has, and understand what she needs to find out about in order to develop as a support worker.

Serena wants to move all areas of her knowledge to Box A – knowledge that she is conscious of and can use effectively.

	Strategies that Serena could use
Box B	Request training Obtain resources about this – books, internet, library Ask other professionals
Box C	Reflect on all areas of her work and identify knowledge that she is either not making good use of or underusing Try to use this knowledge more in her daily care practice
Box D	Think about her job in a very broad way to identify aspects of it that are underdeveloped Consider what the experience of the service user is and develop a holistic approach to supporting them Ask the service user, other professionals, family members etc. what they feel would make a difference to the individual Access information from organisations that advocate for older people through telephoning them or through the internet

In order for any of these to happen, Serena needs to be proactive about her work, she needs to have that sense of accountability to the service user and her organisation and take responsibility for self-development. She needs to be motivated to address her own learning needs and to understand how she can change.

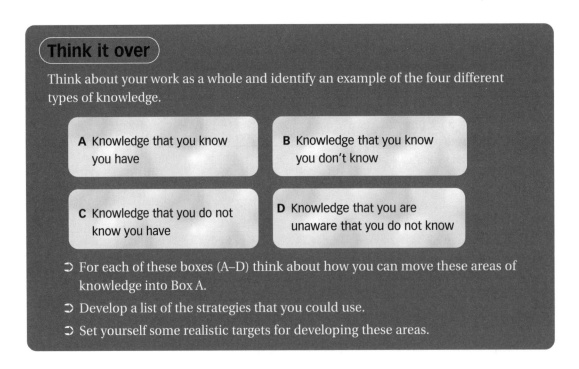

Think it over

Think about your work as a whole and identify an example of the four different types of knowledge.

A Knowledge that you know you have

B Knowledge that you know you don't know

C Knowledge that you do not know you have

D Knowledge that you are unaware that you do not know

> ⟳ For each of these boxes (A–D) think about how you can move these areas of knowledge into Box A.
> ⟳ Develop a list of the strategies that you could use.
> ⟳ Set yourself some realistic targets for developing these areas.

We have identified that knowledge, skills and understanding, whilst being discrete areas, are dependent on each other, and all interlink. We turn now to skills.

Skills

Skills are what you can do, in work practice they are sometimes referred to as areas of competence.

Whilst skills describe what you can do, rather than what you know, it is clear that the development of skills is dependent on your knowledge. Have you ever thought of a particular task that you have some knowledge about, but you just seem unable to do it? Well with some activities it is not enough to know what you need to be able to do, you need to actually be able to perform the task too! Sometimes this gap between what we know and what we can do relates to

➲ lack of opportunity to practice

➲ the need for further knowledge

➲ support or guidance about changing what we do

➲ development of confidence.

If you have ever done an NVQ (National Vocational Qualification), you will be familiar with the idea of competence. It means that you are able to complete a task or action to the required standard.

A skills model

Dreyfus provides a model of skills acquisition which explores the different levels of ability that we may have with different skills [Tight (1997), page 123].

Figure 2.4 *Dreyfus' model of skills acquisition*

➲ *Novice* This means that you can undertake the task as if it is new to you. You may not have done it before, or only a few times.

➲ *Advanced beginner* This means that you are able to do the task but are still learning about it, so you may still need to be supervised or to check out how to do it each time.

➲ *Competent* This means that you are able to do something in the required way and to the required standard.

➲ *Proficient* This implies that not only can you do the task above the required standard, you would feel confident in your ability to do it and would not need assistance or advice about it in order to undertake it well.

➲ *Expert* This level of skill means that you have developed in this skill to such an extent that you can perform a task well above the required ability and standard. You would undertake a task in a way that others could learn from you.

Think it over

Think about these levels in terms of your job as a whole, or in relation to particular tasks.

1 How long have you been doing your job and what level would you place yourself at generally?
2 Do you feel that you are a novice, competent or an expert in any specific tasks that are required of you; maybe there are some tasks that are new to you, or that you haven't been asked to do yet?

Case Study

How skilful are you at caring?

Des has been a mental health support worker for four years and he feels that he has acquired a number of skills in this area of work. He has just joined a project that is focusing on supporting people with mental health problems who also have alcohol or substance addictions. This is new to Des.

We could say that Des has a general level of competence in the area of supporting people with mental health problems. There will be some aspects of this that he may be quite proficient at. However, he may feel that he is a novice in the area of supporting people with dependencies and addictions.

Think it over

↻ In your current job role think about an example of an area of practice that you are new to. How can you move from being a novice through to becoming competent in this task?

↻ Also think of an aspect of your work that you feel competent in and identify how you can progress from competence through to becoming an expert. This can prove motivational, in striving to see if you can develop expertise in an area.

Understanding

Your approach to your work is not only the combination of the knowledge and skills that you have, but also your understanding of the work, or your values that underpin the way that you carry out your work.

Let us return to the example at the beginning of the chapter:

'I walk into the person's room and prop the door open, as it is then easier for me later to assist her to the bathroom. I don't ask her what she wants to do, as it is the same routine everyday, so it is pointless to me to have a dialogue about it. I then assist the person out of bed; it hurts my back supporting them, but it is quicker than waiting for her to move herself.'

Obstacles to the way we work

There are various factors that prevent us adopting a professional, caring approach to our work. These include

⊃ dissatisfaction with aspects of employment, e.g. pay, hours, holiday entitlement

⊃ problematic relationships with colleagues

⊃ not getting on with managers

⊃ not feeling valued ourselves.

There are ways to overcome these negative feelings and adopt a more positive approach. These include

⊃ seeing the value of doing our job properly

⊃ understanding our jobs in terms of the role that they serve, rather than just as a series of tasks

⊃ having a sense of accountability to the service users

⊃ focusing on the relationship with the service user as a key feature of our role

⊃ being proactive about dealing with issues that are causing concern.

Together these amount to 'being professional'.

Theories of learning

Reflection is a process by which we facilitate learning and support development. In this section we look at what learning is, and how we as individuals learn.

Jarvis provides five meanings for the idea of learning [in Tight (1997), page 23]. Learning involves

⊃ a change in behaviour as a result of experience

⊃ a change in behaviour as a result of practice (more deliberate than in the first bullet)

⊃ the process whereby knowledge is created through the transformation of experience

⊃ the processes of transforming experience into knowledge, skills and attitudes

⊃ memorising information.

Think about the relevance of each of these to any care workers' experience of learning, as shown in the table below.

Type of learning	Explanation
A change in behaviour as a result of experience	What you do today in your care work will have been influenced by the experiences that you have had in the past, both in work and in your own life
A change in behaviour as a result of practice (more deliberate than in the first type of learning above)	You try out a new task and it doesn't go to plan so you try it out several times until you feel that you have got it right
The process whereby knowledge is created through the transformation of experience	The knowledge that you have has not only been acquired through training, reading etc., you also acquire knowledge through what happens when you do something
The processes of transforming experience into knowledge, skills and attitudes	When you have an experience in the workplace it is useful to separate out the knowledge, skills and attitude that influenced that task in order to identify what needs to change
Memorising information	This is where you have to remember certain facts or situations

Think it over

1 Think about what you know, and what you can do in your current job.
2 Think of an example of each of the above types of learning from your own care practice.
3 Work out how you can develop each way of learning so that you are more aware of new learning situations in your workplace.

Reflecting and evaluating as part of learning

To reflect is to think about, to reconsider, look back over what you have done; to evaluate is to make an assessment of, to judge what you have done. We do these in learning about what we do.

Thinking back over something is not necessarily going to improve your care practice. Along with this thinking back there needs to be some evaluation of what you have done and then some learning about what could be done differently.

We may ask what we mean by the word 'learning'? It can be seen as an outcome, as in 'I have learnt how to use the new hoist.' (Yesterday I couldn't use it, today I can.) or as a process, as in 'I am learning how to communicate with people using British Sign Language'. (I am developing in my ability to use BSL.)

If we don't reflect on our work, we are likely to do it in a routine way without thinking about what it is we do. The most important aspect of reflection is that you *learn from it*.

What sort of learner are you?

Learning can mean different things to different people, and can mean different things according to different contexts. Your memories of learning to drive may be very different from your memories of learning history at school. Learning is usually affected by our interest in the subject, our motivation to learn and the way in which we are taught. Much research has been carried out to explore the different ways in which people learn.

> ### Think it over
>
> Before you look at theories relating to learning, think about your own experience of learning in the past.
>
> 1 Identify a positive learning experience you had and identify what made it positive. How could you make sure that you have more learning experiences like this in the future?
>
> 2 Identify a negative learning experience you have had, and think about what made it negative. What could you do to make sure that this type of experience is not repeated?
>
> 3 Think about something that you found it easy to learn.
>
> 4 Think about something that you found it difficult to learn.
>
> When you reflect on these what are the differences you can identify from a variety of learning experiences?

There are some factors that prevent or disrupt learning. These include

- ⊃ emotions
- ⊃ lack of motivation to learn
- ⊃ time
- ⊃ environment.

There is a theory that learning takes place according to how our bodies and senses respond. It suggests that some people have a preference for whether they learn through seeing, hearing, doing or reading what they need to learn.

- ⊃ *Auditory* (What we hear) Have you ever had the words to a song you have heard on the radio go round and round in your head even if you do not particularly like the song?
- ⊃ *Visual* (What we see) Have you ever described someone's appearance to a friend even if you can't remember that person's name?

⊃ *Kinaesthetic* (What we physically feel and actively do) Have you ever been surprised that you were able to complete a task, because you have previously done it once?

⊃ *Written* (What we read) Have you ever remembered what was written on an advert on a bus or at a train station even though you were not making an effort to read it?

Think it over

Answer the following examples of questions that can help you to think about what type of learner you are.

1 When learning how something works do you
   ⊃ follow a diagram or picture (visual)
   ⊃ need to be told how to put it together (auditory)
   ⊃ try to fit the pieces together until it all fits (kinaesthetic)
   ⊃ read the instructions (written)?

2 When cooking a new dish do you
   ⊃ try to make it by trial and error, tasting it as you do it (kinaesthetic)
   ⊃ watch a video of TV chefs Delia or Jamie (visual)
   ⊃ follow a recipe in a book (written)
   ⊃ remember what a friend said you should do (auditory)?

3 If you are visiting somewhere new, do you prefer to
   ⊃ follow a map (visual)
   ⊃ have written instructions (written)
   ⊃ visit there with someone else as a trial run (kinaesthetic)
   ⊃ be told how to get there (auditory)?

These three types of questions are not likely to give you a complete and accurate answer to which learning style you have, but they may help you to think about how you like to learn new things. Learning does not happen in isolation. We do not always get to choose what method of learning we use; it is usually imposed on us.

Case Study

Learning styles

Think about the following scenario. What types of learning style are expected of Lucy on her second day at work as a care worker?

Lucy arrives at the Disability Resource Centre. As part of her learning she does the following:

⊃ She **reads** *the policies and practices folder* to learn about health and safety issues.

- She ***watches*** *how one of the other care workers* assists one of the service users at mealtime.
- She ***talks to*** *some of the service users,* ***adjusting how she*** *communicates* in line with the feedback she is getting from them.
- She ***listens*** *to how she should move the hoist,* and then is expected to move it back to a person's bedroom.

Even when Lucy has been in her job for days, weeks, months or years it is likely that she will be expected to carry on using all these methods of learning on a regular basis.

Enhancing your capacity for learning in all these styles will improve your overall performance. However, you may not be in a situation where you can choose the method of learning to use, as in the context of work or when you go on training courses, sometimes we don't get to choose which style of learning to use.

Think it over

1 If you need to learn something new at work do you prefer to
- sit in the office and read about it
- watch a colleague
- listen to someone telling you what to do
- practise it yourself?

2 Give examples of each from your own experience. Think about how your choice relates to the four styles above.

3 What are you usually expected to do when you need to learn something new?

4 What implications does this have on your learning in the workplace?

You may never have thought of work as a learning environment. We tend to think of learning as something we do on a training course or in reading a book. However, there are many opportunities to develop in our understanding, knowledge and skills through our experiences at work. The activity that you will carry out on Kolb's reflection (page 80) should enable you to do that.

Think it over

Think about the following statements and which ones you are more likely to say.

1 'I take pride in doing a thorough, mechanical job.'

2 'The present is much more important than thinking about the past or the future.'

3 'The key factor in judging a proposed idea or solution is whether it works in practice or not.'

4 'I like to relate my actions to a general principle.'

5 'I tend to solve problems using a step-by-step approach, avoiding any fanciful ideas.'

6 'I do whatever seems necessary to get the job done.'

7 'I like to ponder many alternatives before making up my mind.'

8 'I enjoy the drama and excitement of a crisis.'

Honey and Mumford identified four different types of learning style: reflector, pragmatist, theorist, activist. According to this you might have chosen the following styles to match the statements in the exercise above.

1	Reflector	2	Activist
3	Pragmatist	4	Theorist
5	Theorist	6	Pragmatist
7	Reflector	8	Activist

The following are some of the general characteristics of the learning styles.

Learning style	Some general characteristics
Reflector	Cautious. Likes to collect information and think over the past before taking action
Activist	Open minded and will try anything once. Acts first and considers the consequences afterwards. Likes new challenges
Pragmatist	Likes to try out new ideas and see if they work. Likes problem solving and making practical decisions
Theorist	Perfectionists. Likes to think about things in a logical way.

Once again it is not possible here to provide the full interpretation of these styles, but hopefully this snapshot gives enough for you to think about your own approach.

When your manager asks you to undertake a new task which of the following responses are you most likely to have?

	Positive	Care staff	Negatives
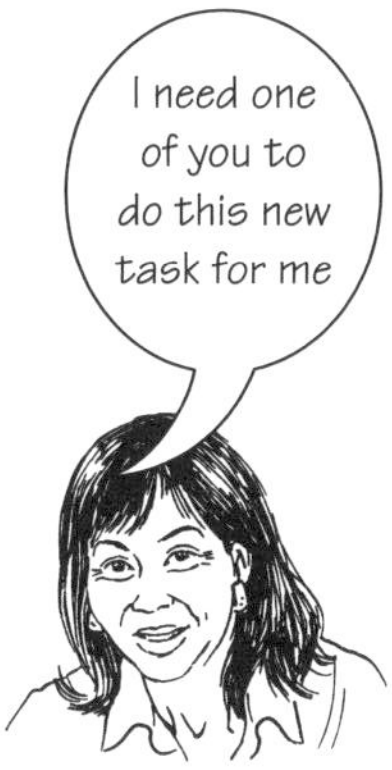 *Manager*	The job gets done, and done quickly	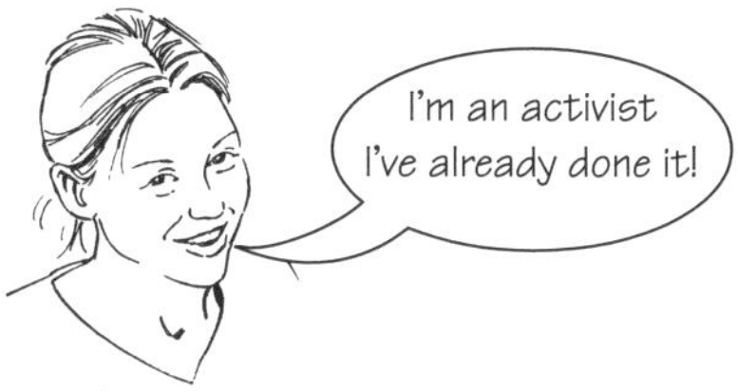 *Vicky is an activist*	You might not complete the task in the best way
	The task will be thought through in a systematic way and relevant theories applied to it	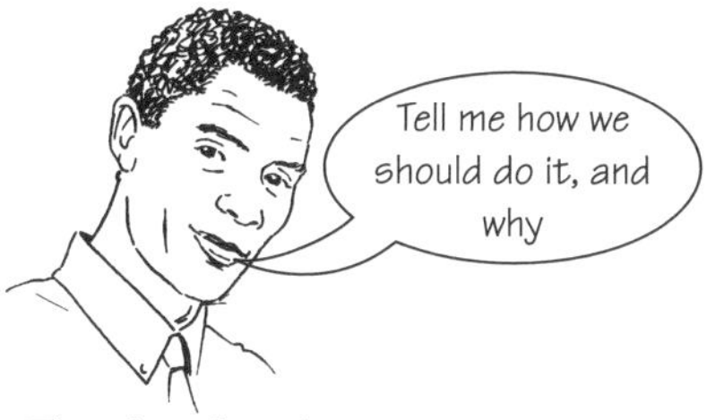 *Theo is a theorist*	May feel uncomfortable making subjective judgements about what to do
	The job will be done thoroughly	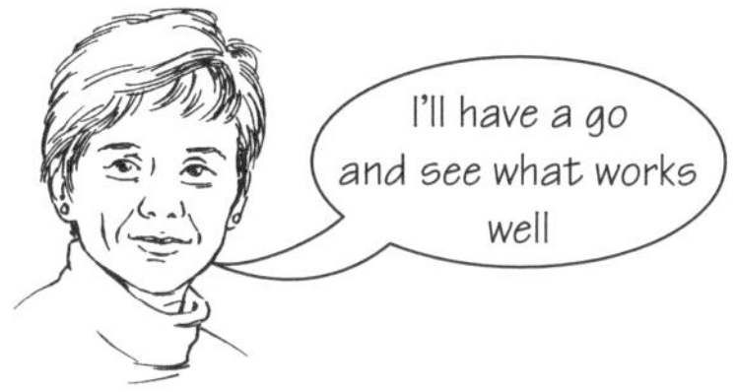 *Aggie is a pragmatist*	Trial and error, may prove a real trial, and lots of errors
	I know you will think about the best way to complete the task based on what you have done previously	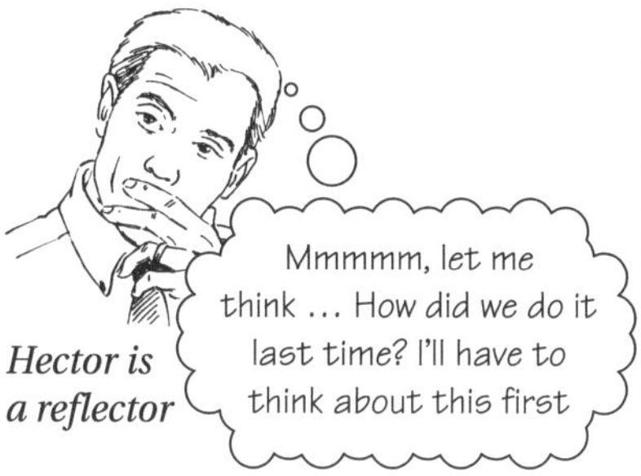 *Hector is a reflector*	I have to wait for you to do the job when you have had a chance to think about it

Figure 2.5 *Learning styles*

Looking at the advantages and disadvantages of each of these learning styles, it becomes clear that it might be useful to draw on each of these as appropriate. Depending on what style you naturally have, there may be barriers to overcome in adopting a different style.

The value of identifying your own learning style is that you can consider ways of developing a more reflective style.

Models of reflection

Kolb's model of reflection

We now explore some models of reflection that can be used as a framework for reflection. A well respected theory of experiential learning is provided by the Kolb cycle. This explores the stages through which a person must progress in order to complete what he calls a cycle of reflection.

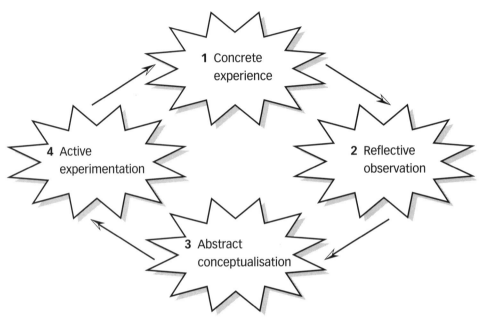

Figure 2.6 *The Kolb cycle*

Stages of the Kolb model

The stages are:

Stage 1 Concrete experience This is the initial experience: what has happened, what you did, what the outcome was. It is the description of a work activity that you look back on.

Stage 2 Reflective observation This takes place after the event or occurrence at work. This stage involves thinking about the experience, trying to look at it from a number of perspectives or from different angles.

Stage 3 Abstract conceptualisation This stage involves analysing the experience, unpicking all the detail of what happened. It involves identifying theories that could relate to the experience and seeing the connection between what you did and what could have been done. It also includes making reference to relevant theories that explain this situation, or identifying models that could be used to structure your future work. →

Stage 4 **Active experimentation** This stage involves applying the theories that you have identified in Stage 3. It includes testing out the new ideas that you have thought about as a result of your thinking in Stages 2 and 3, and putting into practice the new way of undertaking a particular task.

After Stage 4 we revert back to Stage 1 so that you progress through a constant cycle of experience and reflection.

If you have never gone through this cycle in a formal way then there are some ways of starting this process and making it more effective. Let us look at each stage and identify strategies to maximise what happens in each.

Strategies for reflection

Stage 1 Concrete experience

- Being more aware of what is happening at the time that it is happening. Being conscious of what you are doing.
- Thinking about what you are doing, whilst you are doing it.

Stage 2 Reflective observation

- Making time to reflect when the experience is fresh in your mind.
- Making a few notes about what happened and how you feel about it.
- Being aware of how valuable this process can be will help you to allocate time to do this.
- Not dismissing an event as inconsequential.
- Not making too big a deal of it. If you think you have got to set aside two hours to reflect then you will probably never get round to it. Set yourself 10 minutes and then if necessary you can build on this. Not starting to reflect is the main stumbling block.

Stage 3 Abstract conceptualisation

- Making sure you have access to a range of theories and models that may relate to this experience.
- Keeping up to date with ideas about your work.
- Practising thinking about your work from different angles or viewpoints.

Stage 4 Active experimentation

- Being prepared to try out new things.
- Having a structured approach to applying these theories that will then provide the next learning opportunity.
- Having open and supportive discussions about trying new ways of working with your manager and colleagues.

As with many aspects of care work caution needs to be applied to certain aspects of this cycle of reflection:

- ⊃ In Stage 1 a concrete experience for you would usually involve other people. That experience does not become yours to reinvent. It remains a fact that they may also be going through this cycle of reflection and may come up with different conclusions.

- ⊃ During Stage 2, reflecting on a situation can sometimes lead to negative feelings about your own ability to perform a task or role effectively. Inertia can then set in, and we spend a disproportionate amount of time reflecting instead of getting on with a new task. This approach can be overcome by focusing on the aims of reflection, and that you are reflecting in order to change what you do in the future, so you need to think about what to do with your reflection.

- ⊃ Whilst undertaking Stage 3 you need to remember that theories are possible ways of looking at a situation; they do not necessarily provide a factual account of why something happened. It may be inappropriate to adopt a theory wholesale and then pretend to be an expert on a particular situation. The same applies to models of working; these may have to be implemented with caution and sensitivity.

- ⊃ In Stage 4 individuals you work with are not meant to be part of an experiment, so trying out new things needs to be done with the best interests of the service users in mind.

Case Study

Cycle of reflection

Brenda is a deputy manager at a day service for learning disabled adults.

At work one day she is disappointed in the way she handles a team meeting. She needed to discuss some important changes that are going to be taking place, and she really wanted to involve everyone in the team. Once again two support workers on the team, who she has been trying to get more involved, created a situation beforehand that they said they needed to sort out, and therefore did not attend the meeting. Brenda feels frustrated that this has become a pattern, and feels annoyed with herself that she has 'allowed' this to happen.

Let us take Brenda through the stages in Kolb's model of reflection:

Stage 1 Brenda describes what has happened. She planned a meeting, two members of staff did not want to attend and they manufactured a problem to excuse themselves from the meeting.

Stage 2 Brenda reflects on this experience and identifies the key points:

1 Two members of staff did not want to come to the meeting – why?

2 Two members of staff were able to avoid the meeting – how?

3 The meeting went well as far as those who attended were concerned.

4 The people who Brenda feels will have issues with the changes were not part of the team discussion – this does not bode well for the future.

Stage 3 Brenda considers different ways of looking at this situation and tries to identify ideas or theories that may help her to understand what happened with more clarity.

She explores possible reasons why the two support workers are not team players (e.g. in supervision with individual staff Brenda discusses the person's approach to working with the team and finds out that they just do not like team meetings. One support worker says that she thinks they are a waste of time).

1 She looks for different views on how she could approach this situation.

2 She discusses it in supervision with her manager.

3 She asks her peers who manage other services.

4 She thinks about how she handles other situations and what she could learn from previous work settings and how she has observed other managers handle things in the past.

5 She gets a book out the library on managing meetings.

Stage 4 The big test: the next team meeting. Brenda takes the following action:

1 She anticipates possible problems and changes the time of the meeting.

2 She posts an agenda on the staff notice board and encourages staff to put their own agenda items on the list. This way staff will feel that it is their meeting.

3 She plans a rota so that staff will take it in turns to be 'on call' during the meeting if any issues arise; in this way it is not the same person missing the meeting.

Of course we do need to be aware that sometimes we try new things and they do not work either. This can be de-motivating but should not prevent us from continuing through the cycle of reflection and developing new ways of looking at a situation and new strategies for handling it.

The benefits of this reflection impacted on the whole staff team and not just the one staff member who Brenda had concerns about.

Brenda valued the process of reflection, and although it was painful to realise that she had not been handling things in the best way the outcome was very positive.

Think it over

Choose something that has happened in work recently that you are not happy with. It could be a disagreement with a colleague, or a discussion with a relative that didn't go well, or an intervention with a service user that you think was not effective.

Work your way through Kolb's cycle of reflection. It would be most productive to actually write these points out so that you can refer to them.

1 Describe what happened.
2 Think about the reasons behind what happened. Make a note of any thoughts that come to mind.

3 Identify some theories that may be relevant to this situation. There may be examples in this book that you could use.

4 Work out a new way of dealing with this situation, think about what you would do differently and then try this out.

5 When you have tried this out think about what you have learned from this process so that you really consolidate this experience.

Johns' model of reflection

Johns' model of reflection [in Davies *et al* (2000), page 85] provides a structured set of questions to help you explore what you think about a situation or event. It focuses on the need to identify different aspects of information in order to learn from what happened. The questions provide a way of learning about an event.

Johns' model of reflection

⟲ *Core question* What information do I need access to, in order to learn through this experience?

⟲ *Cue questions* to help you identify this information are divided into five sections:

1 Description of experience

    1.1 Phenomenon – Describe the 'here and now' experience

    1.2 Causal – What essential factors contributed to this experience?

    1.3 Context – What are the significant background factors to this experience?

    1.4 Clarifying – What are the key processes (for reflection) in this experience?

2 Reflection

    2.1 What was I trying to achieve?

    2.2 Why did I intervene as I did?

    2.3 What were the consequences of my actions for

        2.3.1 myself

        2.3.2 the service user/family

        2.3.3 the people I work with?

    2.4 How did I feel about this experience when it was happening?

    2.5 How did the service user feel about it?

    2.6 How do I know how the service user felt about it?

3 Influencing factors

    3.1 What internal factors influenced my decision-making? →

3.2 What external factors influenced my decision-making?

3.3 What sources of knowledge did/should have influenced my decision-making?

4 Could I have dealt better with the situation?

4.1 What other choices did I have?

4.2 What would be the consequences of those choices?

5 Learning

5.1 How do I now feel about this experience?

5.2 How have I made sense of this experience in the light of past experiences and future practice?

5.3 How has this experience changed my *ways of knowing*?

Note: The word 'patient' has been replaced with 'service user'.

Think it over

1 Think about a situation at work that you do not feel entirely happy with, it could be a one-off incident or something ongoing.

2 Go through the questions in the Johns' model of reflection.

3 Think about whether this process of reflection has been of any benefit to you.

Connecting learning with our care practice

This section looks at how we can make the connection between theories of learning and models of reflection. In order to do this we draw on work developed in general care practice, nursing, education and social work.

> Professional exercise consists in instrumental problem solving made rigorous by the application of scientific theory and technique. [Schon (1983), page 21 in Romer (2003)]

If we think about this statement in relation to care work it is saying that we have to think about what we are doing and make decisions about how to act on the basis of our knowledge and skills that are useful to working with service users.

Reflection provides opportunities to

- *acquire knowledge and understanding*. Experience in the workplace can provide new knowledge. We can learn new facts about the service user group that we work with through daily contact with them. We can understand how to communicate with a person through our knowledge of what has worked in our previous communication with them.

- *apply formal knowledge*. When we read something new or go on a training course and learn something new we are sometimes invited to put it into practice, to test it out. Have you ever read anything in a book and thought, 'Well that wouldn't work where I am'? Sometimes it can be challenging to think about trying new theories out.

Research

Research does not occur in isolation to other events that happen in an organisation. It is affected by social processes, for example some research is carried out because of the need to cut the funding of a service, perhaps to identify periods in the day when staffing levels could be cut back.

In the evaluation process we can separate out the difference between producing evidence and making judgements.

To produce evidence we need to obtain information. This can be influenced by the reason for gathering evidence. If we have already made a judgement about something then this may alter the way that we collect evidence.

When we make judgements we look at the evidence and form some conclusions based on that evidence. Caution is needed to make sure that all the evidence is interpreted in an unbiased, professional way. It is easy to overlook negative comments, or to dismiss them as the views of a minority rather than acknowledging their significance and to do what we need to.

Research into performance

What does the word performance mean to you? If you have children at school or have an interest in your local hospital you may have read the league tables that are meant to indicate the performance of that school or hospital compared to government set targets or other schools and hospitals. The social services performances are also measured, by way of annual star ratings. This is explored in more depth in the chapter on the context of care (Chapter 1). League tables and star ratings may be focused on a particular aspect of care, but they will relate to the ideas of efficiency, effectiveness and economy.

How do we measure performance, and who are the judges of good practice? [Everitt and Hardiker (1996), page 85] suggest the use of performance indicators as 'tin openers' to prompt questioning of good practice. This idea of using performance indicators as 'tin-openers, not dials' emphasises the need for them to not be a comprehensive measure of what we do or a standard to be aimed at, rather they should provide a means of suggesting changes to practice rather than explaining what good practice is. The use of triangulation, where a variety of methods are used to find out information, can establish a comprehensive and accurate picture of a service. This is discussed later in the chapter. In care service delivery we could add to this list the principle of equity.

The inspection process for care homes includes sending evaluations to professionals, relatives and residents. The comments made by service users are included in the overall assessment of the care home in meeting the National Minimum Standards.

Care work is very focused now on the needs and wishes of the 'customer' of care, the service user. Consumer-led care needs to be provided by workers who are committed in their delivery of a professional service, and responsive to the messages that they are getting about what is not working well.

Reflection 'is imbued with values', according to Everitt and Hardiker (1996). What they are saying is that care workers cannot necessarily evaluate in an isolated way, that is not influenced by other values. An organisation's emphasis on performance can give undue weighting to some types of information than others, sometimes to the detriment of the service users. It may, for instance, be linked to monitoring what is going on within the organisation.

Further Research

Locate the performance indicators that relate to your role and the service that your organisation provides. To start with you may want to consider some generic ones that apply to all care workers, such as the General Social Care Council's code of practice

1 Over the next few weeks select an area of these codes.
2 Compare your own practice to these by reflecting on what you do and whether it meets the expectations of these codes.
3 Identify what other policies and performance indicators relate to this same area of work.

Evaluation is a means of highlighting what is really happening, making decisions about this and making sure that future outcomes are managed. Evidence-based practice implies that there is research involved. The research will produce the evidence on which to base future practice. Research usually involves obtaining information by people who are within the organisation, or external to it. There is increasing recognition of the value and importance of involving people who are involved in the delivery or receipt of the service in the research process; one method of this is known as action research.

> Action research is the study of a social situation carried out by those involved in that situation in order to improve both their practice and the quality of their understanding. [Winter and Munn-Giddings (2001), page 8]

Care organisations now acknowledge the significance and importance of what is known as user-led research.

Information, or data, is sometimes referred to as 'hard', as in statistics, or 'soft', as in the views and opinions of the service users. Quantitative data is measurable, and is often presented in the form of figures, tables etc. Qualitative data may be more subjective, and may include comments and anecdotes. It should not be thought of as less valuable.

Researching into care performance

Mahmud is a care manager in a sensory impairment team. The managers of all teams have been asked to find out how satisfied people are with the service. How would they be able to find this out? They could do it by

1 asking service users what they think of the service (qualitative data)
2 seeing how many complaints have been made in the last year (quantitative data).

They could also look at some statistics to do with

3 how quickly people obtain the equipment, living aids and adaptations they require
4 whether people benefit from the service in the short term and long term.

The care manager would not need to be an expert in research in order to carry out this exercise. Winter and Munn-Giddings (2001) emphasise the importance of not seeing research as an activity exclusive to professional researchers. You are doing research when you ask colleagues about what they do, or if you go on a course and ask someone from a different organisation what they do. This is referred to as research-mindedness.

Feedback on care performance

In a care home for adults with learning disabilities, individuals made the following comment one evening:

'I like going on holiday but I don't like going with the others.'

What could a reflective practitioner do with this information? Would they

➲ ignore it, as it is only one comment; people are allowed to make comments, but we cannot act on what everyone says
➲ think that care work was easier before service users started having a say
➲ think it is not significant; if they say it again in a few months I'll mention it

or

➲ make a note of it
➲ explore what the individual says in more depth
➲ make sure that the person gets to choose exactly who they go on holiday with.

Objectives

Objectives are statements that indicate a final result, or what is being aimed for in the delivery of a service. It is helpful to have an objective as it provides a statement for care practice or service delivery to be measured by. Objectives need to be SMART: Specific, Measurable, Achievable, Reliable, Time oriented.

The following make objectives difficult to work with.

Objectives can be:	Example	Issues
Multiple	Individuals have regular access to a full range of local social activities in the community	Regular, full range, local, in the community If one of these is not met does that mean the whole objective has not been met?
Ambiguous	Individuals will have access to local social activities	They may have access to them, but never actually go What is meant by local? We all travel to get to some social events
Vague	Services users enjoy the provision that is offered to them	Who judges whether something is enjoyed by others? It may be enjoyable, but there may be other aspects that could be improved
Conflicting	A client's right to privacy will be respected by them having locked bedrooms Clients will have more control in the management of their home	If an individual chooses not to lock their room does this mean their right to privacy is not being respected?
Displaced	All service users attend the residents meeting	Some individuals may be unable to leave their room due to their health needs. There may be other ways that their views can be taken to the meeting, and they be informed of what is discussed at the meeting

Think it over

1 Identify the aims and objectives of your organisation. These can be found in its mission statement, statement of purpose, or similar document.

2 Reflect on how these objectives are put into practice.

3 Who actually monitors this?

In the care management process (see the chapter on care planning) there are process outcomes which relate to the involvement, participation and control of individuals in the development of their own care plans. These may not be recorded as actual care objectives, but they are an intrinsic part of the process and would make a considerable difference to the individual's experience of care planning.

Triangulation

Triangulation is the use of different types of information to ensure that our assessment is valid and reliable. For example, in making a judgement about whether the meals provided are nutritious you could look at

⇥ how healthy individuals are

⇥ how the meals compare to Department of Health guidelines

⇥ the views of a nutritionist.

Each type of information can either confirm or challenge the other. If each type of information we obtain confirmed the others then through triangulation we will have demonstrated our assessment to be a valid one.

What to reflect on

We all reflect on our work, often without realising it. Even if you have not been aware of the formal process of reflection you might have left work and wondered about something that has happened and ask yourself 'What did I do wrong?' or 'Why did that happen?'

Reflection can be based on the following:

⇥ A single incident (e.g. an uncomfortable encounter with a colleague). It can be important to think about something that happens in isolation, even if we anticipate never being in that situation again. The reason is that we may need to reconcile ourselves to what has happened so that we do not dwell on it to the detriment of our future actions.

⇥ General performance about one aspect of my work (e.g. how I relate to relatives of the individuals that I support). Having been doing a job for a while we may not think there is any need for, or room for, development. We may be very proficient in an area of our work, but it is unlikely we are doing it to perfection. From how we do this work we could learn to develop a different area of work, or help others to do so.

↺ A series of repeated events (e.g. whenever we have a team meeting I always leave it feeling that I haven't said what I want to). If you ever feel as though you make the same mistakes over and again then it may be useful to challenge why this is happening. We can be guilty of labelling ourselves in this way. Have you ever said 'Oh I'm always like that. I can't help it, it's just me' or 'I'll never change, its who I am.'? Well, for some things it may be best not to stick to the same behaviour and passively accept the role we attribute to ourselves, but to identify what it is that we are regularly doing and why, and then to change our behaviour. In the chapter on values in care practice (Chapter 3) we discuss the idea of labelling.

Problem solving

Reflection can also be issue based. The earlier quote by Schon [(1983), in Romer (2003)] about professional exercise refers to problem solving as an activity that we need to engage in if we are to develop as practitioners. This is not a negative concept; we do not need to think of every situation we are presented with as being a problem in a negative way. This approach provides a framework for considering how to view new or difficult situations and a model of working our way through them to arrive at a successful conclusion. A first step in reaching new conclusions that are likely to be effective is to reflect on what has happened in the past, and prevent the same old mistakes, or the same old problems, arising.

Frameworks for evaluation

Whether we are reflecting on our own or with others there is literature around to facilitate our reflection. In this section we look at examples of guidance, which can provide us with tools for measuring our performance, as a 'tin opener', to use Everitt and Hardiker's (1996) phrase.

Case Study

Reflection on performance

Alex

Alex works in a home for learning disabled adults.

1 He could go through the National Minimum Standards for Care Homes (Adults 18–65) and consider his role in addressing these. Achieving the NMS is the responsibility of everyone in the home, not just the registered manager, and Alex could reflect on what contribution he is making, and if there are any areas that he is not very effective in. For example, Alex looks at the standards in relation to care planning and asks to discuss these with the registered manager to identify any areas that he could look into more. He may then take responsibility for exploring a particular aspect to develop the practice of everyone in the care home. For example, he may visit another home in order to find out how they produce their care plans.

2 Alex could also look at the document *Valuing People* and reflect on whether his role and actions support the principles identified in that White Paper.

He may consider what contribution he is making to the debate about the future of services, and whether there are any individuals in the home who would benefit from a move to a supported living environment?

3 Alex could look at the mission statement of his care home, as what this contains is pertinent to the role of everyone in the home. How is his practice ensuring that people are provided with what they are entitled to, and to the standards required?

4 If Alex was fairly new to his job he could reflect on whether his practice is meeting the requirements set out in the TOPSS Induction and Foundation Standards.

5 Alex could also read through the General Social Care Council's code of practice for social care employees and identify whether he is complying with the statements in this.

6 The National Occupational Standards also provide a way of measuring performance. Alex could request to work towards achieving an NVQ so that he is assessed on his competence.

7 Within the organisation the individual service user care plans would provide statements relating to the care that individuals expect to receive. Alex could consider whether the way that he performs his role is effectively supporting the organisation in meeting the care objectives as specified in the care plan.

Charlie

Charlie works at a day service for older people.

1 Charlie could look at the National Service Framework for Older People (see Chapter 1, The Context of Care, for more discussion on National Service Frameworks). He could think about the standards that are relevant to the service he works for.

2 He could also look at research on care practice carried out by the organisation Age Concern, by going to their website.

3 Charlie asks the health professionals who come to the centre what he could do to support individuals more. He learns about the emphasis on rehabilitation, for example. Charlie then suggests a regular service user meeting in order to find out what changes the day service could make to more effectively support people.

4 Charlie could also read some information about care for older people by visiting his library or asking his supervisor for any resources that the day centre has.

There are lots of opportunities for Alex and Charlie to be proactive in their reflection on how their performance is addressing the aims of the organisation and the needs of individuals. They do not need to wait until their managers direct them in change. Some of the many benefits for Alex and Charlie are that they

- no longer feel novice in their work and they develop in a particular area of expertise
- feel valued within the organisation
- develop more of an interest in their work
- apply their new knowledge and improve their skills in working with people.

Another method of ongoing reflection is to keep a diary or work journal.

Professional journals

A professional journal is a diary of work, containing a collection of entries about work events. Some people find it useful to reflect on what has happened in work each day, whilst others prefer to select significant events to write about at infrequent intervals. Contained in a work journal may be the following, which the worker would make a note of.

- *Anecdotes* These may be brief, or quite lengthy accounts of situations at work, for example 'Had a successful meeting with … It made a difference that I had written down my questions, as I felt more relaxed amongst the other professionals from the health service.'
- *Interpreted stories* The writer may discuss a series of events or an ongoing issue with their reflection on what is going on and why, for example 'There is some tension amongst the staff team developing. I think this might relate to the changes I am making to the keyworker system. I think I need to have a meeting and bring some issues out into the open with the team, nip it all in the bud.'
- *Critical incidents* These are significant events which the worker thinks should be reflected on. For example, 'I made a mistake today by telling a relative about their (adult) son changing activities at the centre, which meant they had to explain to their father who was unhappy about the change. I know why it happened, the parent has always been so involved and the son is very close to them. I need to think before I speak to relatives and stop myself from disclosing information casually, it was careless of me.'
- *Interpretation of the significance of an event* The writer may put down in words their thoughts about why or how something happened in work and why it is important, for example 'A new policy has been introduced which is likely to have an impact on our work by … '
- *Methods of analysing incidents* The writer will discuss different approaches to analysing what has happened in work.

This method of reflective practice has a number of benefits for the care worker. If someone is keeping a journal then it means that they are setting time aside to reflect, which is valuable in certain ways:

- It can provide a skill for lifelong learning, which is currently a theme in all areas of life and in all work sectors. This can facilitate learning and development as a person in many areas of life, not just in the development of good care practice.

⊃ It can also be a necessary skill for effective learning in the context of work. As with any work situation there may be times when we feel that we are not testing out new skills or acquiring new knowledge. Writing a professional journal can provide a way of making learning happen for you.

⊃ It also has the potential to add value to formal learning. Have you ever been on a course and then a week after being back at work you have forgotten everything, or it all seems irrelevant outside of the classroom? Well, if you were to write a journal you may develop a structure for applying your learning from the course or training event to the workplace.

Always remember to ensure privacy and confidentiality when producing any work that relates to your care practice. Never mention specific names and be aware that people and organisations should not be identifiable; anonymity of service users, colleagues and others needs to be respected.

Your development through this chapter should enable you to make more effective use of knowledge and skills that you acquire through any work-based training, college or university care courses, your own research and reading. Learning how to learn is an important stage in anyone's development.

Further Research

Keep a journal as a tool to help your development as a reflective practitioner.

Don't set yourself unrealistic targets, it would be easy to spend an hour writing your first entry and then on day 5 you are down to writing 'Nothing happened much at work today'.

Try this for at least a fortnight and then use it to reflect back and analyse your performance.

Evidence-based practice

Evidence relates to information about how things should be done, the best forms of working, and the types of intervention. It provides a reason for acting in a certain way and gives a justification for doing so. This justification is the available evidence that a proposed course of action is the best one.

Evidenced-based practice has become an important dimension of care work and is being applied more systematically in nursing and social work. [Muir Gray (2001), page 11] introduces evidence as a motivation for practice alongside values and resources. Muir Gray argues that the three combine to inform practice, but that more emphasis should be placed on evidence as pressures to focus on resources often dictate opinion-based decision-making.

Your organisation may engage in systematic evaluation of service provision before it tries to understand the need for, or implements, change. This is because it is searching for evidence to identify what changes should occur, and to support the introduction of these changes.

Integration of theory and practice

Theories are ways of understanding; they attempt to provide an explanation of how and why something happens. Theory is sometimes removed from the context in which we need to apply that theory. Have you ever read anything in a book and thought 'But it is not like that where I work, that's not real life'? Eraut (2003) discusses the importance of seeking out the relationship between the theory and practice. This helps us in exploring the use of theory in the workplace so that we are not disillusioned when the reality of care practice doesn't appear to relate at all to what the theory is telling us.

SWOT analysis

SWOT analysis is another process for considering all the different angles on a situation before you commence a task. It involves exploring the strengths, weaknesses, opportunities and threats associated with a situation.

- ⊃ Strengths are the advantages that we identify for taking a particular action.
- ⊃ Weaknesses are the disadvantages that we identify for taking a particular action, or the barriers that will prevent us from taking a particular action.
- ⊃ Opportunities can include the resources or support that we have to support us in taking a particular action, and enabling us to overcome the barriers.
- ⊃ Threats are the blocks to us making effective use of these opportunities; they might obstruct our progress.

If I do a SWOT analysis on reflecting on my care practice it may look like the following:

Strengths	I want to reflect I am motivated
Weaknesses	Not knowing how to reflect – what do I do? Not having time to reflect
Opportunities	To learn how to, I can read this chapter to learn about it To overcome the issue of time I can use my journey home each day to start off with
Threats	I might give up if I find it difficult I might lose interest

The value of working through the negative aspects is that you can confront, challenge or address them. If we were to just focus on the positive side, we may be unable to realise our good intentions in the long term because of the practical difficulties. Focusing on the negatives gives you a more realistic chance of being positive in the long term.

Use of research

Research is the structured collection of information about an organisation or group of people, or about a situation, in order to come to some conclusions about it. Some organisations have their own research workers. You may have been involved in research yourself. For example, have you ever completed a questionnaire about how good or poor a service is? Do you use service user surveys in your organisation?

We mentioned earlier that the Commission for Social Care Inspection sends questionnaires to care homes for service users, relatives and other professionals in order to obtain information about what others think of the service provided.

Research can also be carried out by people outside the organisation. An organisation may invite another organisation to conduct research into a particular project or service. Research that has been carried out in one organisation can be useful to others. Research may be written up in the form of a report for an organisation. It is also often discussed in professional magazines such as *Community Care, Care and Health* or in journals.

Further Research

Obtain a journal/professional magazine that relates to your own area of care practice. Find an article that interests you, that is describing what happens in a different organisation. Make a list of what you could learn from this research.

Who you reflect with

Reflection need not be a solitary activity. Having a positive approach to reflective practice will enable you to incorporate feedback from people who are involved with your work (service users, informal carers, relatives, other workers, colleagues, managers). It could include all those you are accountable to, and it can make you feel more able to respond to the level of autonomy that you have.

Reflecting by yourself

This kind of reflective practice is about 'counter-discourse', the conversation that it is useful to have with yourself. This is not as odd as it sounds. Just asking yourself 'Why did I do that?' is a big start to reflective practice.

Reflecting with your line manager/supervisor

This kind of reflection may take place in regular formal supervision and annual appraisals. The supervision session belongs to you, and you will get more out of it if you think about it beforehand. You will usually be provided with forms to complete prior to these meetings, but if not, a SWOT analysis provides a useful framework to think about your work. Structured formal supervision and appraisals can be made more effective if you prepare in advance and reflect on how well you are doing in your job, what areas could be developed and those that you feel you need more support with.

You may also talk to your manager informally; perhaps they are completing a work activity with you, or working a shift with you. Feedback that is *ad hoc* can be as informative and relevant (about what your strengths are and the areas you need to develop) as more formal arrangements. Requesting more regular informal feedback and comments from your manager may just be a case of asking them now and again how they think you are doing when they are around or working alongside you.

Reflecting with your service user/s

Earlier we referred to the importance of 'soft' data. So don't dismiss the 'throw away' comments from service users as these can provide a valuable insight into what matters, what is working well, and what needs changing. (Chapter 4 on working with service users has a section on skills which explores the importance of communicating with people.) An organisation reviewing how well it is doing in its care practice would usually involve its customers in that process, so service users are a key to discovering this. This should not involve token gestures that are not meaningful to the service users.

There may be issues about how you obtain information about this. Let us consider some of the ways your organisation may obtain feedback from the individuals that it provides a service to. Formal complaints procedures should be accessible to the individuals they are targeted at, with questionnaires and structured feedback, such as that obtained through service user meetings.

Informal carers

People who provide care to individuals, neighbours, friends and relatives can and should play a significant part in the evaluation of service provision. The care professions perspective on the relationship that they have with relatives has changed, as is discussed in the chapter on working with service users (Chapter 4). There are now more boundaries to consider and issues of confidentiality, which we did not have to be so aware of previously; relatives were automatically told about all aspects of their family member's care. Now we need to consider whether the individual wants information about their care arrangements divulged to relatives. However, relatives remain an important source of information about service users and where individual service users are unable to articulate their own wishes, relatives can play a vital role in shaping support in a way that values their knowledge and benefits the service user.

Reflecting with colleagues

Discussion at handovers

Handovers to colleagues can sometimes be very task oriented with the aim of getting the handover 'over and done with' as quick as possible. This may be understandable after a long shift, but it is not excusable. It may not actually take a lot more time to discuss service users in a more informed way and to question the way that support is provided, or to raise suggestions as to new approaches of working with people.

Think about the different outcomes of the following scenarios.

Jo is handing over to Errol, having just got back from a visit to the Resource Centre with Philip.

Jo: 'He wouldn't get out the car again when we got to the Resource Centre; it took ages and yet he loves it when he is in there.'

Errol: 'Everyone has that trouble, don't worry about it.'

Here is a different conversation between the same two workers:

Jo: 'Philip wouldn't get out the car again, it took ages, I don't know what I could do to make him feel more comfortable about getting out. Do you know what other staff do?'

Errol: 'I make sure he really understands where he is going by talking about it throughout the journey. I also always make sure I go the same route so that he can begin to understand where he is going. I then sit in the car with him for a few minutes when we get there while he gets used to being outside the Resource Centre. I reassure him about who he sees there so he feels familiar with it. We see other people going in who he knows which helps him. Try that next time and let me know how it goes.'

Jo: 'Thanks Errol, that's really helpful having that chat about it, I wish I had mentioned it sooner.'

The outcome of the second conversation, which took only a few seconds longer, is that Jo knows she is not on her own in making decisions and problem solving about appropriate support for Philip. Even if Errol's suggestion does not work, Jo may feel more able to ask again, now that she knows that someone else is taking an interest in the way that she does things with Philip. More communication between people who support Philip in the same activity is always going to be of benefit.

Formal meetings

The more you participate in meetings, the more you will get out of them. Participating means listening to others as well as making contributions yourself. If there is something that you have found difficult, either a practical task, or perhaps a relationship or communication with a particular service user, then it would be useful to share these and find out whether others have the same experience or can provide you with a new way of working that will be more effective. Whilst you may not want to dominate a team meeting you may be able to suggest an agenda item which focuses on an issue in work that you feel needs to be discussed. You may need to be the first person who acknowledges that they don't quite know how to do things, or that you have been struggling in how to support a particular person.

Informal meetings

Observing what others do, the way that they communicate with a person, or the way that they provide physical assistance can introduce you to new ways of working. Asking a colleague for feedback when they have observed you working can give you regular ongoing support. It can provide reassurance about what you are doing well as well as suggestions as to what to do differently. It is important, but not always easy, to avoid being defensive when a peer makes suggestions about how we could change our practice. If someone seems to do something differently to you ask them why they are doing it that way, and if they have tried other ways. Tell them how you do it and ask them what they think. Discussing your work whilst you are doing it will have several benefits, it may

- stimulate you, and those you are working with
- develop the relationship you have with colleagues
- ensure that you are learning from the working environment
- be a means of accessing support over difficulties
- make it easier to bring things up that are difficult
- help you cope more effectively with difficult or stressful situations.

Other professionals

Care work is not a competition between different service providers. Different professionals and different agencies should work together for the benefit of the service user, as discussed in the chapter on collaborative working (Chapter 5). If professionals have identified a strategy of intervention that is effective for the individual then it makes sense for everyone to be making use of this strategy. We have a lot to learn from each other. Asking other professionals why they are adopting a particular method of intervention can be helpful. We are very good at making assumptions about what role different professionals play.

Why reflect?

There are many advantages to developing reflection.

1 We develop self-awareness.
2 It enhances our problem-solving skills.
3 It supports our development as 'life-long learners'.
4 We can attribute more value to our care role.
5 It can increase our self-esteem.
6 We are more able to handle responsibility in the workplace autonomously.

The impact of reflection on practice

Ghaye and Lillyman (1997) state that there are different effects of reflection on care practice (through professional journal writing and analysing critical incidents). They divide these into the following:

1 *Technical aspects* Structured reflection can support the development of our potential as accountable and professional care workers.

2 *Practical aspects* Reflection can increase our ability to make sound decisions based on competent and ethically informed judgements.

3 *Emancipatory aspects* Reflecting on our own care practice can promote our ability to think about, question, and be critical of what we are required to do.

To provide further justification of our need to develop a reflective approach to our individual practice, we can consider the implications of not reflecting, as set out below.

Implications for the care worker	Implications for the service user
⊃ Staying at a minimum level of competence	⊃ Being supported by unthinking or even un-thoughtful workers
⊃ Repeating mistakes	⊃ Feeling that you have to get used to poor practice as nothing is going to change
⊃ Never changing what we do until others tell us to	
⊃ Becoming bored (or boring to work with)	⊃ Not feeling valued, that people who support you don't care about how they do it, feeling like you are just a task to complete
⊃ Losing interest in our work	
⊃ Being very task focused without fully appreciating the people aspects of the job	⊃ Not being given new opportunities or being allowed to take risks
⊃ Diminished career prospects	

Service users have the right to the best possible care outcomes. To ensure that this happens we need to be innovative in the way that we work with people. Innovation involves the ability to look at new ways of doing the same things, or sometimes new ways to avoid doing the same things.

As with all dimensions of care practice there are issues that have to be thought through regarding reflection.

Ethical issues in reflection

There is an emotional dimension to reflection. As you are an individual who cares about your work it is important to reflect in a way that doesn't dwell on negative issues as this can be debilitating. A more productive and positive approach to reflection will focus on what the outcome and purpose of reflection is. Negative emotions, such as guilt, anxiety, or a feeling of never achieving what you need to achieve, will not support your own development or the achievement of more positive outcomes for the service or its users.

> These are not particularly comfortable processes, which may lead (care workers) to personal distress and conflict. [Quinn in Davies *et al* (2000), page 89]

The term 'care workers' replaces the term 'students' (nursing).

There are also practical issues to the process of reflection. It is a means to an end and should therefore not become the focus of your care practice. Think back to the Honey and Mumford roles discussed earlier in the chapter. A reflector should still be able to achieve outcomes as they look back, in order to move forward.

A further issue is to recognise that you do not have sole responsibility for the quality and standards of care provision in your organisation. Your individual or collective reflection is one means of supporting quality and improvements, but it does not replace the responsibilities of management through organisational structures.

When should I reflect?

Here we will consider the advantages of reflecting at a number of different points and different periods of time that will suit us in different ways. There is a value to reflecting in all the following time periods.

Reflect before you act

This chapter has focused on reflecting, that is thinking back over what you have done with a view to improving your care practice. Have you ever advised someone to 'Look before you leap', or has someone advised you to 'Think before you speak'? This advice aims to make people stop and think before they actually do something.

If you work your way through Kolb's cycle of reflection and continue to use this model in your care practice then you will be developing an approach that means you systematically reflect before you act, as well as after.

Even if you are starting a completely new care task you can still reflect on what to do before you perform that task, as you can

- ⤴ reflect on the tasks that are in some way similar to the new one
- ⤴ reflect on the skills that you have that might relate to this new task
- ⤴ reflect on how you have observed others performing this new task.

Reflect as you act

Schon (1983) describes this as 'reflection in action'. Depending on what you are doing, you may be able to think about how you are carrying out a task and if it is working well as you are doing it. Have you ever said, 'Stop, let us start again'? If you have, this may be because in the middle of doing something you have realised that it is not the best way to do it and you want to try a better way.

You may get feedback from an individual about the appropriateness of support you are giving them at the time and as a result adapt what you are doing. You don't need to adopt a 'I've started so I'll finish' approach. Remember, changing mid-course can sometimes save time afterwards.

Reflect after you have completed a task

There are different points after doing a task when it is valuable to reflect on what has happened.

⊃ *Immediately after a task* The advantage of reflecting on a task immediately after doing it is that it is fresh in our minds, so that our recollection of what happened will not be distorted by any changes in our perception of it. Of course, our working lives would be much easier if we had time to sit and think after every task we carry out. What we are not suggesting here is that you halve the amount of work that you carry out in order to make time to think about it as this would not be fair to colleagues. We need to incorporate reflection into our busy working and home lives in a fashion that is manageable and productive.

⊃ *Shortly after a task* There may be periods in the day when you are carrying out practical tasks on your own which do not require full concentration, such as washing up, making a bed or if you take a short break. These could provide opportunities for reflecting on other tasks you have done. If this is not possible then you may be able to reflect on the way home or whilst you are getting ready for work the next day.

⊃ *After a period of time* Sometimes we forget about a situation at work (unless we are keeping our professional journals!). We may be prompted to think about it again when the same situation arises again, or a colleague tells us they had the same experience. Reflection is valuable and is a better option than simply dismissing a situation as having occurred too long ago to bother thinking about. But there may be more limitations. One of the problems with this is that our memory of events may be affected by a time delay. We may be unclear about details or our perception of what happened may be influenced by our feelings about it, so that we do not have an objective description of it.

Theories and models of care

A theory is a way of explaining something that happens. It provides a possible explanation or interpretation of a situation, event or condition. There are several theories discussed in this book in other chapters which could

⊃ influence your understanding of a situation and therefore help you to approach the situation in a new way

⊃ provide you with a clear explanation of why something happened and so enable you to make sure it doesn't happen again.

Further Research

You have already considered theories of learning in this chapter. Now identify a theory from one of the other chapters that you feel could be useful to your own care practice.

Read through the theory and think about it in relation to your own work. You may need to explore this theory in more depth by looking it up in a library or on the internet. Reflect on how this theory could influence the way that you work with people, service users and colleagues.

A model is a framework for action. It provides a structure as to how you respond or intervene in a situation. If you like the idea of a model of working you can adopt it and use it to shape the way that you work.

Think it over

You have already used models of reflection in this chapter. Now identify a model from one of the other chapters and think about how useful it could be in developing your own care practice. You may need to discuss it with others at a team meeting before you introduce it as a framework for your own work.

It is important to feel positive about reflective practice. Thinking about the work that you do can however also involve having to think about negative aspects, that is things that are not going so well. But if you focus on the idea that you are doing this in order to improve your practice then it will help you to feel positive about the overall experience. If you reflect on something and it becomes clear that you did not handle a situation well, or that you made a mistake in what you did, then the important thing is that you have identified this, which opens the door for changing what you do next time. There are several ways of handling negative reflection. They are to

- ↻ focus on the positive aspect of identifying a difficulty in your work – you don't have to wait until someone else points it out
- ↻ focus on the benefits that the people you work with will experience (both service users and colleagues) as a result of you thinking about your work and how to improve
- ↻ talk to your colleagues about what you have discovered – sharing your experience may encourage others to share what has not gone well for them, which is helpful
- ↻ talk to your line manager about it – you are not on your own in terms of your responsibility for doing a good job.

Supporting your peers and developing others

Reflective practice can be contagious! If you open up discussions and start talking about your own practice, you may find that your colleagues start to do the same. This will create a healthier environment, as individuals will not be afraid of doing something wrong. It will also mean that the service users benefit, as care workers are more open to changing what it is they do. It can be a gentle process of initially just asking questions about the 'What, When, How and Why' of care tasks.

You can make a difference in developing a culture of reflection in your organisation just by asking

'What do you think about the way we ......?'

'I have difficulty doing ......, How do you do it?'

'Has anyone got any better ideas on how we could ......?'

If you observe colleagues in areas of practice that you think are particularly good you could invite them to share this with you so that you can develop the way you do things.

Adopting a reflective practice approach to your work will enable you to utilise more effectively the knowledge that you acquire. It will also enable you to transfer your learning from one situation to another with more ease and to better effect.

Maslin-Prosthero [(1997), page 40] summarises the process of reflection quite succinctly as

Figure 2.7 *Summary of the process of reflection*

It is important for you to now think about the difference your understanding of reflection can make to your role in care work.

- ⊃ **What?** Here you have learnt about the importance of reflection and some strategies to facilitate your own reflection.
- ⊃ **So what?** This is important as it could enable you to become a more effective care practitioner.
- ⊃ **Now what?** This is down to you. What are you going to do in order to put these ideas into practice?

Think it over

1 When you read another chapter in this book start by exploring your own understanding of the subject area. Think about 'What do I know already?'

2 Then, when you are reading that chapter become familiar with how you can apply that knowledge to your own work practice. The exercises within each chapter should help you with this.

References and further reading

Britton A and Cousins A (1998) *Study Skills: A Guide for Lifelong Learners*, London, Distance Learning Centre

Department of Health (2001) *Valuing Lives*, London, HMSO

Everett A and Hardiker P (1996) *Evaluating for Good Practice*, Basingstoke, Macmillan

Ghaye T and Lillyman S (1996) *Learning Journals and Critical Incidents: Reflective Practice for Health Care Professionals*, Salisbury, Quay

Maslin-Prosthero S (1997) *Ballière's Study Skills for Nurses*, London, Balliere Tindall

Muir Gray J A (2001) *Evidenced-Based Healthcare*, London, Harcourt (Churchill Livingstone)

Pedler M *et al* (2001) *A Manager's Guide to Self-Development*, London, McGraw-Hill

Quinn F M in Davies C, Finlay L and Bullman A (eds) (2000) *Blackwell Encyclopedia of Social Work*, Oxford, Blackwell

Tight M (1996) *Key Concepts in Adult Education and Training*, London, Routledge

Winter R and Munn-Giddings C (2001) *A Handbook for Action Research in Health and Social Care*, London, Routledge

values in care practice 3

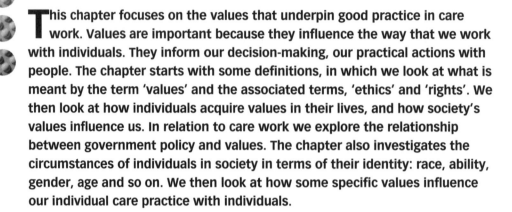

This chapter focuses on the values that underpin good practice in care work. Values are important because they influence the way that we work with individuals. They inform our decision-making, our practical actions with people. The chapter starts with some definitions, in which we look at what is meant by the term 'values' and the associated terms, 'ethics' and 'rights'. We then look at how individuals acquire values in their lives, and how society's values influence us. In relation to care work we explore the relationship between government policy and values. The chapter also investigates the circumstances of individuals in society in terms of their identity: race, ability, gender, age and so on. We then look at how some specific values influence our individual care practice with individuals.

This chapter addresses the following areas:

- ⟳ Definitions: values, rights and ethics
- ⟳ Why values are important in care work
- ⟳ Sexuality
- ⟳ Ability
- ⟳ Age
- ⟳ Health status
- ⟳ Class
- ⟳ Discrimination
- ⟳ Stereotyping
- ⟳ The policy context
- ⟳ Race
- ⟳ Gender
- ⟳ Mental health
- ⟳ Religion
- ⟳ Criminal convictions
- ⟳ Geographical location
- ⟳ Oppression
- ⟳ Prejudice
- ⟳ Anti-oppressive practice and anti-discriminatory practice
- ⟳ Multiple oppression
- ⟳ Service users who express their prejudices
- ⟳ How identity, value and rights can affect the experiences of care workers
- ⟳ Care values
- ⟳ Standards of care

After reading this chapter it is hoped you will be able to

1 understand the terms values, ethics and rights
2 know what values underpin good care practice
3 understand issues of identity in terms of people's race, ability, age, gender, sexuality, religion and other characteristics
4 be able to work in an anti-discriminatory manner
5 be able to practice confidentiality.

This chapter links very much with the chapter on working with service users (Chapter 4), as values are at the heart of your individual intervention with clients.

Definitions: values, rights and ethics

Before we investigate what we mean by values, ethics and rights, let's look at what we mean by 'care'. The word care can have many meanings, some negative and some positive. It depends on the context and the individual. The stressed mother who threatens her children with 'being put into care' is using care almost as a form of punishment. We will use it here to describe the range of activities that are intended to support an individual who, for different reasons, is considered vulnerable and cannot meet their own needs without assistance.

For some the very term 'care' imposes a value on the nature of these activities. This is because 'care' emphasises the role that 'professionals' are engaged in when supporting people. It has associations of a parent–child relationship. It smacks of dependency and power imbalances. The care industry has traditionally been established on a 'them and us' relationship. This has increasingly been questioned and resisted in recent decades. The categorisation of workers as professionals and those cared for as 'patients', 'service users', 'clients' or even 'consumers' reflects a set of beliefs about what the care relationship is or should be. The language of care is laden with values. These need to be both explored, and, where necessary, challenged.

Values

Values refers to the ideas that influence the way we work. They are beliefs about the way that we should 'care' for others. Values guide our approach to those who need care. Below is a list of values that are commonly supposed to underpin good care practice. We will be looking at each in more detail later in this chapter. However, so that we don't simply take them for granted, reflect on what each of these values means to you. Write a few sentences on what you understand by a particular value, and try to provide examples from your care practice to illustrate your answer.

1 Individuality and identity	2 Rights
3 Privacy	4 Choice
5 Independence	6 Dignity
7 Respect	8 Partnership

Ethics

Care work is a complex human activity which raises all kinds of moral decisions and dilemmas on a daily basis – sometimes without our even realising it. Having a knowledge of ethics and different ethical positions can help us approach the dilemmas and decision-making in care, less on the basis of simple common sense, or 'intuition', and more on the basis of something more thought out and therefore more justifiable.

Ethics is the branch of philosophy which concerns itself with questions such as what is the morally right course of action to take in any given situation. How do we know what is right and what is wrong?

Allmark [in Fulford *et al* (2002)] provides an interesting discussion on whether there can actually be an 'ethics of care', a right and wrong way of caring.

> The ethics of care says that we should care, that caring is a moral quality and that we should encourage conditions which create care. What it means is that *we should care about the right things in the right way* and encourage the required qualities. But, by focusing on care as a moral quality in itself, something it is not, the ethics of care can tell us nothing of what those right things are. (page 68)

Think it over

1 How, as care workers, are we meant to know what the right things to care about are, and then how are we to know how to care about them in the right way?

2 Think about the various factors that influence the way that you do your job and the approach you take to it.

You may have identified some of the following:

⊃ What your manager asks you to do.

⊃ What you see colleagues doing.

⊃ What the service user asks you to do.

⊃ What you have read about, or learnt on a course.

⊃ What you think you would like if you were in need of that care.

Out of the factors that you have identified, what do you think is the most important influence on how you carry out your caring role?

Rights

Rights are statements that indicate what a person is entitled to have.

> Most modern democracies accept that there are some basic rights and freedoms that are so important and so fundamental that everyone should enjoy them – just because they are a human being. [Home Office (1998), page 2]

Think it over

1 Which of the following do you feel that you are entitled to?

⊃ Deciding how you spend your money.

⊃ Freedom to say what you want.

⊃ Choosing who comes into your own home.

2 Think about how you would feel if you had some of your rights to these taken away from you. Do the people that you support in your care work have these rights?

Ethical theories

Deontology

Deontology is concerned with the nature of moral duty and the rightness of actions. Kant, the German philosopher, made the classic statement of the deontological position when he said 'Let justice be done even if the heavens fall.' In other words, if you can be sure that your decision is morally right then go ahead and do it whatever the consequences may turn out to be. Political leaders often use deontological arguments to justify their arguments. For example, when asked why they led the country into war, causing great death and destruction, they reply 'Because it was the right thing to do.' Therefore, the key to this ethical position is the belief that if what we are doing is right, it is our moral duty to do it. Worrying about negative or unfortunate consequences should not be part of the decision-making – we must 'grasp the nettle'. This approach sees moral decision-making as based on reason and on being able to argue that a particular course of action is self-evidently the right one.

Utilitarianism

A different position to this is proposed by a group of philosophers who are known as utilitarians. People with these ideas consider that a way through dilemmas and ethical decision-making is to consider that the best outcome is likely to be the result of the greatest good occurring to the greatest number of people, Jeremy Bentham being one such proponent of this idea. This idea focuses on the importance of the consequences of actions. Have you ever heard (or said) the phrase 'The end justifies the means'? If you have, you are working within a utilitarian framework of ethics. In our field of work it is important to think about the process of ethical decision-making; these are not just fancy ideas for the philosophers. As a professional involved in the lives of individuals you may be required to make important decisions.

How can these theories benefit the care worker? Well they may not provide conclusions to how we should behave but they can provide a framework for understanding the dilemmas that arise, and enable us to understand our motivations, as individuals, organisations and as a society as a whole. They can provide us with a new way of looking at complex issues relating to values.

The following example of how these theories may be applied to care situations looks at an issue in a care home. Read through the case study and the exercise to help you think about some of these issues.

Case Study

A moral dilemma

After many years of living on her own Mrs George, who had a stroke, has just moved into a care home. She likes the idea of having more company, having been quite isolated in recent months due to spending a lot of time confined to bed. Mrs George frequently experiences a lot of pain which causes her to cry out for periods of time. There are eight other residents who have lived in the home for a while. They are upset by the noise, do not like it and have indicated that they would prefer Mrs George to spend time in her own room when she is distressed and making noise.

Questions

1 Thinking about the theories we discussed earlier, how can the ideas of Kant and Bentham guide us in deciding the correct course of action? Think about how they would suggest resolving the situation.

2 What would be your recommendation of a solution to this dilemma?

⊃ That the eight people who have lived in the home for some while should have their wishes respected and not have their time interrupted by this one new person?

or

⊃ That the new person has as much right to stay in the communal area with the others even if she experiences distress at times?

There seems to be no clear solution that will satisfy everyone, which is why we refer to it as a dilemma. People may approach this situation from different value bases, which can then have an impact on the process of decision-making.

As we discuss in the chapter on reflective practice (Chapter 2) it is important for care workers to utilise the tools available to them in order to maximise their effectiveness; as well as making use of values to inform their practice it is also important to make use of research, policy guidelines, evidence from own practice and self-reflection. Awareness of our own motivations in analysing situations and coming to conclusions can improve your effectiveness.

Influences on values

Our value base is not something we are born with, neither is it fixed at any particular stage in our lives. Neither is it, for most of us, something coherent or particularly well thought out. The values that we hold have their origins in a range of different influences which occur during the course of our lifetime. If we want to develop a set of professional care values then we must start by evaluating our own personal value base. This inevitably requires us to be reflective. We look at this in more depth in the chapter on reflective practice (Chapter 2).

There are several ways in which values become a part of our own lives. In our early development we are introduced to ideas from family, school education and friends by the process of socialisation. As we grow older we may acquire new values, as some of our earlier beliefs are challenged by new ideas that we are introduced to. If you were to write a list of the things that you think are important now then it is unlikely that these are all things that you have been passionate about all your life; some of these may be values that you have acquired more recently.

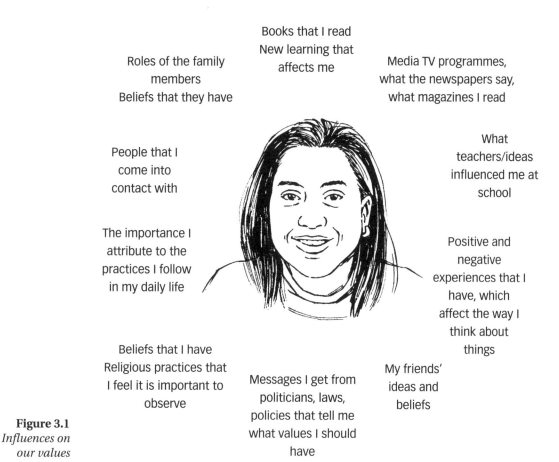

Roles of the family members
Beliefs that they have

Books that I read
New learning that affects me

Media TV programmes, what the newspapers say, what magazines I read

People that I come into contact with

What teachers/ideas influenced me at school

The importance I attribute to the practices I follow in my daily life

Positive and negative experiences that I have, which affect the way I think about things

Beliefs that I have
Religious practices that I feel it is important to observe

Messages I get from politicians, laws, policies that tell me what values I should have

My friends' ideas and beliefs

Figure 3.1
Influences on our values

For example, if you have a strong sense of family support you may impose expectations on other family groups who do not share the same values. It is important to be aware of the impact our own values can have on others and how easy it is to articulate this. This will be discussed in more depth in the chapter on working with service users (Chapter 4), but for now consider what values are implicit in the following communication between a client and care worker.

Care worker: 'Aren't you going to stay with your daughter for Christmas?'
Individual: 'No'

If the person did not have a relationship with their daughter that meant they wanted to stay with them they may feel guilty about this. If their daughter did not want to have them to their home the person may feel upset.

Care worker: 'Isn't your father going to stay with you over Christmas?'
Relative: 'No'

This dialogue is also making the assumption that an individual thinks of Christmas as a special period of time, as well as assuming that family members are important.

It is tempting to believe that as long as we don't intentionally behave inappropriately towards someone in our care then this is good practice. As we have seen though, if we don't stop and think about values and assumptions that we take for granted, we could easily offend others without even realising it. For example, asking someone who is Jewish or Muslim 'Can you tell me your Christian name?'. This is why it is so important to be aware of our own influences and remember that everyone won't always share similar beliefs and see things the same way.

You need to be conscious of your own actions in order to be able to understand where you are at with your own values, and to really be able to assess what impact your values have on others. We all have prejudices and beliefs that may influence our behaviour with others and it is important not to underestimate their impact.

Society's values

Our society is culturally and ethically diverse. Each group has its own beliefs and values, but we know they don't all carry the same weight. Sociologists talk about dominant cultures and dominant beliefs. These are the values and beliefs of certain majority groups that tend to ignore the standpoint of others. Two examples of dominant beliefs within society that have an impact on the way people in society usually think and behave are ethnocentrism and heterosexism.

Ethnocentricity is where the values and practices of one ethnicity are considered to be the norm to such an extent that all other ethnicities are ignored or considered to be irrelevant. This may seem inevitable when social processes and the need for societies to develop norms is considered, but it needs to be acknowledged and attempts made to expose the effects of this process. An example is where Christmas is recognised as a period of celebration, but an individual may not be supported to take time off work to celebrate their own religious festivals that are relevant to their own faith.

Heterosexism is where the dominant values and practices in a society reflect a view that all people are heterosexual, ignoring the possibility that individuals may be homosexual. Society has not historically recognised, valued and included individuals who are homosexual, and their existence has sometimes been completely ignored. An example is where official forms ask for details of husband or wife. If you think about the experience of a homosexual person when faced with constant images of heterosexuality then it is clear that they may feel that their sexuality makes them inferior, as it is not validated by society as a whole. Another example is always asking women when we first meet them if they have a husband. This places the onus on the person to state 'I am different' rather than just answering the question in the same way a heterosexual person might.

Ethnocentricity and heterosexism are both based on and perpetuate stereotypes of minority groups. Difference is constructed negatively. This, in turn, colours the outlook of other people in society, creating a cycle of prejudice.

Instead of disapproving of difference, 'celebrating diversity' is about recognising the significant and valuable contribution that all groups can make to society often because of their differences.

The policy context

When considering your own experience of values as a care worker we can look at three levels:

- ➲ legislation and policy
- ➲ organisational procedures
- ➲ your own individual practice.

In the chapter on the context of care (Chapter 1) we look at the current legislative framework for the delivery of care, and the policies that are shaping care provision. How do values influence these policies and legislation?

Further Research

In the table below there are some examples of the values that have influenced two policy documents.

- ➲ Find out more information about these documents and think about what other values are intended in these government policies.
- ➲ Find copies of the policies that are referred to in your own work most frequently and identify the values that are implicit or explicit in these.

Policy	Theme	Values
Valuing People 2001	Emphasis on working in partnership with service users and promoting their rights, choices and control	➲ Respecting individuals ➲ Valuing the rights of individuals
Carers (Recognition and Services) Act 1995	Assessment of individuals who provide care to other adults in their own home	➲ Rights of carers ➲ Challenging dependency within families

The Care Standards Act 2000 provided a comprehensive review of standards within the care sector that were based on care values. The practices of a care organisation will then need to capture these values. Some organisations will try to be very transparent with their values, making sure that potential users of their services are clear about what they should expect. Other organisations may have a very clear written statement of values but this may not be evident in the daily practices of the care staff that work there.

> The registered person conducts the home so as to maximise service users' capacity to exercise personal autonomy and choice. [Department of Health (2000), page18]

Think it over

Locate the mission statement of your organisation and identify what values it claims to be important. Then think about what values are evident in the daily delivery of care. One way of thinking about this is to consider what values the service users would state were most evident, and then to reflect on whether these match with the ones that the organisation claims to be promoting.

How do you promote values in your own work? There are some areas of care practice where you need to acquire new knowledge to work more effectively with people. Values are an area that underpin all care practice and it is important to consider where you are professionally in terms of your own understanding of these values.

There is a much clearer framework now for discussing care values, as there is more written policy on it. Recent years have seen increased willingness by government to put standards of care practice into written documentation, both legislation and policy guidance. The Care Standards Act 2000 provided the necessary legislation for some values to become more formalised and developed as a requirement of care providers. The government placed the idea of standards within a legal framework and values are an intrinsic part of this.

It is worth noting that health services and social care services have their foundations in different value bases. The integration of these two providers of care as discussed in Chapter 1 on the context of care, leads to a meeting of these value bases.

Think it over

A useful starting point is for you to consider what values you have in your own life. Make a list of the things that you value in life, e.g. being respected by the people that you work with, having your own private space at home etc. Think about how important these values are to you, and what your life would be like if these values went unacknowledged by other people.

Chapter 2, on reflective practice, shows you that as a care worker it is important to keep up to date with government guidance and policies. Some policies provide a good indication of what values are important within the care sector; an example of this is the White Paper relating to learning disability; there are four key principles at the heart of the government's proposals in *Valuing People: A New Strategy for Learning Disability for the 21st Century* [Department of Health (2001)]:

1 Legal and civil rights

2 Independence

3 Choice

4 Inclusion.

If you are working with learning disabled service users this policy will have an impact on any current changes in your organisation, as it contains strong recommendations relating to every aspect of service delivery.

The Sector Skill Council for Social Care, TOPSS (The Training Organisation for the Personal Social Services), which has a significant role in developing the care workforce, has produced a set of induction and foundation standards [TOPSS (2001)] that state a range of values that should underpin the work of all care employees:

   1.1 The values

      1.1.1 Understand the importance of promoting the following values at all times:

          ⊃ Individuality and identity   ⊃ Rights

          ⊃ Choice   ⊃ Privacy

          ⊃ Independence   ⊃ Dignity

          ⊃ Respect   ⊃ Partnership

      1.1.2 Understand the meaning of prejudice and equal opportunities in relation to the service users they will be supporting

You may have a responsibility in your work for ensuring that others work to these care values. We will look at each of these values in turn within this chapter.

The last statement in the list refers to the important area of equality. Equality can be difficult to describe, and professionals need to be clear about whether they are focusing on equality in the provision of health and social care services, or equality of individuals in their experience of health and social well-being. This may seem like the same thing at first view, but the former statement emphasises that there should be equity in the way that care services are organised, funded and delivered – the *process*. The latter statement recognises that by focusing on the care outcomes for individuals, the need for difference in the process of providing care can be achieved. Addressing well-being as an *outcome* may identify that the process of care does not contribute towards this.

Why values are important in care work

Diversity in the UK today

The term diversity refers to differences in the characteristics of individuals within the changing population in the countries of the UK. The population comprises a diverse range of individuals with a variety of races, abilities, religions and cultures etc. The reason for investigating this in this chapter is that care happens in a context and the care worker needs to understand the social context of care in order to understand the circumstances of individuals that they support.

The following table provides some idea of the diverse range of peoples who live in the UK today.

Total population	Males: 30.3 million Females: 28.9 million	
Ethnic minority groups	Asian or Asian British:	2,329,000
	Black or Black British:	1,148,000
	Chinese:	243,000
Religion (77% of population)	Christian:	71.7%
	Muslim:	3.1%
	Hindu:	1.1%
	Sikh:	0.6%
	Jewish:	0.3%
	Buddhist:	0.3%

Source *Social Trends* 2003

Of course there is geographical variation in the percentage of individuals living in a particular area. Consider your own area, how do the statistics above compare to your local environment?

Think it over

Where do you fit into the statistics above?

➲ What characteristics do you have as an individual?

➲ How would you represent yourself in terms of the characteristics that you have?

In one context I may emphasise my nationality. In a different context I may emphasise my gender and see that characteristic as being of greater importance. I may be unhappy by being grouped with other people based on one of my other characteristics.

What makes you who you are, also influences the values that you have.

Issues relating to diversity

The way that services are organised is a response to a general identification of need; that is to say that services are often arranged around characteristics of service user groups. This may sound like commonsense but the characteristics of one individual within a service user group could be very different from others within that group. We mentioned earlier that focusing on one aspect of a person's identity can lead to labelling. Individuals within a client group have similarities and differences in terms of their life experiences and their care needs. Labels and grouping of individuals may better suit the delivery of services rather than the needs of the individual who requires a service.

When considering the context of care delivery the care worker needs to consider the inequality of social experience by members of the public and whether the response by welfare services condones or challenges this. An example of this is that different values have been applied to groups of asylum seekers and refugees compared to others with a similar need. Suddenly society thinks it is OK for individuals to be retained in isolated institutions away from society (reception centres, or in the future offshore boats?), when it has taken years to overturn this policy of segregation with learning disabled individuals and people with mental health issues.

Case Study

Diversity

Meadow Lane Community Centre is holding its Annual General Meeting. On the agenda is allocation of resources for the coming year. There is dissatisfaction amongst some members that resources have not been targeted at the most needy in the local area because the most deprived groups are refugees. Local media have labelled people as bogus asylum seekers and economic migrants who take local people's jobs. Current changes to immigration policy and uncertainty surrounding the government's attitude towards people is not helping.

There are also examples of government policy that do recognise the value of acknowledging the different characteristics and experiences of individuals. The White Paper *Saving Lives: Our Healthier Nation* identified that in improving the health of the population they needed to focus on the worst off groups in society and reduce the imbalance in health, known as the health gap [Department of Health (July 1999)]. This represents recognition of the causal relationship between poverty and ill-health, which has enabled policies to become more focused.

If poverty makes such a significant contribution to the experience of inequality then how does this affect the users of care services?

Care work is not necessarily about working with individuals who experience poverty, and just because a person requires support in some aspect of their lives does not necessarily mean that they experience disadvantage; however many users of care services do find themselves in circumstances of economic disadvantage. We need to have an understanding of the characteristics that can contribute towards poverty, as these include some of the characteristics shared by users of care services – older age, physical disability, mental health.

Race

Race has been an accepted term used to provide biological groupings of individuals. The word has been challenged in recent years as research has evidenced that there is as much biological difference between individuals who share the same race as there is between individuals of different races. Whilst debate about the use of the term 'race' continues it is important to recognise that categorising individuals into racial groups has been used as a means of oppression of groups historically.

Forms of oppression

Racism

Racism is an ideology, a set of beliefs. As an ideology it includes the following ideas.

- ⊃ The superiority of white members of the population.
- ⊃ The inferiority of specific black races due to biological difference.
- ⊃ A justification for different (unequal) experiences of society due to the above.

For some groups of people racism has served a specific purpose; it has allowed individuals to think that the power they assert over other groups is justified and legitimate. Racism also can encourage members of the black population to feel inferior and to accept oppressive actions towards them. Historically, racism has shaped societies, obvious examples include the period of apartheid in South Africa and the oppression of Aboriginals in Australia. Racism was used to justify the oppressive actions of whites over indigenous groups. It was only in 1970 that the Australian policy of compulsory abduction of children with one white and one Aboriginal parent to encourage the development of the white culture was stopped. When you consider individual interaction between people in society today it is important to not underestimate the present significance of history. Individual interaction cannot be separated from the wider social context.

Racist abuse can take the form of jokes which perpetuate images of groups and confirm negative stereotypes, or it can be verbal abuse directed at the individual which has an immediate detrimental impact.

There are several terms used which refer to characteristics of individuals that may be associated with 'race'.

Ethnicity

Smith [in Spybey (1997), page 247] provides a list of characteristics of an ethnic community:

1 A collective and proper name.

2 A myth of common ancestry.

3 Shared historical memories.

4 One or more differentiating elements of common culture.

5 An association with a specific homeland.

6 A sense of solidarity for significant sectors of the population.

Ethnicity refers to the social grouping of individuals, so in addition to race factors such as culture and religion, nationality may account for a person's overall ethnicity. The use of the phrase ethnic minority can be unhelpful in encouraging equality of experience. In some communities people of a particular ethnic group may be in the majority. If services are to be allocated according to needs then even being in a minority of one should not limit your experience of care.

Culture

A person's culture can be the customary practices that they adopt, the lifestyle that distinguishes them from other groups. Culture can be acquired through family and local community influences. Origins of culture may be connected to religious beliefs, place of birth, family practices, nationality, contemporary influences etc.

It is important for care workers not to underestimate the influence of culture on the lives of individuals and to take the lead from individual clients about how important certain customs and practices are. An example is where a dominant value in care practice today is that of informing the client of everything that is happening to them and engaging them in decision-making. Some cultures do not value this process, preferring to involve the family in decision-making practices, especially around death. The care profession has to consider whether it wants to promote the cultural practices of the individual or to interpret them as oppressive and impose western values on the family.

Nationality

Nationality usually relates to the country (geographical and political boundary) that an individual is connected to either from birth or because they have acquired this status by living there. Historically, discrimination has focused on visibly identifiable characteristics such as colour, and white Europeans have not been subject to discrimination in the same way as black and Asian groups. This has recently changed with a focus of discrimination on Eastern Europeans who are seen by the media to present a problem to the countries of the UK.

In the first three months of 2003 there were 16,000 applications for asylum, with Iraq, Somalia, Zimbabwe, Afghanistan and China the top nationalities of applicants. The government has to contend with the emotive use of language by the media when providing asylum policies.

Why do people seek asylum?

- ⊃ *Political oppression* In some countries people do not have the freedom to speak out against the political party that is in power. If a person opposes the government or leader of that country they, and their families, may be persecuted.

- ⊃ *Religious oppression* Sometimes whole groups of people are attacked or threatened and made vulnerable because they have a particular religion.

- ⊃ *War* If a country is used as a site for war it can leave the area devastated and mass populations can be homeless and without any means of supporting their families.

- ⊃ *Natural disasters* Natural events such as famine or floods can cause whole populations of people to be left in an environment which can no longer support them.

Creed

Creed refers to the statement of belief that an individual has. This of course may be associated with nationality, religion etc., but it may be different within family groups.

Language

There are many languages in the world; Chinese Mandarin is the most commonly used, followed by Spanish and then English. Within the countries of the UK other languages are spoken as first languages in addition to English. The effective use of language is a powerful tool for gaining access to socio-economic and political processes, as will be discussed in the chapter on working with service users (Chapter 4). Language as a form of communication can promote a person's participation in society and enable him or her to gain access to the facilities and services that will empower them. In a similar way, not having access to language can disadvantage individuals and limit a person's ability.

British Sign Language has until recently not been acknowledged as one of the languages of Britain, and yet it is the main form of communication of many deaf individuals. If we think about the idea of power and structural discrimination that we mentioned earlier, consider how liberated some deaf people would be if BSL was on the national curriculum and all schoolchildren were able to develop these skills and communicate with deaf people.

The Race Relations Act 1976 aimed to address the negative experiences of individuals from minority ethnic groups in society, especially in relation to employment. Employers had to consider their practices, such as requesting photographs for interviews and monitoring of characteristics of employers to ascertain how successful they are in counteracting discrimination.

The Commission for Racial Equality was established in order to promote racial equality and ensure that there was appropriate representation for individuals within the Race Relations Act 1976 and the more recent Race Relations (Amendment) Act 2000.

Other legislation has promoted the ability of individuals to have appropriate support, an example is the NHS and Community Care Act 1990, which allowed for the delivery of specific services through local authority contracts with organisations who had the expertise to consider the needs of certain groups. This potentially enabled the tailoring of services to meet more local needs and reach groups who had previously had their needs marginalised in 'mainstream' services. It stated that culture needed to be considered when assessing needs and allocating services.

Government-initiated service standards such as the National Service Frameworks and National Minimum Standards policies now identify the significance of race and culture in determining people's experience of care.

Here is an extract from the Domiciliary Care National Minimum Standards:

> Service users have some choice of staff who work with them, such as staff from the same ethnic, religious or cultural background or the same gender.
> [Department of Health (2000), page 34]

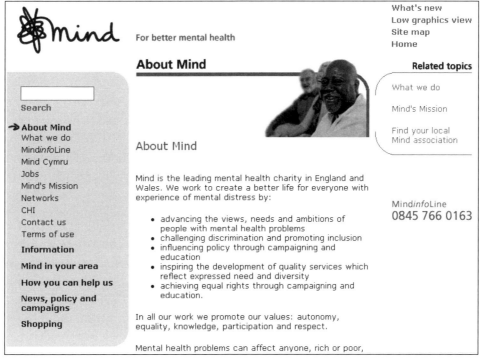

Figure 3.2 *Some organisations have the expertise to deal with the specific needs of certain groups in society*

Sexuality

Sexuality is not a reason why individuals require care, and sexual orientation is not even identifiable in service users unless the individual wants it to be identified. So why is it important to consider the experiences and needs of service users in relation to their sexuality? Sexuality is part of an individual's identity, whether or not they are or have ever been engaged in any sexual activity. As part of individual identity it is an important dimension of individuality for the care worker to be aware of.

Again it is significant to remember that the care profession has not necessarily promoted homosexuality in a good light. The medical profession has at times contributed to homophobia by its persistence in establishing a cause of homosexuality. This has led to its association with mental illness, a view not as prominent now as in the past, but still considered by some. There is an absence of conclusive proof that homosexuality is completely biologically determined and the stance adopted by Stonewall, who are acknowledged as leading campaigners on gay rights issues, is that sexual orientation is likely to be the product of biological and environmental factors.

An important dimension of promoting rights is that of sometimes treating people differently in order for them to enjoy equality of service. Dismissing individual needs as irrelevant to the care task is easier, and still in many instances the needs arising from sexuality are ignored; sometimes, individual service users dismiss their own needs themselves [Wilton (2000), page 6].

A holistic approach to care requires that an individual's physical, social, emotional, intellectual and cultural needs are considered in any area of health and social care delivery. This necessitates respecting people's identity, including their sexual identity. The National Minimum Standards now acknowledge this dimension of individuality.

Remember that one of the TOPSS values is that of privacy; sexuality is not part of the reason for care giving, and it therefore does not need to become the focus of attention when providing care to a lesbian or a gay man. What the care worker needs to be aware of is the heterosexist practices of both themselves and the organisation, and the potential needs of individuals who are homosexual, or bisexual.

Research by Langley (2001) indicated that the needs of older lesbians and gay men were systematically unmet. It did however feel that there was the potential for facilitating appropriate services through established frameworks. This group may currently lack the political or social power for this to happen in a significant way, hence the significance of heterosexism in society, and the value in the care worker being aware of how heterosexism within the care organisation could affect the identity of the individual. Heterosexism can create mental and physical stress in individuals who feel pressurised into presenting a heterosexual identity. The history of homosexuality in the UK has included it being classified as mental illness or a criminal activity. It was only as recently as 1992 that the World Health Organisation declassified homosexuality as a mental illness.

The experience of individuals within care services cannot be removed from their experience in society in general. The report *Queer Bashing* by Stonewall concluded that one-third of gay men and a quarter of lesbians had experienced at least one violent attack during the period 1990–1995. This statistic explains the following findings: that 65% of respondents always or sometimes avoided telling people they were gay and 59% always or sometimes tried to avoid looking obviously gay.

Experiences of care services by lesbians and gay men do not indicate that professionals are at the forefront of innovative responses to this group of people; Wilton [(2000), page177] identified the following experiences within care services:

- Professionals are ill-informed about health issues.
- Many care professionals hold ill-informed and prejudicial views on lesbian and gay peoples' lifestyles.
- A significant proportion of gay men and lesbians receive poor treatment, hostility or abuse by care providers.
- Education for professionals is inadequate and tends to be focused on issues (e.g. HIV/AIDS).
- Medical knowledge can perpetuate negative attitudes.
- Statutory powers can be used to support discrimination.
- A significant number of gay men and lesbians feel unsafe about revealing their sexuality to care professionals and so remain without appropriate treatment.

A significant proportion of young homeless people are made homeless by their rejection by family members when their sexuality is made known [Wilton (2000), page105].

What would be ideal is for gay men, lesbians and bisexuals to have legal equality and social justice. This group experience some severe opposition to their rights presented under the banner of morality or religious beliefs. People sometimes feel morally justified in opposing equal rights for homosexuals on the basis of their religion. This may occur in fostering and adoption.

Think it over

In early 2003, two social workers felt unable to undertake their required tasks due to their individual beliefs about the appropriateness of a child's placement with homosexual parents.

1 What do you think about the actions of these social workers?

2 How should individual values of professionals be balanced against the right of service users to have respect from those who work with them?

When it comes to sexuality there is an assumption that awareness is enough, but as Wilton states, even basic awareness is not prevalent amongst care workers.

Research indicates that the majority of those working in health and social care are ill-informed about issues affecting the well-being of their lesbian and gay clients and/or are actively hostile towards this group. [Wilton (2000), page159]

Whilst much of the original opposition to Section 28 of the Local Government Act 1986, which prohibited 'promoting' homosexuality, has been superseded by education legislation, objection to the 1986 Act remains. The importance of understanding the relationship between policy and values is summarised by the actor who campaigns for the gay rights organisation Stonewall:

If Section 28 and the attitudes behind it remain then society will still believe that gay people are second class citizens and that it is right that they should be treated as second class citizens. (Sir Ian McKellan)

This Act also labels gay family relationships as 'pretend'. The message that society receives as a result of this is very negative.

The government is however introducing legislation to facilitate the same legal rights within a homosexual partnership as with heterosexual marriage. It announced in November 2003 a single comprehensive equality legislation that will address discrimination, including on the grounds of sexual orientation. An all-encompassing law would provide for individuals who have same sex experiences but do not self-identify as gay, lesbian or bisexual, and people who experience discrimination because they are perceived to be gay, lesbian or bisexual, as well as individuals who describe themselves as lesbian, gay or bisexual.

Think it over

How informed are you about supporting an individual's sexual identity? Check through the following to see whether you could improve your practice.

- ⊃ Do you make assumptions that individuals are heterosexual unless they state to the contrary?
- ⊃ Does your language support heterosexism, or are you sensitive to all sexualities?
- ⊃ Do you always challenge homophobic statements from others?

Gender

When you considered your own values you may have identified that some of the origins of these are associated with your gender. Gender is the word used for the social grouping of people where the biological grouping is sex. Care workers need to develop a critical approach to the experience of gender, as with the focus on other equality issues it may be overlooked, or issues which have been on the agenda for years are assumed to have been dealt with. There is nothing wrong with differences originating in gender, but care workers should question what is commonplace and identify the sources of poor practice associated with gender.

Assumptions about gender assume femininity in women and masculinity in men. These assumptions can differ according to a person's culture, age and personal values. Expectations of roles associated with gender can be oppressive, and may serve to exclude individuals from certain roles, services, social networks or support. This is a further example where the importance of identifying need in partnership with clients is important.

Case Study

Gender roles

Consider the experiences of a care manager who fails to acknowledge the importance of gender roles in a couple who are experiencing life-changing circumstances. The husband may be experiencing mental health problems that limit his ability to manage relationships with family members, or to provide financially for his family. The professional would need to acknowledge the importance of the roles that the family members have, even if they disagreed with the values underpinning these roles.

Having an understanding of gender roles can enable the care worker to communicate more effectively with individuals, recognising the fact that some values may have been imposed on people we work with by society. An example of this is where a daughter-in-law assumes the role of carer for her mother-in-law without questioning whether this is her responsibility.

The Sex Discrimination Act 1975 and the Equal Pay Acts of 1970 and 1975 tackled unequal relations between males and females, especially in the workplace where it was recognised that there were examples of overt discrimination. This legislation was furthered in 1986 with an additional Sex Discrimination Act that outlawed discrimination on the basis of gender to even small organisations, and made the age of retirement and pensions equal. In 2003 there are still cases where employers adopt discriminatory practices in relation to employment, pay and promotion of women.

We have looked at theories and models previously to understand a particular issue. Feminism is a perspective, a way of looking at a social situation that focuses on the belief that structures in society serve to oppress women, and that these need to be taken into account in all interaction and dialogue. Feminist discussion has included the desire to politicise the personal and to personalise the political [Thompson (2001), page 54]. This means that individuals should see their own experience of discrimination in the context of wider society, and that society as a whole should acknowledge the significance of the very real experiences of individuals.

The government response to the European Union directive that aimed to address sex discrimination was the policy statement *Towards Equality and Diversity*. This may lead to further legislation in the future, although this is more likely to be a broad-based policy including discrimination on any basis rather than individual laws.

The Equal Opportunities Commission research findings in *Women and Men in Britain: The Lifecycle of Inequality* highlights the significance of interrelated issues. An example of this is the subjects that are predominantly chosen by girls in schools, which then lead them into particular careers that are low paid due to the concentration of women in some jobs. In recent years 90% of students taking

GNVQ Foundation Health and Social Care were female, whilst 81% of those taking GNVQ IT were male. The EOC recognise that the costs of gender stereotyping in occupational choice are

⊃ discrimination

⊃ wasted talent

⊃ skills gaps

⊃ unequal pay

⊃ disaffection.

The report *Women's Incomes Over The Lifetime* estimated that a well-qualified childless woman who had not had a break in employment to raise children will still face a loss of income of £143,000 over their life compared to a well-qualified man.

Ability

In this section we focus on how the ability of individuals affects their experience of life and participation in society. In the UK 15% (8.5 million people) of the population are registered disabled. This may factually mean that statistically they are a 'minority group' but I think you may agree that 8.5 million is a significant number of people, and yet their lives are often negatively affected so that they do not have an equal experience of society as those people whom society does not disable. There have been several words associated with disability and it would be useful to clarify some of these.

⊃ **Impairment** This word relates to the functioning of an individual in relation to a particular physical or cognitive feature. For example, a person with a hearing impairment would not have full capacity in their hearing ability.

⊃ **Disability** A definition of disability provided by the Disability Discrimination Act 1995 is

⊃ a mental or physical impairment

⊃ the impairment has an adverse effect on the ability of the individual to carry out normal day-to-day activities

⊃ the adverse effects are substantial

⊃ the adverse effects are long term (having lasted, or likely to last, at least 12 months).

⊃ **Disabled people** A phrase used recently is 'people with disabilities', and this was favoured as it emphasised the idea that individuals are people first. However the phrase 'disabled people' is currently preferred by some groups as it identifies that the disability is not located within the individual, but that individuals are disabled *by* society and inaccessible environments. Some disabled people's groups use the phrase 'temporarily able' about members of society who are currently without an impairment, in recognition of the fact that the majority of people will at some point experience disability.

Disability can be associated with physical, sensory or learning needs. It can have an effect on individual's day-to-day activities through affecting the following areas of well-being:

- ⊃ mobility
- ⊃ manual dexterity
- ⊃ physical co-ordination
- ⊃ continence
- ⊃ ability to lift or carry
- ⊃ speech, hearing or eyesight
- ⊃ memory, concentration, learning or understanding
- ⊃ understanding of the risk of physical danger.

These aspects of a person's condition relate to the extent to which an individual has the physical, social and psychological ability to participate in their society. When considering this we could focus on the ability and inability of the individual, or we could focus on factors in the environment that affect the person's ability or inability.

Figure 3.3 *The ability or inability of a person can be affected by the environment*

Language has been a defining factor in the history of disabled people. Historically, this group has been labelled as 'imbeciles', 'invalids', 'handicapped'. It is important for the care professionals to respond both to the language that is preferred by disabled people's groups as a whole and by the individual they are working with.

Models of disability

In order to appreciate the experiences of individuals, and understand how society has responded to them previously, we will now look at models of disability. Models provide a way of explaining what is going on, a way of viewing the situation. We shall consider three models:

- ⊃ The personal tragedy model
- ⊃ The medical model
- ⊃ The social model.

The **personal tragedy model** starts with the individual situation of the disabled person. It focuses on the loss of ability in the individual, and emphasises the physiological reasons why an individual is unable to undertake certain tasks. A person is described in terms of what they cannot do. The response from others in society is therefore one of pity and sympathy.

> 'Poor Jenny, she has multiple sclerosis and can't look after herself anymore. She can't get herself dressed and her legs are useless, she needs to use a wheelchair all the time.'

The **medical model** emphasises the pathology of the individual. It focuses on what the body is capable of and how the physical reaction to the impairment can be improved by the care profession. Discussion on overcoming disability would focus on correcting the impairment. Comparisons would be made with what an able-bodied person is capable of, and providing feedback based on the 'norm'.

> 'Jenny has experienced a change in her condition, which means she is currently unable to walk or physically attend to her personal care needs. Her condition is degenerative so her ability to do things herself will decrease over time. There are new medical techniques that we could consider to reduce the effects of this change.'

The **social model** starts from the premise that the environment we live in restricts some individuals in what they can do, and limits some people's access to, and participation in, society. The focus is not on the individual who experiences disability, but on society, which has created barriers for some people. This model is further strengthened by the idea of rights; individuals who are disabled by the communities in which they live have the right to have their needs addressed. It values the individual with the impairment and aims to support them by changing the physical and social environment rather than changing the person's identity.

> 'Jenny has multiple sclerosis, which has affected her experience of society and her environment. Jenny will need her environment to respond to her changing needs, with more appropriate access to buildings and an increase in the practical support that is given to her. Jenny has a right to continue participating in the activities that she has always been involved in and will need advice and support to do this.'

You may be wondering why models of disability are useful for care workers. Their significance is evident from the role that professionals take on when working with individuals. As with the example of Jenny, models impact on both the individual and the response of those around her, including the provision of services by the care worker.

Think it over

Having read through the models and how each one would interpret Jenny's circumstances, think about the impact that each model would have on the attitudes of the following:

- People in society
- Care workers
- Jenny and her family.

Recent models of working with learning disabled individuals have focused on the ideas of normalisation (ensuring that the life of a learning disabled person follows the usual patterns associated with age etc.), social role valorisation (where the role and status of a learning disabled person is valued by society) and ordinary life principles (where people have access to normal daily living and the usual expectations on all of us are applied to learning disabled people). The similarities of these have been that they aim to promote inclusion of individuals in society, and validate the status of learning disabled individuals.

Disability has often been associated with dependence, French and Swain [(2000), page 405]:

> Whose tragedy? For many disabled people the tragedy view of disability is in itself disabling. It denies their experiences of a disabling society, their enjoyment of life, and even their identity and self-awareness as disabled people.

Policies and disability

Studying the history of policies towards disabled people gives a valuable opportunity to identify the significance of the relationship between society's values and government policy.

Period	Focus of policies	Examples
Up to the end of the 1800s	**Containment**	Various means to confine people, exclude people from society
Early 1900s	**Compensation**	A response to people with legitimate industrial and war injuries
From 1950s	**Welfare**	Rehabilitation, to 'normalise' people, by a growing care profession
From 1990s	**Community care**	A response to population changes and economic pressures Preventing moves into institutions and closing of large institutions
	Civil rights	An emphasis on anti-discrimination, citizenship, e.g. the Disability Discrimination Act, Valuing People, Independent Living Fund and Direct Payments

Adapted from Drake (1998)

Drake is critical of a lack of consistency in policy making for disabled people:

> British disability policies have been narrow in scope, largely uncoordinated in implementation and fragmentary in effect. [Drake (1998), page 179]

People with learning disabilities have also been excluded from policy-making due to

- ⊃ the ability of others to exercise power over them
- ⊃ society's perception of the helper–helped relationship
- ⊃ the structure of the policy-making process which excludes disabled people.

An example of how this is changing is the People's Parliament, where disabled people have a forum for raising political issues and then accessing the political system. Practices promoted by the *Valuing People* [Department of Health (2001)] White Paper are also an attempt to address the exclusion of disabled people from policy making, especially when the policies are about them.

Having considered models of disability, and the history of disability policies, let us explore the experience of disabled individuals by all aspects of society and in welfare services.

The experiences of disabled people

Disability is a barrier to employment with just 54% of disabled people 16–59 years of age employed compared to 85% of non-disabled people [Government Statistics (2003)]. People experience inequality in terms of their social relationships, such as not being able to access the local pub or leisure centre when they want to or without great difficulty. Society imposes stereotypes about individuals with disabilities; these range from disabled individuals having no sexuality to being very promiscuous. Disabled people are also treated as a homogeneous group, or they are arranged into a hierarchy of disability. It is important therefore for the care worker to acknowledge their responsibility in addressing inequality.

Disabled people are now not only claiming their rights as people but they are asserting their sense of identity as disabled people. Society disrespects this sometimes and tries to impose values on individuals in relation to their ability. For example, medical advances have enabled technology to overcome some causes of deafness. Within the deaf community there is a mixed response to this as many feel that having corrective intervention to become hearing negates the very positive experiences of deafness by individuals.

The Disability Rights Commission (DRC) aims to raise issues relating to medical practices. There are ethical issues associated with genetic screening, the right to medical treatment and resuscitation, voluntary euthanasia and assisted suicide. The DRC acknowledges the complexities of individuals having a choice if society's practices advocate one thing and make the individual feel like they would be a burden if they opted for a different outcome.

A further example is the availability of screening during pregnancy, such as the amniocentesis test, which identifies 'abnormalities' followed by an option of terminating a pregnancy if 'deficiencies' in the foetus are identified. This can lead to a negative view of individuals who are born with so called 'abnormalities'. These are complex issues relating to values, which disabled people themselves have differing views of.

Legislation and disability

The Disability Discrimination Act 1995 made it unlawful to discriminate against a disabled person in

- ⊃ employment
- ⊃ the provision of goods, facilities and services
- ⊃ education
- ⊃ management, buying or renting of land or property.

Under this legislation discrimination means

- ⊃ the disabled person is being treated less favourably
- ⊃ the treatment is for a reason relating to the person's disability
- ⊃ the treatment is not justified

or that

- ⊃ there has been a failure to make reasonable adjustments for the disabled person
- ⊃ this failure is not justified.

The Disability Rights Commission (DRC) was born out of the Disability Rights Commission Act of 1999. The principles that the DRC propose, that underpin all policies and practice with disabled people, are choice, control, autonomy and participation.

They have statutory duties to

- ⊃ work towards the elimination of discrimination of disabled people
- ⊃ promote equalisation of opportunity for disabled people
- ⊃ take steps as is considered appropriate with a view to encouraging good practice in treatment of disabled people
- ⊃ keep under review the workings of the Disability Discrimination Act 1995.

Criticism of the way the legislation has been enforced claim that there have been cynical interpretations of disability, which focus attention on the individual's ability due to its use of the medical model. 'It could be argued that at present the Disability Discrimination Act 1995 has a narrowly drawn, medically grounded definition of disability.' This has led to what Roulstone (2003) describes as, 'The triumph of legal doctrine over the perception of disabled people's experiences...' (page 127). This may be a further example of structural discrimination that we discussed earlier, where the views of the dominant and more powerful group in society override that of disabled people.

They have also taken on the mission of seeking to achieve a society in which all disabled people can participate as equal citizens. The Special Educational Needs and Disabilities Act (SENDA) 2001 requires educational institutions to promote the inclusion of disabled individuals in education, and provides a legal backing to individuals who experience discrimination.

Sometimes services designed to meet the needs of disabled individuals do not get it right. Marler discusses the complex nature of meeting needs with individuals who have a learning disability and Alzheimer's.

The inflexibility of current service models causes many people with Down's Syndrome and Alzheimer's disease to fall between two stools [Marler in Astor and Jeffreys (2000), page 148].

There are some tensions in care practice relating to individual's rights. The current legislative framework creates conflict between health and safety legislation and the principle aims of community care. The local authority's duty to their care staff overrides their duties towards an individual who requires assistance with mobility, for example. As a care worker it is difficult to work safely with individuals who need practical physical support with their personal mobility when you know they hate using the hoist. The Royal College of Nursing guidance indicates that employees lift manually only in 'exceptional or life-threatening situations'. The Health and Safety Executive has devised a more positive solution for care workers aiming to promote the values inherent in community-based care.

Mental health

Research by Mind indicates that 1 in 4 of the population will experience mental ill-health at some point in their lives. It is a significant area of society and certainly not a 'them and us' situation. The following terms are important here:

- ⊃ *Mental health* This phrase refers to well-being associated with thinking and emotions.
- ⊃ *Mental disorder* This refers to a specific group of conditions that affect mental well-being.
- ⊃ *Mental health problems* This refers to situations and conditions that have a negative effect on a person's mental well-being.
- ⊃ *Mental distress* This refers to ill-health experienced as a consequence of disorders or problems.

The following are models of mental health.

Model	Mental health problems are caused by …
Organic	This model classifies mental health problems into disorders with set characteristics
Psychodynamic	This model suggests that mental health problems can be caused by emotions, conscious and unconscious ones
Behavioural	This model focuses on the symptoms of mental health and how understanding behaviour of individuals is most important
Cognitive	This relates to the thinking processes of individuals. Changes in the intellectual ability of individuals affect their mental health
Social/Political	Society creates situations or social relationships which initiate problems for individuals

Why is it important for care workers to be aware of these models? Whatever client group you work with mental health could be an issue for you to respond to either temporarily or in the long term. As we have seen throughout this chapter, models can have an influence on the way society responds to individual need; our chosen model will then influence the services of an organisation and frame our way of working.

Case Study

Self-managing mental health problems

Tony lives as a tenant in a Supported Living scheme. He has been seeing a psychiatrist on and off for a number of years due to a diagnosis of schizophrenia three years ago. Tony feels he is really benefiting from the current support he gets as it enables him to carry on some aspects of his normal life whilst still getting a lot of support. He doesn't know what effect his medication is having on him, but he knows that the regular group meetings and individual support is making a big difference and helping him to begin to self-manage his mental health.

For example, if we have total faith in the organic model we may see that supporting individuals with a mental health problem should remain the responsibility of the medical profession and psychiatrists, that family, friends or individual support workers have little to offer. There is awareness that a very few individuals have a mental disorder which will necessitate much medical intervention, but the majority of people will benefit from a holistic approach to their support. Some people will experience mental health problems that are not associated with a disorder, and the need for medical intervention may be limited.

The values of the recent Mental Health Bill are questioned by the Disability Rights Commission; they suggest that some proposals could 'entrench discrimination' faced by this group of people. Entrenchment here means that current discrimination of individuals with mental health problems will be condoned and furthered by this proposed legislation. An example of this is the proposal that there should be a different threshold for detention of individuals with mental health problems in cases of future risk of violent crime, than those without a mental disorder. These proposals feed the stereotypes that the media require in order to sell papers. The reality of the association between violence and mental health does not support this proposal; the proportion of homicides committed by people with mental disorders fell steadily and significantly from 35% to 11.5% between 1957 and 1995, which was a period of de-institutionalisation and people being settled into community homes [Taylor and Gunn (1999)].

With rights come responsibilities, and mental health campaigners are clear that both individuals with mental health issues and society in general have responsibilities. People with mental health problems sometimes face stigma from their own families, society, employers and colleagues. Mental health is sometimes viewed as embarrassing to discuss, or not something to bring into the open. When you think about your own experience which of the following statements are easier to say, to family members, colleagues or managers, or even strangers ?

'I feel really dizzy and need to sit down.'
'I don't feel as 'though I can cope at the moment.'
'I feel really down all the time and can't get motivated about anything.'

Even within service delivery there is discrimination about the capacity of individuals who use mental health services to retain control of their decisions. Discussing the low take up of Direct Payments amongst this group of individuals, Carmichael discovered that professionals did not advocate the system with mental health service users due to

⊃ the perceived ability of individuals to meet the 'willing and able' criteria for Direct Payments

⊃ the perception that clients would involve carers in their delusions or obsessions.

Carmichael and Brown [(2002), page 804]

Language has played a significant role in the values associated with mental health. The words 'lunatic' and 'mad' are part of the history of mental health services, The *Sun* was quick to use the headline 'Bonkers Bruno' when the boxer moved to a hospital for mental health reasons in 2003. Some groups prefer to refer to people experiencing mental health issues as being in an 'unresourceful state'; this term emphasises that mental health is a resource for living and changes to a person's mental health will affect this resource.

Age

In many ways society likes to determine our behaviour by categorising us according to age. Issues arising from age occur throughout the life course. Stereotyping of young people creates expectations that they are 'trouble', older people are considered to be a burden.

Young people have experienced lack of continuity in service delivery as they undertake transition from adolescence to adulthood, exampled in mental health and learning disability services. In mental health this is being addressed through CAMHS (Children and Adolescent Mental Health Services). Older age should not necessarily be a reason for coming into contact with care services; some people will go their whole lives not requiring any support from professionals, but many people do need some level of assistance in later life. Older people experience more poverty than other age groups. Political discussions about pensions do not seem real to us until we stop work and become dependent on a low income through our pension. The political weight of older people is weakened by their status in society. Discrimination is even evident within care service delivery as older people receive less mental health support than other age groups from specialist teams when individuals acquire dementias such as Alzheimer's.

Society perhaps feels justified in discriminating against people due to older age, perhaps because it is a characteristic that we may all share at some point. Many images of older people are negative and emphasise that it is the last stage or even the end of life. It may be that this group of people have been unsupported in advocating for themselves and therefore their issues remain on the fringe of society.

Let us look at the factors that influence our perception of older age.

Economic circumstances
Money gives us the means to continue in some activities

Environment
How safe it is for individuals to access their locality

Individual
Ability to maintain lifestyle is linked to wealth

Family situation
Changes in role and relationship with children

Society
Age of retirement is linked to the economy

Biology
Physical ability of the body to undertake different tasks

Psychological changes
Self-esteem may change with change in circumstances

Culture
Expectations of what people do at different stages of life
Old = wise or old = out of touch and past it

Figure 3.4 *Factors that influence how we perceive older age*

In society the emphasis is usually on health and biological factors, so older people are often associated with what they *cannot* physically do any more. Age is frequently a criteria for being allowed or not allowed services: within the NHS you are labelled as being an 'older person' when you are 70 years, within local authorities this age is 65. Means testing legitimates some individuals' access to domestic care or mobility aids at home whilst others go without.

Just as we have looked at models of disability and mental health, let us explore theories of ageing. This should provide an opportunity for you to reflect on your own personal values associated with age.

Think it over

Look at the factors that influence society's perception of age. Think about what your individual view is of age in relation to each of these.

1 What would be the view of age of the service users that you support?

2 In what way does the organisation that you work for influence the staff and service users' views of age?

3 Is this a positive or negative influence?

Theories of ageing

Chronological age refers to the timeline of birth to older age and looks at age as a progressive, and then degenerative, experience. There is an emphasis on how our biology changes with time, and what we are capable of doing is affected by age.

The social construction theory of age recognises that society can dictate what expectations individuals have of what they can or can't do at certain times in their life. For example, when is the 'right age' to marry, have children, go to college or university, start and stop working? There are lots of pressures to conform to what society expects of us. There are ways that society controls what we do, there are laws that say when we can drink alcohol, consent to sex or leave full-time education.

Policies

The proposed new comprehensive legislation on discrimination will encompass age. There are current examples of where age discrimination is being addressed through government policy:

The National Service Framework for Older People

Standard One: Rooting Out Age Discrimination

Aim: To ensure that older people are never unfairly discriminated against in accessing NHS or social care services as a result of their age.

Standard NHS services will be provided, regardless of age, on the basis of clinical need alone. Social care services will not use age in their eligibility criteria or policies to restrict access to available services.

[Department of Health (2001)]

Further Research

Compare the National Minimum Standards for Older People and for Adults and identify the differences between what is required for the age groups 18–65 and 65+.

This standard raises issues as many services are organised around criteria, which provide a rationale for providing services to an individual, as well as an excuse for not providing them to others. This links with the organisation of services and whether we do have a needs-led or service-led provision, as discussed in the chapter on the context of care (Chapter 1).

The government report *Fit for the Future* sought to provide a more positive view of this generation:

⊃ The older population should not be viewed negatively but as a major achievement of the 20th century.

⊃ Old age should be seen as a distinct phase of life which brings new opportunities and developments for both individuals and society. Older people have considerable assets of time and experience contributing to intergenerational interactions, within families and wider communities.

- Social inclusion should be a goal for ensuring opportunities for all citizens to participate fully in society, regardless of age, gender, ethnicity or socio-economic group.
- Policies and practices should reflect the principle of age neutrality and should not use age as a basis for discrimination.
- Strategies must focus on maintaining and enhancing what older people are able to do, rather than what they cannot do.
- Promoting positive values and attitudes should be part of public policy and law.

Sexuality and older age

The impact of the process of social construction on individual perception of age is illustrated through society's attitude towards older people and sex. Bytheway (1995) discusses the negative impact of humour on older people as they evoke ridicule or disgust from others. Older people are not viewed as having a sexuality by people, including many care workers.

Case Study

Sex and older people

Babs and Donald have been married for 67 years. They have been caring for each other for the past three years, but a recent chest infection has meant that Donald is very weak and unable to support Babs any more. Babs and Donald have been assessed and they will be moving into a care home very soon. They had heard that they wouldn't be allowed to share a room, but they are pleased that they can share and this has been arranged for them; they had not spent a night apart since the end of World War Two until Donald's recent spell in hospital.

Religion

Religion may relate to a person's

- faith and spiritual beliefs
- customs and practices
- association with a religious community.

This is an aspect of life in society that has become more in focus in a very negative way recently with increased prejudice against Muslim groups, due to political events. Some people may think that religion is irrelevant today and holds no significance in their own life. However religion may be a very important part of a person's identity and so the threat of intolerance, discrimination and abuse can be debilitating for an individual, even if actual discrimination is not experienced by that individual. Many Muslims reported that their perception of prejudice against themselves in the lead up to the war in Iraq during 2003 rose as a result of negative media reporting against them as a group.

The care worker needs to acknowledge that their own religious beliefs can influence their interpretation of and response to an individual's circumstances. Religion can be an important part of an individual's life, and it should be up to the individual to determine the support they require to access religious practices. This is also acknowledged in the National Minimum Standards for Care Homes, Older People and Adults.

Government proposals that we have previously mentioned will include making discrimination, on the basis of a person's religion, illegal. This area is a little more complex than others as issues are more subjective. There is no absolute definition of what constitutes a religion or faith by individuals in society. Some people would describe themselves as Christian or Muslim without being affiliated to a religious organisation, attending a church or mosque regularly. People who hold the same faith may have differences of opinion about what customary practices should be observed and how strict this observance should be.

Religion is sometimes a criterion for access to schools or jobs as it is viewed practicable to segregate children whose families share the same beliefs. There are different views as to whether this self-segregation serves to perpetuate stereotyping and lack of awareness of different groups, or whether it is a sensible solution for families who share the same religion.

Further Research

1 Investigate the religious profile of people who use the services of the organisation that you work for.
2 Find out more about these religions so that you can be more receptive to the care needs of people.
3 Think about how your own religious beliefs can potentially influence your ability to support others.

Health status

When we looked at disability we focused on examples where an individual's disability would be recognised by other people. There are conditions, which are not obvious to others, that can increase their chances of being disabled by society, such as asthma and diabetes; these are often described as hidden disabilities. These conditions can make a negative impact on the lives of individuals, as there is generally a lack of understanding about how they affect people.

Rayner (2002) discusses the issue of an emerging genetic underclass who experience discrimination by insurance companies when having to declare conditions that they have awareness of through genetic testing:

The Human Genome Project promises a glorious future …. At some point the science should make us healthier, happier people …. For the time being diagnosis is far ahead of treatment and so long as this remains the case, thousands of people will find themselves discriminated against every year.
[Rayner (2002), page 96]

Criminal convictions

Care workers have a responsibility to provide a quality service to whoever is entrusted in their care, and this may include individuals who have criminal convictions. Personal values can be tested in such circumstances and need to be acknowledged when working with an individual who has contravened society's values, and/or those of the care worker, in the past. When supporting an individual, is it realistic for the care worker to say that they are not affected by the history of the individual? It would be important for care workers in such situations to access support to recognise potential issues that may arise and to have an opportunity to discuss their feelings towards the service user so that they do not negatively impact on the task that the care worker is commissioned to carry out.

Think it over

Read the following descriptions of individuals and reflect on what you think about the person and how your own values could influence your ability to provide professional support for them.

⊃ Clarissa has a criminal record for possessing and supplying illegal drugs. She has been diagnosed with multiple sclerosis and needs some practical support.

⊃ Ten years ago Terry served a custodial sentence for sexual abuse of a child. He is now 73 years old and needs an assessment of his needs due to a change in his physical mobility.

Class

Some people feel that we live in a classless society, and that values associated with being working, middle or upper class are no longer relevant. Class is often associated with the economic circumstances of an individual, both in terms of the income and assets that an individual has, and also the lifestyle choices they make on how to spend it. We may have the ability to present ourselves to others as we choose, and can create an impression of our lifestyle, values and status in society. Many service users have intrusion into their lives so that they cannot do this; and it would be easy to make judgements about them based on what we find.

Characteristics usually associated with class are economic circumstances and education.

Economic circumstances

In the year 2000 in the countries of the UK the wealthiest 1% of the population owned 22% of total wealth in the household sector, whilst 50% owned just 6% of total wealth. This unequal distribution of wealth has a significant impact on the life experiences of people. Poverty can affect an individual's ability to participate effectively in the education system, in the work sector and to have equal experience of health care.

So how do economic circumstances affect care today? People's entitlement to an assessment of need does not mean that all those needs shall be met. A person's financial assessment will identify their ability to pay for some of the services that they require and depending on how much disposable income they have this will influence whether they choose to take up that care.

Education

The educational background of individuals is often associated with their class. A sound education can provide individuals with a good start in life, and give them the resources to look for the career that they want. Education can also inspire confidence in people and enable them to represent their views more articulately when dealing with other professionals. Of course service user groups are representative of the population as a whole but there are reasons why people who need care services may have been disadvantaged by the education system.

- Children sometimes miss school due to ill-health.
- Disabled people may not have been provided with an appropriate curriculum in the past when they were children.
- Mental health problems can mean children are labelled as odd at school and they are excluded from social activities; this may reduce their confidence in class.

Geographical location

The government has been criticised for what is described as the postcode lottery associated with geographical location. It may be thought that a National Health Service should provide equity of access and parity of health outcome, but this has been exposed as a misnomer. Choice and access to services is affected by

- the resources of an area, which affect the professional support available or buildings and facilities
- the priorities of a Primary Care Trust or local authority
- the level of eligibility criteria set within the authority's region.

Think it over

We have looked at all the characteristics of individuals that potentially affect their experience of life, and potentially their experience as a service user. Reflect on your own situation:

1 How would you describe yourself in terms of your gender, sexuality, age, ethnicity, race, nationality, ability, religion, educational background, class, health, geographical location?

2 To what extent have any of these characteristics afforded you privileges or given you a disadvantage?

3 How can the experience that you have influence your ability to support others?

Discrimination

Now that we have looked broadly at the identity of individuals in society, let us consider what happens when individuals are affected negatively or disadvantaged due to the characteristics that they have.

Positive discrimination

Before we consider negative experiences of discrimination let's focus on positive discrimination. Positive discrimination is used in the policy of 'affirmative action' in the USA where, for example, in the job application process individuals from disadvantaged groups were given favourable treatment. Some job application processes in the UK will try to increase the number of applicants from disabled people by guaranteeing interviews to applicants with disabilities who meet the criteria.

What is the purpose of positive discrimination?

- ➲ It aims to counterbalance the disadvantage that individuals from minority groups are likely to have experienced in education and previous employment.
- ➲ It requires organisations to consider their institutionally discriminatory practices.

Why is it sometimes considered in a negative way?

- ➲ It has led to the belief that some people are the 'token' disabled/black/female employee.
- ➲ People from minority groups are viewed as jumping the queue and not achieving on the same playing field as others. Achievements go unrecognised.
- ➲ Institutional discrimination may be shielded by the individual.

> **Think it over**
>
> Think about what thoughts you have about positive discrimination.
>
> Is it a good thing? Do you feel it has a place in a society where discrimination is still prevalent? Have you experienced it yourself, or do you know someone who has?

Forms of discrimination

Indirect discrimination This is where individuals are treated the same but some experience inequality as a result of this. An example of this covert behaviour is where staff training is always provided 9–5pm so that part-time employees who have childcare responsibilities are unable to participate. The employer may say that the same thing is on offer to everyone, so what is the problem?

Direct discrimination This is where individuals are treated differently, and as a result some people experience inequality. In relation to the above, an example may be that training is only offered to full-time employees.

The significant factor in any issue of discrimination is what the individuals or group experiences, not the intention of the perpetrator. Not intending to discriminate against someone does not mean that the victim has not experienced discrimination. The important point to remember is that sometimes you need to treat individuals differently in order for them to have the same access or opportunities as others.

I'm a very fair boss and shall be treating you all the same. That's why we only have one size of uniform to wear.

Figure 3.5 *Indirect discrimination*

Levels of discrimination

The different levels of discrimination are individual, institutional and structural.

Individual discrimination is where a person's actions cause disadvantage to an individual or group of people. This can happen regarding people's psychological, social, physical, cultural or economic well-being.

The following is an example of individual gender discrimination. The manager of Bailey Lodge Care Home is recruiting for new care staff, but has not short-listed any male applicants as she thinks they wouldn't fit in with the female staff group.

Institutional discrimination is where an organisation has policies and procedures that condone or perpetuate inequality of opportunity. It does not mean that everyone employed in the organisation acts in a discriminatory way, but systems are not established to pick up on individual or group poor practice and to address discriminatory practice. The Macpherson Report exposed the extent to which institutional discrimination had impacted on the work of the police force, and its findings are now being applied to all areas of society, especially the public sector.

Here is an example of institutional age discrimination. At Bailey Lodge the younger members of the care team are always given any new interesting tasks to undertake, and the older staff are not sent on any training sessions. Everyone seems to agree that it makes sense as the younger staff are more motivated and the older staff are very set in their ways.

Structural discrimination recognises that society has an infrastructure that facilitates inequality of opportunity. If you consider the disadvantage that some groups experience due to levels of deprivation in their communities then it is clearly not just the product of one person acting in a discriminatory way.

The following is an example of structural discrimination affecting people with hearing impairment. A person becomes disabled by a society that excludes them from local schools, does not promote the development of BSL skills amongst hearing people in society and creates an environment that depends on being able to hear. A child's experience is then continued into adulthood when the person has to access public transport, public facilities and employment which are not prepared for people without hearing.

Non-disabled people (or temporarily able-bodied people) have several aids that enable them to function effectively in life and modern technology is constantly improving our ability to access facilities and services, or to undertake tasks in a productive way. However, people with impairment are made to feel that their aids are specialised and make them stand out as being 'special' or different from others.

Oppression

Oppression is linked to discrimination, as it refers to the use of power to make a group or individual feel inferior. Oppression can impact on people in a number of ways and can have its origins in surprising sources. A contentious issue is the relationship that disabled people have to formal charities. Describing disabled people's concerns about the role of large charities as lobbyists, Carmichael and Brown discuss their (disabled people's) dismay

> to see the power for determining how services are to be provided being vested with the traditional charities, ... which have historically been viewed as one of the main sources of disabled people's oppression. [Carmichael and Brown (2002), page 798]

In a society where an emphasis is now placed on rights, questions are raised about the values still attributed to individuals who are offered charity, and whether this reinforces the lower status of individuals with disabilities in society.

Stereotyping

Stereotyping is the process whereby a person attributes the same characteristics of one person to others who share similar characteristics. It is a complex dimension of human behaviour. As humans it is convenient to put individuals into groups and label them with the same characteristics, both positive and negative. This process creates an expectation by the onlooker and the individual recipient of the stereotyping. For example, the media has selectively reported news items concerning individuals with mental health issues. They have chosen to write about just the incidents where a mental health service user has acted violently and killed another person. Because they do not report well on general news about mental health or the fact that 1 in 4 people are likely to experience mental ill-health at some point in their lives, then it makes it inevitable that the general public associate mental health with violence and danger. People are engaged in stereotyping without feeling unjustified. This then leads to discriminatory behaviour by individuals and governments, as will be discussed later.

Prejudice

Prejudice is where an individual pre-judges another person and develops an attitude towards them (positive or negative) that assumes what characteristics they have or what behaviour they are likely to display. Prejudice is a natural human process that it is important for us to acknowledge. It would be a mistake for care workers to claim that they have no prejudices, as this would prevent them from dealing with some of their own attitudes that are inappropriate. In order to understand what prejudice is it is useful to consider some theories of prejudice that attempt to explain individual prejudicial behaviour.

Explanations of prejudice

The **biological explanation** proposes that prejudice is a result of conflict between groups, that it is an inevitable consequence of human nature and the differences in our genetic makeup. Critics of this perspective argue that social behaviour cannot be explained away by reference to genes, and that this explanation assumes individuals have very little control themselves.

The **psychoanalytical group of explanations** suggest that prejudice is the result of deep-seated motives, either as a result of personality formation [Adorno *et al* (1950)] or as a result of innate energies and instincts [Freud (1920)]. Limitations of these theories are their lack of recognition of the complexities and impact of social relationships. Individuals do not operate in isolation; we are influenced to a lesser or greater degree by others in society and this should not be ignored.

The **cultural explanation** explores the historical fact that prejudices change with different time and location contexts. This theory takes into account the object of prejudice and the relationship of one group to another as a significant factor. An example is the scapegoating of some minority groups during periods of unemployment or economic disadvantage. This explanation would account for periods of time in Britain where prejudice has been focused on colour in the past, and more recently nationality. Of course it is important to remember that not everyone within one societal group will have the same levels or type of prejudices as others, so factors within the individual must hold some significance. Asylum seekers and refugees are currently targeted by the media, and blamed for causing the country's many social ills; therefore political debate is distorted against them.

The **socio-cognitive explanation**, such as that proposed by Tajfel [in Hayes (1998)] is based on stages; categorisation is where we classify individuals into groups. This is combined with assimilation of social knowledge where we interpret our evaluations of groups as factual and then the search for coherence where we try to understand and explain (justify) what is going on. This model proposes three mechanisms of prejudice, commencing with the categorisation of people into groups and then the accentuation of difference. This exaggeration of the difference between people then leads to intergroup conflict; group membership then affects individual self-esteem due to differences in power and status.

Whilst it is useful to gain an understanding of processes that may lead to prejudice, these are not provided as justification for the application of prejudice that results in individuals being discriminated against. Discrimination can occur when people who have power exert this power on the basis of their prejudice in order to disadvantage another individual or group. If we are to understand that the development of prejudices is part of human behaviour then why do care workers need to be so self-aware? It is because the combination of prejudicial attitudes and power has consequences for individuals and groups.

Think it over

Think honestly about yourself, and identify

➲ any situation where you have stereotyped others

➲ any areas of prejudice that you have.

What steps can you take to deal appropriately with these?

Effects of prejudice

Prejudice can manifest itself in different ways, as Allport (1954) identified.

1 Antilocution	Verbal denigration of groups and hostile talk about groups
2 Avoidance	Segregation of groups in society to keep some groups at a distance from society as a whole
3 Discrimination	Either through government policies or the experience of minority groups
4 Physical attack	Violence against property and people
5 Extermination	Violence against entire groups, wiping out whole groups in society

Earlier we looked at the experience of different groups in relation to inequality. Now we will consider some general ways in which discrimination can affect people whatever the origins of the discrimination.

Case Study

Discrimination

Amrullah is a doctor from Afghanistan, who has been given refugee status in Britain.

Some examples of the effects of discrimination on Amrullah may include:

Social	Isolation from society, social exclusion, due to his lack of confidence and limited English skills. Unable to work as a doctor due to prejudice in the employment system
Physical	Injury from physical assault by neighbours
Emotional	Fear of verbal or physical abuse, effects on self-esteem and confidence. His awareness of his changed status in British society compared to the value he had as a practising doctor in his own country
Intellectual	Lack of access to professional educational experience, suppression of potential
Cultural	Denying one's own culture, inability to observe important cultural practices for fear of standing out and being picked on
Sexual	Denying one's own sexuality, lack of fulfilment, fear of consequences of expressing sexuality

The discrimination that Amrullah may be subjected to may affect him in every area of his life. Thompson (2002) summarises the effects of oppression as

➲ alienation, isolation and marginalisation

➲ economic position and life chances

➲ confidence and self-esteem

➲ social expectations, career opportunities.

Think it over

1 Consider your own life experience and think about any oppression that you have experienced.

  a How did this affect you at the time?

  b How can you use this experience to improve your awareness of oppression with the people that you work with?

2 What oppression might the individuals that you work with have experienced previously, or be vulnerable to?

A discussion on discrimination needs to include an understanding of what power is and how it impacts on individuals. The relationship between power and discrimination allows some groups to assume a higher status of themselves as a social group in relation to the status of other groups. Some groups have experienced oppression where a dominant group who has more power creates structures in society to maintain their own status and experiences by individuals and groups. This means that they set up education, laws and policing etc. in a way that elevates their own importance over others. This can lead to marginalisation of particular groups and the exclusion of some individuals and groups from participating in society fully.

Whilst service users have a diverse range of individual characteristics, their life experiences often share an element of inequality and discrimination. There is no reason why requiring support as a service user should mean that you experience social exclusion as a matter of course, but this is in fact frequently the case.

As has been mentioned, values inform the creation of new policies and shape people's experience of society. An example of this is that the experience of many older people and individuals with disability is that of poverty. Society seems to accept that this may be an inherent feature of older age and so they do not see the need to address it.

Diversity is a positive aspect of our society and as care workers our role is to promote the rights and experience of individuals whatever their individual characteristics. We shall now consider individual aspects of identity in turn.

Anti-oppressive practice and anti-discriminatory practice

> Anti-discriminatory practice is an attempt to eradicate discrimination and oppression from our own practice and challenge them in the practice of others and the institutional structures in which we operate. [Thompson (2001), page 34]

Anti-discriminatory practice has been described as a form of emancipatory practice [Thompson (2001), page 34]. It provides a framework for working with individuals so that we do not perpetuate the discrimination that individuals face in their lives. As care workers we can unknowingly contribute to the oppression that some individuals experience.

> Anti-oppressive practice describes work that seeks to challenge oppression, or the unjust and harmful exercise of power over someone. [Adams (1994), page 3]

Case Study

Discrimination and anti-discrimination

Read the following and identify both anti-discriminatory practice and the oppressive practice that discriminate and oppress individuals.

Ashbridge Day Resource Centre
The manager of this day service feels that they run a tight ship and that the service users benefit from an efficient service.

Activities are structured so that the men do sports and the women do craft work. Individuals with complex needs spend more time at the centre than those who are more independent and mobile.

A dietician advises on meals, and everyone eats the same so that they have a balanced diet. One of the service users, who they call Art (as they cannot pronounce his name), does not speak much English, but the staff have got used to what he needs based on the little communication that they have with him.

Task

Read the experience of individuals at Ashbridge Day Centre and identify the different levels of oppression.

- ⊃ Personal   The manager
- ⊃ Cultural   The culture of the organisation
- ⊃ Structural   Political, economic and social systems in society

Oppressive practices include

- ⊃ activities being very gender based
- ⊃ everyone having the same meals
- ⊃ Art not being provided with an interpreter.
- ⊃ individuals with complex needs staying in the centre.

Thompson (2001) discusses what he calls 'PCS' analysis, this involves:

P Personal
Individuals have their own values, and some of these form prejudices. These influence their actions towards others.

C Cultural
Earlier in the chapter we looked at ethnocentrism and heterosexism, as examples of the cultural level of oppression. Values and beliefs can be reinforced by groups sharing these values.

S Structural
Society has structures and systems which create an environment of discrimination and oppression, for example the education system disadvantages African-Caribbean children and legislation has not recognised same-sex relationships. This level refers to the social, political and economic framework of society.

Thompson is clear that whilst society values need to be considered in order to understand individual behaviour, they do not necessarily determine individual actions. The manager is individually responsible for his or her behaviour; he or she is not excused because they are influenced by structural oppression.

Working with individuals in a care setting, be this the individual's own home, a day resource, or a care home, often means that as an individual you are charged with a certain amount of autonomy and responsibility for what it is that you as an individual do with service users. You are responsible for addressing your own practice, but also for challenging the practices of the organisation that you understand to be oppressive.

A first stage in anti-discriminatory practice is recognising the social position of the individuals that you work with, and the relative power that they have in society, and in relation to yourself as a worker. Understanding the experiences of individuals will also enable you to adopt sensitivity in your approach with people. For example, if you are working with a refugee who had their life uprooted during ethnic cleansing in their home country, the experience of discrimination that they now have here needs to be considered in this context. The social position of this individual has been influenced by

- the individual's experience of discrimination (extermination of friends/family) in their own country
- media reporting of the 'masses of bogus asylum seekers'
- UK government policies that denigrate individuals and confirm this group's low status in comparison to others (i.e. voucher systems)
- complexities in accessing appropriate support.

In a similar way an awareness of the oppression experienced by lesbians and gay men over the past 40 years would enable you to develop more understanding of the current status of older people who are lesbians or gay men.

Ignoring the different social positions and assuming everyone is the same will not provide you with a sound attitude for making progress with an individual. When working in an anti-discriminatory way it is important to be aware of the actions of others. You should not be content with getting your own house in order; you should be actively questioning what is going on around you. If you are not part of the solution then you are a part of the problem is a helpful way of viewing this.

It is not always easy to challenge the practice of others, and there may have been times when you have wanted to speak up but have had difficulty doing so. If this is the case then you may find the following useful to guide you in challenging poor practice.

Remember that sometimes people can commit oppressive actions without deliberate maliciousness. For example, adult children may assume control of an older parent's finances, and start making decisions for them because they think it is in everyone's best interests. The social position of older people in society does not encourage adult children to challenge this assumption, but in supporting the older person you may be able to facilitate a different perspective from the older person and their family members.

The Macpherson Report highlighted the ease in which a culture of poor practice can lead to institutional discrimination. Whilst this was the result of an investigation into the police force, all organisations are required to apply its findings.

So far we have looked into the individual reasons why people may experience discrimination or oppression. Of course individuals do not have single characteristics and so sometimes experience oppression in a multiple way.

Multiple oppression

It is important for us to acknowledge the life experience of individuals and understand that some people experience discrimination and oppression at a number of levels.

We should not just focus on the here and now when we are working with people, we should acknowledge an individual's life history and the experiences that have shaped their identity.

Service users who express their prejudices

As we discussed earlier, an understanding of prejudice can be useful to us in understanding ourselves and dealing with inappropriate feelings, and also in supporting other people to confront their own values. A client may still be able to accept responsibility for their own actions and behaviour if they behave inappropriately. Being a client does not excuse us from such behaviour, and just because it is a client that you observe being racist, you are not excused from challenging them. We should not make excuses for clients because they are older or disabled. This is not empowering them as individuals. Individuals that we support should be empowered to accept their responsibilities in supporting other people's rights, as well as enjoying their own rights.

How identity, values and rights can affect the experience of care workers

Discussion on discrimination within the care sector should not only focus on the experiences of the people the sector is set up to serve. Employees within organisations can also experience discrimination.

There is a lack of disabled individuals who work within the care profession. Where people have gained access to employment and training they are often working with individuals who share the same disability and are faced with difficulty when attempting to work with a different client group.

> 'Young and enthusiastic' or 'Young and inexperienced'
> ' Old, experienced and wise' or 'Old, set in their ways and past it'

I don't know how old you are, and you don't know how old I am. Is it significant? Within professions people can be knowledgeable and skilled whatever their age, or they can lack knowledge and skills whatever their age. As is discussed in the chapter on reflective practice (Chapter 2) the value of experience is as much about being able to reflect and respond to evaluation etc. than just clocking up the years. A young care worker may be labelled as being inexperienced, or if they demonstrate particular skills in an area may be described as a young upstart. This may lead to discrimination by a senior worker who feels threatened. An older person may be excluded from training or bypassed for particular projects. They may be labelled as 'out of touch' or 'set in their old ways' rather than being attributed with being experienced.

Research into the lives of 120 people in the North West found that older people with learning disabilities (50 years+) are offered fewer opportunities than younger people to develop personal skills and take part in community activities or develop social networks. Older people with learning disabilities also fall between services for older people and services for people with learning disabilities as they are 'too difficult', disabled or too young for the former or too old for the latter [Walker, Ryan and Walker (JRF)]. Some age-based discrimination relates to sex discrimination, for example access to pensions, which the government proposes to make the same.

The care profession is a female-dominated profession, so it is important to consider the experience of male colleagues. The reason why care work is low paid compared to other professions is often cited as being its association with the natural care-giving ability of females. Whilst legislation has been productive in addressing specific individual cases of discrimination, the EOC is critical of the ability of the SDA to

- promote good practice
- prevent unwitting discrimination
- be effective in putting things right after an issue of discrimination.

Recent debate about involving more men in childcare employment found that whilst women favoured the inclusion of more men in employment, negative stereotyping about the motives of men in childcare remain prevalent and mitigate against more males from joining this area of work.

Some care workers who do not have the same ethnic or cultural characteristics of those they work with may experience more intrusion into their personal lives, as there is a focus on them as a novelty. Organisations are not excused from addressing ADP because they employ someone who shares the same religious practices as one of their service users.

A fair and just profession needs to challenge discrimination that staff experience as well as the clients. Issues have arisen where patient empowerment has led to individuals requesting support from particular care workers. If it is appropriate for an individual to request an Asian Muslim worker who may understand their needs more, is it appropriate for an individual to request a white female care worker? What would be the impact of promoting this for other care workers and clients, or for the service as a whole?

It is also important not to be naive about racism. Discrimination does not just occur when people make an oversight, or fail to see the significance of something; there are people in society who are actively racist, and they feel very comfortable about this. The British National Party claim not to promote racist views, rather that they are promoting a return to a national identity; these claims are presented as the acceptable face of their party. The BNP have won seats in a number of places over the past two years, indicating that there are sections of society who are supportive of their ideals and values. Care work happens in this context, our service users are not immune to what is going on in society, and neither should we be.

Further Research

1 Look at the websites or contact the organisations that have been mentioned that are responsible for monitoring equal opportunities and discrimination to obtain more information.
2 Identify what policies your own organisation has that relates to these areas.

Care values

At the beginning of the chapter we mentioned a list of values that TOPSS had identified as being important for all care workers when they start working in care. Now we will explore these in more depth.

In each section we will look at what that value might mean to an individual, what policy guidance is on that value, and also good practice in relation to this value.

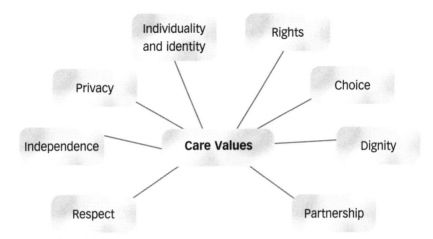

Figure 3.6 *The care values that are important for care workers*

Individuality and identity

> Service users choose their own clothes, hairstyle and makeup and their appearance reflects their personality. [Department of Health (2000), page 34]

You are unique. Even if you have very similar siblings or an identical twin you are an individual in your own right – there is only one of you. That is a very special fact within humanity. What makes you unique are the characteristics that shape your personality and your appearance; some of these you may have been aware of throughout your life, whilst others may be characteristics that you have acquired as an adult. Life experiences influence the development of you as a person. Think back to the exercise where you described who you were. If you had to place these characteristics in order of importance to you then you may find that some of them have a higher priority. Some of these characteristics may become more prominent depending on who is asking you, or when you are asked.

This chapter has explored the diversity of individuals that we work with. Each person that you come across is also unique. Individuals who use care services are frequently grouped together for the convenience of arranging care delivery. This may not seem problematic, and would be viewed as a sensible stage in the process of organising care. However for the individual person, they may find themselves labelled as a 'learning disabled person' or an 'older person'. Other characteristics may be seen as secondary, and will therefore not be prominent in shaping the care professionals response.

The National Minimum Standards for Domiciliary Care states that, 'Service users are addressed by their preferred name at all times.' [Department of Health (2000), page 16]

This may seem like a minor detail but there have been incidences where individuals do not have their request respected. The effect that having your individuality ignored can have on people is immense. It may affect a person's spirit and sense of self. If a person feels that they do not matter as an individual and they are just one of a group then they may feel devalued and insignificant.

Diversity should be seen as an asset according to Thompson (2002), who also acknowledges that 'the way organisations work will either support or inhibit the affirmation of diversity' [Thompson (2002), page 39].

Labelling

Labelling is the process whereby the individuals that we work with are grouped together and given a label that then becomes their defining characteristic. This process is considered by some professionals to be necessary in order for individuals to access the services that are categorised in the same way. But a different view proposes that it is often very unhelpful to attribute a label to an individual that then shapes all the services, intervention and professional relationships that they engage in.

> These words that lump us together – 'the disabled' 'spina bifida' 'tetraplegic' 'muscular dystrophy' – are nothing more than terminological rubbish bins into which all the important things such as people get thrown away. [Thompson (2001), page 126]

Figure 3.7 *Should people be labelled?*

Labelling can also serve to reinforce and perpetuate characteristics that may be assumed by the person doing the labelling. For example, if you are an agency member of staff working a new shift at a place and you are told about a service user who is 'difficult', then you may pre-empt situations and create a type of interaction that confirms what you have been told. Many care workers will tell you of examples where a service user's notes state negative patterns of behaviour that new staff groups have not experienced. In the past labelling has served a purpose in grouping individuals together for the purposes of service delivery. The aim now should be for services to be shaped around the identified need of individuals, not just focusing on the category of client group that they come under.

Recognition of the variety and different needs of individuals will enable you to respond to individuals in a more appropriate way. Individual identity has a strong association with a person's self-worth. If an individual has elements of their personality or character affronted this can have an impact on their overall self-esteem. Historically, individuals who lived in large institutions may not have considered themselves to be individuals. The values in the profession at that time did not facilitate what we now would consider to be appropriate staff support; an example of this would be the sharing of clothing by people who were the same size. People who lived there may not have had the opportunity to see themselves as individuals. The idea of personhood, which relates to the importance of individuals having value as individual people, was not a feature of care work at that time.

Ways of encouraging individuality will be different with everyone. For one person it may be supporting them to bring their own possessions into a new care setting so that their room reflects their individuality. For another person it may be enabling them to develop self-awareness about what they like as an individual so they don't always feel they just do things as a group. Being able to represent yourself is an important aspect of this.

Rights

The idea of rights links closely with the ideas proposed by philosophers. Rights are a fairly new idea in relation to care provision. Historically, the language of care was to do with caring, supporting individuals who have needs.

Concerning society generally, people began to talk about tolerance and integration of different groups. Assimilation and integration was a policy designed to ensure new groups joined in with the dominant culture and adapted their own lifestyle and beliefs in order to fit in; the onus was on individuals from minority groups to change and accept a new way of life. Multi-culturalism followed from this with the promotion of different cultures and the idea that it was beneficial to society as a whole to have different groups. Anti-discriminatory practice recognised that the language of tolerance was in itself a contributory factor in the negative experiences of minority groups; it failed to place any responsibility for changing the experiences of individuals on society. Inclusivity is a term used to describe the importance of individuals who are disabled by society becoming included in usual activities.

It is useful to consider a history of disability policies. Four approaches to disabled people are identified by Drake (1999), who sees that historically the issue has been to deal with the 'problem of disabled people', mainly through segregation and based on a political consensus around the medical model of disability. We will be looking at these approaches later on in the chapter when we focus on disability.

The campaign for human rights generally was initiated through the civil rights protests in the USA and has recently been affirmed in the countries of the UK through human rights legislation.

Individuals have a right to their own citizenship; citizenship is a concept that relates to the relationship an individual has to the political process. Remember that one of the principles of the recent policy on learning disability, *Valuing People*, was that of legal and civil rights.

If someone has a right then at least one other person must have duties towards that person. [Banks (2001), page 113]

We will be considering this statement when we think about who has responsibility for ensuring that rights are respected, but firstly let us think about what the word 'rights' actually means.

Rights can be divided into positive rights and negative rights, as explained by Banks (2001):

Negative rights (liberties) relate to the freedom to do something without interference.

An example of this would be having your privacy respected without someone invading your personal space.

Positive rights (claim rights) claim against someone to do something.

An example of a positive right would be someone saying the care organisation had not provided appropriate support.

Think it over

Think of an example of the liberties and claims that you promote in the work that you do.

1 What role do you have in supporting the individual's negative rights?
2 What rights could individuals claim they are entitled to from your service?
3 How do you ensure that people are aware of the rights that they are entitled to?

A further distinction is made between *legal* rights, which are framed within a legal code or customs, and *moral* rights, whose origins are in a moral code. It demonstrates that in theory there should be a relationship between moral codes and legislation. Moral rights may be much harder for us to discuss in care work because we have individual interpretations of the importance of different values. If you have ever known anyone be very concerned about a particular issue affecting them but thought to yourself 'I don't know what the fuss is all about', then this may be an example of differences in moral views.

For the care worker, rights are significant because you work in a social and legal context and there are many grey areas concerning the idea of rights. Individuals may feel that they have rights in respect to something and it is important to take this into account. In your own practice, think about what difference it makes to assume a paternalistic caring role for individuals based on the idea that they need care support and you sympathise with them in providing it, to adopting a more rights-based approach.

Legislation and rights

There is much more reference to the idea of rights within legislation today. Some policies are designed to provide a framework of rights for particular service user groups, such as the National Minimum Standards or National Service Frameworks. There are examples where individual ideas about rights may create a conflict with the implementation of official government standards. The implementation of the National Minimum Standards in Care Homes for Older People was reviewed due to the awareness that individual residents were losing the right to decide whether they were content with the provision they received.

In 1998 the countries of the UK introduced the 1998 Human Rights Act in order to bring our legislation in line with European law. This would enable UK courts to deal with issues of human rights rather than cases being referred to the European Court of Human Rights. The ECHR had been established to provide a legal framework of rights with member states. The main purposes of the European Convention for the Protection of Human Rights and Fundamental Freedoms are to

- be an instrument for the protection of individual human beings
- promote the ideals and values of a democratic society
- promote and guarantee rights that are practical and effective
- ensure that in its interpretation courts reflect the sensitivity of the public to the fair administration of justice
- expect courts to give the words of the Convention their ordinary meaning.

The 1998 UK Human Rights Act requires all legislation to be interpreted and given effect as far as compatible with the Convention rights. These rights must be taken into account by the UK courts in all cases brought before them and in the development of common law (developed through individual cases and the setting of precedents.). The Act also makes it unlawful for a public authority to act incompatibly with the Convention rights and cases may be brought before the UK courts if they do.

European Convention Rights

The Convention rights are described as articles and protocols:

Article 2 The right to life

Article 3 Freedom from torture or inhuman or degrading treatment

Article 4 Freedom from slavery or forced labour

Article 5 Personal freedom, the right not to be deprived of liberty

Article 6 Right to a fair trial

Article 7 No punishment without law

Article 8 Right to respect for private and family life

Article 9 Freedom of thought, conscience and religion

Article 10 Freedom of expression →

Article 11	Freedom of assembly and association
Article 12	Right to marry
Article 14	Prohibition of discrimination
Protocol 1 Article 1	Peaceful possession of property
Protocol 1 Article 2	Children's right to education and parents' right for their beliefs to be respected in the education of their children
Protocol 1 Article 3	Free and fair elections
Protocol 6	Abolishes the death penalty
Articles 17 and 18	These relate to appropriate interpretation of individual articles so as not to limit any of the other rights.

Impact of human rights legislation on care practice

You may already be aware of the potential impact that the Human Rights Act 1998 has had on your individual work, or that of the organisation and service users. If you look at the list of articles it is clear that some relate to key aspects of care delivery. Within the countries of the UK many of the articles were already provided for in our legislation, but some of the articles are new and potentially have an impact on care work.

An example would be Article 5 and the right not to be deprived of your liberty. Care organisations have to be more explicit now about any reasons for depriving an individual of their liberty with clear risk assessments and written documentation of safety being the reason for not allowing someone free access. An example of service users who may need this to be considered would include individuals who are learning disabled or older people with dementias.

A further example is in relation to Article 8 and the emphasis on privacy. Care homes would need to provide the means for individuals to have individual security in their rooms and for others not to have free access or opportunities to take possessions.

Choice

> For choice and control to be meaningful, service users and carers have to have clear information. [Department of Health (2001)]

This may seem like a very simple value but it has its foundations in a number of other values such as respect and rights. The value choice was recognised by O'Brien (1981) as one of his 'accomplishments' for learning disabled people. It may seem like a trivial aspect of life, or a very simple one, but actually supporting individuals to access proper choice can be a complex but empowering process.

Think about how many decisions about your own life you make in one single day. Take today for instance, did you decide

⊃ what time to get up? (maybe not if you started your shift at 7am!)

⊃ whether to have a bath, shower, or quick wash?

⊃ whether to have breakfast? (fruit and cereal or a big fry up in café).

If I continued this list of the decisions you make about your activities in one day it would be very long. Now looking at these, they may not seem important but if I was to tell you what you were going to do, what time you were going to do it, and how you were going to do it, then this may have a big effect on how your day goes. Your sense of control and responsibility for yourself would very quickly become eroded.

Choice is a complex concept partly because it is necessary for us to include the ability for an individual to make inappropriate choices and to take risks. Choice enables an individual to retain ownership of their lives through decision-making and control. Choices do however need to be real. Asking someone if they want A or B may make the organisation feel that they are giving choices to a person, but it still means that the care organisation is keeping control of those choices. The issue for care services is how to support individual choice and control in the process of providing services to groups.

One of the main benefits, as identified by the Social Services Inspectorate, of using the Direct Payments system has been the choice it has given to individuals. You may work with individuals who present you with the challenge of providing access to choice in a meaningful way.

> People with learning disabilities with more complex needs had a more difficult time getting choice and control over their lives than those with less complex needs, who in general were able to participate more easily in assessments and reviews. [Social Services Inspectorate (2003), page 22]

In the chapter on working with service users (Chapter 4) we will be exploring strategies, such as empowerment advocacy, that can be tools for promoting choice with individuals. We develop these points in more depth and discuss Direct Payments and care planning in the chapter on planning care (Chapter 8).

Privacy

Is there anything that you don't want me to know about you? Have you ever been fined for not paying your television licence, or caught speeding, or is your home a mess unless you have people coming around? Recently there has been an interest in a Big Brother approach to entertainment with the general public joining game shows where they are on view all the time, or fly-on-the-wall documentaries monitoring a period of time for people. People who use care services sometimes have their whole lives exposed to others whether they choose to or not; every success or achievement, every failure and mistake may be discussed at meetings, written about in reports, and reminded of at a later date.

This is not usual in life; we all have an element of control over whether we make the same mistakes, what information about our past we share with new people we meet, how we represent ourselves to others etc. Imagine what new social situations would be like if every person you met had been briefed about your good points and bad points.

It is therefore important to retain an individual's privacy wherever possible. This relates to both the physical and social aspects of their care. A frequently used example is that of not leaving their bedroom door open so that others cannot look, or go in. Less obvious examples of privacy relate to information about the person, i.e. not telling the neighbours that the service user is going to a home for respite care next weekend. Individuals should own their personal information, and a care worker should encourage the person to manage the information that relates to them where this is possible. This links with empowerment, as will be discussed in Chapter 4.

A difficulty with this value is that people have different expectations of the idea of privacy. Have you ever thought a person to be withdrawn or unsociable if they prefer to have long periods of time on their own?

As you saw under the section on rights, privacy is acknowledged as an important dimension in life as it is contained within one of the Human Rights Convention articles. UK government policy has also recognised its significance, as evidenced for example in the National Minimum Standards for Domiciliary Care:

Standard 8
Personal care and support is provided in a way which maintains and respects the privacy, dignity and lifestyle of the person receiving care at all times with particular regard to assisting with:

- dressing and undressing
- bathing, washing, shaving, oral hygiene
- toilet and continence arrangements
- health and medication requirements
- manual handling
- eating and meals
- handling personal possessions and documents
- and entering the home, room, bathroom or toilet.

Think it over

Think about the following physical environments in which care may be provided. Identify some ways in which you could create more privacy for individuals or facilitate the use of space to encourage more privacy.

- An individual's own home.
- A day centre for people with a learning disability.
- A large care home for older people with dementia.

Confidentiality

Confidentiality relates to the need to make sure information is not accessed inappropriately. As care workers we are privy to much information about individuals.

Article 8 Human Rights Act 3.70 Study Guide states:

> Your right to private life can also include the right to have information about you, such as official records, photographs, letters, diaries and medical information, kept private and confidential. Unless there is very good reason, public bodies should not collect or use information like this.

You may already be familiar with issues of confidentiality, it forms part of the induction standards and there are statements in policy, such as in the National Minimum Standards for Domiciliary Care:

Confidentiality
Outcome: Service users and their carers or representatives know that their personal information is handled appropriately and that their personal confidences are respected.

As a care worker it is helpful to remind yourself of why you are privy to some information. You work on behalf of an organisation and the information that a client shares with you is communicated because of your role in that organisation. You may develop close relationships with service users over time.

The Caldicott Principles were developed for use within the NHS but they are very relevant to social care practice.

Principles	Explanation
Purpose of the information	This principle asks why the information exists and suggests that each piece of information should have a clear purpose
Use of identifiable information	There should be justifiable reasons why named information is used
Reduction of identifiable information	The less information available the easier it is to manage confidentiality. This principle suggests that organisations reduce the amount of named information that they produce
Accessibility to information	Within an organisation there should be a rationale for why each person has access to information. Some information should be kept locked away with limited access. This includes information held on computer files
Responsibilities	Each individual should be aware of their responsibilities with information and the need to keep information confidential. There should be identified people to monitor issues of confidentiality within an organisation
Compliance with legislation	All care organisations are required to adhere to not only care legislation and policies such as the National Minimum Standards but also the Data Protection Act 1998

The **Data Protection Act 1998** supersedes previous data protection legislation, providing a comprehensive policy relating to both written and electronic information. It requires that individuals have access to data that is held on them, and where appropriate a request should be made to view this information so that reference to other people can be removed from documents before they see it. It relates to all forms of information, paperwork and files on the computer.

The **Public Interest Disclosure Act 1998** provides an important framework for individuals to disclose information, which would otherwise be confidential, where there are concerns regarding well-being of individuals or groups. It facilitates whistle-blowing, where an employee may require protection as a consequence of their actions to inform authorities of poor practice.

Your organisation should have policies and procedures that enable you to work responsibly with the information that you are privy to.

The issue of confidentiality is complex. Within the care sector it is recognised that good communication between both professionals and organisations can lead to sound continuity of care and consistency in service delivery. It is sometimes difficult to balance this with not wanting to share information that is not relevant. This issue will be discussed in the chapter on collaborative working (Chapter 5).

Once information is obtained it attracts a legal duty of confidence. This information can only be used in a manner that breaches confidentiality if

- ⊃ there is a statutory requirement

- ⊃ there is a court order

- ⊃ there is a robust public interest justification.

Under Department of Health guidelines there are three types of consent for using information:

	Explanation	Some issues
Consent	Agreement either expressed or implied based on knowledge of the likely consequences	Does an individual really understand the consequences? How is consent implied?
Express consent	Consent which is expressed orally, in writing or through other forms of communication	Evidence of consent if provided orally? Communication ability of the individual consenting?
Implied consent	Consent which is inferred from a person's behaviour	Potential for misinterpretation of an individual's behaviour?

[Adapted from Crown Copyright (2001)]

As the chapter on working with service users (Chapter 4) discusses, it is important to establish trust in your relationship with the individual. To this end it is therefore important that the individual is aware of your requirements regarding information that is shared. There may be some secrets that it is appropriate to keep in the spirit of the relationship that you have with the service user, for example if they have bought a present for someone as a surprise etc. A care worker should never make indiscriminate promises to keep a secret as this could compromise their position in the future.

Independence

Think back to the last time that you learnt a new skill. How did this make you feel?

- ⊃ A sense of achievement?
- ⊃ A feeling of pride?
- ⊃ A sense of capability?
- ⊃ Motivation for learning something else new?
- ⊃ Increased self-esteem and sense of value to self and others?

If these are feelings associated with achievement of skills then consider the feelings that may arise when you are not given any opportunity to acquire new, or maintain existing, skills.

> Indeed, the term 'care' perpetuates the view of disabled people as separate and dependent beings, reinforcing their exclusion from mainstream society.
> [Carmichael and Brown (2002), page 806]

What is care work? Doing things for people, caring for people, supporting individuals, enabling people to do things for themselves? Care work has changed from an exercise where care workers were doing things for people who society felt could not do things themselves, to enabling individuals to maximise their own abilities and retain their own independence with appropriate levels of support.

> ## Case Study
>
> *The importance of independence*
>
> Compare the life of Elisabeth who was born 57 years ago. Her parents were told that she would not be able to do anything due to her disabilities and that it was best for everyone if she stayed in a hospital. She lived in Mapledene Hospital with other children who had disabilities and was looked after, but not given much opportunity to develop her own skills. When the hospital closed 10 years ago she moved to a smaller home in the community and has been given different support from her care workers so that she can develop new skills. If Elisabeth was born today she would be given a different start in life that would aim to promote her ability to gain independence in her personal care, mobility, home management; she may always still need support but every chance would be provided for her to gain some independence.

Independence is given differing levels of value according to the client group and care setting. With older people there is a tension between whether support at this stage of life involves hotel-type facilities in a care home or being encouraged to continue the use of their skills in care home settings. With people under 65 the emphasis is usually on continuing the use of established skills, and developing new ones. There is an emphasis on the development of personal living and social skills with people who are learning disabled, whatever the care setting. This value may apply to older people who live in their own home, but for some reason it alters where group living arises in a care home, perhaps this is partly because it is more difficult to manage the environment and ensure individuals have the potential to develop their own skills on such an individual basis. The values of society have a continuing impact on the type and level of support that individual older people receive compared to younger service users.

Another dimension of independence is that of self-determination. This also links with the value of choice, as a principle of ensuring that individuals have control over their lives. As stated in the Human Rights guidance, 'Your Article 8 Rights include matters of self-determination.' [Home Office (2000), page 18]

Care workers should question the extent to which their actions promote dependency in service users, dependency that includes decision-making as well as practical dependency.

The way that services are organised can have an influence on the level of independence that an individual aspires to. This is borne out through recent use of the Direct Payments system, which was introduced through the Community Care (Direct Payments) Act 1995. Research has shown the impact that this policy has had on the implementation of values:

> The quality and flexibility I now have is because I have an individually designed package to suit not just myself but also my family and lifestyle and it is worth any second of any stress. [Carmichael and Brown (2002), page 800]

Dignity

Just as service users are exposed to more intrusion into their lives they experience more situations that others would find humiliating, but as service users they may be conditioned to accept that behaviour. The care process may lead to situations which expose individuals to potentially degrading situations, and care workers need to be aware of this. A sense of self-worth is accompanied by inner respect and self-esteem. If you have assaults on your dignity that indicate a lack of respect from others, this can lead you to doubt your own worth. Think back to the exercise where you identified the characteristics that made you who you are.

Promoting someone's dignity means that care workers do not engage in any intervention that is demeaning or that devalues the individual. The amount of intrusion into an individual's life increases the opportunity for this. The social status of individuals who require our support may also make them more vulnerable to assaults on their dignity.

The following are examples of not respecting dignity with different service user groups.

A learning disabled person	Inappropriate clothing that is not age appropriate
A person who is registered blind	Doing things in front of them that you would not do if they had sight
A person who uses a wheelchair	Leaving the door open when you are assisting them in the bathroom
A person with mental health problems	Talking to the individual as though they have lost the capacity to use any skills and make any decisions
An older person	Dismissing the fact that the individual's life story and history is important or valued

Respect

All staff are instructed during induction on how to treat service users with respect at all times. [NMS Care Homes (Older People) Standard 10.5]

Some groups use this term frequently today and people are generally more aware of its significance in life. Many believe that respect needs to be earned from individuals so how can it be an automatic value for the care worker. Describing what respect is can be difficult, so it may be easier for us to consider what occurs when individuals are not shown appropriate respect. The actions that indicate lack of respect may include not acknowledging an individual when you walk into their personal space and carrying out care tasks without involving the person. How would you feel if you had two support workers who were talking about something between them when they were assisting you to move from your bedroom to the dining room? It would be more appropriate to talk to the person and involve them in the process more. The potential affect on the individual may be that they feel like an object being moved around.

Having respect for individuals can benefit the care worker by enabling them to perform their tasks appropriately. It will inspire the need to be honest with clients, and to develop trust within the relationship. Respect will enable affirming the person's values and taking into consideration the individual's account of what they want to happen.

Respecting an individual will lead to supporting them in their choices, recognising what dignity means to that particular individual.

Dignity also relates to keeping aspects of care personal. An older person may not want all their relatives knowing that you are concerned about their incontinence. This information should only be shared with others if the individual so chooses.

Partnership

Working in partnership with service users should be a main feature of any work with clients, and a goal of care workers whatever their role. This involves communicating with clients and enabling them to communicate effectively with yourself and others, so that they are instrumental in identifying their own needs and strategies to meet their needs. At the beginning of this chapter we raised issues related to the role of the professional as the 'expert', which needs to be questioned as service users are involved in defining their own care delivery. The idea of partnership is at the heart of this challenge.

This value is not dealt with in great depth here as it is a significant feature of the chapter on working with clients (Chapter 4). Partnership will also mean engaging with other professionals and agencies, as will be discussed in the chapter on collaborative working (Chapter 5). Partnership can operate on a large scale, as with the introduction of Learning Disability Partnership Boards, or on an individual level where professionals aim to empower individuals in their communication rather than assuming the role of expert.

Case Study

Promoting a care user's values

Read through the following case study and think about how this individual would need support in order for their values to be respected. You can consider each value that we have discussed in turn. If it helps and is relevant you can focus on your own role as a home carer/care manager/day service worker/residential care worker etc. and identify what part you could play in making sure that Mr Dakshy's values are promoted in this time of transition.

Mr Dakshy is an 82-year-old man who has been living at home, and has recently been assessed as needing to move into a care home. Mr Dakshy is a private man who doesn't always share what is going on with him with his family, although he would say he was close to them. He is Hindu, following certain beliefs and practices, although he hasn't participated in the local Hindu community for a long while due to his restricted mobility. Mr Dakshy can communicate very well verbally, but is disappointed he cannot read and write well anymore due to his sight, as he cannot keep in touch with family members abroad.

Questions

Now think about one person that you work with and answer the following questions:

1 How do you know what values are important to this individual?

2 What issues arise when supporting this person relating to the promotion of their rights and values?

3 What can you do as an individual care worker in order to ensure that their values are respected?

Further Research

Read through the following information from the General Social Care Council about the social care workers' code of practice and find out some more information about what values care workers should promote and what standards they should work to.

Standards of care

The Care Standards Act 2000 initiated the government agency the General Social Care Council (GSCC), which has responsibility for regulating the workforce. They have devised a set of standards for employees and employers of care:

The General Social Care Council's Code of Practice for Social Care Workers

1 As a social care worker, you must protect the rights and promote the interests of service users and carers

    1.1 Treating each person as an individual

    1.2 Respecting and where appropriate promoting the individual views and wishes of both service users and carers

    1.3 Supporting service users' rights to control their lives and make informed choices about the services that they receive

    1.4 Respecting and maintaining dignity and privacy of service users

    1.5 Promoting equal opportunities for service users and their carers

    1.6 Respecting diversity and different cultures and values

---

We have been looking at what values are important in care work and you have completed some activities to give you a chance to think about how these apply to care work. We are now going to focus on your own relationship to these values.

Case Study

Skills required to support values of care user

Look at the following values that are important to the individual. For each value, make a list of the skills that you would need if you were supporting this individual, so that the values were respected fully.

About me	Values that are important to me
I am a 28-year-old man who has cerebral palsy. I love living on my own, having moved out of my parents' home six months ago. I need a lot of assistance in personal care and daily living tasks, and use a wheelchair at home as well as when I go out. I have an advocate who, with my care manager, has supported me in using Direct Payments to employ my own personal support worker. I am vegetarian, love watching football, and like going down the pub for some real ale.	'Being able to live in my own home.' 'Having a say in who comes into my home and works with me.' 'Being able to make bad decisions and do the wrong thing on occasions!' 'Having areas of my life that I can control.' 'Not everyone knowing all my business all the time.' 'Not being told I'm a fire risk when I go to new places, and having a toilet around that I can actually get into.'

Some activities that would enable a care worker to support any individuals in promoting their values include

- finding out relevant facts about the individual
- considering your own values in respect to this person, so that these do not impact negatively on the care process.
- ensuring that the individual is engaged in their own care
- increasing your knowledge base about the individual's care needs and practical ways of supporting him or her
- making sure that you let relevant people know of what values need to be observed
- not making assumptions about what the individual would want or what could enable the individual (i.e. 'He's too old for glasses' etc.).

The chapter on working with service users (Chapter 4) will explore this in more depth as it focuses on practical skills when working with individuals. If you take responsibility for developing good practice, recognising gaps in your own experience and the service you provide, then acquiring new knowledge about diversity and rights should lead you to more productive and effective practice. Learning from the experiences of service users and other professionals will make a key contribution to this.

It is important not to underestimate the impact you can make as an individual. As one person it would be easy to think that you cannot overcome discrimination, that it is part of society anyway irrespective of what you do. The phrase that we used earlier that 'If you are not part of the solution then you are part of the problem' may be useful here, as this attitude will mean that you remain working in a discriminatory way that fails to address values issues.

Care workers also have a responsibility to question established practice where we think that it goes against an individual's values. Social control is an idea from sociology (the academic discipline that studies society). It claims that some practices in society, either by governments, organisations or individuals, aim to influence or indeed manipulate the behaviour of individuals or groups in society. Some policies have an impact on individuals in a way that makes them a contributor to the idea of social control. This means that the policy dictates the professional practice or influences the behaviour of recipients of services in either an overt or covert way. As agents of welfare, care workers should recognise the contribution they make to perpetuating the values of society, government or the care organisation, rather than promoting the values of the client. It is important to enable the service user to identify their own values and to empower them to assert these values in the way that care intervention is received. This idea recognises the significance that power plays in the relationship that service users have not only with the state, but also with the individual care worker.

There have been issues raised with the implementation of the Direct Payments policy, with an individual requesting that their support workers, known sometimes as personal assistants, purchase alcohol and the support worker has felt that the service user is drinking too much. Who defines what is too much? Does the individual service user have the same rights as other people, including you and I, to drink 'too much' in the privacy of their own home? Or does the individual have the right to support that assists them in challenging the amount of alcohol that they consume? This brings us back to the idea of right and wrong in care work, the ethics associated with the dilemmas inherent in care practice. Observing the fundamental values of care that we have discussed can help us to provide the best care with the best outcomes for individuals.

References and further reading

Adams R (1994) *Skilled Work with People*, London, Collins

Astor R (2000) *Positive Initiatives for People with Learning Disabilities*, Basingstoke, Macmillan

Banks S (2001) *Ethics and Social Work*, Basingstoke, Macmillan

Carmichael A and Brown L (2002) 'The future challenge of Direct Payments' *Disability and Society*, Vol 17, pages 797–808

Department of Health (1999) *Saving Lives: Our Healthier Nation*, London, HMSO

Department of Health (2000) *National Minimum Standards for Care Homes (Older People)*, London, HMSO

Department of Health (2000) *National Minimum Standards for Care Homes (18-65)*, London, HMSO

Department of Health (2000) *National Minimum Standards for Domiciliary Care*, London, HMSO

Department of Health (2001) *National Service Framework for Older People*, London, HMSO

Drake R (1999) *Understanding Disability Policies*, Basingstoke, Macmillan

French S and Swain J (2000) 'Towards an affirmative model of disability', *Disability and Society*, Vol 15, No 4 June

GSCC (2002) *Code of Practice for Social Care Workers*, London, HMSO

Hayes N (1998) *Foundations of Psychology: An Introductory Text*, Surrey, Nelson

Home Office (2000) *Study Guide to the Human Rights Act*, London, HMSO

Langley J (2001) 'Developing anti-oppressive empowering social work practice with older lesbian women and gay men', *British Journal of Social Work*, 31, pages 917–32

O'Brien J (1981) 'Framework for accomplishments', quoted in Tyne A, *Five Values for Every Care Package, Care Plan*, March 1981, Positive Publications

Rayner (2002) in Fulford *et al* (eds) *Healthcare anbd Human Values: An Introductory Text with Readings and Case Studies*, Oxford, Blackwell

Roulstone A (2003) *How Disabled People Manage in the Workplace*, Joseph Rowntree Foundation

Social Services Inspectorate (2003) *Fulfilling Lives: Inspection of Social Care Services for People with Learning Disabilities*, London, HMSO

Spybey T (1997) *Britain in Europe: An Introduction to Sociology*, London, Routledge

Taylor C and Gunn J (1999) 'Homicides by people with mental illness: myth and reality', *British Journal of Psychiatry*, Jan 1992, 174 pages 9–14

Thompson N (2001) *Anti-Discriminatory Practice*, Basingstoke, Palgrave Macmillan

Thompson N (2002) *Understanding Social Care*, London, Russell House

Thompson N (2003) *Promoting Equality*, Basingstoke, Macmillan

TOPSS (Training Organisation for Personal Social Services) (Date) *Induction and Foundation Standards*, London, HMSO

Wilton T (2000) *Sexualities in Health and Social Care*, Buckingham, Open University Press

working with service users 4

This chapter focuses on the relationships that you are engaged in with individuals and looks at the tasks that you carry out with them in your care worker role. We will be looking at the purpose of these relationships, what influences them and how care workers can develop skills to make relationships productive and effective for the people that they support. What will become evident is that whilst we can discuss approaches that care workers can adopt when working with people, it is more difficult to describe in detail the range of practice that is necessary in order for care workers to successfully fulfil their roles. However, this chapter introduces some care activities and explores some of the issues for a care worker to consider and it also offers some practical advice regarding appropriate support (emotional, social, physical and intellectual) to individuals in their lives.

This chapter links particularly with both the chapter on reflective practice (Chapter 2), and that of values in care practice (Chapter 3).

We mentioned previously that the relationship of the 'professional' to the service user has changed over the years. Historically, care work was about doing things for people who were unable to do things for themselves. Care workers would feed, wash and dress people who were not given an opportunity to develop these abilities themselves. This has changed now so that there is an understanding that 'care' work is about supporting individuals who require assistance in some aspects of their lives. Values are a key component of these tasks; a care worker's approach to the task is as important as the skills that they use to carry it out. Working in partnership with service users is also an important dimension of this. Whichever service user group you work with, there may be different skills required by us to promote the ability of the individual. We also consider the professional role and boundaries associated with working with people.

This chapter addresses the following areas:

- ⊃ Factors that influence care relationships
- ⊃ Why do individuals need support?
- ⊃ Policy guidance on the relationship between individuals
- ⊃ Understanding people
- ⊃ Relationships
- ⊃ Relationships with service users
- ⊃ Supporting individuals through change
- ⊃ Principles that underpin the professional relationship

- Skills in relationships
- Barriers to communication
- Communication needs of individuals
- Empowerment
- Assertiveness
- Advocacy
- Working with others involved with service users
- Supporting people
- Managing yourself in a relationship

After reading this chapter it is hoped you will be able to

1 know some of the reasons why individuals need care or support

2 understand the nature of the professional care relationship

3 communicate effectively with individuals in a care context

4 support individuals in physical, social, emotional and intellectual well-being.

Factors that influence care relationships

Care work involves working with people, and in working with people it is necessary to have a relationship with them. This relationship will be very different depending on several factors, which we shall now consider.

There are differences between our usual relationships and those that we have with people who use care and support services:

- We have a specific *role* that shapes the relationship.
- The relationship exists for the *purposes* of the service user.
- The service user and us do not always have *choice* in the relationship.
- The relationship may be *time* limited.
- There are *boundaries* to the relationship that we have with service users.

Case Study

Influences on relationships

Kevin works in a day centre for people with learning disabilities. He has particular responsibility for recreation, sports and leisure activities. His job has developed over recent years. He used to set up whole group activities in the centre; there is now an emphasis on smaller groups and individuals participating in community-based activities rather than providing whole group sports events at the centre. Kevin makes sure that a risk assessment has been carried out for each individual involved in any activity; he also makes recommendations for training events for staff to ensure that activities observe health and safety guidelines.

Factors currently influencing the relationship Kevin has with the people who use the day service:

Kevin's knowledge of what people's needs are and his professional experience in meeting those needs

The amount of time that Kevin has. The resources and facilities available to Kevin. The physical environment and the local community

Kevin's characteristics – his personality, sense of humour, experience, knowledge, his style in communication

Kevin's values which influence his approach to working with people, the respect he has for them, how much he values their choices and ability to make their own decisions

The service user's characteristics, personality, expectations and needs
- Gender
- Age
- Ethnicity
- Culture
- Religion
- Personality traits, e.g. patience
- Physical ability
- Communication skills

Policy guidance
- Government guidelines
- Modernising social services, valuing people
- legislation
- National frameworks
- Current thinking and research

Kevin's role with the individual as defined through
- his job description
- the service user's care plan
- supervision
- policies of the organisation

Kevin's relationship with others in the centre, the manager and colleagues, and with other professionals

Questions

Having considered Kevin's working relationships with service users, think about your own.

1 What are the characteristics of the relationship that you have with people?

2 What aspects of your role affects relationships with service users?

3 Draw a spidergram, similar to the one above, noting all characteristics of this relationship. How do the tasks that you carry out affect relationships with individuals?

The tasks that you carry out with individuals will influence the development of the relationships in several ways. Let us look at the differences in the relationships that the following care workers and the service users have.

	Maggie is the home support worker for Mrs Phillips	Reggie works at a support centre for refugees. Renata has just arrived at the centre
Purpose of relationship	To assist Mrs Phillips in getting up in the morning personal care and breakfast	To identify what support that Renata will need in order to get established in her new local community, to provide information, counselling, peer support
Expected duration	Ongoing until Mrs Phillips' circumstances change, or Maggie leaves the job	Determined by Renata and whether she needs continued support
Period of contact	45 minutes	30 minutes
Setting	The service user's home	Community centre
Skills required	Communication skills Moving and handling skills Physical care skills	Communication skills Problem solving Advocacy Emotional support
Knowledge required	Dietary needs Practical care Hygiene Mobility needs Health and safety	Services and community groups in the area Awareness of situations that refugees have Legal issues
Characteristics of the care worker	Sound experience Enthusiastic Playful sense of humour Age 29, female White British	Age 25, male Bangladeshi British Fairly new to the job but very organised and a positive attitude to people
Characteristics of the service user	Age 83, female Black British	Age 36, female Eastern European Limited English language Fearful of the future

The relationships that each of these care workers will have with the service users will be very different.

One feature of the relationships relates to the care or support tasks that you carry out with individuals. These are influenced by

➲ the care or support needs of the person

➲ the principles that underpin the relationship that you have with individuals, e.g. the philosophy of care that underpins the organisation that you work for

➲ models of working with individuals.

Why do individuals need support?

Before we start looking at individual ways of working with people let us consider the reasons why individuals require support. This usually focuses around the needs of people. Whilst there are many additional reasons why individuals require support we will focus on learning disability, mental health, physical ability and older age.

Learning disability

Learning disability is a label applied to individuals who experience a cognitive impairment before reaching adulthood that has a sustained impact on them throughout their lives. As a term there are problems associated with the label 'learning disability'. People may be able to function perfectly well if society did not present barriers to people, or provided appropriate support to enable people to overcome these barriers. There is a range of causes of learning disability:

1 There has always been awareness of the *biological determinants* of learning disability, including

➲ genetic influences, such as those related to Down's Syndrome

➲ non-genetic prenatal factors such as those that cause learning disability with cerebral palsy

➲ trauma during birth that then affect the cognitive development in the child.

2 *Social factors* that can affect the learning and development of a child may include the experience of significant events in childhood, such as illness or accidents, abuse or neglect. Oppression and discrimination can also affect a child's development negatively.

3 *Environmental factors*, such as poverty and deprivation, can contribute to the development of a child and introduce delay in skills that are then associated with cognitive ability.

It is important to acknowledge that a person's ability to participate in society is associated with the way that society is set up, for example what expectations are placed on individuals to support themselves as much as possible. Learning disabled individuals may have jobs, drive cars, gain academic qualifications and establish successful personal relationships, including being parents. The values that society attaches to particular behaviour are significant, and how this influences the label 'learning disabled'.

Mental health

There are also changing approaches to understanding what 'mental health' might mean in today's world. Mental illness is a contentious term. In a lot of care situations it is used to describe a situation where a person has a severe and enduring mental health problem, which adversely affects someone's ability to function in daily life. Mental illness is greatly affected by labelling as discussed in the chapter on values in care practice (Chapter 3).

Mental illnesses are often categorised as:

○ *Psychoses* These are distortions in the perception of reality. An example of a psychotic mental illness would be schizophrenia. The person may experience delusions or hallucinations and lack insight into their illness.

○ *Neuroses* These are severe forms of experiences which are considered to be part of normal life. An example would be a phobia, anxiety attacks or compulsive behaviours.

○ *Organic* These cause conditions like dementia, caused by physical deterioration in the brain.

People may experience mental health problems as temporary features of their life. Mental health is not a static condition; anyone of us can experience mental health problems at some time in our lives.

There are several ways of viewing the causes of mental ill-health.

○ **The disease model**
This explains mental illness in terms of identifiable disorders. Mental illnesses are classified as disorders and there are identifiable treatments, including prescribed medication, associated with each of these.

○ **The functional model**
– *Psychodynamic* This explanation of mental ill-health states that emotions, often from early life, have not been expressed or resolved. Childhood experiences often have a deep impact on our emotions and behaviour in adult life, although as individuals we may not be aware of their influence, or understand why.

– *Behavioural/Cognitive* This explanation states that mental ill-health can be understood through looking at the symptoms and behaviour of individuals. It explores the reasons for that behaviour or those thoughts.

○ **The social model**
This model includes attributing the cause of mental ill-health to life events that we are presented with. Relationship problems, poverty, loss, and other situations can present stress or conflict to people.

○ **The political model**
This model acknowledges that the organisation of society contributes to the mental well-being of individuals, and can therefore also have a negative impact on people's mental health. The experience of oppression and discrimination can affect a person's psychological well-being and provide feelings of depression, or despair.

Our understanding of mental health is more influenced now by the experiences of individuals and their narrative of what influences their experience. For example, people who hear voices were often labelled as having schizophrenia, whereas now there is recognition that some people may hear voices without having an associated mental illness.

Physical ability

A person's ability to function effectively in their environment depends on how responsive that society is to adapting to their needs and how empowered individuals are to overcome the remaining barriers to their participation. Some people have physical characteristics that initiate this need for particular support. A person's physical ability may be affected by:

1 **Genetics** There are some conditions that are determined before birth when the foetus is developing, which may or may not be hereditary. These may be evident from birth, or develop in later life.

2 **Problems occurring during birth that affect oxygen to the brain** Our ability to function physically is related to the functioning of our nervous system, including our brains. If our brains experience any damage then this potentially can have an impact, temporarily or permanently, to our physical ability. For example, if an adult has a stroke.

3 **A condition acquired through**
   - illnesses that affect our body's ability to undertake usual tasks. For example, a person who has Acquired Immune Deficiency Syndrome may experience changes in their physical functioning as the condition develops, and their general health and mobility is affected.
   - accidents that may cause physical damage to part of the body, or affect the nervous system. For example, a person may have damage to the brain, which then affects physical functioning, or they may acquire a physical injury to part of their body which then affects functioning and mobility.
   - changes associated with lifestyle and behaviour. A common condition that affects many people is that of backache. There may be a gradual deterioration in the strength or condition of the spine, sometimes due to continuous inappropriate lifting. This can then limit an individual's capacity to undertake certain tasks.

4 **Life stages** Our bodies change as we progress through the life stages. This happens at a different rate with people, and contributing factors such as health and lifestyle can affect the rate of change. Some of these changes may affect a person's mobility. It is only the reluctance of society to adapt the environment to suit the needs of older people that means that people are disabled by these changes.

5 **Cognitive ability** Physical ability may also be affected by a person's level of awareness and understanding. For example, a learning disabled person may need continued support to promote their independence at mealtimes, even though physical functioning in their limbs is fine. An example of how mental health can affect someone's physical ability is that of dementia. The person may forget how to perform certain tasks or not remember to undertake them.

It is these circumstances that initiate the needs of the individual and prompt the level and type of support that is required from us as care workers. Some service users require physical support in order to undertake certain activities; others may need assistance with the development of new skills through rehabilitation with the aim of one day performing these tasks independently.

Think it over

Think about the care activities of

➲ supporting an individual in making their own lunch

➲ assisting a person with their personal care in the bathroom

➲ listening to a person describing how distressed they are feeling.

1 Identify the reasons why these individuals might need support.

2 How might a care worker provide support to these people?

Care covers such a wide range of activities from physically carrying out tasks for people to supporting individuals in gaining the skills they need to be able to perform them themselves.

What sort of help can you give to a learning disabled person whose physical ability is limited?

Policy guidance on the relationship between individuals

We said in the introduction that the nature of relationships with service users has changed over the years, and part of this change has been the policy framework of care provision. The chapter on the context of care (Chapter 1) describes the history of care services and the provision of 'care' in large institutions. It also explores the current context of care and the policies which currently shape the way that we work with people. This section in this chapter provides a few examples of these as a way of illustrating how policy influences the way that we work with people.

The Community Care (Direct Payments) Act 1995 provided the means for local authorities to give cash payments to individuals for them to purchase their own care. This has enabled individuals to set out the specific requirements they have for the support that they receive.

The possible effects of this are:

➲ The service user sees themselves as the employer.

➲ A more direct relationship between the person requiring care or support and the care worker.

➲ The service user has more influence in what role the care worker has, and the tasks that they perform.

➲ The service user is able to dismiss a care worker if they are dissatisfied with the standard of their work or unhappy with any aspects of the relationship.

The Care Standards Act 2000 provided a comprehensive base recognising the importance of standards in care provision. Through National Service Frameworks and National Minimum Standards there are specific statements about the way that care should be provided; this in turn can shape the relationship that the professional has with the service user.

The Data Protection Act 1998 influences the care profession's observation of confidentiality and has changed the ownership of patient/service user information. People have more access and control over the use of information about them.

Supported Living arrangements have altered the identity of learning disabled people or individuals with mental health problems in supported tenancies. The organisation that provides their accommodation may differ to the organisation that provides a care/support service. This is a different arrangement to other care home or hostel arrangements for living.

Further Research

Identify the policies that have an impact on the working relationships that you have with people.

Include documents from within your organisation, as well as national policies. (If you are unsure where to start think about the policies that are discussed in the chapter on the context of care – Chapter 1.)

Understanding people

Developments in the way that care workers are expected to work with people are due to changes in how we understand human behaviour, disability, illness, psychology and the role of professionals. The chapter on values describes the changing perception of disability from one of sympathy for incapable people to one of challenging society's ability to discriminate against some groups and empowering individuals in order to participate.

Theories can provide us with a way of explaining why people behave in a certain way, or why their circumstances are affecting them in a particular way. In the past the predominance of theories was based on the idea that professionals knew best. Now, recognition is given to an individual's perception and own interpretation of their behaviour. Whilst we still have a long way to go in this area, it has helped to shape current discourse on some areas of individual experience. An example of this is the situation of people who 'hear voices'; they have challenged the clinical diagnosis of people who hear voices as having schizophrenia; their account of their experience is that they are voice hearers without an associated mental illness, so it should not be labelled as a symptom of schizophrenia.

The following table gives a summary of approaches to understanding people.

Approach	Explanation
Behaviourist	Emphasis on the relationship that individuals have with their environment, behaviour being related to the responses that individuals have to stimulus
Humanistic	Emphasis on the self-concept and the individual's understanding of themselves
Psychoanalytical	Emphasis on the significance of stages in early development

Behaviourist

A behaviourist approach to understanding a person would focus on their learning. It emphasises the role that conditioning can have on people, where you learn how to behave due to the responses you have previously received when you either behaved like that, or differently. It focuses on the relationship that humans have with stimuli (what happens to you) and responses (how you react).

There are variations of this theory. As responses can be learned and therefore unlearned, we can be trained to manage our response to certain stimuli which are unfavourable. The context of a situation can be a significant factor in shaping our response.

Humanistic

These theories emphasise the individual's self-concept and the importance of the psychological well-being of a person that then influences their behaviour. The idea of the 'self-actualising' person is characterised by

- realistic perception
- rationality
- personal responsibility
- self-regard
- capacity for good personal relations
- ethical living.

Again there are various approaches within this broad grouping:

- Person-centred approaches.
- Transactional analysis explores the relationship between the parent, child and adult that is present in all of us, with reference to early experiences.
- Reality and rational emotive therapy explores the individual's perception of what the situation is and seeks to manage their thoughts.

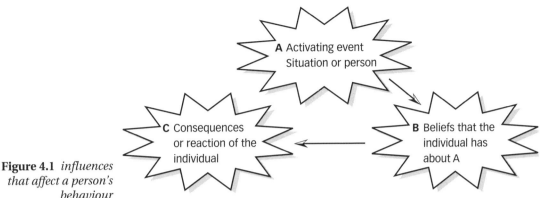

Figure 4.1 *influences that affect a person's behaviour*

The assumption made above is that A causes C. However Step B is where the individual has developed beliefs that A will influence C, but these beliefs may be ignored when the reasons for C are considered.

Psychoanalytic

This set of approaches to understanding people explores the relationship between early experiences and how people then respond in adult life.

Freud identified three areas of a person's consciousness:

➲ The *id* relates to an individual's impulses and biological instincts.

➲ The *ego* acts as the mediator between the id and the external environment, it manages reason and common sense.

➲ The *super-ego* contains the demands of the id through moral influence on the ego.

People's behaviour is sometimes influenced by defensive mechanisms, which continue to operate after they have fulfilled their initial usefulness. People then have different responses to new situations. Earlier experience may influence this:

Repression	Information in the mind is not allowed to enter the conscious thoughts of the individual Information is pushed into the unconscious
Sublimation	Displacing impulses into more socially acceptable behaviour
Reaction formation	The person feels strong impulses which are opposite to the existing ones
Denial	The person ignores or disregards information that would be painful to acknowledge
Fixation	A person fails to move on to the next stage of development due to anxiety or insecurity
Regression	An individual returns to an earlier phase of development
Projection	In order to avoid acknowledging feelings within oneself a person externalises these feelings, and their awareness of such characteristics in other people becomes heightened

So what use are these theories if we apply them to our care work? Well in the first place caution has to be displayed in applying a little knowledge we have acquired that is used in specialist professions. These theories may be useful in opening up our understanding of people, but not in providing a strategy for working with people, for that you would need to investigate these in more depth than can be provided for in this book.

Case Study

Understanding relationships

It is 9.20 am at Pine Lodge Care Home for Older People. Mrs Dakshy and Mr Stringer are engaged in a disagreement about something. You don't want to interfere and you observe the following.

Mrs Dakshy feels that Mr Stringer is bossy and accuses him of bullying her into going to watch TV in her bedroom.

Mr Stringer says that it is all in Mrs Dakshy's imagination, and he only suggested that it would be better for her to watch the programme without any distractions. Mrs Dakshy says she is used to men like him and that she will sit where she likes. If he doesn't want to watch the programme, she feels that he can move. Mrs Dakshy feels upset and in the end she does go to her own room. Mr Stringer is asked about what happened and he says everything is fine, he doesn't realise that Mrs Dakshy is upset.

Task

Consider what happens between these two people and explain the causes of this interaction based on each of the theories

- ⊃ from a humanistic point of view
- ⊃ from a behaviourist perspective
- ⊃ from a psychoanalytical perspective.

Power imbalances are not always straightforward. There are other factors to consider in the dynamics of this interaction – gender and race. If you want to explore how these may impact on the dialogue between them, you could go to the relevant sections in the chapter on values in care practice (Chapter 3).

The case study above illustrates the importance of distinguishing the person from the behaviour, and the behaviour from the feelings. In doing this we can seek to support people more appropriately.

Further Research

These theories of human understanding are worth exploring in more depth. A psychology A Level text will provide a summary of each. Look into these further, as it will provide you with more knowledge to understand possible explanations of why people behave in the way that they do.

Relationships

We will now look at what relationships with service users are all about. Here we focus on the stages that these relationships may progress through. Your own experience of these stages may influence your relationship with service users.

For each stage we will look at your relationship with the people whom you support, and also how you can support individuals in the relationships that they have with other people.

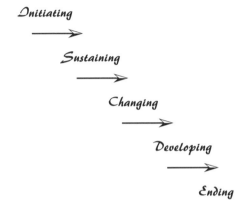

Figure 4.2 *The stages of a relationship*

At the beginning of this chapter we identified that relationships with service users are different to the other relationships that we have, and this affects the progression through these stages.

Think it over

Think about and compare the following scenarios.

Mrs Galloway has a care worker visit her first thing in the morning to assist her with getting up, she then spends most of the day in her front room until a care worker assists her in the evening.

Care worker A 'Hello Mrs Galloway, I am Jo, what do you prefer me to call you?'... 'I'm an agency member of staff so this might be my only visit to you but make sure I do things how you like them, tell me if I get it wrong won't you' ... 'Can I read your notes in your care plan to check what you need me to do?'.... 'I see that the nurse visited the other day, is everything all right to do with ... '

Care worker B 'I let myself into the house, I let Mrs Galloway know that I was there and then I read the care plan and got on with the tasks that I was required to do. I didn't chat to the service user as I was only going to visit her the once, it was pointless getting to know her.'

The service user's experience of these encounters would be very different, and this is significant; care tasks can be very personal activities, and the care was taking place in Mrs Galloway's own home. A further fact is that on this particular day the contact with the care worker was the only social contact that Mrs Galloway had.

Think it over

Reflect on your own relationships with service users.

1 How do your relationships with service users progress through these stages?

2 What are the characteristics of these stages, and how are they influenced by your role (e.g. influence of time, tasks that you perform, other professionals)?

As care workers it is easy to view the relationships that we have with individuals simply in terms of our role and the approaches that we use. It is however very important to consider the experience of the service user.

Mrs Galloway's account of the two separate mornings are as follows:

About *care worker A*, she said, 'Another new care worker this morning. Still, she was very pleasant and cheered me up first thing. Made me feel very safe and wanted, I felt like we began to know each other a bit. She even asked me if she was doing everything right – never been asked that before! I hope she comes back another time.'

About *care worker B*, she said, 'I was woken up this morning by a person, don't know her name, I suppose she knew mine though as she read my notes. I wanted to ask her what the weather was like outside as I had not slept well due to the wind, but she didn't seem interested in chatting so I didn't bother.'

Relationships with service users

What was your first contact with the people that you support? You may work in an environment where the people who use the service are very constant, such as in a care home, or it may be that you are a care manager in a hospital and you are introduced to new service users on a regular basis. Can you remember the first time that you met your best friend, your partner or your manager? How important was the first contact? It may have shaped the beginning of the relationship, and may have continued to influence it.

Think about the various ways you can start to establish a relationship with the people you have to care for

Case Study

Starting relationships

Read the following case study and think about what feelings Douglas is likely to have that will have an impact on the way the relationship starts.

It is Douglas' first day at the Day Resource Centre. It was suggested that he try it to see how he gets on. Douglas is 73, he has cerebral palsy and has a personal support worker but it was felt that he would benefit from some social contact through the Centre.

What thoughts are likely to be going through Douglas' mind as he waits outside?

What can the support workers do to ensure that Douglas feels positive about this new situation, and the new relationships that may develop?

In starting relationships with service users it is very important that the care worker does not trivialise the feelings that the individual may have about the circumstances of the relationship.

Do

➲ be clear about what the aims of the relationship are, and what role you as an individual have with that person

➲ be clear about the potential duration of the relationship – this will range from supporting someone for a couple of hours to a life-long commitment

➲ remember that being a service user doesn't make it easier to cope with new situations

➲ remember that you are there for them, they are not there for you

➲ support the person to assert their own expectations on the relationship. This may range from 'I'd like to be called Mr Bain' and 'Call me Douglas' to 'I want support with dressing, but I shall choose what I wear myself.'

Don't

➲ make promises about the relationship that are not within your role and that you will be unable to honour

➲ negate the experience of the individual prior to their relationship with you and your organisation.

Supporting individuals in relationships

The people that you support may not have the same motivation, confidence or opportunities to initiate relationships in the same way that we do. The more support required to attend to a person's physical well-being makes it easier to overlook their social needs and relationships.

The care plan will guide your relationship with each person. The development of your role with the person will also be affected by the impact of other relationships that the person has, both professional and otherwise. All relationships need nurturing. As we saw at the beginning of the chapter, relationships are affected by the amount of time spent on them; of course mostly this time is limited and outside the control of the individual care worker.

It may be that individuals can be encouraged to be

⊃ more confident,

⊃ more in control,

⊃ more assertive

in the relationship that they have with you, other carers, family, and socially.

The purpose of the relationship should be regularly reviewed to ensure that it is meeting the needs of the individual. Are the skills of the service user being developed, as they become more confident in their independence?

Think about what you would be aiming to achieve in developing your relationships with those people you have to care for

When we think about the relationships that the service user develops with other people we can consider these features:

1 Content	What activities the people in the relationship do together
2 Diversity	What range of different activities the people in the relationship take part in
3 Quality	How people in the relationship approach interaction
4 Patterns	What type of interaction takes place, and their frequency
5 Reciprocal or complementary	Whether the roles adopted by people in the relationship are similar or very different
6 Intimacy	Self-disclosure and revelations
7 Interpersonal perception	The way that the individuals in the relationship view the other person
8 Commitment	How each person sees the relationship in terms of its longevity, or whether it is temporary

Hayes N (1998)

Insights into the relationships between clients and others can create dilemmas for workers. On the one hand, it is not appropriate to make a judgement about family or friendly relationships and the worth of these, and yet, on the other hand it may be important to identify potential situations where taking advantage is actually a situation of abuse.

Case Study

Sibling relationship

Sunita has always had a close relationship with her sister Milu, and Sunita talks of her with affection; she always asks her advice and looks to her for guidance. As a home support worker you visit Sunita in her home to assist with personal care in the morning and evening. One evening you arrive and Milu is just leaving, the sisters have been arguing and Sunita tells you that Milu is telling her what to do.

This is not untypical in a sibling relationship, lots of sisters argue and there may be one sister who tries to dominate the other. On just this information it would be wrong to come to conclusions that there is anything wrong in the relationship. Service users are as entitled to problems in relationships as the rest of us! If the upset that was caused by one argument developed into continuous distress caused by constant harassment then this would be cause for alarm.

As relationships develop, they also change. Within the care worker/service user relationship it is useful to consider who has control over any changes. It may be that the role you have develops due to changes in the skills, or the well-being of the user, so that the role you used to perform is no longer required, so that you have to adapt what you do.

Supporting people through conflict and difficult relationships

Relationships do not always go to plan, and the care worker/service user relationship may experience similar tensions and issues that arise in your own life.

The following are some of the relationships that service users have.

Occasional professionals   Regular professionals   Advocates   Close family members   Distant family members   Employers and work colleagues   Key worker

Other service users whom the individual is indifferent to

Other service users whom the individual dislikes   Volunteers   Friends

Other service users whom the individual is friends with   Neighbours   Managers of organisations

Figure 4.3 *Relationships that service users have*

Think it over

What potential is there for conflict in the following relationships?

Daughter 'Mother never accepts that I know what is best for her.'

Care home resident 'Coral always gets more attention because her hearing is better than mine, the staff don't get fed up with talking to her.'

The cause of conflict may be

- ↻ in the past or recent or current
- ↻ real or imagined
- ↻ temporary or permanent
- ↻ with the service user or with the other person/people.

The following chart illustrates that there is no single way of responding to conflict. It focuses on extremes in the assertiveness of each person in pursuing their own goals, and how co-operative each person is in pursuing the goals of the other person. The ability of an individual to respond to conflict in an appropriate way will be influenced by

- ↻ the relationship that they have with that person
- ↻ their sense of self
- ↻ their communication skills.

The following are ways of handling conflict.

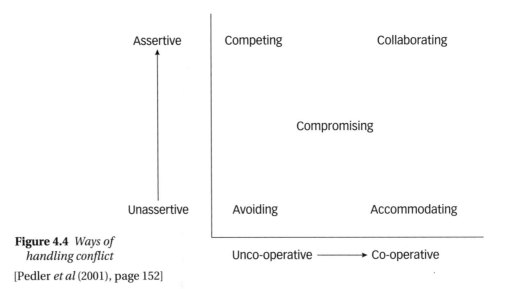

Figure 4.4 *Ways of handling conflict*

[Pedler *et al* (2001), page 152]

If difficulties in relationships remain, there are several strategies we can use to manage problems:

Strategy	Description	Issues for service users
Exit	This can involve leaving the relationship physically, or just mentally	⊃ Do people have a choice? ⊃ Is a person physically able to leave a relationship? ⊃ Are people supported in articulating their desire to end relationships? ⊃ Are decisions, made by the service user, acted upon?
Voice	Discussing the issues	⊃ Experience of the person in communicating dissatisfaction? ⊃ Is the person's view taken seriously? ⊃ Are changes going to be made?
Loyalty	Waiting and hoping for improvements in the relationship	⊃ Is the service user able to establish a point when they will wait no more, or is this a constant situation?
Neglect	Allowing the relationship to dissolve gradually, making no attempt to address issues	⊃ Does neglect of relationships happen because the service user needs support in actively maintaining relationships? ⊃ Is this related to self-esteem?

Hayes N (1998)

Loneliness

Many people who use care services experience physical isolation, possibly due to changes in physical mobility. Some people experience emotional isolation, either due to being isolated at home, through withdrawing from their usual activities, or through changes in mental health. Situational loneliness is due to changes in circumstances. A geographical move can create temporary isolation until you become established and more confident in an area. A change in mobility can cause practical difficulties in continuing usual social contacts. Situational loneliness needs to be recognised, acknowledged, and the individual needs it to be supported in self-managing so that they can overcome their loneliness.

Chronic loneliness is more related to long-term emotional well-being. This type of loneliness is not necessarily associated with lack of social contact [Hayes (1998), page 356].

Case Study

Loneliness

Mr Bahrami moved into Maple Green Care Home three months ago. He is feeling very cared for in terms of the personal care that he receives, but has a deep-seated loneliness that has made him very withdrawn. His move was associated with the death of his wife, who had been his main carer. She also was the main person that he communicated with in Farsi. Although he moved to Britain from Iran 10 years ago and can speak some English, his dialogue is very limited.

Questions

1 What are the causes of Mr Bahrami's current emotional well-being?

2 How could this potentially affect him in the long term?

3 What could be done to prevent Mr Bahrami's current loneliness becoming chronic?

Supporting individuals through change

During their life a person experiences changes in

- ⊃ physical health or functioning
- ⊃ mental health
- ⊃ relationships
- ⊃ death of a partner or close friend
- ⊃ geographical location
- ⊃ living conditions, e.g. loss of home
- ⊃ financial situation.

Some of the above may be positive or negative experiences. A negative change can produce some positive effects. A very positive, welcomed change can also illicit some negative effects. Change is associated with push and pull factors, and what we are trying to do is to establish some level of equilibrium. The reason why some individuals become users of care services is because they experience change in their lives.

Change is sometimes described as *transition*, in recognition that it is a process that people are involved in.

Think it over

Make a list of all the changes that take place for the people you support and think about how effective you are at supporting people to

- ⊃ recognise the transition that they are experiencing
- ⊃ to manage the change.

Figure 4.5 *People react differently when facing change*

Case Study

Facing change

Marjorie is an 84-year-old woman whose husband died three weeks ago. They had been married for 61 years, he supported her with some aspects of her personal care as her mobility changed since her fall 18 months ago. Marjorie relied on her husband to keep her in touch with all the news; he would read the newspaper to her each day and tell her what he had chatted to family about on the phone.

The changes that Marjorie has experienced recently may have affected her in the following ways.

Change	Effects
Marjorie's husband dying	Loss of ⊃ life long partner ⊃ living companion ⊃ practical support in the home ⊃ emotional support ⊃ social company ⊃ stimulation – discussing the past, family, current affairs
Previous change in mobility	Loss of ⊃ health ⊃ physical mobility ⊃ confidence Changes in ⊃ social activities ⊃ dependence on husband

Loss and bereavement

It has long been recognised that loss is not just associated with the death of family or friends, it is also a feature of other changes that occur in our lives. Grief is the process associated with loss.

The following are components of grief.

Shock	Disbelief, numbness
Disorganisation	Inability to perform usual daily tasks
Denial	Not acknowledging the death
Depression	Despair, pining
Guilt	Blaming oneself
Anxiety and/or panic attacks	Complexity of emotions becomes too strong for the person
Aggression	Anger may be directed at self or others
Resolution	Form of acceptance
Re-integration	Reorganisation of new life, formal acceptance of the loss

A care worker who is supporting someone through the grieving process may need to consider

- ⊃ the need for both physical and emotional space and privacy
- ⊃ the effects of changes to routines and patterns of behaviour that have been disrupted
- ⊃ the desire or ability of the person to express their feelings when in the company of others – as service users people can be frequently in the company of people who they may not feel close to
- ⊃ not making assumptions about the worth of any relationship – people may feel a variety of emotions about a person when they die
- ⊃ supporting family members who you come into contact with, accepting their feelings or behaviour without being judgemental
- ⊃ not fussing over individuals or feeling the need to interpret every aspect of the person's behaviour as a symptom of the grieving process.

Relationships can develop in a natural way, usually as a result of spending more time with a person. In some care roles this is not always possible and the care worker needs to be more focused on how they can influence the development of the relationship.

Ending relationships

There are many reasons why relationships with service users come to an end; some are related to the care worker, and some to the circumstances of the service user.

- ⊃ The service user is no longer eligible for a service.
- ⊃ The care worker moves to a different job.
- ⊃ The care worker changes job in the same organisation.
- ⊃ The organisation changes its focus or budgeting priorities.
- ⊃ The needs of the individual changes, so that they no longer benefit from the organisation that you work for.
- ⊃ The person's financial status changes so that they are either not entitled to the services of the organisation or they cannot afford to purchase the care provided.
- ⊃ The death of the service user.
- ⊃ The individual moves to another area outside of the geographical area that the organisation covers.

People respond differently to change, including changes in relationships.

Think it over

1 Reflect on the relationships that you have had in your life that have come to an end. Some of these may have come to a natural end and you felt OK about this, however there are others you may not have felt so comfortable about.

2 Identify what is important for you in the way that a relationship ends.

3 How do you support service users in managing the endings to relationships?

Sometimes it is really important to feel OK about the end of a relationship. The idea of closure relates to the ability to resolve in our own minds the end of a relationship, so that feelings related to it do not re-surface later. Being able to say goodbye to people is a step in addressing this issue. Not saying goodbye to people and ending the relationship inappropriately may affect people in the long term if they do not have the opportunity to explore this.

It is important to acknowledge each person as an individual, and to recognise that service users have a variety of expectations about relationships, as you or I do. An individual may want to end a relationship because they feel that the relationship is no longer progressing. The phases in relationship breakdown are listed below.

Intra-psychic phase	Dissatisfaction in the relationship The relationship is questioned
Dyadic phase	Expressions of uncertainty and indecision about the relationship continuing
Social phase	Practical implications are worked out
Grave-dressing phase	Individual accounts of the break up are developed

The importance of relationships can be underestimated by professionals; we may make assumptions about one person's view of another.

Case Study

Loss of a friend

Bill and George, who attend the same luncheon club, are always arguing over who sits where, and what activities should be put on. We may assume that they would not miss each other if one of them wasn't around. However, when Bill dies George actually misses him more than anyone else; he always valued the banter that they shared, and he felt the arguments were a reflection of the respect they had for each other. He misses the stimulation he got when Bill was alive.

Relationships with service users may last for a couple of hours, or they can last for years. You have a responsibility to make sure the relationship is effective for the purpose that it is meant to serve, however long it lasts. It is important to be sensitive to the way the service user experiences the relationship. For example, it would be easy to think that as you are only covering a shift as a one-off it would not be worthwhile to invest in a relationship with a service user during that time. From their experience, the service user may believe that every service worker has that attitude, and they may easily feel as though they are an inconvenience. Your individual approach will influence this person's experience.

Now that we have considered what factors influence the relationship that care workers have with individuals we shall think about the principles that are required to support people effectively.

A person's values influence their attitude to others and the approach they have to working with people. Attitude can influence the way you work on a one-to-one basis, and this will have the biggest influence on the welfare of the person receiving care.

Principles that underpin the professional relationship

Having explored some of the reasons why individuals might need support and the approach to understanding people, we now turn to consider some of the underpinning principles that should inform the practice of the care worker.

Power

How do you think that power affects the relationships that you develop with service users? The care worker should always consider the position of power within the relationship. In the chapter on values in care practice (Chapter 3) we look at the significance of power in the status of individuals in society. Now we shall look at the impact of power on the relationship that you have with individuals.

There are different types of power.

- reward
- legitimate
- expert
- coercive
- referent
- informative.

Power of course is about control. Care workers can have considerable control over the nature of the interventions they provide. Recognition of this power can lead us to address the power imbalance and work with people in a manner that develops their control in the relationship.

Direct Payments is an example of a policy that has provided the impetus for individuals regaining control over managing their lives, making decisions about who provides care, when and in what way. These are fundamental aspects of a person's life.

Think it over

Think about your own work and identify situations where you potentially exert power over individuals.

1 Which of the above types of power are implicit in the relationships that you have with service users?

2 What factors are influencing the power balance between you and the people that you support?

3 What steps could (a) you and (b) your organisation take to address this power balance?

Values

Underpinning the care relationship should be the values that are discussed in the chapter on values. They are

- respect
- confidentiality
- promoting independence.
- dignity
- partnership

Other dimensions to the relationship include *trust* and *honesty*.

> To be genuine in a helping relationship means to be honest and free of pretension, to be transparently real. [Poindexter *et al* (1998), page 55]

It should also encourage a feeling of being relaxed as this creates the best environment for communication to take place.

This can be a difficult area, as whilst it is important to be open and honest with people there may be situations where issues arise.

Case Study

Trust and honesty

Mrs Hedges' granddaughter has recently had an accident. Mrs Hedges' children do not think it is appropriate to tell their mother the full extent of her granddaughter's condition, as it will cause great distress. They inform you, but say that they do not want their mother to know. Mrs Hedges often asks the staff if her granddaughter has called, as she was used to her popping in sometimes on her own. The staff understand the reasons for the family's wishes, but are feeling very unsettled by not telling the truth. They feel that Mrs Hedges is anxious about not seeing her granddaughter.

Questions

1 Identify the issues for the following in their relationship with Mrs Hedges:
- relatives
- manager of the care home
- care workers.

2 What could be done to address this dilemma so that the relationships with Mrs Hedges are not compromised?

Skills in relationships

There are a range of skills that care workers can use in order to meet the requirements of the relationships that they are involved in. The skills that we shall look at are:

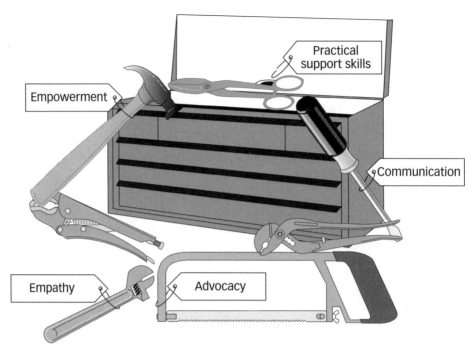

Figure 4.6 *Skills required for developing relationships*

Communication skills

Communication skills can enhance the ability of any person to do their job well, irrespective of what kind of work they are involved in or what job role they have. Such skills are also a resource for living in that all of us use communication to function in our own lives. Communication is important in care work as we need to

⊃ understand what specific communication needs the people we work with have

⊃ utilise the skills that we have to maximise the support we are providing for people

⊃ develop our skills.

Communication is about giving and receiving messages. There are numerous reasons for conveying messages to other people; they may be expressions of feelings or giving or requesting information. Sometimes we convey messages without wanting to, or without realising it; others can pick the subtle signals that our words or body language convey.

Figure 4.7 *Body language may convey a different message from the one the person is conveying verbally*

There are codes in behaviour. Communication is laden with values and influenced by the context in which communication is taking place. If a friend says to you, 'I don't think that you should do that' when you are out socialising with them, it has a different meaning than if your manager says exactly the same words.

Case Study

Communication issues

Read through the following and identify what the communication issues are in each scenario.

1 **Mick**

Mick has just arrived at work in a care home and has been told by his manager to change his weekend shift. He is angry about this. When he goes into the lounge to support one of the people who live there he doesn't really listen to what they are saying because he is thinking about the change to his shift.

2 **Cecil**

Cecil has an acquired language disorder (dysphasia) as a result of a stroke. This affects his choice of words and his ability to structure sentences together. He has a new care worker who finds it difficult to understand what he is saying.

In the first of these scenarios, Mick's communication is being affected by his emotions. His anger is stopping him from paying attention. In the second, Cecil's communication is being affected by the awareness and skills of the other person. He is clear in what he is saying, but the other person is unable to receive that message.

The diagram shows how messages and feedback flow.

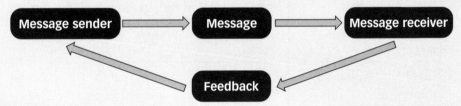

Questions

1 What would improve the communication in the above scenarios of Mick and Cecil?
2 What messages are the following people providing?

You can probably tell from the drawings above that the individuals are unhappy or angry about something. You will have been able to identify this even though you cannot hear the words they are saying. This is a non-verbal message, i.e. the body language, which you see just from the photos. The verbal and non-verbal messages need to be considered together, but we will explore them separately in this section.

The balance in the importance of the verbal and non-verbal message will be influenced by the communication needs and skills of the persons giving and receiving the message. You need to consider how relevant the points being made in this section are to the people that you support.

Verbal communication

This relates to the content of what is said. There are various reasons for communicating orally. It is usually the most immediate and efficient way of communicating with another person. Where possible it can also be the most effective way to establish a relationship with that person.

There are several categories of verbal behaviour.

Seeking ideas	What can we do about the medication issue?
Proposing	I think it would be a good idea if Joan became Adam's keyworker when Susan leaves
Suggesting	Why don't we try it this way?
Building	Good idea, we could also ask relatives to join in
Disagreeing	I don't think we should
Supporting	I think that would be a good idea
Difficulty stating	I'm not sure that we can manage without them
Seeking clarification/ information	Could you point to where it is most painful
Clarifying/explaining/ informing	I'm just letting you know that the GP is visiiting you later this morning, after her surgery has finished

Questioning

The nature of questioning in care work has changed over the years along with other aspects of the relationship between professionals and individuals who require care services. Changes have taken place in the nature of questioning in the caring professions, from narrow, closed, biomedical and technical questions that are asked of the individual to broader open questions relating to psychosocial and lifestyle issues. There is a new emphasis on the importance of the service user's narrative, their own account and story of their situation. We value what an individual has to say about themselves rather than just focusing on a professional's point of view. We challenge the idea of the care worker as the expert in the chapter on values, and this approach to communicating with individuals reinforces this debate.

There are different types of questions that can be used.

- ⊃ *Open* This invites a response from the person without suggesting what that response might be, 'What do you want to do this afternoon?' The person being asked is free to come up with an answer.

- ⊃ *Closed* This question implies an answer, which can potentially affect the decision-making of the person. 'I don't think you'll like going to the sports centre, do you really want to go?' This question is inviting just a yes or no answer, and the person asking the question has made it clear what response might be best. It might be difficult for the person to say 'Yes I do want to go.'

- ⊃ *Clarifying* This is where you check what the person has said. There are various ways of doing this. You can simply ask 'Can I check what you meant…?'

- ⊃ *Reflecting* is also a way of clarifying, where you say back to the person what they have just said. It gives them an opportunity to think about what they said and to potentially change anything if they were not able to accurately articulate what they meant.

- ⊃ *Paraphrasing* is where you summarise what has been said to you and say it back to the person in your own words. It can act as a buffer between listening and responding, and will enable you to clarify or confirm what has been said to you. It helps the person to think about what they have said.

You may think you have put your message across clearly, but it is always useful to reflect on how well you have communicated.

Think it over

'I thought that you were assisting Michael this morning.'

What is the key point that someone is making here? Read through the statement again (out loud if possible), emphasising the words in bold italics each time. See how it changes the meaning of the sentence. The differences in the message are indicated by the paralanguage, for example the tone and pace of communication. These form part of the non-verbal communication.

'I thought that you were assisting Michael *this morning*.' (not *this afternoon*)

'I thought that you were assisting *Michael* this morning.' (not *Jimmy*)

'I thought that you were *assisting* Michael this morning.' (not *doing* something for him or *instead* of him)

'I thought that *you* were assisting Michael this morning.' (not *me*)

'*I* thought that you were assisting Michael this morning.' (the *manager* thought differently)

We all have different styles of communication. If communication is at least a two-way interaction then the communication is influenced by not only the style of the person giving the message but the communication needs of the other person. For some people their ability to communicate is affected by impairment – sensory or physical ability.

Staunton (2003) describes the six Cs of communication as being clear, concise, courteous, constructive, correct, and complete. You need to find the most effective way of conveying your message to the person or people who are going to be receiving that message.

Speaking to someone should convey

- clarity
- empathy
- warmth.
- accuracy
- sincerity

Ways of encouraging the above can be through creating a relaxed dialogue, and being aware of your appearance. We have all felt tense in situations and this can affect our ability to communicate effectively. Being relaxed does not mean being laid back or slovenly, it means being aware of encouraging the other person to be relaxed through your careful use of language and non-verbal cues.

In order to use the above speaking skills, I suggest that you need to consider the following:

- Think about what you are going to say before you say it.
- Be aware of your feelings towards the person and their situation, and the context of the communication. Manage these feelings to facilitate the communication. We do not need to like everyone we work with in order to be able to work effectively with or for them.
- Be aware that you are communicating through more than the spoken word; there are subtle clues in the tone and pace of your words, and your whole body will be transmitting a message.
- Don't fancy things up or use jargon – use the best words for what you want to communicate; these are usually the simplest words.
- Be sensitive to the individual's expectation of language because of the differences in generation, culture, sensory abilities.
- Be aware of how what you are saying is interpreted by others. A message is only clear if the other person receives and interprets it in the way you wanted.

Think it over

This exercise will help you to reflect on your best use of language.

1 Try to rephrase these sentences using more effective use of language:

'We have a multidisciplinary conference for all stakeholders in the service that we would like service user representation at.'

'We need professional support in identifying a more appropriate package of care that addresses your current mobility requirements.'

2 Think about the phrases that are used in the organisation that you work for, either in meetings or on documentation. Are you confident that all the language used is clear to the service users?

Developing appropriate vocabulary can provide you with a tool to make more effective use of yourself. It will also make you more able to control the potential problems associated with communication.

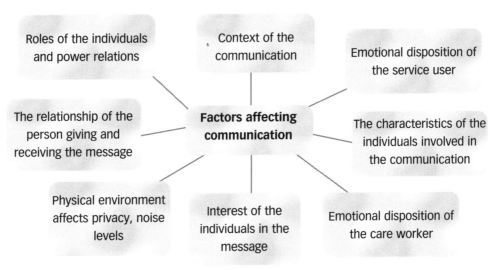

Figure 4.8 *Factors affecting communication*

Listening

How good are you at listening? Listening draws on a number of skills – cognitive and interpersonal ones. A first step to becoming a good listener is actually valuing what the other person is saying. A positive attitude and appropriate values are essential if you are going to listen to someone else.

Listening can be improved by

➲ *preparation* Knowing some background to the person or situation can help you in understanding new information they give you. Listening involves the use of schema; by interlocking knowledge that we utilise in everyday conversations we can accommodate new information. Think about why you are listening to the person and the overview of what they are saying.

➲ *being interested* Be proactive about learning about the needs of the people that you work with, or the views of the colleagues in your team.

➲ *being open-minded* If you are closed about what you think, then you will be reluctant to actually hear what someone is saying to you. Don't anticipate what they are about to say.

➲ *identifying the main ideas* Identify the main points the person is making, as it is not always appropriate or possible to have a notebook with you to write these down.

➲ *being critical* This doesn't mean being negative, it means thinking about, questioning and analysing what is being said as a way of understanding and coming to know it.

➲ *avoiding distractions* Try to overcome internal distraction, such as being preoccupied, and external ones, such as feeling you need to answer the telephone.

- *taking notes* Record what someone says. In care work this is an essential way of maintaining continuity and ensuring that individuals are supported in the best way.
- *helping the speaker* You can do this through the questioning and use of body language that are discussed in this chapter.
- *holding back* Resist jumping in with your own views or interpretation of what the person is saying. This will disrupt their thinking and also make them think that you are not interested in them.

Small talk

Small talk can provide a way of identifying common ground or avoiding having to talk about intimate personal things straight away. It can be used as a tool in situations where initial contact is problematic. It should not be used in a careless way, but as a way of building a relationship with a person, enabling them to relax into the conversation perhaps, rather than feeling pressurised from the first contact.

It can be useful for individuals to be able to continue conversations that you have had with them previously, in that it

- establishes a bond
- makes them feel valued as you demonstrate your interest in what they have been doing
- provides more depth to the small talk that the person engages in
- is less likely to be repetitive of conversations they are having with others.

Humour

Use of humour can improve communication, but before you consider it as a communication tool in your work you may need to reflect on your ability to use it in your personal life.

Humour can be used

- as a stimulus, to initiate dialogue
- as a response
- as a disposition, an approach to communication.

[Chapman and Foot in Hargie (1997), page 260]

Humour can be appropriate to reduce tension in a situation or to distract the person's focus on the negative side of a situation. It needs to be used only when the relationship and the context suit the use of humour. Where used inappropriately it can be interpreted as disrespectful. Being a care worker is about being a professional person who thinks about what they do, and how they do it. Never think, 'Oh that's just how I am, they will have to get used to me.' It may be you that needs to adapt.

Self-disclosure

Some service users may be seeking mutual self-disclosure. If you work in a care home or day service where you see the individuals on a daily basis and know what they are involved in, they may feel that it is part of usual conversation to ask, 'What are you up to at the weekend?' It may appear rude if you do not engage in conversation with someone about this. Talking about yourself can serve a useful purpose in helping to develop the rapport that you have with individuals. However you do need to consider whose needs you are meeting when disclosing information about yourself to a care user. You need to be cautious, because discussing your own life can potentially affect the relationship in a negative way, if it

- dominates the conversation
- affects the relationship with the service user
- becomes a distraction to the core tasks.

It is also important to remember that if you invite a person to be interested in what you are doing in your personal life then it may be difficult to withdraw this offer when it doesn't suit you for them to know.

Think it over

This exercise should help you to explore the impact that communication can have on the other person. Elisabeth is upset, she has just heard that her cousin has died. Read through the following responses and decide how appropriate each one is.

1	I didn't think that you liked your cousin anyway?	Insensitive, inappropriate, judgemental
2	You haven't seen them for ages, they can't have been that important	Imposing assumptions about a person's feelings
3	You must be very sad, let me know if you want to have a chat about it	Considerate, to invite discussion if the person wishes, but tells the person how they feel
4	Oh my cousin died last year, I know exactly how you feel	Me, me, me! My feelings are more important. Assumes that they know how the person feels
5	That's sad. Good job you are going out today, that will cheer you up	Being cheered up may not be an appropriate care response to bereavement

Which responses would you say are most appropriate?

Using a person's name will depend on your role with the individual. It is always best to ask the person how they would like to be referred to, as some people prefer to commence relationships more formally and then may invite you to call them by a different name. Differences in people's ideas about this may be influenced by their culture, age, and their perception of the relationship they have with you.

Metacommunication

This refers to all the non-verbal behaviour which contributes to communication. We established at the beginning of this section that non-verbal communication plays the most significant part in the communication process. There are different ways of viewing this, either as a feature of personal characteristics or as a set of skills that individuals can develop and use. Whatever the origins of non-verbal communication it is important to acknowledge that it is also a tool that can be used with people. The care worker's knowledge of a person's non-verbal communication will increase their ability to observe the subtleties of communication and to pick up significant messages. Skilful use of non-verbal communication can also control the signals that you give to support your own communication. It can

- ⊃ assist speech, give emphasis to the attitude or emotions that we are expressing through speech, e.g saying 'I'm so pleased to see you', with a smile and a big hug
- ⊃ replace speech, e.g. looking very displeased without saying anything. For some people speech is not an option in communication, either due to physical or cognitive impairment, or perhaps temporarily due to current emotions.

This refers to all the communication that takes place other than the content of what is said or written. The physical and sensory ability of individuals needs to be taken into account when thinking about non-verbal communication. For example, a person who uses a wheelchair may be restricted in their control over proximity and the ability to use their posture to encourage warmth in the development of a relationship. They may need to rely on the verbal message more. A person who is deaf and uses British Sign Language may not pick up on the subtle emphasis of words that hearing people do. A person who has not lived in this country all their life may not understand the historical references that are made in conversation, and the context of conversations that take place.

Body language

You are confronted by someone with their hands on hips or arms folded. What messages do these two images convey? As we have seen, only a small percentage of a message is actually conveyed through the spoken word. As we walk around, meet people and talk to them we are not always aware of our body language, we don't usually have to be.

Why do you think an understanding of body language is important to the work you do?

Care workers need to develop their awareness of body language for two reasons.

1 We need to understand how our own body language supports our ability to communicate with others.
2 We need to be able to interpret the body language of others.

Proxemics

This refers to the distance that we maintain when interacting with another person. Individuals have personal preferences about proximity that will be based on their culture, experience, and the relationship that they have with the person. There are social norms relating to how close we stand to people that we want to communicate with them according to

⊃ what our relationship is to them

⊃ the context of the communication

⊃ what the message is.

Distances may be:

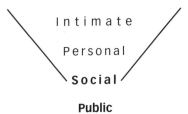

Figure 4.9 *The distance of relationships between people*

Some people may not be able to influence the distance that they have with other people during communication due to their physical mobility, or others may need support in identifying what is appropriate space due to learning needs.

Proximity is also a feature of different types of care. If you are involved in providing personal care then the people that you work with may have to accept very intimate physical contact and proximity with a range of people, which is untypical. Some service users have little personal control over proxemics; they may not like it when a new care worker stands physically close to them to introduce themselves, but because of their physical mobility they may not be able to move away or indicate unease with their body language.

Always

⊃ be sensitive to an individual's expectations of proximity that relates to cultural, generational or gender differences

⊃ encourage service users to assume control over proximity, e.g. walking into a person's house and then asking, 'Where would you like me to sit?', rather than just assuming a position.

Posture

Posture is not something that we are always aware of, and people naturally have different ways of holding themselves. Be respectful when working with individuals, as your posture will be interpreted as part of the message. For example, some people would consider it insulting if you lounged in front of them rather than adopting a more formal posture.

Be aware of the posture of those that you work with. Changes in mobility or the commencement of pain can change the posture of a person, and it may be that some assistance or advice would prevent long-term posture issues.

Gestures

Gestures are very context specific; there are geographical variations as well as cultural.

With some people who have multiple communication needs, gestures may be a part of their intentional or unintentional communication. It is important for care workers to be receptive to gestures and to recognise communication in others, and not to dismiss messages.

Always

- ⊃ use gestures to reinforce what you want to say, and make sure they are not contradicting what you want to say
- ⊃ use gestures that are familiar to the individual
- ⊃ use gestures that are appropriate, especially if the person may choose to use them with other people.

Facial expressions

Have you ever been told 'Its written all over your face' when your verbal message is clearly at odds with how you are feeling? Some people are less able to control their facial expressions but may still be able to communicate. Have you ever smiled when you are not happy or pleased, or laughed when you really don't find the joke funny? We have learnt how to manipulate our facial expressions to convey the message that we want – we have control over this.

For people who communicate a range of emotions and needs through their facial expressions, continuity of care is very important. You need to keep accurate records so that the person's needs are met consistently. It is important not to diminish the significance of this.

Eye contact

People can sometimes avoid eye contact because they find it difficult to not betray how they are feeling with their eyes. People who have multiple communication needs may rely on eye contact to communicate. Eye contact can be a very personal aspect of communication – too little and you can appear rude or uninterested, too much and you can be accused of glaring. Eye contact can encourage communication in others, as it is a way of inviting a person to continue speaking.

Mirroring non-verbal behaviours

Copying the body language of the person that you are talking with can be used to establish rapport with an individual. It may also be possible to test whether rapport with an individual has been established by ceasing to copy them, and then seeing if the person starts mirroring your own behaviour. There can be a certain element of unease about this as you may feel that this is manipulative, and an abuse of the knowledge that you have about communication.

Appearance

You may work in an environment where you wear a uniform which means you have less to think about in terms of your appearance. Society tends to judge people and make assumptions about them based on their appearance. You may need to consider the balance between expressing your own individuality, promoting an image consistent with the values of the organisation that you work for, and respecting the feelings of the person you are working with.

It is dependent on the care context. Very formal dress may be impractical in a care environment where close personal care is provided. Appearance is influenced by and is a reflection of culture. Individuals you support may have their appearance affected by their current circumstances. For example, some clothes are easier to put on and take off, so the decision by the individual (or is it the carer deciding?) to wear a particular item may influence this.

Having an awareness of these aspects of body language will enable you to

⊃ adjust your body language to support your communication more
⊃ pick up on the subtle meanings in the communication of others.

> **Think it over**
>
> Think about your current skills in each of the above areas. Identify the needs of the individuals that you support in terms of the way that you should be communicating with them. Make a note of any strengths that you have, and think about if there is anything you need to adjust.

Barriers to communication

At the beginning of this section we looked at two scenarios where communication had been affected by internal factors relating to the communicator, or the person receiving the message, or external factors outside either person's apparent control. Of course communicating can be difficult. All of us will have had encounters with people where we feel that communication has not really taken place, either because we don't understand the other person, or the person has not understood us.

Figure 4.10 *These are some of the barriers that can affect communication*

Distractions will include the following:

➲ Noise – it may be possible to reduce distracting noise by closing a door or window, or suggesting the communication takes place at a later time or in a different place.

➲ Thinking about something else – this will probably show in your body language! It usually means that the communication is going to be wasted, as you will not receive the full or even part of the message.

➲ Lack of interest in communicating either due to personality differences or preoccupation with other issues.

Being proactive and acknowledging that there is a communication difficulty does not need to sound rude either. Consider the following:

'I'm a little preoccupied with something else I have to sort out at the moment, could we talk about this later, you suggest a time.'

'I don't know about you but I can't concentrate in here, shall we go to a different room where there is less distraction?'

'I'm too anxious to discuss this now, can we talk about it tomorrow?'

In the last example it is the emotional state of the person that is potentially going to affect the communication.

Communication needs of individuals

The following is not an exhaustive list. It is important to identify the individual needs of each person, and these are some points to consider:

1 Communication needs associated with English language skills

Don't

- ↻ assume the person has little to say just because they can only say very little
- ↻ interrupt when the person is pausing to think of how to say what they are thinking or feeling
- ↻ rely on family members to interpret, as this is usually not appropriate
- ↻ avoid communicating with the person.

Do

- ↻ access an interpreter
- ↻ access information in the person's own language
- ↻ make use of all messages that are being communicated to you: non-verbal communication etc.
- ↻ ensure your body language is encouraging for the person to communicate at the pace that they need to.

2 People who have a hearing impairment or who are deaf

Don't

- ↻ all speak at once
- ↻ shout at the person
- ↻ make assumptions about how the person will be communicating or will need you to communicate
- ↻ talk loudly to the person about personal or confidential information when others are around.

Do

- ↻ ensure that others who are communicating with the person are aware of the individual's needs
- ↻ be aware of lighting and the position of yourself in relation to windows – the individual will advise you about the best position
- ↻ face the person consistently
- ↻ speak a little slower than usual
- ↻ think before you speak – it is easier if you don't change your mind halfway through a sentence
- ↻ learn appropriate communication skills, and/or access interpreters
- ↻ access professional advice so that you can maximise communication opportunities.

3 People with visual impairments or who are blind

Don't

- ↻ use body language (gestures etc.) that the person will not be able to access
- ↻ make reference to visual objects without using description that is meaningful

Do

- ↻ check with the person what you need to do to support communication with them

- introduce yourself and others as people enter/leave the room
- state names at the beginning of each communication until the person is familiar with everyone's voices.

4 People who have dual sensory impairment

Don't

- assume that someone is not communicating just because you don't understand them
- exclude people from conversation
- talk about people without including them through your body language and use of language, be respectful.

Do

- be aware of only using communication that is meaningful to the person
- use a total communication approach.

5 People whose behaviour is described as challenging

Don't

- label the person as difficult to work with – if you do you may be contributing towards the problem
- contribute to the problem by being complacent about your own communication and behaviour
- ignore positive aspects of the person and the skills they have
- assume that all behaviour is part of the 'challenging behaviour', some behaviour may be an indication of abuse, discomfort, unhappiness, being physically unwell or in pain.

Do

- take responsibility for your role in the behaviour and review your communication methods and skills
- teach relaxation and a positive mental attitude through your own approach with the person
- encourage social skills
- communicate with others to ascertain patterns of behaviour
- communicate with the person to enable them to identify the causes of their feelings and behaviour
- access appropriate support for the individual.

Think it over

What are the particular communication needs of the people that you support? Think about all aspects of communication and whether there are any areas of your own skills that you could improve.

Empowerment

Earlier we looked at the significance of power on relationships with service users. In this section we shall be looking at the tool of empowerment, and how care workers can support individuals to regain control in their own lives.

Empowerment is a broad concept that encompasses a range of ideas. It focuses on the idea that individuals who need support can frequently lack power and control over their lives. Care workers can develop skills to ensure that they are competent in working with the service users that they support in an empowering way. Braye and Preston-Shoot [(1995), page 113] identify the building blocks of empowerment as:

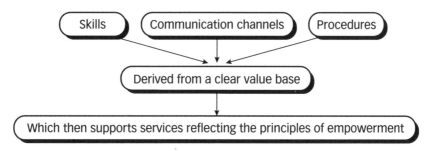

Figure 4.11 *The building blocks of empowerment*

An empowerment model of working with people can lead them to self-determinism, whereby they have control over their own decisions and feel that they are shaping the course of their own lives in the same way that you and I are. Of course we all have limitations on our freedom and our ability to control everything we do. Many people would not want to get ready to go to work on a Saturday night, but responsibilities to the care home, and the need to be paid at the end of the month dictate that they do. Developing power and control in your life is not an easy process. People who come under the broad umbrella term of 'service users' may need to be supported in developing these skills and becoming more assertive due to both their individual and their collective life history of not having access to such control and responsibilities. In an empowerment model of working with an individual, it is their definition of their needs that is significant.

The aims of empowerment can be achieved in different ways according to the setting and the needs of service users. You will need to consider what are the most effective techniques for ensuring that the people you support feel empowered. It is useful to consider practices that potentially disempower:

- Asking for service users' opinions on existing services rather than encouraging innovative proposals for new provision.
- Use of a professional's agendas and professional jargon.
- Ignoring or minimising comments that individuals make about their care.
- Only allowing one person to represent others.
- Making individuals or groups an addition to the main agenda of a meeting, as any other business.

The positive ways you can help empower your clients:

➲ Enable the service user to see themselves as an agent of change. You are not doing this for them; they are the pivotal part of this process.

➲ Help the service user to use the knowledge and skills that they already have.

➲ Help the service user to access professionals and to use their knowledge and skills.

➲ Help the service user to change the power dimension of the relationships that they are in through effective communication, assertiveness etc.

➲ Involve service users in the evaluation of their experience of the service.

In supporting individuals in the self-empowering process it is necessary for professionals not to patronise service users and act as though they should remain dependent on them. Some disability rights organisations are critical of disability organisations that are not led by disabled people themselves. They want to challenge the assumption that change needs to be led by professionals, and they can only be participants in this process. Individuals do not need to be rescued by professionals, and professionals need to acknowledge whether they are one of the obstacles that individuals face in assuming responsibility and controle

Case Study

Empowerment

Let us consider some examples of how care workers can be more empowering to services users.

Using Direct Payments

A physically disabled woman employs a personal support worker through the use of Direct Payments.

Some of the issues to do with empowerment and home care are

➲ the person's potential lack of control over who comes into their home

➲ the ability of the person to access their local community facilities

➲ how providing practical support potentially influences power in the relationship.

Think about how the Direct Payments system can support empowerment in this area of support.

Claude

Claude is a volunteer working for a mental health befriending scheme with a 54-year-old man.

➲ Individual communication can promote empowerment, through choice of language.

➲ Empowering the carer who lives with the person through a carer's assessment.

Some service user groups have expressed issues regarding the very existence of charities. The idea of dependence on these is also difficult for professionals to relate to in an era of rights and empowerment.

Solomon [(1976), in Payne (1991)] discusses the idea that powerlessness is created through negative valuations. People become negatively valued through their membership of a stigmatised group and being labelled along with that group. Empowerment should therefore focus on working with an individual to reduce the powerlessness that is experienced.

Aims of empowerment

These are the aims of empowering service users.

➲ It is important for service users/patients to be active in the process of addressing their needs, not passive recipients of care services.

➲ Professionals should be seen as a resource for the service user to access.

➲ Professionals should be viewed as peers, adopting a partnership approach to working with service users.

➲ Service users should be able to acknowledge the power structure, but see that it can be influenced.

Think it over

1 What response does the organisation that you work in have to empowerment?

2 What strategies can you take on as a care worker to ensure that you are working in a way that empowers service users or patients in your individual interaction with them?

Principles of empowerment

The following four principles were identified by Solomon (1985) for Black empowerment, but they can be applied to other groups who are disempowered.

➲ *Enabling* Making sure the service user recognises what strengths and resources they have that are useful.

➲ *Linking* A professional may support a service user/patient in accessing support networks and making connections. This assumes that collective power can be gained by joining with others.

➲ *Catalysing* The resources and strengths that a service user or patient has may need an additional resource before they can become useful.

➲ *Priming* This principle aims to promote more positive relationships and interactions with organisations by individuals or professionals informing others of potential difficulties before they arise.

Think it over

1 Consider the four principles and relate them to your own place of work. Think of an example of each of these principles from the service user group that you work with.

2 What skills do you have in order to promote empowerment? Think of what you do in your workplace and how you work with individuals.

Models of empowerment

Consumer model

This approach to empowerment sees people as consumers. Empowerment is developed through expanding the choices available to people. Dissatisfaction with services can be encouraged and acknowledged through complaints procedures.

Democratic model

This approach includes the role that individuals have in the development and organisation of services for them, rather than just a choice between services established by professionals. Information needs to be provided to people.

Neither of these models acknowledges the power issues that people who use care services face. Care services users experience substantial social exclusion and limited opportunities to participate in decisions that affect them. Sharkey stresses 'the desirability of collective empowerment strategies through involvement in self-help groups and community development' [Sharkey *et al* (2000), page 124]. Although it is not just to do with individual activity, empowerment must be seen as including individual activity so that we as professionals take responsibility for our individual action to support empowerment. The idea that if you are not part of the solution then you are part of the problem seems pertinent.

The following is a ladder of empowerment.

Manipulation	Creating an illusion of participation resulting in disempowerment
Informing	Telling people what is planned
Consultation	Offering options and listening to feedback
Deciding together	Encouraging others to provide additional ideas and join in deciding the best way forward
Acting together	Deciding together and forming partnerships to act
Supporting independent community interests	Helping others to do what they want

[Barr *et al* (1997), in Sharkey (2000), page 120]

This ladder illustrates that sometimes we can think that we are empowering individuals when in fact our actions serve to perpetuate the circumstances of them.

O'Brien (1981) suggested that empowerment can come from the following sources:

➲ *Choice* Individuals need to have access to alternatives and real choices, not just options from a predetermined list. Acting on individual choice leads to a sense of control.

↪ *Competence* This relates to the development of skills that support an individual in their independence. Being able to do something reduces your need for others to be constantly supporting you. The development of skills should influence the role that professionals have with people.

↪ *Presence* We have discussed in other chapters that people who require support have often been excluded from society. Today children who are learning or physically disabled may attend schools alongside other children. Their presence is valuable in many ways, including that they feel part of society.

↪ *Participation* People who require the support of care/support services are often marginalised in their participation in society and sometimes excluded from active involvement.

↪ *Status* Society comprises different individuals who have a different level of power, control and respect from others. These influence their status in society. Older people, mental health service users and disabled people are not always respected by society or considered by others as being of any importance.

Think it over

Discuss how each of the above aspects of empowerment relates to your place of work. Identify some of the issues, e.g you may think that presence is affected by the mobility needs of a person. It would be important to acknowledge that legislation places the onus on organisations to address access issues and by withdrawing service users from the physical environment care workers may be colluding with society.

What steps can you take as an individual worker to ensure that you are promoting these principles?

Assertiveness

This is a skill that is useful for you as a care worker and also for the individuals that you support.

The following table reveals the distinctions between being passive, assertive and aggressive.

Passive	Assertive	Aggressive
Valuing others more than yourself	Valuing both yourself and others	Not recognising the importance of others
This leads to: Acceptance of others, interpretation of a situation Others not knowing what you want	Discussion regarding an appropriate solution to differences	Only valuing your own interpretation of a situation

Advocacy

Advocacy can facilitate empowerment of individuals and groups. The Alleged Lunatics Friend Society was set up in 1845. This might be considered one of the first examples of an advocacy group. Advocacy is a process that supports individuals in managing their lives and the decision-making process around them. It involves accessing information, negotiating decisions, protecting people from being exploited.

The principles of advocacy

There are different views on advocacy. Southgate (1995) identifies five activities within the process:

- *Nurturing* Supporting the person in their development, encouraging them.

- *Witnessing* Acknowledging what a person's experience is, recognising their circumstances.

- *Protesting* Registering dissatisfaction with a situation, making it clear that you or they are not happy with a set of circumstances.

- *Translating* Interpreting what is going on.

- *Supporting* Working alongside the person to achieve positive outcomes.

The skills required for advocacy include the following:

- *Listening* This means really listening and accepting the person's account of the situation, not adding your own view.

- *Informing* This may be just stating the facts about a situation, but in a manner and language that is meaningful to the person.

- *Encouraging* This involves developing the confidence of a person, motivating them to continue in a particular course of action.

- *Liaising* Identifying who is going to be a key to accessing the support the individual needs and then setting up situations for communication to take place.

- *Mediating* If communication does not happen in an effective way then it can mean that the advocate needs to identify strategies to enable communication to continue, by identifying common areas of discussion or possible routes to resolve a situation.

- *Negotiating* Some people have negotiation skills that are well developed, perhaps because it is part of their job.

- *Representing* This should be working alongside the person, representing with rather than acting on behalf of.

Using advocacy to support a care user

Dave is an advocate for Adrian. Adrian has bi-polar affective disorder. His anxiety is exacerbated by situations in which he feels under pressure. Adrian meets with Dave in a local café, which he feels is neutral and relaxed. He does not like attending the day centre and wants to get back into employment. Adrian has a formal review coming up where he will meet with a number of professionals. At the last meeting he felt overwhelmed and was unable to articulate what he wanted to say.

Tasks

1 Identify how Dave might support Adrian by using the five tasks stated above.

2 After you have considered these tasks think about how they may have an impact in your care work. Think about the skills that you have, or would need to develop in order to effectively engage in the process of advocacy with an individual.

Types of advocacy

The aim of advocacy is to develop the ability of a person to represent themselves effectively in any situation. This is a tall order for many of us, as different situations present different challenges. All of us sometimes depend on others for support and guidance. Advocacy comes in a number of forms, including:

- ⊃ *Self-advocacy* An individual is able to represent themselves. This requires a number of skills. Self-advocacy should be the aim of people.

  Self-advocacy may be carried out by one individual or by a collective of people who share some common characteristics, circumstances or aim.

- ⊃ *Collective advocacy* People can provide support to each other in a group and convey the sense of feeling about an issue. This may enable a person to feel part of the norm.

  A political or organisational framework may act against an unstructured system, i.e. a body of people that does not have a structure. There is dissatisfaction sometimes at the idea of two or three representatives attending larger meetings where the balance would remain with the organisation.

  In theory the aims of all other forms of advocacy could be to promote advocacy by self as the main objective, however long term that might be in reality.

  People First and Mind are examples of organisations which represent individuals, the former a learning disabled organisation and the latter mental health. A group approach can be a means of developing the self-advocacy skills of individuals; such groups can provide positive role models and motivation to aspire to. The idea of the People's Parliament is to encourage and facilitate access to the political agenda through national group participation in discussing issues relating to disabled people.

- *Advocacy by relatives or friends* An individual is represented by a relative or friend. There may be a need to consider the extent to which a relative or friend can be objective about an individual service user and disregard their own interpretation of what that person needs or wants.

- *Peer advocacy* An individual who has shared a similar experience or is in similar circumstances may be a useful resource as an advocate. As well as the immediate practical support they can provide, they also can facilitate the development of skills to enable self-advocacy.

- *Citizen advocacy Valuing People* set a target for each local authority having at least one citizen advocacy group by 2004. This involves a one-to-one relationship, the development of a partnership. The advocate needs to be aware of the dynamics of power in the relationship and would need to acquire appropriate skills and to have access to the legal framework to ensure successful outcomes.

- *Professional advocacy* These are paid individuals, usually employed by an organisation to be an advocate for a person. They should always be independent of the relationships and organisations that are involved in providing care, so as to avoid a conflict of interest and ensure that the person is being provided with the most effective advocacy.

- *Cause advocacy* This type of advocacy may focus on a particular issue. It can draw people together who have different circumstances but who want to focus on a particular concern.

- *Legal advocacy* This may be a solicitor, barrister or advice worker. They can focus on knowledge associated with, for example, benefits or discrimination. They have specialist knowledge of the law and legal system in order to support and negotiate a person through the complications of this.

Bateman (2000) states that advocacy 'requires both persistence and assertiveness' (page 99). This is true whichever form of advocacy is used.

Case Study

Advocacy for care user

Faith lives with her sister and brother-in-law. Her sister is a carer for Faith, and has had an individual carer's assessment.

Marcia is an advocate for Faith. Marcia feels that being a Black British woman with a Caribbean heritage she is able to recognise some of the issues that Faith has. Her aim is that Faith may not need an advocate in the future, that Faith will develop her ability to articulate her own needs, and handle disputes over decision-making in the home that could affect her detrimentally. Faith has benefited from Marcia's support as she now understands more the options that are available to her, including potentially moving out of her sister's home; previously she had not even considered this.

Formal advocates can be provided by organisations to support people. This can create tensions with staff who feel their position with the person is undermined. Advocacy is not about setting up power issues, but in exposing existing ones that professionals may overlook.

> ### Think it over
>
> 1 If the individuals that you support have advocates consider the benefits that this brings to them.
> 2 In what ways could you promote this amongst other service users?
> 3 What are the benefits or advantages of each type of advocacy, and the potential limitations?
> 4 How could the service users that you support benefit from access to advocacy?

Bateman identifies some useful principles, which are described as a 'code of ethics for advocates in health and social care':

➲ Always act in the client's best interests.

➲ Always act in accordance with the client's wishes and instructions.

➲ Keep the client properly informed.

➲ Carry out instructions with diligence and competence.

➲ Act impartially and offer frank, independent advice.

➲ Maintain confidentiality.

[(2000), page 63]

He also identifies that formal advocacy will involve

➲ putting things in writing

➲ viewing an individual's problems as symptomatic of a wider malaise

➲ regarding it as positive to complain

➲ considering the role of publicity to change matters

➲ having a good understanding of the facts

➲ having a good understanding of any relevant technical, procedural or legal aspects.

(page 107)

As with many features of care work there are issues relating to advocacy. In the absence of formal advocates, care professionals may consider they have an advocacy role. For example, in a care home a key worker may see that they support the particular interests of an individual in whole home decisions. Of course care workers do welcome the employment of independent advocates and the consequent distancing of the advocacy role from the organisation. Decisions are taken in a context and care workers, despite the best of intentions, may find it difficult to think beyond what are the issues for the organisation as a whole. It can allow for broader thinking and discussions that are not limited by obstacles and foregone conclusions.

A further caution is in ensuring that the growth of formal advocacy does not preclude the development of self-advocacy.

Working with others involved with service users

Service users may have varied contacts with people; some of these relationships will overlap with the relationship that you establish with a service user. This will include

- informal carers
- relatives
- parents
- children
- siblings
- neighbours
- friends
- volunteers/befrienders
- other professionals.

Recent policies have helped bring about a shift in the dynamics between parents and their adult children. For example, some parents of learning disabled people have had to get used to not being involved in decision-making about their son or daughter, or not having automatic access to information about them. This can be difficult for the parent to adapt to; they may have had years of feeling unsupported and feeling that they have to make all the decisions for their child. Changes should be managed sensitively, by explaining in plain language the new requirements of policy and the aims of this in that it values their son or daughter's right to privacy.

Tensions can arise in this aspect of care work as some people may be used to having control over a relative. People may feel that they are acting in the best interests of the service user by trying to make decisions for them, but as the care worker you need to focus on the rights of the individual that you are commissioned to support.

Your relationships with individuals may be very task-focused, and we will now look at how focusing on relationships can facilitate the fulfilment of the care tasks that are required.

Supporting people

Having looked at some features of relationships with service users we turn now to the specific aspect of care that you provide. When you described the tasks that you carry out with service users you may have focused on one of the following areas: physical, emotional, intellectual or social support. Whichever service-user group you work with, people may need support across all these areas. A physically disabled person will have intellectual needs, a person with mental health problems will have social needs, etc.

	Example of care tasks	Other dimensions to these care tasks
Physical	Assisting an older person with their mobility, to have a bath and get dressed in the morning	➲ Providing personal care in a way that supports the person's emotional well-being ➲ Communicating with the person to stimulate their interest
Social	Supporting a person with mental health problems to access community facilities	➲ Empowering ➲ Providing practical support in new situations
Intellectual	Supporting a person with learning disabilities to learn budgeting skills to enable them to live independently	➲ Facilitating the development of numeracy skills ➲ Coaching them to develop confidence
Emotional	Listening to a physically disabled person express their disappointment at recent health news	➲ Emotional support ➲ Encouraging contact with others for social support

In this section we focus on each of these areas. This chapter cannot provide a comprehensive guide to working with individuals in every aspect of care; however, it will raise some key points to consider and introduce some guidance on suitable approaches to fulfilling a range of care tasks with different service-user groups.

Providing physical support

Sometimes people need physical support to undertake what we would describe as the usual daily tasks, such as getting up and dressed in the morning. This may be due to their

➲ physical strength

➲ mobility due to impairment

➲ manual dexterity

➲ hand–eye co-ordination.

Physical mobility

People may need support with their gross motor movements (large body movements by their limbs) or with manual dexterity (finer movements, such as with the hands). There are a number of issues for us to keep in mind when supporting people in a practical physical way.

What sort of things do you have to think about in supporting people in a practical physical way?

Touch

Providing physical care often means that you will need to touch people. Touch is a very personal dimension in any relationship and it has different purposes in different contexts. Think about the role that touch plays in the care relationship, and the amount and type of touch that you may experience in a usual day. For most people touch is controlled and appropriate to the amount that is desired, and it is provided only from those that it is wanted from. For example, you may hug a friend you have not seen for a while, but just greet other work colleagues politely after a break from seeing them. As we saw in the section on communication skills, touch may be used to express emotional connectedness. It can convey

- ⊃ support
- ⊃ love
- ⊃ sexual feelings
- ⊃ anger.

In care work touch can be necessary for the care worker to support the person. It may be an essential component of the care task to physically touch or handle someone. If so, it is important to do this in a way that conveys respect for the person's personal space, to facilitate a sense of dignity and to ensure the person feels safe and secure, both physically and psychologically.

Pain and comfort

An individual's experience of pain cannot be measured accurately by someone else. Some people's mobility is affected negatively by pain. Pain management is a complex area and one where the care worker may need to access support from others. The role of the care worker can be to ensure the individual has access to professional help. There may be structured interventions and advice concerning posture or movement that can reduce a person's pain. Medication may not be the first choice of the individual, or the professional, but can be an option.

Care plans can ensure that an individual does not experience additional problems as a result of their current circumstances. It ensures that all people involved with the person are aware of what is important. An example is if the person's mobility has affected their movement in bed or when they are sat still. The potential for developing pressure sores is great if care plans are not monitored and adhered to.

Assisting with mobility and handling

As with the other physical care tasks it is important to empathise with the individual regarding how it feels to be physically moved around and to be limited in how you can adjust your position. The principles of moving and handling have developed as guidance regarding the safety of staff and the needs of people who require support has changed. Local authorities and independent providers are employers of care staff. As such they have the complex task of balancing service user care and support needs with preserving staff from injury [Mandelstam (2002), page 203].

Care staff should always adhere to organisational guidelines, as these will be based on legislation. The principles of moving and handling change with legislation and good practice guidance regarding safe techniques. You need to communicate with the team and managers about potential issues in meeting the guidelines.

Mandelstam (2002) discusses the need for accurate and consistent interpretation of guidelines to ensure that risk is managed appropriately and that the person's rehabilitation and mobility needs are not compromised. As an employee it is important that any risk assessment with regard to manual handling involves you so that any limitations on you providing support due to your own health can be considered. You should always inform your manager if there is any reason why you are unable to carry out the tasks required of you. The phrase 'reasonably practicable' refers to the balancing of risk against the cost necessary to remove or reduce that risk.

Physiotherapists can provide sound advice and support for both the individual and care staff to ensure that a person is supported safely and in a manner which maximises opportunities for rehabilitation.

Using hoists is now a requirement to move individuals who are unable to manoeuvre in a safe way. Any piece of equipment can be a hazard if used inappropriately, so it is important to have proper training and to feel confident that you can use equipment. When using equipment it can be difficult to manage the safety of the service user whilst at the same time respecting and securing their dignity, but this should always be the aim.

The accountability of the care worker to a number of other parties can influence their relationship to the service user. It can be difficult if an individual prefers you not to use the hoist when you are required to, and you know that it is in your own and the service user's best interests to do so. The introduction of Direct Payments has implied that the employment of the care worker is the responsibility of the disabled or older individual. However test cases have confirmed that the local authority is ultimately responsible as they are the initiating body in terms of assessment of need. If they are not satisfied that the monies from the Direct Payments system is being used in a way which meets the requirements of legislation then they can stop the payments [Mandelstam (2002), page 100].

There has been criticism that the rigid interpretation of health and safety legislation has meant a negative impact on disabled people's lives. There remain unresolved tensions in this area.

Negligence is referred to where

- there was a duty of care with the alleged perpetrator
- the duty was breached through carelessness or lack of reasonable competence
- the harm was directly caused by this breach of duty.

You can follow this basic guidance that requires you to

- empathise with the individual; it is not always pleasant being handled by other people
- be clear about your responsibilities and follow care plans
- plan through the whole action before you start so that problems do not arise
- look after yourself
- use the equipment that is provided
- inform people when you anticipate difficulties
- keep up to date with guidance on techniques; these are what are referred to in court decisions.

Assisting people with daily living skills

The care task may involve supporting an individual in developing the capacity to manage independently in ordinary daily living skills. There is additional support for people in this area: occupational therapists provide expertise in identifying what skills a person could develop and provide strategies or assistive devices to support this development.

The pathway to introducing an assistive device is shown in the following diagram on page 225 [Pain *et al* (2003), page 203].

The occupational therapist can work with the individual in order to maintain a person's occupational performance, or to rehabilitate a person to return to a previous level of functioning.

Many people need assistance if they have had a change in their ability due to ill-health or an accident. Through the assessment of a care manager they can access

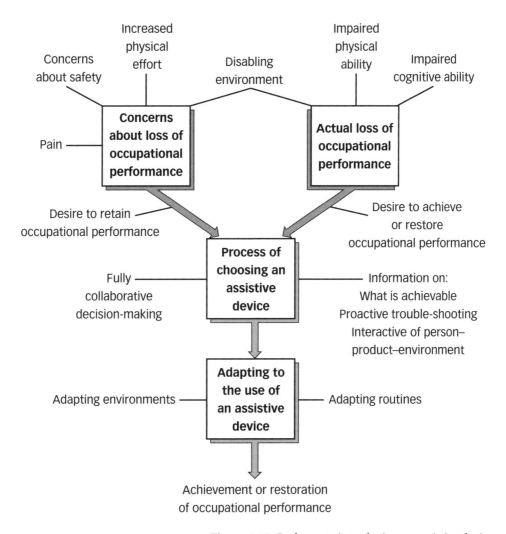

Figure 4.12 *Pathway to introducing an assistive device*

the additional support of other professionals. If you work in home care you may be familiar with this process. It enables some people to stay in, or return to their own home. It is important that all care workers involved with the person know their role in supporting the rehabilitation of the person; the major changes over months cannot happen without the small daily progress.

Personal care

You may have had experience of someone looking after your personal care if you have had an accident or illness that has reduced your ability to self-manage. If you have not, then it would be worthwhile to think about what it would be like to need support in the areas of your life that are usually the most private.

It is important to understand what routine the individual desires with regard to their personal care. Individuals who are supported in the community may find that they are provided with care support at times not of their choosing; there is often little that the individual care worker can do to overcome this except to inform their managers, and to enable the person to manage the time as best they can.

Some general principles would include:

- ➲ Encourage a sense of dignity in the person. An individual may say, 'Oh don't worry about closing the door', because they are either used to other staff members not worrying, or because they don't want to cause you too much trouble. We should encourage or re-instil self-respect in individuals. Only expose areas of the body as necessary.

- ➲ Prepare yourself properly – plan tasks all the way through to avoid any unnecessary interruptions to the task.

- ➲ Always encourage independence and responsibility, on whatever scale the individual can manage. If the person needs total physical support then this may be through asking them to make decisions about what they are going to wear etc.

- ➲ Communicate with the person throughout the task; make sure that it is clear that you are focused on them.

- ➲ Be aware of how the individual will be experiencing the situation, don't become complacent.

- ➲ Enable the person to take as much responsibility themselves, position them so that they can see their clothes, or take out some clothes from the wardrobe for the person to decide, as it is often difficult to choose without seeing. Let the person consider what they will be doing that day, and let them look out the window to see what the weather is like in case they want to go out.

- ➲ Think about whether there might be some aids to assist the individual in dressing independently.

- ➲ Consider how the environment supports or restricts the person's independence.

- ➲ Small physical adjustments to a person's physical environment and space can promote their independence.

Be aware that the person may need support in their personal care at other times during the day. If they have guests coming to see them, or they are doing a completely different activity, such as sports, then it may be appropriate for them to change their clothing.

Promoting continence

Continence is described as 'being able to pass urine or faeces voluntarily in a socially acceptable place' [White in Swiatczak and Benson (1995), page 67]. For some people this is not possible, either as a temporary or chronic condition. There are various causes of incontinence, among them

- ➲ changes in the physiology of the person that may affect their muscle control

- ➲ ill-health or infection that can affect the urinary tract or bladder

- ➲ emotions that can influence continence, e.g. anxiety or as a symptom of abuse.

The types of incontinence are:

- *Stress incontinence* This is where there is a leakage when the body exerts itself. The muscles and bladder can usually be strengthened through exercises.

- *Urge incontinence* Developing a pattern of rushing to the toilet and emptying the bladder frequently can soon become a habit, and then a problem. Such a pattern of behaviour can usually be adjusted through a programme of help.

- *Overflow incontinence* Continuous leakage, which could lead to infection and embarrassment. There may be a physical cause, which will require treatment.

- *Reflex incontinence* If the nervous system is damaged for any reason then it may stop monitoring the need to use the toilet and so the bladder empties without any warning message passing to the brain. The timings of this may be monitored so that the person becomes more aware of when it is likely to occur, or continence aids may be required temporarily.

- *Functional incontinence* This is where there is no physiological cause of incontinence, but the capacity of the person to respond to the need to use the toilet is affected. Making sure that the person is near to a toilet and that they are able to undo clothing easily can help.

Identifying the reasons for incontinence is vital to providing the correct intervention and support.

Incontinence can cause

- embarrassment

- a feeling of unease or disgust

- an unwillingness to take part in social activities.

Support with continence is available from professionals. Continence advisers can provide valuable expertise in care homes or day services, with advice to other professionals as well as the individuals who are affected. Assurances about the availability of toilet facilities can encourage a person to resume social activities. Whenever you assist the person in visiting somewhere new make sure that they know exactly where the toilet is. Being able to talk about their feelings can help some people, whereas others simply do not want to talk about it. A person's age should not preclude them from developing skills to manage their own incontinence.

Hygiene and infection control

Hygiene and infection control is the responsibility of everyone involved in the care profession. The first point to consider is that we should respect the service user's own hygiene routine and how it is influenced by culture, religion or just personal preference. The care plan should indicate the approach that is required. Your organisation will have specific guidelines it requires you to follow, depending on the care setting. These should be adhered to and you should inform your manager if there are issues to do with your ability to adhere to policy. The organisation is responsible for providing appropriate equipment such as gloves, aprons and hand-cleansing products, and you are responsible for making sure that you use them. Make sure that the people you support are aware of the reasons for you doing things so that you are not compromised in your actions. This can be particularly true if you work in a person's own home. It is also important that you understand why you are required to do certain things. Knowing 'why' can enable you to fulfil the task appropriately. For example, putting on some disposable gloves at the beginning of the shift may be appropriate if you are about to support someone in their personal care. However, wandering around the care home providing personal care for four individuals, opening doors and cupboards before you take them off an hour later, is not addressing the hygiene issues, and you would be contributing to an infection problem.

Never underestimate the importance of hand washing. Hands are the primary transmitters of infection in any environment, and thorough hand washing can make a big contribution to improving the hygiene issue. Support the individuals that you work with in taking responsibility for hand washing as well.

Case Study

The need for physical and personal care

Maureen has Parkinson's disease. She experiences difficulty in her physical construction of language due to dysarthria. This means she understands exactly what she wants to say but has difficulty in physically producing the words. She also needs support in many aspects of her physical and personal care, due to her lack of self-awareness and physical mobility. She lives on her own and has support workers visit her three times each day.

Questions

1 Identify all the support needs of Maureen.
2 What feelings might the individual have in relation to all aspects of their needs and abilities?
3 What skills would the care worker need in order to work effectively with Maureen?

Meals

Supporting an individual with mealtimes may involve developing a working knowledge of the particular choices that they would make in respect of their culture. Eating a meal is often part of a social situation, and the aim should be that it is a pleasant experience, and should not be rushed or viewed as an obstacle in the day. The emphasis should be on promoting independence, making sure people have access to the cutlery and crockery that is going to enable them to self-manage. This support and encouragement to develop skills needs to be consistent. Where people need total physical assistance then they should be focused on and involved in the meal, by talking to them about what the meal is and other conversation that relates to them. It can be disrespectful to turn around, and get up and leave the table halfway through supporting a person with their meal.

If the consistency or texture of the food needs to be altered the individual may still want the different foods to be kept separate so that they can still taste the different ones rather than have a mixed up meal.

People should be supported to have meals where they would like to, and to move to a different area, such as a dining room, if they choose. Decisions about where people eat should be made with the person involved, based on their choice, not the convenience of the organisation or individual care staff. If the food drips onto an individual's clothing this should be dealt with immediately rather than leaving the person with dirty clothes for the rest of the day. Some people may choose to wear an apron; these should be used appropriately and not left on throughout the day.

The cultural needs of an individual may dictate their choice of food, and when they eat. It should be recognised that a textbook guide to a religion may not represent each individual's preference. For example, in the Hindu faith some people will not eat meat or fish at all, whereas others do eat lamb, chicken or white fish. It is unusual for Hindus to eat pork or beef and some Hindus fast for one day each week. In the Islam faith pork or products of carnivorous animals are not usually eaten, and alcohol is not usually allowed. During the 30 days of Ramadan there may be a period of fasting for healthy adults.

Case Study

Managing to entertain

Carlton is a 57-year-old man who had a stroke 12 months ago. He lives at home with his wife who has been assessed as his carer. He used to enjoy entertaining people at home before his stroke, and it has taken him a while to develop his skills so that he can invite people to his home again without feeling embarrassed. He still doesn't like to eat in front of other people; he finds that he makes a mess when he eats and it doesn't do much for his self-image. He has always prided himself on his appearance and likes to look smart.

Questions

Imagine what feelings Carlton has about his current situation.

1 If you were going to support him in his care needs what factors would be important to consider?

2 How do you think the changes in Carlton's ability might have affected his wife?

Providing social support

Social activities are usually an important part of life. For some people their dependence on others limits their potential for actively participating in a full range of social activities.

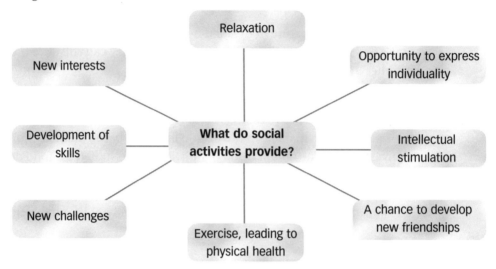

Figure 4.13 *The importance of social activities*

'Supporting and enabling friendships requires consistency, creativity and persistence, but can make a real contribution to personal quality of life and general well-being.'

This quote from the Foundation for People with Learning Disabilities can be applied to other service-user groups. What is clear is that relationships and social activities are important in all of our lives.

Some people find they engage more in social contact with care workers or the people that they live with than they do with other people; they may have quite a closed circle of friendships. Some people also feel that whilst they participate in social activities that are the norm, or visit the same recreational facilities as others, they always do so in a segregated way, at a time allocated to them as a group. Leisure opportunities for people with learning disabilities are often segregated from usual activities that other members of the public engage in, but it is now recognised that they should

- be responsive to the interests and wishes of the person and support real choice
- be available to all, including those individuals with high support needs
- offer practical help to enjoy the activities
- enable use of facilities the same as others
- be available evenings and weekends as well as day time as appropriate
- allow a choice of people to spend time with.

The emphasis is on individuals accessing community facilities in the same way that you or I may choose to.

Social activities can provide us with valuable shared experiences and memories. Some of these may need to be recorded, so that a person's history is represented through photographs and other media that are meaningful to the person. The person should have control over these, and ultimately be able to destroy memories if they choose to. New hobbies can be a way of developing relationships between people, and widening the contacts that an individual has.

The National Minimum Standards for Older People and 18–65-year-olds specify the need for people to have access to a range of social activities in recognition of its importance as part of the function of care providers.

Case Study

A sense of belonging

Suzanne is 28 years old and has just started a cookery class at her local college. She likes attending the class because no one there knows that she has recently spent some time in hospital following a period of severe depression. She likes the conversations that she has there as they focus on how people are getting on with their cooking; she feels no pressure to talk to people about herself, and she has a sense of belonging. She has developed a friendship with Andy who attends the class. She feels relaxed in that environment with him but secretly hopes that she will develop the confidence to see him when the classes stop in six months.

Supporting people in sexual relationships

It is clear that many people with learning difficulties are not being supported to develop friendships and relationships, and even less are being supported to exercise their sexual rights. [Carson and Docherty in Race (2002), page 151]

When it comes to supporting people in relationships, there needs to be an appropriate balance between the assessment of risk and the empowerment of individuals to take control of their own circumstances. Care workers need to work within legislation and be aware of the limitations of their own role. Ordinary life means that people sometimes make poor judgements and decisions that they later regret. Individuals have the right to make mistakes in their own lives, and care workers should not impose their own values, assumptions and judgements on people. People have a right to develop relationships whether they are an older person, have a cognitive impairment, mental health concerns or are physically disabled. The idea of risk is discussed in more detail in the chapter on assessment (Chapter 6). The role of the care worker is usually to ensure that people have access to appropriate advice, be this in the form of literature or professional health or counselling support. As a care worker you should not take on responsibilities that are outside your area of expertise.

Providing intellectual support

This chapter has emphasised the need to support people in a way that promotes their independence and ability to self-manage. This usually entails supporting them in learning how to do something or practising a new skill. The chapter on reflective practice (Chapter 2) provides some guidance on the process of learning that we can consider in relation to supporting service users.

This section provides some additional factors to consider.

- The context of learning is important. Acquiring new skills may be required due to the sudden loss of ability, so it would be important to be aware of the emotional dimension to learning when the person is coming to terms with their loss of ability.

- Motivation can be a real driver to an individual's learning; this may influence the sequencing of learning that you initiate. Sometimes it may be useful for the person to independently finish the task that you have started with them, to give them a sense of achievement, and then to gradually withdraw the support earlier on in the task.

- The practice of over-learning produces reinforcement of a sense of achievement before moving on to the next stage, and it can enable a person to move towards independence in a particular skill.

- The principles of feedback include beginning and ending with positive comments. Any suggestions for development that focus on negative aspects of the skills should be included in the middle. The reason for this is that learning is closely associated with self-esteem and motivation.

Supporting an individual in their learning of skills should be based on the following.

- Plan interesting tasks that are meaningful and appropriate for the person. Break down the whole exercise into individual actions that need to be carried out. Identify the skills required to undertake each task.

- Provide short sessions at a length and pace to suit the individual. Think about the ability of the person, the skills that they currently have, and their ability to learn the new skills that are required.

- Access specialist support from psychologists, physiotherapists or occupational therapists to enable you and the person to develop an action plan.

- Set short-term targets that can be achieved and take small steps that provide early achievement and are rewarding and motivating. It sometimes works best for a person if they develop their independence in completing rather than starting the task, and then on the next occasion the support is gradually withdrawn at a earlier stage.

⊃ Provide regular encouragement in a manner which suits the situation and is meaningful to the person. Learning often provides intrinsic rewards; a person may feel a deep sense of achievement when completing a new task.

Providing emotional support

We have already explored that there is an emotional dimension to most of the other areas of support. We will now focus on what emotional support entails and how we should provide it.

Psychological support requires an understanding of what the needs are of the individual and acknowledgement of the value of the person who is to receive appropriate support. Support should be tailored to the particular needs of the individual. At the beginning of the chapter we looked at some of the reasons why people need support, one of which was due to dementia. The following table, on pages 234–5, describes some of the behaviours associated with dementia and suggested responses from care workers.

What sort of skills do you need for counselling?

Being a care worker does not entail taking on a counselling role with people; counselling is a specialised field of work that requires substantial training and the development of skills. However, parts of this knowledge and skill base can be useful for all care workers in their care or support role.

An important dimension of supporting individuals in their emotional well-being is to acknowledge and accept them as an individual. In the chapter on assessment (Chapter 6) we look at Maslow's hierarchy of need and the idea of 'self-actualisation', i.e.when people reach their potential in terms of their psychological identity. Individual interaction can go a long way in promoting this. By empowering an individual who is feeling very unworthy and unskilled it can inspire confidence and a sense of control.

Behaviour	Possible reasons	Suggested responses
Repetitive questioning	Short-term memory loss Anxiety or insecurity about ability to cope	Answer in a tactful way Distract with an exercise Leave the room for a while
Repetitive phrases or movements	Discomfort, due to thirst, hunger, heat or cold, constipation	Check that the person is not in discomfort Try to alleviate any boredom through stimulating activities Reassure the person
Repetitive behaviour	Behaviour may relate to previous occupation	Try to ascertain what the exercise relates to as a prompt for conversation Try to provide an exercise that will relieve any boredom that is similar to the behaviour the person is carrying out and uses the skills that they have
Trailing and checking	Memory loss means that a few moments may seem like hours Only feeling safe when in company of others	Don't be sharp with the person If you need to get on with a task away from the individual then keep talking to the person or sing as reassurance that you are still around Be aware of how draining this can be on you, the care worker
Shouting and screaming	Physical illness or pain Hallucinations Lonely or distressed Anxiety about failing memory	A night light Talk to the person about their past Stimulating occupation and engaging in activities together
Laughing and crying	Hallucinations Delusions Brain damage due to dementia	Reassuring the person Some people may prefer these episodes to be ignored
Lack of inhibition	Failing memory General confusion May be due to specific brain damage	Remain calm and respond in a reassuring way Take them somewhere private and ask about the need for the toilet Distract the person, provide something for them to be involved in with their hands

Pacing up and down	Discomfort, pain, hunger, thirst, constipation Wanting to use the toilet Feeling ill Side-effects of medication Boredom or excess energy	Find appropriate activities and exercise that the person can engage in They may like a quieter room Ensure that the person, and others, are safe if the pacing continues, shoes, flooring Offer snacks and drinks to encourage regular rest from pacing Offer different environments to pace in (garden?)
Fidgeting	Need for more exercise Discomfort Boredom Damage to a person's brain	Try to find the reason for feeling upset Distract with an interesting exercise Provide some objects for the person to fidget with
Hiding objects or losing them	Insecurity may lead the person to hide objects so that they are safe, or can be found later (e.g. food)	Make sure important objects/documents are not accessible for the person to hide/lose Have spare keys Make a note of hiding places that the person uses so that you can support them in future to find things Be aware of food that may be hidden
Suspicion	Fear and insecurity Inability to recognise people Failing memory The person trying to make sense of what has been happening	Try to avoid arguing or distressful conversation State what you know to be true in a calm manner Be aware that there may be some truth in the person's statements, and not to dismiss them automatically

Note: Table created using information from the Alzheimer's Society website

Rogers (1961) identified that there is a difference between who a person is known as their 'self' and their 'self-concept', or their perception of self. He proposed that relationships should have the following features:

1 *Unconditional positive regard* This is where a person is respected without any conditions or expectations on their behaviour. A person feels valued because of who they are rather than what they do, or what role they perform to others.

2 *Genuineness and congruence* The messages that a person with mental health concerns receives should confirm to them the support that you are providing in a way that is sincere.

3 *Empathy* provides a tool for supporting people in any situation. It can be particularly relevant to supporting a person's emotional well-being. Tilbury (2002) identifies the following 'axioms' of empathy in relation to supporting people experiencing mental ill-health:

   (a) Empathise with the sufferer's reality and the responses it generates. This means that you do not dismiss what the person says is their experience or how they are feeling.

   (b) Help the person to keep in touch with reality by focusing on either general well-being, management of symptoms or creative self-expression. In order to promote well-being and an ability to self-manage it is important to support the person to focus on real situations and the practical issues in life that need to be managed.

   (c) Relate to the person not the symptoms. The symptoms of mental illness can sometimes distract others from who the person is, and the hope that at some point the symptoms will no longer exist.

   (d) Promote the person's skills to manage themselves and their lives so as to
       (i)   prevent any loss of skills
       (ii) reinforce skills that could diminish
       (iii) compensate for lost skills by reviving others
       (iv) renew skills that promote self-sufficiency.

It is not always appropriate or necessary to medicalise some mental health conditions; all of us can experience changes in our mental health. Where a person is receiving structured intervention through care management or the care programme approach, it would be important for the support worker to ascertain exactly what their individual role is and how they can promote the mental health of the individual through the tasks that they perform with that person. In the chapter on reflective practice (Chapter 2) we look at what the function of care tasks is.

An important step would be to understand the treatment that a person is receiving. Interventions that are available to support people include:

➲ **Talking treatments** This group of interventions includes both short-term counselling and long-term psychotherapy. The emphasis is on exploring the cause of the current mental health problem with the individual in order to promote change and an ability to cope. There are different models of therapy based on the schools of thought that the therapist is working to.

↪ **Physical or physiological treatments** These include:

1 *Medical intervention* Whilst not commonly used, electro-convulsive therapy is still a recognised form of treatment by the medical profession. It produces an electrical stimulus through the nervous system, which can induce an epileptic seizure and create a desired change in the individual.

2 *Medication* Some drugs are prescribed in order to affect the chemical balances in the brain. They may induce sedation, or act as a stimulant, depending on the diagnosed need of the individual.

An emphasis in supporting people with mental health problems today involves recognition of self-management techniques, so that the support people are provided with does not take away any independence that they could develop. Mental ill-health creates an unresourceful state for the person; any intervention should aim to facilitate a return to resourcefulness rather than creating dependency on any intervention regimes.

Care workers need to ascertain the role they play in supporting individuals to manage change. They will need to acknowledge that people may experience transitions themselves as intervention progresses through different stages. Information about the type of intervention can enable the care worker to be more understanding of changes and developments.

↪ Check your understanding

Think about the role that you have with the individuals that you support. Reflect on the different areas of support, emotional, intellectual, physical and social, and identify if there are any areas that you could develop for the benefit of the individual.

Managing yourself in a relationship

Boundaries

Remember that whether you are a volunteer or salaried employee, you are part of an organisation. Your role with the service user provides a function that has been identified, usually through an assessment.

If you ever feel that your relationship with a service user is compromising your role, either due to its closeness or negative feelings, then it is important that you seek advice from a line manager immediately.

Stress

Any job that involves working with people can be stressful, and care work is no exception. Even if the environment is pleasant and working relations are good, there can be an emotional cost to supporting people if we do not access support ourselves.

Stress can be evident through physical symptoms such as

↪ backache

↪ tiredness

↪ other muscular strains

↪ regular ill-health.

Other symptoms include

- inability to concentrate or listen to others
- making regular mistakes
- snapping at people uncharacteristically.

We are all individuals and need to find our own ways of managing stress at work. Some suggestions include

- anticipating tricky situations and planning support
- recognising stress in yourself, both physical and psychological symptoms
- not bottling things up, be prepared to talk to others
- reflecting on work in a constructive way.

Further Research

Identify the emotional needs of the service users that you support. Think about all the people you support. For more depth seek advice from other professionals, find out what you can from your formal and informal support networks, and reflect on possible concerns.

References and further reading

Barr A, Drysdale J and Henderson P (1997) in Sharkey P (2000) *The Essentials of Community Care: A Guide for Practitioners*, Basingstoke, Macmillan

Bateman N(2000) *Advocacy Skills for Health and Social Care Professionals*, London, Jessica Kingsley

Braye S and Preston-Shoot M (1995) *Empowering Practice in Social Care*, Buckingham, Open University Press

Hargie O (ed) (1997) *A Handbook of Communication Skills*, New York, Routledge

Hayes N (1998) *Foundation of Psychology: An Introductory Text*, Surrey, Nelson

Mandelstam M (2002) *Manual Handling in Health and Social Care*, London, Jessica Kingsley

Payne M (1991) *Modern Social Work Theory*, Basingstoke, Macmillan

Pedler M *et al.* (2001) *A Manager's Guide to Self-Development*, Maidenhead, McGraw-Hall

Poindexter C *et al* (1998) *Essential Skills for Human Services*, Brooks Cole

Race D (ed) (2002) *Learning Disability: A Social Approach*, London, Routledge

Southgate J (1995) quoted in Brandon D (1995) *Advocacy: Power to People with Disabilities*, Venture Press

Staunton N (2003) *Mastering Communication*, Basingstoke, Macmillan

Tilbury (2002) *Working with mental Illness: A Community Approach*, Basingstoke, Macmillan

White H in Swiatczak L and Benson S (1995) *The Handbook for Hospital Care Assistants and Support Workers*, London, Hawker Publications

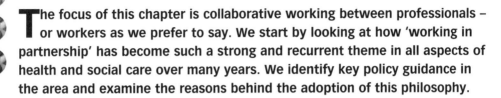

collaborative working

5

The focus of this chapter is collaborative working between professionals – or workers as we prefer to say. We start by looking at how 'working in partnership' has become such a strong and recurrent theme in all aspects of health and social care over many years. We identify key policy guidance in the area and examine the reasons behind the adoption of this philosophy.

The chapter considers some of the various overlapping terminology used and asks whether, at bottom, the same principle is at stake whatever the language. We follow this by taking a detailed look at the kinds of problems that occur when agencies do not work together effectively. Reflecting on and understanding these difficulties leads us on to an in-depth discussion of what lessons we can learn from research in this area. We then focus down to 'worker level' in more detail. We investigate the various reasons why, despite the strong messages from above, working in collaboration doesn't always work 'on the ground'.

To conclude the chapter there is a detailed section which considers both useful methods and the specific skills needed to ensure that the policies of working collaboratively can be put more meaningfully into practice.

This chapter addresses the following areas:

⊃ Why work collaboratively?

⊃ Collaboration – definitions and debates.

⊃ Problems when agencies and workers do not work together effectively.

⊃ Reasons why working collaboratively doesn't take place.

⊃ Ensuring that collaborative working is effective as possible.

After reading this chapter it is hoped that you will be able to

1 understand the reasons why collaborative working has been placed on top of the care agenda in recent years

2 be aware of the various reasons why collaborative working between agencies has not always happened

3 appreciate the difficulties that can occur when effective collaborative working does not take place

4 examine ways for workers to facilitate successful collaborative working.

Why work collaboratively?

Within the field of social care, the theme of working collaboratively has a long history particularly when it comes to bridging the divide between health and social care. Webb (1991), cited in Means and Smith (1998), observes, somewhat depressingly:

> Exhortations to organisations, professionals and other producer interests to work more closely and effectively litter the policy landscape, yet the reality is all too often a jumble of services fractionalised by professional, cultural and organisational boundaries and by tiers of governance. (page 141)

The reasons for this state of affairs can almost certainly be traced back to the way the welfare state was set up and developed after the Second World War. The NHS came into being in 1948 and substantially took over the running of hospitals and primary care services. Local authorities retained certain functions such as the provision of health visiting, mental welfare officers and hospital social workers. Local authority welfare departments were given responsibility for areas such as residential care for older people and services for disabled people. On the housing side, separate local authority departments – usually at district rather than county level – had responsibility for the provision of social (known as council) housing. Over successive decades, we have seen several major reorganisations in the way the NHS is run. The National Health Service Act 1973 brought major change, for example it took district nursing out of local authority control and put it under the charge of the newly formed District Health Authorities. Prior to that, in 1970, there was a major reorganisation of how social care and social work was organised and delivered with the creation of local authority social services departments. Since the 1980s, housing departments have more or less been relieved of their role as direct providers to be mainly replaced by housing associations.

In 1982, the Barclay Report on social work stated that 'dealing with a vulnerable person with a complex problem often entails the development of a network of collaborative relationships between social worker, client, family, the local community, others who may be concerned and one or more of the public, or voluntary agencies that have relevant interests or resources' (8;2, page 113). This prompted social services towards a move towards 'localisation' but this hardly got underway before community care legislation pushed it off the agenda.

Vocational and professional training in all these areas has evolved too. In the field of social care and social work, a variety of qualifications and types of training have come and gone. For example, CQSW, CSS, ISSC, PCSC, City & Guilds, BTEC and NVQs are just some of the ways in which workers have been trained and certificated both currently and in the past.

Given the diversity of welfare services in terms of different professions, different departments, different training, changing roles and functions, it is little wonder that despite the best efforts of many, effective collaboration between different agencies has been hard to achieve. Much of the time different agencies have been pulling away from each other rather than pulling together. The government made this blunt observation in its 1998 document *Modernising Social Services*.

> Sometimes various agencies put more effort into arguing with one another than into looking after people in need.

Next, we will look at how, since the late 1990s, New Labour governments have been determined to ensure 'joined up' government and 'joined up' ways of working and have made certain policy statements to back up the need for agencies to work in partnership. However, first you should be aware of where your own workplace fits into this agenda.

Further Research

What guidance have you had about the need to work collaboratively? You will need to locate your own organisation's mission statement or statement of purpose and find out what it says about working collaboratively. What about other manuals, practice guidance or operating instructions? Read them through – especially the introductory sections. What evidence can you find that there are moves to ensure more effective collaborative working?

It would be surprising if your research did not inform you that the requirement to work collaboratively is embedded in all kinds of policy documents. As indicated earlier, *Modernising Social Services* is the original New Labour blueprint for working collaboratively. However, before that, the need for health and local authorities to prepare Joint Investment Plans had already been established resulting from the *Better Services for Vulnerable People* guidance issued in 1997. In 1998, two significant developments took place. The government set up the Health and Social Care Joint Unit, whose job it is to develop policy on joint working between health and social services. It also published a discussion document called 'Partnership in Action'. In the foreword Ministers for Health explain:

> All too often when people have complex needs spanning both health and social care, good quality services are sacrificed for sterile arguments about boundaries. When this happens people ... and those who care for them, find themselves in the no-man's land between health and social care services. This is not what people want or need. It places the needs of the organisation above the needs of the people they are there to serve. It is poor organisation, poor practice, poor use of taxpayer's money – it is unacceptable.

Although the document goes on to say that 'major structural change is not the answer', subsequent legislation has paved the way for far-reaching structural and organisational change. For example, the 1999 Health Act gave both health and social care agencies powers to pool budgets and delegate functions to enable provision and lead commissioning. This impacted more at management level. The Health and Social Care Act 2001 introduced changes that would affect workers at all levels. This Act created a new body – the 'Care Trust'. The aim of this radical step was to achieve integration of health and social services for vulnerable people. Instead of persisting with the line that two separate agencies must work more closely together, the creation of Care Trusts meant the dissolving of existing organisational boundaries and creating new integrated organisations. To some extent, the way had been paved by the earlier phasing in of Mental Health Trusts which operate on a similar integrated principle. However, the tradition of multi-disciplinary working through the Community Mental Health Team made this change less of a culture shock.

It should not be assumed that the concept of partnership working is simply about health and social care, important as these two elements are. The National Service Framework for Older People, for example, set up Local Strategic Partnerships, whose role is to 'bring together the public, private, voluntary and community sectors' into a single 'overarching framework'. The document assumes that the various standards it sets can only be met by all relevant services working together. Therefore, issues of housing, transport and a range of other services have to be coordinated at a strategic level.

As far as actual working practices at the front line level are concerned, collaborative working has been signalled in just about every policy document concerned with health and social care. For example, *Valuing People*, the government's major policy document for people with learning disabilities, under the heading 'Integrated Professional Working', makes this statement:

> (Learning Disability) Partnership boards should review the role and function of community learning disability teams in order to ensure that
>
> ⊃ all professional staff become a resource for the local implementation of the White Paper and to help achieve social inclusion for people with learning disabilities
>
> ⊃ organisational structures encourage and promote inclusive working with staff from the fields of housing, education, primary care, employment and leisure.
>
> [Department of Health (2001), page 110]

It is clear that the principles of *Valuing People* can only be achieved if staff work collaboratively.

Standard 2 of the National Service Framework for Older People is about 'Person-centred care'. Its stated aim is that

> NHS and social care services treat older people as individuals and enable them to make choices about their care. This is achieved through the single assessment process, integrated commissioning arrangements and integrated provision of services, including community equipment and continence services.
> [Department of Health (2001), page 23]

Both managers and 'professionals' are told that they must 'provide co-ordinated and integrated service responses'. We have to remember that an important reason that the National Service Framework was introduced in the first place was to eradicate unnecessary delay and duplication of effort – this implies a commitment to working collaboratively. In a similar vein, the National Service Framework for Mental Health embodies the same principles. It states that people with mental health problems can expect that services will 'be well co-ordinated between all staff and agencies'.

Therefore, we can see quite clearly that in all areas of care the need to work collaboratively is clearly stated in official documentation. Over and above this, we have seen that in the field of health and social care, the government has been prepared to make radical changes to organisations to try to ensure that the old barriers to collaborative working practices might be dismantled.

The case for collaboration at 'grass roots' level

We have seen how successive governments have set out the case for working collaboratively. This wisdom is handed down from 'on high'. There is no reason to accept this view uncritically. Many writers have commented on the dearth of hard evidence that supports this view. In fact, some have challenged the idea that collaborative working is inherently a good thing. Concerns have been raised about blurred accountability as well as questioning whether claims of comprehensiveness and seamlessness are justified [Leathard (1994), Loxley (1997), Hudson (2000)].

Therefore, we need to proceed positively but with a degree of healthy scepticism. If we reflect on our own experiences in social care, these can almost certainly provide many reasons to work collaboratively. We should ask ourselves what working in care would be like if we were compelled to work completely on our own. How successful or effective would we be if we were denied the advice, knowledge, opinion or any other type of input from other workers? How are our clients benefiting from workers working in isolation from each other?

It is perfectly possible that some workers do not think there would be any problems. They presumably enjoy the freedom from the interference of others, content in the knowledge that they are capable of sorting out all aspects of their client's care on their own. Sometimes we work with people assuming that we are the only worker that matters in their lives. This raises a key question – are we always aware of who else is involved in our clients' lives and what they do?

Think it over

1 Think about your own work. With the clients that you work with, make a list of all the other workers, of any description, who have in some way had some input or influence in those clients' lives. Remember you don't have to see or speak with these workers personally; communication could be through referral or report, letter, fax or email. You may even be aware of their existence but have never communicated with them.

2 Group these other workers under main headings such as health, education, social care, housing, benefits, other.

3 Compare your list with someone else from another area of work, if possible. Either on your own or with another, go through the workers under each heading and identify:

➲ Who do you have most contact with?

➲ Who do you enjoy the best working relationships with?

➲ Who the least?

➲ Who have you got on your 'other' list? Are they from statutory agencies such as the police, voluntary organisations or private agencies such service providers?

Completing this exercise should have brought out how many different workers may be involved with our clients. Some clients have many involvements, for others you may be the only worker. The exercise probably showed we work more closely and more frequently with some workers than others. There also might have been other observations, such as frequent contact with certain workers doesn't always mean that you have a good working relationship with them. You may even have started wondering more about what exactly it is that those other workers do! The basic premise of this chapter is that client care improves if there are good working relationships between all workers involved. Have any of your thoughts or discussions so far suggested otherwise?

Collaboration – definitions and debates

A theme throughout this whole book is the need to be mindful of the language we use. We need to ensure clarity when we are communicating with others but we have seen that different words convey different nuances of meaning to different people. The temptation in this chapter is to talk in terms of 'other professionals'. We prefer not to use this term but instead use the more general term 'worker' because it is less exclusive and more accurately describes the full range of workers who get involved with our clients. For the purpose of this chapter, 'worker' refers not only to paid workers but also to unpaid workers, such as an advocate or volunteer.

Using phrases to clients such as 'we've had a meeting of professionals' may sound impressive but it is potentially belittling and disempowering to them and their families. It also calls into question who exactly is a professional anyway. There is too much 'us' and 'them' in this phrase. Such use of the word professional may possibly exacerbate tensions between, say, a senior residential care worker and an occupational therapist – both of whom play an equally valuable role but have had different training.

This is obviously quite a subjective area. However, for the purposes of this chapter the chosen term to denote anyone with a formal role with the client is 'worker'. It is currently quite fashionable in social care discourse to refer to 'stakeholders' in the context of working together. Use of this word will mainly be avoided in this chapter for the reason that 'stakeholder' usually refers to both formal and informal involvement, and the main focus of the chapter is collaborative working between formal workers – that is, workers who work for some form of organisation – not families, neighbours or friends.

Mostly, the organisations that those other workers work for will be referred to as 'agencies'. This is an unfamiliar term for some people and can be difficult to get to grips with. Clients can mistake what you mean because they may associate the term with other types of agencies they are more familiar with, such as travel agencies or estate agencies. The term also has its limitations when referring to where, say, GPs or district nurses work. We might prefer to use the term surgery, practice or even primary health care team. However, when we talk about 'inter-agency', collaboration between, say, health and social care or social care and housing, we mean all those workers who work in that area of service provision.

What do we mean by collaborative working?

Literature in this area abounds with different words and phrases for what is essentially the same thing. We could talk about collaborative working, joint working, cooperation, working in partnership, working together, inter-agency working, multi-disciplinary working, networking, coalition, integrated working, or even consultation. Each of these terms could be said to have its own particular shade of meaning and, in certain contexts, there may be significant differences. Nevertheless, in the context of this chapter, we are essentially using the terms interchangeably. Our basic idea is that they are all used to refer to the notion of collective actions by individuals or their organisations which produce more benefit for clients than each could accomplish as an individual player.

If anything, collaborative working has been chosen mainly because this is a book primarily written for frontline workers. Other terms like joint working or working in partnership are often more associated – at least in some people's minds – with working together at a higher organisational level, such as joint investment, joint commissioning, pooling of budgets and so on. We will, however, return later to discuss the different levels on which collaborative working can take place even between frontline workers.

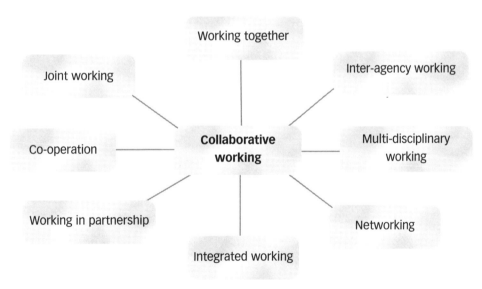

Figure 5.1 *Types of collaborative working*

Think it over

What would your favourite term be for workers working together to promote the best interests of their clients? What term do you use where you work?

The reality of collaborative working

So far, we have established that, ordinarily in social care, several workers from different agencies work with vulnerable people. We have also seen that over a long period successive governments have urged that to promote better, person-centred care the various agencies – and the disciplines within them – need to work a lot more closely together. Government has also backed this up with key policy changes.

Whilst understanding the reasoning behind these exhortations, frontline workers, in their various workplaces, should be asking themselves what it actually means for them. Does it, for example, mean that we should team up with colleagues from other agencies and approach our work as a kind of double act, a kind of care version of Starsky and Hutch, or if you're from a slightly younger generation – Dalziel and Pascoe ?

Figure 5.2 *Collaborative working involves working together with other agencies*

It is one thing to extol the virtues of working collaboratively, it is another thing to put this into meaning for people.

> ### Think it over
>
> When you see statements urging you to work more in partnership, work collaboratively or work in a 'multi-disciplinary' fashion, what does it actually conjure up in your mind that you should be doing? Try to write down how you understand this term.

Were you undertaking that activity 'collaboratively' with another worker, it would be interesting to share your views and compare your different responses. This in itself would be an example of one form of collaboration. We are sure you have found that there are many meanings that can be attached to this whole area. If we were to arrange the various ways of what working collaboratively could mean in some sort of order or hierarchy, it might look like the following.

7 As below, but in addition different agency staff are invited to each other's team meetings, other means of communication are used such as group emailing, newsletters, study days etc. The purpose of this being to move forward together in terms of information sharing, raising of issues, giving access to certain resources, breaking down of any boundaries.

6 As below, but also routinely meeting with other key workers (either in professional groups or on the basis of locality or both), so that as well as specific cases, more general issues in common can be raised, discussed and sorted out.

5 As below but, where relevant, setting up joint visits with another key worker, such as a district nurse, CPN, or housing worker, so that issues in common can be agreed and worked on jointly. Also, with client's permission, sharing case information with other agencies.

4 As for level 3 but also discussing your client's needs more fully with them and their carer(s) – referring on to other relevant agencies, explaining what your involvement is and what you would like them to do.

3 Making a point of finding out who is currently involved – clarifying exactly what their role is and establishing contact with them, also explaining what your involvement is.

2 Being aware of the existence of other workers, having a clear idea of their role. Making a point of letting them know you have a client in common – where it's relevant.

1 Being aware of the existence of other workers, having a rough idea of their job role. Referring to them and communicating when it is obvious that the occasion calls for it.

Figure 5.3 *A ladder of collaboration*

The hierarchy above can be drawn in many different ways with plenty of other stages built in. It's not definitive by any means. However, the point we are trying to make is that there is a spectrum where at the least collaborative end a worker will be mainly independent, reacting to other's roles only where it is clearly obvious and usually just on the specifics of one case. At the other end, the approach is more proactive and thinking outside of the details of a particular case; here the worker is consciously seeing themselves as part of a wider network.

Working together

Gavin Chadwick is a 29-year-old quadriplegic. He became paralysed after a swimming pool accident when he was at university. He was keen on all types of sports. He lives on his own and has a 24-hour carer paid for by social services. He has read about Direct Payments and would like to take this further.

You go and see him to discuss things in more detail. It becomes apparent that there are other issues in his life. He is bored on his own with nothing to do, his main contact being with his family. He is also fed up with the bland diet that 'the medics' originally recommended he follow. He doesn't say so but you think he is depressed. His car is off the road and he is having problems with the motability scheme so he can't get it replaced to go anywhere.

You are not that experienced in how Direct Payments work. You are also put off by the paperwork.

Questions

1 From the details you have, what would be the *least* collaborative working response to Gavin?

2 How might working more collaboratively benefit not only Gavin, but other people in similar positions and other workers as well? Give specific suggestions and explain your reasoning.

⊃ Check your understanding

1 Note down four other expressions we could use to describe the act of working collaboratively.

2 Describe two reasons why it might be that despite the best efforts of many, effective collaboration between different agencies has been hard to achieve?

3 Identify four recent government initiatives that urge closer working between health and social care.

4 In your own words, explain the two ends of the ladder of collaboration.

Problems when agencies and workers do not work together effectively

Although our focus in this chapter is primarily adult social care, there are nevertheless key lessons that can be learnt from the reports published in respect of child abuse tragedies.

We are probably all too aware of the number of inquests and enquiries that have been held when child abuse tragedies have occurred. One of the most high profile ones was the investigation into the death of Maria Colwell in 1973. The findings showed that a major contributory factor in Maria Colwell's death was the lack of interprofessional co-operation. On the back of the Report major changes were made to Britain's child protection system, and inter-agency working was built into the system. However, the new system could not prevent the death of Jasmine Beckford in 1985 and the huge problems in Cleveland in 1987 when the authorities overreacted in response to concerns about widespread sexual abuse. A new major set of guidelines was produced in 1988 called *Working Together* which was followed by the Children Act 1989. In 1995, the Department of Health published *Child Protection: Messages from Research.* This contained the following findings from Hallett and Birchall:

➲ Dealings between social workers and the police seemed remarkably friction-free … by comparison with the testy relationship that existed between many social workers and doctors.

➲ Friction to do with tasks or priorities or role confusion within and between the professions was very evident and was responsible for unrealistic or incompatible ideas about what individuals were supposed to do or were capable of doing.

➲ Beyond the early phase of an investigation, inter-agency co-ordination declined.

➲ The most prominent form of co-ordination was information exchange, which was abundant at the referral and investigation stages, but less apparent in case intervention, and at reviews.

Think it over

Study the list of findings from Hallett and Birchall's research. What, if anything, might be applicable to your area of work? Explain.

Unfortunately, the various initiatives to improve inter-agency working have not been able to prevent the deaths of children known to the authorities, the most high profile case in recent years being that of Victoria Climbie.

A striking feature of the vast majority of the inquiries that have been reported stands out above all others – it is each committee's conclusion that inter-agency communication was flawed. Typically, there were crucial mistakes identified where agencies did not pass on or share information with each other. These reports show that tragedies occur not only when a single piece of information of major importance is not passed on properly but when the passing of any information doesn't take place – however seemingly insignificant – thus preventing workers in various agencies from building up a full picture of what is going on. The same 'small' thing happening many times is as important to know about as a 'big' thing happening once. This was evidently a problem in child protection, but can equally be a problem in work with vulnerable adults. The outcomes might not always have such seriously tragic consequences but could be very distressing or harmful nevertheless. The significance of one 'small' piece of information may not be appreciated until it has been collated with other 'small' pieces of information.

Figure 5.4 *Effective collaborative working depends on the pieces of information fitting together*

The pooling and sharing of case information is vital if collaborative working is going to take place effectively. There are reasons why this doesn't always take place as we will examine in more detail later on in the chapter. Failure to share information effectively can often lead to problems. However, equally important is the need to make sure that the other worker or agency understands the significance of any information given to them.

Case Study

The need to pass on information

Arthur Robins is an 80-year-old diabetic who also has Alzheimer's disease. He has domiciliary care at home but his 81-year-old wife Ada tends to keep an overall eye on him. Ada is rushed into hospital with suspected angina. The request is made by the GP to social services that Mr Robins must be found emergency respite because he has Alzheimer's and cannot be left on his own. The GP also says that with Mr Robins there is often a risk of hypoglycaemia.

Mr Robins is quickly assessed and taken to a nearby residential home for a two-week stay while his wife undergoes investigations and treatment. The day after his admission Mr Robins becomes quite ill. Social services are also telephoned several times by his daughter wanting to know why he had been admitted to a home when her own daughter would have been able to stay in the house for at least a week. Both the district nurses and the daughter make a strong complaint that the home were not informed about Mr Robins' diabetes and that he could have been kept at home given the amount of distress it has caused him.

Questions

Think over the case study details.

1 What information is not passed on and why?

2 Why do you think this is?

3 How do you think the whole situation could have been improved – paying particular attention to the communication of information between different workers?

Key lessons to be learnt from the kind of case described above are:

➲ Time taken to build up more information about Mr Robins' situation would have led to better decision-making. The impulse to do something quickly needs to be avoided.

Workers from social services did not feel able to further interrogate the opinion of the GP. Is this a sign of professional power imbalance? In any event, the GP and social services have not collaborated very well.

➲ Information about Mr Robins' health and how best to manage it was not fully made clear.

➲ Too much is taken for granted and insufficiently clarified to all concerned.

➲ Information about Mr Robins' family network was not fully investigated and shared.

➲ The views of Mr Robins, his wife and his regular carers don't seem to have been explored in any great detail.

There are other points that you could make about this kind of case but it shows the perils of making decisions and embarking on courses of action with too little information and the information that is known not being used correctly. The case study suggests a certain 'remoteness' between the workers involved. It doesn't seem as they have developed any real trust or mutual understanding – as a result, client care has suffered badly. If, as in the chapter on assessment, care is increasingly about the assessment and management of risk, then not only must this process be informed by an adequate flow of information between concerned parties but workers should make others clearly aware about what they consider the risk factors to be. As we discuss in the assessment chapter, for all kinds of reasons everyone doesn't have the same perception of risk – it should not be taken for granted that if, say, you drop the term 'hypoglycaemia' in a discussion that the other will know what the significance is. On the other hand, the person hearing the term 'hypoglycaemia' needs to clarify its significance and what to do about it.

What lessons can be learned?

How might the different workers react to this situation? Here is one scenario:

➲ The GP becomes exasperated by what has happened and makes this clear in discussion with her colleagues at the medical practice. They regret the lack of basic health care knowledge possessed by social care staff.

➲ The social services workers lament the autocratic style of the GP blaming them for passing on partial information.

➲ The residential home staff feel a mixture of guilt and anger about the way Mr Robins' admission to their home was managed. They have been presented with a man who they weren't able to look after properly. They blame both the GP and the social services.

It would be nice to think that such defensive and blaming reactions would not take place. However, we all know that in reality they often do. We would suggest that the whole process would have gone better and there would have been less cause for recrimination if all parties concerned knew each others' ways of working and were familiar with and trusted each other *before* the incident takes place. A key lesson is that it is hard to work effectively with people who you don't know or are not sure about.

Therefore, while it is not hard to demonstrate that client care suffers when workers don't work collaboratively, it needs to be recognised that another more insidious problem is that each failure, like the one seen in the case study, can quite easily lead to a more entrenched view from one set of workers about another. Less trust and more suspicion are likely to further inhibit the good working relations needed to work collaboratively.

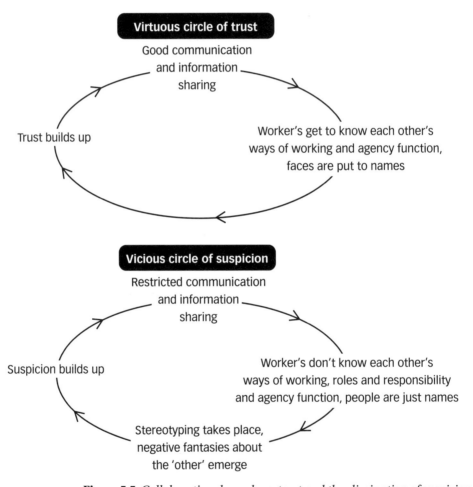

Figure 5.5 *Collaboration depends on trust and the elimination of suspicion*

Think it over

Reflect on your own work. Think about occasions where collaborative working did not take place effectively. What sorts of problems emerged? Who were they a problem for and why?

Your reflections might have thrown up several different kinds of problem. The next one we shall look at is confusion.

Case Study

Confusion

Danny Miles is 25. He has Down's Syndrome, his learning disability is categorised as mild to moderate. He lives in a group home run by a housing association and staffed by an independent care agency. He has a key worker at the group home. He also has a care manager employed by the local Learning Disability Partnership. Five days a week, he attends a life skills course at his local FE college. There he has a personal tutor, Mike. Danny's parents live about 15 miles away and see him at least once a month.

At lunch time, Danny has got into the habit of occasionally augmenting his lunch money by leaving the college, walking into town and telling passers-by that he has lost his lunch money. Sometimes he goes to the nearby pub and offers to buy drinks for others at the bar. Mike knows from first-hand experience that Danny has a very low tolerance of alcohol. The local pub has an arrangement with Mike that should they see this happening they will let him know. Mike then goes over informally to the pub to collect Danny. He reminds him that there are risks and 'morality' problems with what he's doing. The behaviour then usually stops for a while.

The college tutor has never passed this information on to anybody outside the college. This is mainly because he doesn't know who exactly is involved with Danny and also because he regards it as 'college business'. In any event, he thinks that the existing arrangement works fine. Every year Mike is invited to a case review held at the group home. Mike couldn't get to the last one because he was teaching.

Unbeknown to Mike, Danny also frequents the pub at the weekend when he goes with a small group of residents under the supervision of a group home worker. It's mainly soft drinks and bar games they go for.

On one occasion, however, a new member of the bar staff serves Danny and his new 'friends' at lunch time. He then continues serving other customers. After half an hour Danny is drunk and involved in a brawl with two other men. Danny ends up being violently sick. The member of staff calls the police who, in turn, call the social services. Danny's care manager is baffled by what's happened and takes Danny round to his GP for a medical examination. Eventually, after many phone calls the situation is sorted out and Danny is taken home. The following day, Danny's parents insist on talking to the group home manager – wanting to know how such an incident could take place.

Questions

1 Who is responsible for this episode – are Danny's parents talking to the right person?

2 If you were the care manager, how would you ensure that similar misunderstandings did not occur?

It would seem that a key factor in the scenario above was not only the lack of information passed on or the failure to do a proper risk assessment, but the general confusion about who has responsibility for Danny's welfare, and what that responsibility entails. As a result, Danny found himself in a very vulnerable situation. It would be tempting to simply blame Mike, the college tutor, but it is more than that, it's more of a system failure. The overall network around Danny had broken down – or, as it appears, never been properly established. Working collaboratively would have entailed interested parties meeting, talking through what Danny is like and what he likes to do, the risks involved and, more importantly, discussing how to manage the situation collectively. This could have forestalled a very unfortunate incident.

Duplication of effort

The final problem we are going to focus on when people don't work collectively is that of duplication of effort. In the chapter on assessment we discuss the introduction by the Department of Health of the Single Assessment Process. This initiative, as much as anything, recognises that vulnerable adults usually have several social and health care workers attending to them. Also, when more than one worker becomes involved with somebody, that person can often face several assessments – all asking for a lot of the same information. This is a waste of time for all concerned and potentially both tiring and irritating for the person concerned.

Figure 5.6 *We need to avoid wasting time and effort by duplicating the information we gather about a client*

The single assessment process may go some way in cutting down on duplication at the assessment stage, although this has yet to be fully researched. However, the initial assessment is only one area where, because of uncoordinated inputs, duplication of effort can take place. It also doesn't include all areas of involvement – just those from the statutory health and social fields. Unnecessary duplication can take place at every stage of care involvement. The result is always wasteful but often there are other negative consequences – confusion and alarm for example. If we go back to Danny's case, if all of the people involved with him had decided, for one reason or another, to contact his parents, the parents could have easily felt overwhelmed and much more concerned.

Information gathering and contact with clients and their families are two areas identified where duplication of effort takes place.

Think it over

From your own practice, identify areas of work or procedure that are often unnecessarily duplicated by more than one worker. Consider these questions.

1 What are these areas?

2 How much is the duplication you have identified to do with individual work practices and how much is a consequence of organisational procedures?

3 In both cases, how could such duplications be avoided?

On the level of individual worker, we would suggest that there are reasons why work is duplicated. Firstly, it may be that one worker isn't aware that another is involved. Secondly, they might not trust the other workers to do the task properly. Thirdly, agency working practices may not permit the sharing of information. In each case, the development of better collaborative working relationships could help deal with each of these problems – to the benefit of all concerned. There are clearly limits to what extent frontline workers can change agency procedures, but that doesn't mean there aren't many areas where improvements could be made.

⊃ Check your understanding

1 Identify three major problems that can occur when workers don't work together effectively.

2 Explain why, sometimes, simply passing on information to another agency isn't always going to promote client care.

3 How would you put the vicious circle of suspicion and the virtuous circle of trust in your own words?

4 What types of confusion might occur in a case where several workers are involved?

5 Describe three reasons why work with clients can be unnecessarily duplicated.

Reasons why working collaboratively doesn't take place

Several studies have investigated the many barriers to effective collaboration that exist. Nearly all of them point to factors that run much deeper than the practices of individual workers – such as different organisational cultures or professional philosophies. Each of these factors will be examined in more detail later on. However, because this is a text written primarily with frontline workers in mind, we therefore acknowledge that at 'coal-face' level there are obvious limitations to how much the individual worker can influence organisational structures or cultures. Nevertheless, this should not be an excuse to shrug our shoulders, fail to take responsibility and put it down to being a 'management thing'.

We would argue that in many cases, collaborative working doesn't succeed because of a combination of factors – involving organisational, cultural, philosophical *and* personal factors. There is usually an interrelationship between one or more of these factors. The justification for saying this is that often, even when relationships are poor between agencies, there are some workers who still manage to establish good working relationships with others despite the barriers they face. Conversely, there are situations where two agencies might be committed to joint working. They could have many systems in place to ensure that this happens but there are still problems at the interpersonal level. Consequently, the situation is a complex one and needs to be tackled on many fronts and at many levels.

Personal factors

As we discuss in the chapter on assessment (Chapter 6), as individuals we all bring our own personalities, backgrounds and values to our work – this we called our personal context. We also argued that we should try to develop a degree of self-awareness about our personal context in order to ensure that it didn't interfere with the goal of being focused on our clients' needs. It is worth returning to this as we seek to explore why sometimes problems emerge when we try to work collaboratively.

Good cop–Bad cop

The purpose of the exercise below is to try to draw out the different aspects of our job role and to reflect on how we feel about these different aspects. If we experience role conflict (where the job demands conflicting things from us) or role ambiguity (confusion about what it entails) this can make us feel psychologically uncomfortable. In addition, if there is incongruity – or lack of fit – between the various aspects of our job role and our personality or self-concept, we will experience difficulty performing all aspects of our role satisfactorily. For example, a teacher may be a good communicator but struggle with the idea of authority. This will cause them difficulty when they need to be an authority figure as part of their job. The difficult parts are those where we can experience problems when it comes to working with others.

Think it over

1 In no particular order, write down all the various ways you see your job role.

Helper
Gatekeeper
Bureaucrat
Sign poster
Accountant
Consultant
Pen pusher
Parent
Paper shuffler
Computer programmer
Nosy parker
Fixer
Listener
Authority figure
Advisor
Whipping boy
Carer
Sponger
Crawler
Policeman

2 From doing the exercise, how clear are you about what exactly your job role is? Are there conflicting parts to it? Are there any ambiguous parts to it – i.e. aspects that you're not really sure about because they could be seen in different ways?

3 Next, sort out those aspects of your job that you like to do and that you're proud of, those you're neutral about and those you actually dislike doing and that make you feel bad about yourself.

Clearly, depending on our jobs and personalities, we're all going to have different responses. It would be odd, however, if there were no ambiguities, conflicts or aspects of our role that we were uncomfortable with. We need to explain why the exercise was called Good cop–Bad cop. When we see this familiar routine on the TV, the 'bad' cop is harder, more unpleasant and less bothered by the distress of the 'interviewee', the good cop (a nicer person) uses the nastiness of the 'bad' cop to form a closer relationship with their interviewee, they get their confession and the titles roll. This can only work for the two cops if they are both reasonably comfortable in their respective roles. If you had two good cops one would have to work at a greater level of personal discomfort as they'd be working against their personality. They would probably be only too willing if they could reverse their roles – letting the other do the dirty work.

What has this got to do with care? Well, as we saw with the exercise above, there are several 'faces' we need to present to our clients and their carers. There are several aspects of our job roles which we feel more comfortable with than others. Sometimes, it's very tempting to try to pass the more difficult or uncomfortable sides to our role onto others. That way we have less role conflict, less ambiguity, less inner tension and more peace of mind. When working with other workers we can sometimes fall into this trap. If we can make them the 'bad cop' then we (having shuffled the difficult part onto our colleague) can relax in the role of 'good cop'. For example, we can present ourselves as the genuine helper, only too willing to help, whilst the other is the bureaucrat telling the client that they can't have a particular service. There are many scenarios in which one worker tries to find a way of dealing with the perceived negative aspects of the case by projecting them onto or associating them with another. In this way, workers can try to improve their relationship with a client by deliberately disparaging the work of others.

Case Study

Failure to work together

Joe Simpkins is a care manager. He has a case where the client is 88 years old, barely being maintained at home and desperately in need of a permanent nursing placement. The client's family are putting Joe under constant pressure to get it sorted out as soon as possible. Joe has done his assessment and completed all the necessary paperwork, funding has been approved.

The problem is there are no nursing beds in social services contracted homes within a 40-mile radius. There is a private nursing home but their fees far exceed the social services benchmark figure. The family take every opportunity to lobby whoever is involved, to 'get the thing moving'. Joe has explained on several occasions that the private bed can't be used unless the family want to top up the fees, but they are unable to do this.

District nurses visit regularly, they are also feeling the pressure. The district nurses understand the situation perfectly well but when confronted by the increasingly distressed family members they occasionally lapse into saying things like 'If only social services pulled their finger out', or on one occasion 'I'm not sure whether Mr Simpkins quite understands just how risky the situation is'.

Questions

1 Do you think Joe and the district nurses are working together effectively? Give reasons.

2 What effect do you think the nurses' statements have for Joe, the client, the family?

3 What effect do you think the comments have for the nurses?

4 How could collaborative working be improved in this case?

This type of displacement activity can take place in any area of work. Much of the time it isn't carried out that wilfully or consciously either. In stressful and difficult circumstances, it can be seen as an attempt to find a personal comfort zone at another worker's expense.

In the case study we have just looked at, there are likely personal factors at work but these can put in the wider context of scarce resources and different organisational cultures. This is a good opportunity to look at some of the research which has tried to understand why inter-agency collaboration has not always worked particularly successfully.

Philosophical and professional barriers to collaboration

Recent work by Van Eyk and Baum (2002) encapsulates many of these difficulties. They found that:

1 Staff normally feel loyalty and commitment to the agency in which they work. However, this can make it more difficult for them to think or work at an inter-agency level, which could potentially involve shifting resources or services between agencies. The addition of institutional and professional politics (both within and between agencies) can contribute to this difficulty. The research showed that there can be a 'them and us' attitude both *within* and between *different* professional groups, which can work against inter-agency collaboration.

2 In some cases, 'them and us' attitudes can be attributed to a response to new and threatening experiences and approaches. In other cases, they can arise from pre-existing views about other professional groups or approaches.

3 Tensions between professional groups and between agencies are accentuated at times of budgetary difficulties, when services are overstretched and under-resourced, and when staff feel that they are under threat because of the possible transfer of their responsibilities or services to another professional group or agency.

[10 (4), pages 262–5]

Hudson (1987) puts the failure of different agencies to collaborate effectively into a broader context, saying

> From an agency's viewpoint, collaborative activity raises two main difficulties. First, it loses some of its freedom to act independently when it would prefer to maintain control over its domain and affairs. Second, it must invest scarce resources and energy in developing and maintaining relationships with other organisations when the potential returns on this investment are often unclear and intangible. (page 175)

It would appear that because agencies have not been convinced of the possibility of 'collaborative advantage', they have tended to adopt a defensive posture towards inter-agency collaboration and have not fully committed themselves to joint working. In addition, to take Hudson's second point further, developing and maintaining relationships with others certainly does require the investment of energy, time and other resources such as training. In order to commit themselves to this, individual workers need to be freed up. If this doesn't happen then the worker's other commitments will suffer as a result and the whole experience will be stressful and will more than likely undermine collaborative working rather than support it.

1   What are the expectations from within your agency that you, as a worker, will invest energy, time and other resources in developing and maintaining relationships?

2   If the answer is that there are clear expectations, how much have you been freed up to properly commit to this task?

3   If you haven't got enough time, energy or other resources, how could you improve your situation?

Doubtless, different workers will have their own individual responses to the activity. However, some general points can be made.

1   If agencies commit themselves to collaborative working at the top level *and* back this commitment up with the training, time and other support necessary for their workforce to make it happen, then the chances of this being successful should be relatively good – assuming that the other agencies are similarly committed.

2   If, on the other hand, agencies commit themselves to collaborative working at the top level and *don't* back this commitment up with the training, time and other support necessary for their workforce to make it happen, then the chances of this being successful must remain doubtful. The reality will not live up to the rhetoric.

3   We have already hinted at a third possibility, which can probably best be summed up by the phrase 'it takes two to tango'. If one agency is fully committed to collaboration, with all the necessary support, but the other agency isn't ready or willing to collaborate – or is, but only on a rhetorical level – then the chances of successful collaborative working are slim.

Case Study

Barriers to collaboration

A social services team is contacted by a senior district nurse from one of the local surgeries. The district nurse wants to speak to the team manager, however he is busy and asks the duty social worker to pick it up. The district nurse explains that with two new staff starting soon, they would like, as part of their induction programme, to spend some time with the local social services team. The duty social worker takes down the request and passes it on to the assistant team manager to attend to. Amongst all the new referrals to sort out, the assistant team manger doesn't mange to get back to the district nurse until the following week. The district nurse repeats her request. The assistant team manager says he's sorry but it might have to wait because things are so stretched at the moment, no one's really got the space. The district nurse decides to leave it. Things move on and the two new district nurses never make their visit.

Earlier, we acknowledged the difficulty faced by individual workers because they have to work within an organisational structure and fit into a certain work culture. Where there is a strong 'top-down' management style, the power of individuals lower down the hierarchy to effect change is limited. However, whatever the management culture of the organisation we work in, what occurs at the level of interpersonal relationships still matters. In order to explore some of the interpersonal difficulties that emerge we turn to research published by Means *et al* in 1997. They found that the following factors were significant:

⊃ Stereotypes

⊃ Cultural differences between professions and organisations

⊃ Disagreement about roles and responsibilities

⊃ Misunderstandings.

We now look at each of these factors in more detail; you should try to think how they might apply to your work situation.

Stereotypes

Different professional groups often hold negative stereotypes about each other. The more entrenched the stereotypes – particularly if they are negative – the harder it will be to develop joint working.

It is worth reflecting on why the urge to stereotype is so powerful. The term social stereotype dates back to the 1920s when the American psychologist Walter Lippman described stereotypes as 'pictures in our heads'. Lippman saw stereotypes as a means whereby people protect their relative standing in society. So, for example, in what was then a white-dominated society, Lippman said that white people used negative stereotypes of black people to justify their dominance. These days, we might say stereotyping is the means by which we control 'the Other'.

Psychologists say that we are all constantly engaged in mentally categorising (or constructing) the world. We do this in order to make sense of the sheer diversity and complexity of what is all around us. Stereotyping is a way of categorising people in that it involves putting them in boxes – we are 'encapsulating' them. A feature of stereotypes is that they are more rigid and resistant to change in the face of contradictory evidence than are other categorisations. They are less easily amended and updated. Stereotyping 'fixes' and homogenises people. Stereotypes also tend to distort by oversimplification – which is part of their power. These days, to talk of stereotyping is to imply a narrow-minded, inflexible and prejudiced way of thinking. However, a study in 1989 by Hill *et al* found that stereotypes are easily developed by anyone and can be both powerful and pervasive in their effects. All of us stereotype all of the time.

To relate stereotyping back to our theme of collaborative working, we should remind ourselves that through stereotyping people lose their individuality. We can see stereotyping people as an attempt to control or have power over them. Placing people in 'a box' and attributing certain general characteristics to individuals merely because they have a certain look, accent, title, job or role helps us deal with fears, anxiety or uncertainty. It establishes our position in relation to 'the Other'. By saying, for example, 'that's typical of a doctor!' we are communicating to others (but also to ourselves!) how familiar with and unthreatened we are by them. It helps us to think we 'know' them and what they are about. We have put 'the Other' in a box. Stereotyping is a both a functional and dysfunctional activity because whilst it helps us feel less threatened by a complex and potentially overwhelming world, at the same time it also locks us into both a rigid and distorted way of looking at things.

Think it over

1 Do you agree that to stereotype is put 'the Other' in a box? What other reasons might explain our need to stereotype?

2 Write a list of all the other workers who you come across or work with.

3 For each of them write down what the stereotyped view is of their role – this can be positive or negative.

4 Which workers are most stereotyped?

5 In your workplace, how strong do you think the stereotyping of others is and what effect, if any, do you think it has on collaborative working?

To conclude this exploration of how different groups of workers stereotype one another, we must recognise that if we are stereotyping others, then the chances are they are stereotyping us. We are not immune. In which case we need to be able to break out of our box and assert our individuality. If we can do this, we greatly improve our chances of developing productive professional relationships.

Think it over

Think about your job. What ways do you think it might be stereotyped in the eyes of others? Do you think the stereotype varies according to which type of other worker is doing the stereotyping?

It is not enough just to feel aggrieved by being stereotyped by others – irritating as it might be. All this will probably lead to is more stereotyping! We need to be able to take steps to ensure that others find it difficult to lapse into a stereotyped picture of who we are and what we do.

The first point to realise is that if we are suffering from a stereotyped image, it's nothing personal. Blaming the other is not helpful either because, as we've seen, everyone stereotypes at one time or another. It's therefore usually not malicious. The most effective way of combating others' stereotyping of us is to ensure that they get to know us as an individual. This means that we have to think of strategies to have more contact, and preferably contact that is not always linked to specific cases. We discuss various ways of improving relationships in the next section.

Cultural differences

In addition to stereotypes, there are real and very important cultural differences between professional groups in terms of how they understand and respond to need. The same could be said for different organisational cultures. It is important to be aware of such cultural forces because the pressures to conform for individuals who are subject to them is very strong. In reality, it is unlikely that an individual worker could operate freely from the pressures and constraints of the work culture they are in. Therefore, a worker wishing to work collaboratively with others, but who works within a culture where this isn't valued or supported, would experience serious problems. These cultural differences include the use of jargon particular to each profession. In terms of joint working between health and social care professionals, tensions can also arise from differences in the dominant model of care each worker works to. The medical model and the social care model, for example, differ over how best to respond to the needs of service users and how clients should be treated.

We discuss the implications of workers within a medical or social model in the chapter on assessment. Having earlier discussed the dangers of stereotyping it is worth reminding ourselves that not all health workers approach their work according to a strict medical model. Neither, for that matter, do all social care workers understand and fully embrace the social model. It would be too easy to caricature the work of others in this way. Medical and social models are not the only agency cultures that we need to consider. For example, the statutory social care sector, with its local government traditions, together with its tradition of means testing and charging for services, is a strongly bureaucratic culture. Care providers in the private sector have more of a commercial/business orientated culture. Voluntary agencies have their own culture, often more flexible and less profit-minded than the others we have mentioned. Over and above these broad sectoral organisational cultural differences, all workplaces and agencies are bound to develop their own 'micro cultures' depending on factors such as the individual management style, the make-up of the work force, location, availability of resources, type of agency and so on.

Types of organisations

Case studies of organisations reveal that one of the main features of the classic bureaucracy is rigidity. However, more flexible organisational structures and cultures have also developed.

In their classic study of the Scottish electronics industry, Burns and Stalker (1961) examined the emergence of a more flexible form of organisation. They called this the 'organic' organisation and contrasted it with the more traditional 'mechanistic' organisation, which they also found within this industry. Their findings can be applied to all areas of work.

The following table illustrates the characteristics of the mechanical and organic forms of organisation

Mechanistic	Organic
Rigid division of labour	Flexible tasks
Hierarchy	Network
Authority based on position	Authority based on expertise
Obedience to authority	Collective problem solving
Instructions	Advice and consultation
Defined duties/responsibilities	General commitment to goals
Vertical communications	Lateral
Stability	Change

Adapted from Burns and Stalker (1961)

Think it over

1 Have a go at describing your own professional/organisational culture. Use any of the terms from the list given plus any others that you think are appropriate.

> client focused, caring, bureaucratic, organic, mechanistic, medical model, social model, innovative, entrepreneurial, creative, siege mentality, defensive, cost-conscious, oriented to customer satisfaction, hierarchical, rigid, flexible, open, closed, dynamic, undynamic, responsive, warm, impersonal, businesslike, efficient, wasteful, client knows best, worker knows best, empowering.

2 Because our theme is collaborative working, take a look at your list and identify those aspects of your professional/organisational culture that help collaborative working and those that don't.

The value of this exercise is that it can help to know the obstacles we face in forming effective collaborative relationships. We shouldn't, for example, accept or attribute personal blame for what are larger, cultural factors. Trying to understand the points of friction between your professional or organisational culture and that of those you need to collaborate with can make it easier to develop links. This is because you can not only understand better the other worker's ways of working but you will be aware of the controls and constraints they face. If the overall cultural differences are too strong then, as we have argued, the individual faces a very difficult task.

Jargon

A key aspect of organisational and professional cultural differences is that different work groups develop and speak their own jargon. Jargon is a kind of specialist language that groups use. Using jargon has the effect of excluding those outside of the group because they don't know what the specialist terms mean. As such it is disempowering and a definite barrier to communication.

When people enter residential care it is good practice for their GP to send in a medical report outlining the patient's physical and mental state of health, any medication and any specialist involvements. Quite often these reports are peppered with medical jargon such as 'suffered several TIAs over last two years', 'ca lung in remission', 'recovering from ARF', 'sups to be given PR'. It is not uncommon for the care home staff to have to ring up the surgery for a translation. Either that or they discuss it amongst themselves and proceed on the basis of informed guesswork. This is not only to save the time in having to call the surgery but often to avoid the embarrassment of revealing ignorance to a fellow worker. It is also not uncommon for residential care staff to ring the social services care manager to find out what a certain piece of medical jargon meant. Usually they cannot help but it is more time wasted.

It isn't just health workers who use jargon unthinkingly. An occupational therapist following up a referral to her local social services was told quite bad temperedly 'If it doesn't come in on a Soc 358 it won't get looked at.' There are plenty of these examples and the effects vary. However, to summarise, the use of jargon can

  ⊃ lead to people's needs not being met properly

  ⊃ exclude other workers, the client and their carers

  ⊃ disempower other workers, the client and their carers

  ⊃ create unnecessary barriers to communication

  ⊃ waste time

  ⊃ cause unnecessary irritation

  ⊃ lead to misunderstandings with injurious consequences

  ⊃ lead to a hardening of professional boundaries.

Figure 5.7 *You need to avoid jargon in dealing with clients*

Think it over

1 Think about your own agency or place of work. Are you a jargon-free zone or do you use jargon at times? What is it?

2 What about workers from other agencies – do they use jargon? If so, what is it and what effect does it have?

3 If you do face jargon from others, think of constructive ways in which you could ensure that colleagues in other agencies could be educated out of it.

Disagreement about roles and responsibilities

Another finding of Means *et al* was that if professionals disagreed over their respective roles, responsibilities and competences, then this was likely to be an obstacle to effective joint working at the local level.

We have already talked about the importance of workers being clear about their own job role. However, the principle of close collaborative working raises some important issues around roles and responsibilities. Individual workers might well be clear about their own role but that can still leave 'territorial' disputes about 'who does what' when there is potential for more than one worker to perform a particular task. The experience of different types of multi-disciplinary team is often that whilst workers retain certain key specialisms, there is also some blurring of professional boundaries. Many of the tasks carried out for clients are 'generic' – they do not require a particular professional specialism and can be performed by any member of the team. How these so-called 'generic' tasks are allocated can be the source of friction. The blurring of professional boundaries around generic tasks suits some workers better than others. Workers are reluctant to give up high status work for something which might be considered lower status.

What are high and low status tasks? Clearly, there is some room for discussion here. However, under high status work we might include

- tasks that require specific professional expertise
- tasks that allow the worker to use their professional discretion and judgement
- tasks that can be carried out autonomously or with a high level of autonomy
- tasks that can further our career (good CV material!).

Under lower status tasks we might include

- routine form filling and paperwork
- tasks that have a low skill content and permit no professional discretion
- tasks that allow little or no autonomy
- tasks that add nothing to one's CV.

Multi-disciplinary working can sometimes end up as an exercise in the 'cherry picking' of the high status tasks and its corollary – the avoidance of as many low status tasks as possible. Many collaborative working situations in care involves a lot of valuable but nevertheless, low status tasks – these are the 'bread and butter' of care work. This can provoke friction and disagreement amongst workers when it comes to negotiating who takes on this work. Often, the worker with weakest professional identity loses out. When we use the term 'professional identity' here, we mean the sense workers have of what their professional skills and knowledge are. This would also apply to how clear workers are about their professional roles and responsibilities. A strong professional identity is where the worker is clear and confident about their particular skills and knowledge base. The opposite would be the case when the professional identity is weak. This discussion raises questions:

- How is it decided and agreed which tasks are generic?
- How are boundaries drawn around each worker's role and responsibilities?
- Who decides who is competent to perform certain tasks?
- How should the low status tasks be shared out?

Ironically, successful collaborative working can often stall over the 'bread and butter' matters – to put it bluntly it is about who does the donkey work. This is because the obvious specialisms are taken care of, but the mass of generic tasks are not so clearly allocated.

Case Study

Working out roles and responsibilities

A community mental health team has recently become part of a Mental Health Trust. The team management has embraced the principle of collaborative working and has urged the team members to work as generically as it can. The team is made up of community psychiatric nurses (CPNs), occupational therapists, a psychologist and social workers. 'Territorial disputes' arise in the team when it is explained to the CPNs that when they feel that one of their clients would benefit from home care or day care, they must commission it themselves and complete all the necessary paperwork. The CPNs make it clear that they resent having to undertake a task they expect the social workers to do. They claim 'they are not bureaucrats' and it is a waste of their time and expertise. When things come to a head, they argue that because the social workers are not sufficiently well trained to the CPN's job (e.g. check medication and other clinical issues) they don't see why they should do what was traditionally a social work task.

Questions

1 How can this dispute be seen in terms of high status and low status tasks, strong and weak professional identities?

2 How do you think the social workers should respond to this dispute?

In attempting to answer the second question and at the same time promote the cause of collaborative working, the social workers could make several responses. An understandable but ultimately unhelpful response would be for the social workers to take umbrage and embark on a frosty relationship with their fellow team members. What they really need to do above all is to speak to each and clarify in their own minds what their role and responsibilities are and to be clear what their specialisms are. If the social workers can work on strengthening their professional identity, e.g. by establishing their assessment and interpersonal skills, their values and identifying what their particular areas of expertise are – for example dealing with adult abuse or complex legal matters – then the subsequent discussions can be more of a negotiation between equals. The trading can take place with more equanimity if each party can respect the professionalism and expertise of the other. It would help with the process of sorting out who does their share of the mundane tasks. To be uncertain and unconfident about one's job role and responsibilities is no position to bargain from.

Misunderstandings

Workers often have only limited knowledge about other professional groups or other organisations with which they wish to liaise and work. They simply misunderstand the priorities, organisational structures, cultures and working practices of fellow professionals. There is a lack of 'network awareness'.
This point returns to the discussion at the very beginning of the chapter, where we asked 'Do we know who else is working with our clients?'

From this we have to acknowledge that:

1 In the first place, there are times when we simply don't know who else is involved.

2 On other occasions, we have a vague idea of who is involved but are not clear about what the nature of their roles and responsibilities are.

Think it over

Let us briefly explore the first point in more detail. What reasons are there for not knowing who else is involved?

One obvious reason probably springs to mind: the client and/or their carers does not communicate this information to us. This is because either they are unwilling, unable or they don't think it's relevant. For many people, it suits them to compartmentalise their lives. It might be easier for them to deal with different workers in isolation. To some extent, if this is a preference we shouldn't simply ignore it. Quite often people complain about workers coming along 'poking their noses into their business'. If this is their attitude, they might well withhold information about other involvements. This desire to protect one's privacy is not an uncommon feeling amongst service users. We should accept that it poses dilemmas for workers. We need to think seriously about whether and in what circumstances we need to seek someone's permission in order to share information about them. What is collaborative working for us may feel like 'plotting behind their back' to clients.

This links us to the second point about being aware of involvements but not being very clear about what they are. If we rely on clients and/or carers to inform us precisely on what others' involvement is the information we get may be very limited. People can be less than forthcoming for the kinds of reasons set out above. Apart from problems with memory and confusion, or communication problems, they may choose to be deliberately vague. This, almost certainly, is not out of a mischievous desire to play games, it is more likely an attempt to retain some sort of control or power over the situation when they are feeling at their most vulnerable.

People in crisis or distress have to 'lay themselves bare' to strangers. It can be a humiliating and exposing experience. It is often something they want to remain silent about, particularly when they are faced with yet another stranger.

Case Study

A misunderstanding

The care manager goes to assess Albert Jackson. He is an elderly man whose wife has recently died. The neighbours are concerned and think he needs opportunities to get out and meet more people. When the care manager gets there Albert admits to being lonely and missing his wife but turns down the offer of day care. The care manager tries to get as full a picture of health and social care needs as possible but Albert says that mainly he is OK and he'll be in touch if he needs anything. The care manager is on the point of 'closing the case' the following week when the district nurse rings up. She didn't know that the care manager had visited but wanted an assessment to be carried out for personal care as much as anything. This, she explained, was because she visits regularly to assist with Mr Jackson's colostomy bag. His personal hygiene has become noticeably worse since the wife died, in addition dirty laundry is just piling up in the bedroom.

Questions

1 Why do you think Mr Jackson failed to mention such an obvious involvement to the care manager?

2 What lessons does this teach us about relying on the person concerned, their carer or even the referrer to inform us about other involvements?

We have now established that discovering the make-up of someone's care network is not always straightforward. It might require not only time and effort checking various sources, but also having to deal with dilemmas about respecting privacy. However, even when we are aware of various involvements, the second point we need to address is that workers can often possess limited knowledge about other professional groups or other organisations. For example, even if we are aware that, say, an occupational therapist, a member of the 'Rapid Response' team, or a day services support worker is involved with one of our clients, this doesn't mean that we are always entirely clear about what they do and what they are responsible for. This clearly poses problems for effective collaborative working. One obvious problem is how to ensure that the expectations we have of other workers is realistic and vice versa. There are many reasons why we aren't clear about others' roles and responsibilities; and this suggests that we should ask how we discover such knowledge.

Think it over

1 Write down a list of the workers who become involved with your clients.
2 Now, write down a score against each worker on a scale from 0 = I know nothing about this role, to 10 = I know just about everything there is to know about this role.
3 Lastly, for each worker, write down *how* you actually gained that knowledge.

It would be entirely reasonable to have a range of scores. Hopefully, there are no 0s! It is interesting to reflect on how we know what we know about each other's roles and responsibilities. Those whom we actually meet regularly and work alongside the most frequently probably score the highest. However, we might also acquire our knowledge of, say, a GP's role from our own personal contact as patients – that wouldn't be unreasonable.

What about those workers who you scored lowly? You might, with some justification, expect a textbook such as this to be able to fill in the missing details. That, after all, is what we expect from books. If you think about it, is this the best way to familiarise yourself with the specific roles and responsibilities of those working in your locality? For example, across the country there are groups of workers with names like 'Community Support Team', 'Crisis Intervention Team', 'Community Resource Team', or even 'Assertive Outreach Team'. They all are working in the field of social care for vulnerable adults. However, depending on the locality they could be doing completely different things for different client groups. There are workers with job titles such as GP Liaison Worker and Assistive Technology Officer. What one does in one area may not apply in another. In some areas the NHS might have a Falls Coordinator in others they might be called The Falls Prevention Officer, each with slightly different responsibilities. No single textbook, however well researched, is going to adequately cover this plethora of different roles. This means that workers need to gain the necessary information in ways that are appropriate to them and where they work. Workers need to take responsibility for finding out this information on the ground for themselves, there is no better alternative.

Figure 5.8 *You may need to go in search of the information you require*

With your lists from the previous exercise think about how you personally could get a clearer picture of what those workers do. We discuss some methods for doing this in the next section.

Lastly, a further complicating factor is that whilst certain individual workers have a particular talent for networking, others have the capacity to undermine joint working through what is sometimes called 'street level bureaucrat' behaviour. This is to say that some people are simply not 'clubbable'; their overall approach to other workers is to put their backs up with a bureaucratic, officious, often pedantic manner. They will either lecture others on what their responsibilities should be, talk at length about why doing their job is 'not as easy as you think', and generally maintain a 'yes but' attitude to approaches to work collaboratively. When you encounter such people, if all else fails, it is often simpler to work around them rather than waste further time and energy.

Having to work across different administrative boundaries

In recent years, particularly to advance the cause of 'joined up' government, attempts have been made to make the various health authority and local authority boundaries coterminous – that is to say that the boundaries of responsibility for health authorities and local authorities have been redrawn to match the same geographical area, be it a town, region or county. There are unfortunately still quite a few exceptions. This means that a health authority can have responsibility over, say, the whole of one county, the southern part of another, and the western part of another. A single health authority is therefore dealing with three different local authorities, or maybe more if there is a unitary authority embedded in a larger county authority. A local authority might have two or more health authorities with responsibilities in different parts of its area of responsibility. This can cause problems at the level of strategic planning. These need not be insuperable but it just means more people to meet with, negotiate with and to agree plans with, and more chance of getting wires crossed.

At a more local level, it is usually the case that several GP surgeries operate within the boundaries of a single local authority. However, the way that a local authority divides up its area, for example in East, West, North and Central divisions, can often mean that one surgery has half its patients in the East division whilst the other half are in the West division. Here, the problems are having two different managers and two sets of workers each with their own subtly different ways of working. Twice as many links to make and maintain.

At ground level, care practitioners are not always sure whether a person living in a particular street is Dr Smith's or Dr Jones' surgery. Health workers refer to one locality social services team when they should be referring to another because they are not entirely sure where the boundaries are drawn. The possibilities for confusion and the wasting of time are made more complex again once the different catchment areas of housing and education authorities are factored in.

As we have seen, the government is in favour of a seamless service and Care Trusts are meant to be an important step towards this. In addition, other initiatives such as NHS Direct and Care Direct are meant to create one-stop 'portals', whereby the person needing help only has one door to go through. It is too early to say whether these initiatives have solved the problems caused by lack of coterminosity.

Think it over

Think about the various agencies involved in your area. As far as you know are they working 'coterminously' or do they straddle one or more areas? Are there any problems? Explain.

Data protection and confidentiality issues

All workers should be legitimately concerned about data protection and confidentiality issues. However, an eagerness to keep information safe can lead to an unwarranted withholding of information. Timely and effective interventions can sometimes be badly stalled by an overprotective mentality towards information sharing. How different professional workers share information between themselves is a far from settled area. Different agencies are still reluctant to share information electronically for example, because there are concerns about security. Proper 'fire walls', passwords, and other access arrangements need to be put in place before one agency is prepared to pass its case information across a computer network to another. However, IT security concerns are not the only problem.

Case Study

Sharing information

A locality social services team receives a rather vague referral about a man said to be in his 50s. He is a reclusive character. He walks very unsteadily and has been seen to fall over in the street outside the flat (14 Bracken House) where he lives. His flat is in a very poor state of repair. He is often heard shouting to himself in an unintelligible way. This gives rise to suspicions that he is suffering from a form of mental disorder.

Neighbours haven't seen him for some days and there are concerns about his well-being. It is believed that his name is John Bailey. The duty worker taking the call feels that more information needs to be gathered. She rings the local GP surgery enquiring whether they have a Mr John Bailey of 14 Bracken House registered with them. The receptionist says that for data protection reasons she is unable to give confidential information out about a patient without their consent. When the duty worker explains they are from social services and outlines their reason for ringing, the receptionist says they will need to ring them back through the social services main switchboard in order to establish that they are a genuine worker. When the calls comes back to the duty worker, the receptionist says that they will have to contact the medical records department at the health authority. The duty worker calls the medical records department. They take details and ring the duty worker back with the relevant GP information.

Questions

1 What are your comments about how information is shared in this case study?

2 What do you understand by the receptionist calling it a 'data protection' issue?

3 Have you had any similar experiences trying to obtain information from other agencies? If so, what were they?

4 How can such long-winded and over-protective procedures be avoided?

The situation in the case study is not that complex but it does raise some interesting issues. It shows that a certain interpretation of 'data protection' can practically stop collaborative working in its tracks. Whilst confidentiality is an essential principle of good care practice, it can also be a cloak to hide behind if another, for whatever reason, is feeling uncooperative. Confidentiality is about respecting people's privacy and the responsible management of information about that person. This scenario raises questions of what exactly is 'confidential' information. The receptionist has interpreted this to mean the information about whether John Bailey is registered with that practice. Remember, the duty worker was not asking for case information but trying to establish who John Bailey's GP was. The receptionist is within her rights not to give out information over the phone to strangers, although GP surgeries are at liberty to say whether they have certain people registered with them.

Workers exchange case information all the time, particularly over the phone, often without seeking the subject's consent. To a degree, this is a matter for professional discretion, the justification being the common law principle of it being in the interests of the person's welfare. Often information is given without checking the credentials of the person asking. This is bad practice. If anything, the case study shows a lack of trust between the two agencies. If there had been a designated liaison worker known to the surgery this almost certainly would have led to better communication. The receptionist referred to it being a 'data protection' issue and it is essential that all care workers know about the Data Protection Act 1998 (DPA) because this covers all aspects of the recording, handling and disclosing of personal data that is held on people whether it be within the NHS, social services or any other agency. All organisations should draw up their own policies and practices on confidentiality and data protection. These need to conform to the principles and provisions of the DPA. Guidance issued to social services in 2000 states:

> Care is necessary when making oral disclosure that conversations cannot be overheard and that individuals to whom personal information is disclosed are aware of the confidentiality implications of such disclosure. Use of the telephone as a means of disclosing information, especially confidential information, should be avoided where possible. A record of all oral exchanges of information should be kept and confirmed in writing. (page 39)

Data protection and confidentiality issues are very important. Collaborative working can only work effectively if those involved are clear about what can and what cannot be shared with each other, in particular what information requires the subject's consent before it can be passed on. Problems occur when workers aren't sure what the position is and react either by being too casual with confidential information or being too withholding.

Further Research

Track down your agency's policy on data protection and guidance on confidentiality. Thoroughly familiarise yourself with the contents.

⊃ Check your understanding

1 Give an example of how the 'Good cop–Bad cop' factor can create problems when trying to work collaboratively.

2 Briefly, summarise the *three* areas which Van Eyk and Baum found impeded inter-agency collaboration.

3 List the *four* factors that Means *et al* found created difficulties in working in partnership.

4 Why might stereotyping pose problems in professional relationships?

5 Give *two* examples of how different professional or organisational cultures may get in the way of successful joint working.

6 Explain why, in multi-disciplinary teams, disagreement over roles and responsibilities can lead to friction.

7 Explain why workers don't always know why others are involved.

8 How can having only a vague idea of other workers' roles and responsibilities impede working together effectively?

9 What does 'coterminous' mean and what effect can a lack of 'coterminosity' have?

10 What does data protection legislation tell us about the way information on clients is recorded, stored and managed?

Ensuring that collaborative working is effective as possible

In the previous section we discussed a range of problems that can create obstacles to successful collaborative working. Some of the solutions are beyond the powers of the individual worker and are more appropriately the responsibility of politicians, policy makers and senior managers. However, there are clear messages and lessons to be learned for workers at every level.

Collaborative working is most likely to be effective if certain key principles are followed.

Figure 5.9 *Principles for effective collaborative working*

If we can work to the spirit of these basic guiding principles then overcoming some of the obstacles we have identified should be easier. Our effort to work collaboratively will benefit both from acquiring and practising certain skills and adopting certain methods and strategies.

Important skills and ways of behaving when working collaboratively

Let us start with a brainstorm. Given all the possible pitfalls we've uncovered, make a list of all the skills and qualities you think are needed to ensure that we can establish good working relationships with other workers.

Your list is probably very similar to a list that you would make if asked what skills and ways of behaving you need to work in care. This would typically contain the following:

- ⊃ Being a good communicator
- ⊃ Having good interpersonal skills
- ⊃ Being non-judgemental
- ⊃ Being genuine.

Therefore, we're not necessarily talking about the acquisition of specific new skills. However, in the light of some of the potential difficulties we have discussed in earlier sections, the following skills and ways of behaving are going to be particularly important:

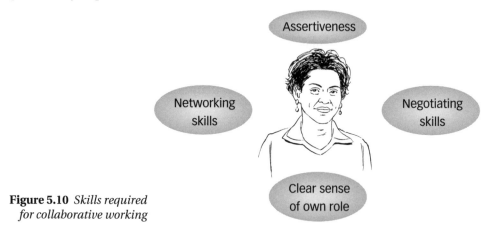

Figure 5.10 *Skills required for collaborative working*

Assertiveness

Assertiveness is a vital ingredient to working in social care and particularly when it comes to being effective in partnership working. The non-assertive worker denies their own rights and will forever find themselves in a subordinate (inferior) role with others accommodating their interests, needs and wishes to the detriment of their own.

Assertiveness is a state of mind which requires you to know who you are and what you want. It is a way of behaving that enables you to communicate this knowledge clearly and effectively to others. It runs wider than just the ability to say 'no'. Assertiveness is often confused with selfishness or aggression, with putting our own needs before other people's and pursuing them regardless of the effect on others. This is not assertiveness. Let us look at what assertiveness really is and compare it to other ways of relating to people's aggressiveness, passivity and being manipulative.

Assertiveness

➲ Recognising our needs and asking openly and directly for what we want.

➲ Recognising and respecting the rights and needs of other people.

➲ Relating to people in personal and working situations in an open and honest way.

➲ Feeling responsible for and in control of our own actions.

➲ Not seeing situations in terms of win or lose, but being prepared to compromise.

➲ Being able to resolve difficulties and disputes in a way that feels comfortable and just to those involved.

➲ Expressing views coherently whilst being prepared to listen. →

Aggressiveness

➲ Expressing feelings and opinions in a way that punishes, threatens or puts the other person down.

➲ Disregarding the rights and needs of others.

➲ Aiming to get our own way no matter what.

➲ Views made forcefully to the point of rudeness.

➲ If we 'win' and get what we want aggressively it probably leaves someone else with bad feelings, making it difficult to relate to them in future.

Passivity

➲ Not standing up for our rights. Allowing others to take advantage of us.

➲ Avoiding responsibility for making choices – leaving others to make decisions for us.

➲ Not being in control of our lives. Seeing ourselves as helpless victims of unfairness and injustice.

➲ Feeling that our view is less important or valid – backing down even when we think we are right.

➲ Avoidance of conflict at all costs.

Being manipulative

➲ Unable to ask directly for what we want.

➲ Trying to get what we want indirectly, by playing games or trying to make people feel guilty.

➲ Expressing views in a covert manner. Often using snide remarks, gestures and facial expressions.

In becoming more assertive we develop an awareness both of what we say and how we express ourselves.

Think it over

Which approach(es) do you have: aggressive, manipulative, passive or assertive?

Basing your decisions on what is described above, reflect on which approach you adopt in your day-to-day dealings with other workers. Which approach most characterises the way you are? Does it vary according to who the other worker is? Explain.

What do you need to do to become more assertive?

Becoming more assertive

If you found that you were able to be properly assertive with other workers, whichever agency they are from, that is fine. If, on the other hand, in some situations you find this difficult, you need to do some work.

Some basic guidelines to becoming more assertive

Verbal aspects in becoming more assertive:

➲ *Aim to personalise pronouns* Use 'I' statements rather than 'You', 'It', 'We', 'One'.
  When we use the personal pronoun 'I' we acknowledge that the statement is true of our experience and that it may be different from other people's.

➲ *Changing verbs* Change 'can't' to 'won't' where 'can't' isn't an appropriate restriction.
  This change of verb encourages us to take responsibility and to be aware of what we can and can't realistically do, and that we can make a positive choice when we decide whether or not to do something.
  Change 'need' to 'want' and differentiate between the two. This change of verb encourages us to be realistic and responsible about what we need and want.
  Change 'have to' to 'choose to'. These changes in verbs acknowledge that we make a choice about what we do and are therefore responsible for the choice. This realisation that we have choices is an important part of becoming more assertive.
  Change 'know' to 'imagine' when a fact is a fantasy. Often we state we know something about someone when in fact we base this 'knowledge' on fantasy. It is important to differentiate between what we know, imagine, feel and think when making clear and assertive statements.

➲ *Changing passive into active* We put ourselves in a passive role when we talk about something happening to us. Part of becoming more assertive is recognising that we are responsible for things that happen to us. For example, 'I allow people to take advantage of me and often feel angry' is very different from 'Things keep happening to me that make me feel angry', in which we blame things/others for how we feel.

➲ *Changing questions into statements* Questions such as 'Don't you think?' are often indirect ways of stating 'What I think...'. When we are clear and direct in our communication we are more assertive with ourselves and others.

There are non-verbal aspects to becoming assertive:

➲ *Eye contact* How a person looks at someone conveys how they feel about themselves and what they are saying.
  It is a powerful form of self-assertion to look someone directly in the eye. A person will often give their power away by looking away. When a person looks directly at who they are talking to they communicate that they are alert and present in themselves.

➲ *Posture* How a person stands or sits also communicates how they feel about themselves and what they are saying.   →

When a person is standing talking to someone or addressing a group of people it is important that they stand with both feet firmly on the ground. This means that they are both centred and balanced in themselves.

You can assert yourself by saying no to whatever you dislike or disagree with. But why do we find saying 'no' difficult? There are many possible reasons but some common ones are:

- ➲ We don't want others to think us unkind.
- ➲ We want to be popular.
- ➲ We think we should be all things to all people.
- ➲ We think our refusal might devastate the other person.
- ➲ We may have been bought up to think saying no is impolite.

Hints for saying 'no':

- ➲ Get the word 'no' out early in your response, if possible make it the first word.
- ➲ Give reasons if you need to, but don't make excuses; others will see through them.
- ➲ Don't apologise unnecessarily.
- ➲ Keep your non-verbal message assertive; maintain good eye contact and don't smile inappropriately.
- ➲ When you've finished making your point, find a conversation 'closer' such as 'Okay?', 'Thank you for being so understanding' etc., or just change the subject.

  Remember, you are turning down a request not rejecting a person – you have the right to say no!

How to criticise or challenge someone assertively:

- ➲ Before you start work out a sound inner dialogue to make sure the criticism is specific and not a personal attack.
- ➲ As you criticise introduce a topic and (if appropriate) say why you are raising it.
- ➲ Specify what the problem is.
- ➲ Get a response to your criticism.
- ➲ Ask for suggestions to rectify the problem.
- ➲ Summarise suggestions agreed.

How to respond assertively to criticism or a challenge from someone:

- ➲ Listen to the criticism carefully, rather than rejecting it or arguing with the person.
- ➲ Ask yourself whether the challenge is valid/invalid and/or whether it is in the form of a put-down. →

If the criticism or challenge is valid:

⊃ Acknowledge that it is true.

⊃ If it is generalised then ask for more specific information.

⊃ Ask other people for information, whether or not they experience you in a similar way.

⊃ Decide whether or not you are going to change your behaviour as a consequence of the criticism.

⊃ Thank the other person for their challenge/criticism.

If the criticism or challenge is invalid:

⊃ Say so and assert yourself positively, for example
'You have made a mistake in your assessment.'
'No, that isn't true. I am usually very careful.'

⊃ When criticisms are made that are invalid, affirm yourself.

If the criticism is valid and in the form of a put-down:

⊃ Acknowledge that it is true! Challenge the put-down and assert yourself positively.

It is important with put-downs to respond assertively and to confront the put-down, for example
'Typical of you – you never return my emails.'
'Yes, I have not yet responded to the last two. However, I am usually respond to all my emails as soon as I can and I don't like your put-downs!'

If the criticism is invalid and in the form of a put-down:

⊃ Say so. Challenge the put-down and assert yourself positively, for example
'No, that isn't true, I have answered all my emails and I don't like your put-down!'

Our discussion on assertiveness has probably made you realise just how important our use of self is in conducting effective relationships with other workers. It should also have reinforced how important it is to possess a clear professional identity. Low professional self-esteem and successful working in partnership are incompatible.

Clear sense of own role

We have seen how difficult it is to be assertive and therefore work effectively in collaboration with others if we have self-doubt about our own worth, our own competence and what our role is. It is therefore of paramount importance that, as workers, we clarify what our job role is and what responsibilities it carries with it. This question will have been raised many times throughout the book but let us make sure that the lessons have been learned.

Think it over

Imagine you have been asked to give a talk to a group of service users, your colleagues and other workers. You have fifteen minutes to make it absolutely clear to all of them what you do, what you are responsible for, what you are *not* responsible for, in other words what the function of the organisation who work for is and your role within it.

How would you structure your talk? Write down your headings together with what you would say. Make a point of identifying areas where you specialise.

If you found that exercise difficult it might suggest that you would benefit from doing some research. Look out your agency's mission statement and any other relevant documents that could help you summarise what business you are in exactly. What is the agency's literature saying it is about? Look out your contract and job description. What are your core tasks and key responsibilities? What leaflets or other publicity does your agency have for the public? What do they say about the agency purpose and your role within it? If you are still unclear because, for example, you don't recognise what you do on a day-to-day basis from the official job description, then you should raise this at a staff meeting or some other appropriate forum. There is no shortage of people who are happy to tell us what social care or social work is or should be. Unless we want our roles limited and defined by others we need to have a clear idea of what the purpose of what we do is.

Then we can assert ourselves effectively.

Negotiating skills

To negotiate is to try to reach a mutually acceptable agreement with another party (or parties), usually through discussion. Negotiating is at the heart of social care work. We need to reach agreements with others on a range of matters, some relatively trivial, others more serious. These could be times of meetings, dates when care starts, where to have a meeting, when to have the next review, who is going to take key responsibility or even who is going to give someone the bad news! What we're trying to do is achieve a 'fit' which all those involved are reasonably comfortable with. Because most of these decisions are reached with little or no dissent, we can often take what we're doing for granted. But clearly even the most straightforward of decisions don't happen automatically. Somebody needs to take the lead, identify what needs to be done, offer suggestions and then make an appropriate response, even if the minimum amount of negotiation is required.

From time to time, we will find that it is hard to obtain a 'fit' or a happy medium and that is when the ability to negotiate becomes very important.

What happens if someone has poor negotiating skills? We've probably all been on the wrong end of situations or 'agreements' that have been badly negotiated. This can leave us with feelings of anger, injustice, being cheated, put upon, outmanoeuvred, or even bullied. This is because the so called 'agreement' has been settled on the other party's terms. Goodwill soon disappears in such circumstances. It is also equally true that if we impose our decisions on others without the possibility of negotiation, then they too will feel a similar sense of grievance. Collaborative working can only work properly if agreements are negotiated on terms that everybody is happy with.

Case Study

Negotiating a care plan

A care plan has been drawn up for Joyce McCullough, a 41-year-old with schizophrenia. When Joyce, who lives on her own, goes through occasional periods of instability, members of the Community Mental Health team make a point of visiting twice a day to ensure that any risk is managed. The key worker is Adrian, a CPN, and he has asked Janet, one of his social work colleagues, to share the task. In the spirit of working collaboratively, Janet agrees. Adrian then draws up a rota for visiting which requires Janet to visit at 6.00 pm each day whilst the Adrian visits Joyce at 9.00 am on his way to work.

Janet would have preferred the earlier visit because the 6.00 pm visit conflicts with a range of other tasks she wants to do – including going home! Initially, no comment is made as Adrian says it will only be for a few days. After a week, Joyce is still unstable, and it is clear that Adrian has no intention of offering to share the 6.00 pm call. When Janet half raises the issue of changing times, Adrian says that the earlier call is more important for him to do because he checks medication – something Janet wouldn't be able to do. Janet feels trapped.

Questions

1 What options are open to Janet?
2 Can a more suitable agreement be negotiated, if so, how?

In your responses you should have been able to link this situation to points we have made previously about power imbalances, professional identity, assertiveness and the need to have a clear job role.

Outcomes which would *not* promote effective joint working would be for Janet, the social worker, simply to

- ➲ withdraw
- ➲ go straight to the team manager, or
- ➲ continue but vow never to help that particular CPN again.

Another approach could be for Janet to refer Joyce to the psychiatrist for a case review, and use this as an opportunity to disengage from the situation. This wouldn't really be negotiating with Adrian though, it would be working round him. This could be considered manipulative even if it is in Joyce's best interest. Going straight to the manager would be a later option if negotiation proved unsuccessful. Working collaboratively is about trying to forge reasonable working relationships with colleagues, not trying to outsmart them.

Situations like the one outlined above should be resolved by negotiation wherever possible. In order to negotiate successfully in any situation we need to know what we want – it is no good simply grumbling, we must have our own clear proposals. We need to think about what our ideal solution would be – i.e. What would be the best possible result to come out of the negotiation? We then need to be realistic and be prepared to concede some ground. This involves having a 'fall back' option – i.e. What is the least satisfactory solution we would give our agreement to? We need to be clear that we will not go over this line. If someone tries to force us beyond our fall back position then we need to be clear what we will do. This might involve taking things higher or simply refusing to cooperate further, it depends on the situation. In any event, it is no good having a fall back position if it is ignored.

Having clearly set the parameters of what is acceptable in our head, we need to be able to successfully argue for what we want. We need to be able to show that our proposals are fair, reasonable and rational. We need to have arguments that reflect coherent care values. They can't be arguments that can be attacked for being selfish or overlooking clients' needs.

The way we negotiate is as important as the quality of the arguments we use to negotiate with. This inevitably brings us back to assertiveness. If we try to negotiate in a way that is aggressive, angry, manipulative or passive we will greatly reduce the chances of success. If we aim to negotiate in a way that shows us to be open, flexible and reasonable then this too will be conducive to effective collaborative working.

Successful negotiation checklist

➲ Am I clear about what I am trying to achieve?

➲ Am I clear what my fall back position is?

➲ What will I do if I am pushed beyond my fall back position?

➲ How will I conduct my negotiation – what arguments will I use?

➲ Have I got a case which can clearly be seen to promote client care?

➲ How will I negotiate in a way that is assertive and not aggressive, manipulate or passive?

➲ Am I being open, flexible and reasonable?

Networking skills

Here we see networking as an umbrella term which includes a range of activities, all of which have 'contact' as an important feature. They include:

Figure 5.11 *Networking skills*

Networking is not a precise science, in many ways it is more of an art. A common way of describing networking is to compare it to a bee busily buzzing around picking up pollen from one flower and depositing it on another. In their research, Means and Smith (1998) found that good networkers or reticulists as they are sometimes called (from the French word *réticule* meaning network):

> ... tend to feel comfortable working above their hierarchical position, and they are willing to operate in a way not bounded by narrow organisational self-interest. (page 143)

How to network

Good networking might be as much a product of personality than a set of skills we can learn. It requires a certain mindset. To put it rather crudely, good networkers are 'chancers' and opportunists, they exploit situations for all their 'contact potential'. They are both active and proactive in their approach.

Therefore, to be able to network effectively, we need to see the value in making contacts.

Networking is about building up contacts and sharing ideas and information. The more knowledge we have of what is available and who is out there to help, the more our clients have to gain.

In order to exploit situations, we need to have a raised awareness to the possibility of making contacts and be able to seize possible opportunities. We also need to actively create openings and not just wait for them to come to us.

Case Study

Networking

David Toole is a new care manager for a locality team. He keeps hearing from his colleagues how the rapid response team are always moaning about how slow the locality team is in picking up the work which they want to hand over. There is quite a backlog of unallocated work. David is a bit unclear about what the rapid response team do, but knows that the two teams have quite a strained relationship. Whenever a member of the rapid response team rings up David feels defensive and apologetic even though he personally has done nothing wrong. When a district nurse rings about a client, David decides to ask whether there is any feeling among the district nurses that social services aren't picking up work quickly enough. The nurse starts to talk about certain cases, some of which David also knows the rapid response team are involved with. David decides that he needs to go and meet with the rapid response team and contacts their team leader. They welcome the opportunity for a 'clear the air' talk.

Questions

1 What are your comments on David's action? Is he networking? Give reasons.
2 If David wanted to take his networking further, what should he do?

Just about any situation can be used as the basis for networking. David could involve both the district nurses and rapid response team in regular meetings. Meeting together could help to foster a better understanding of each other's roles, work pressures and organisational cultures. This in turn could promote trust and facilitate problem solving. The network can also be enlarged as other interested parties such as GPs and home care providers might have some useful input. The case study illustrates that by dealing with the problem directly, being proactive and making personal contacts you can increase the chances of making collaborative working run more smoothly.

Methods of promoting collaborative working

In social care work there are several formal methods which bring different workers together to discuss cases and wider practice issues. Some common methods are now discussed below.

Case conferences/meetings

Case conferences are used widely in all aspects of social work and health and social care. In certain contexts, case conferences have a clearly laid down name, purpose and set of procedures that govern them. An example of this type of case conference would be the Initial Child Protection case conference. Official guidance covers all aspects of such a conference: when it should be called, who should be invited, what agenda should be followed and so on. However, in other settings the term is used in very general terms to mean a gathering of relevant workers involved in a case coming together to discus details of the case. In the spirit of fostering user involvement, it is expected that the client, their carer and/or any other representative or advocate will be invited to attend part or all of the conference. Therefore, as a worker, if you felt that a case would benefit from a formally constituted meeting of those involved, you must invite the service user or their representatives. If you do not, you should have a very good reason why this would not be appropriate.

If your meeting is not a conference called as the result of official guidelines or procedures, but simply because a sharing of views and information would be a good idea, it might be better to drop the term 'conference' and call it a case meeting instead. This will stop people being confused about its status. Case meeting sounds slightly less formal and official than case conference. Nevertheless, if a case meeting is going to promote collaborative working it should still be conducted in a proper manner.

> ### Think it over
>
> Earlier (page 253) we looked at the case of Danny and his lunchtime visits to the pub. Imagine you were the care manager, explain how you would organise a case meeting so that the various issues could be sorted out. Key decisions that you will need to make in such a case would be:
>
> ⊃ Whom to invite?
>
> ⊃ Where to have the meeting?
>
> ⊃ When to have the meeting?
>
> ⊃ Who will chair the meeting?
>
> ⊃ How will the agenda be settled?
>
> ⊃ How will the meeting be recorded?
>
> ⊃ What accountability, if any, will there be in any decisions taken?

These questions raise several interesting issues for working collaboratively. The chairing and agenda setting inevitably raises questions of power, e.g. who decides what can be discussed, the recording question raises issues of confidentiality, e.g. will minutes be produced, how will they be disseminated and where will they be kept? Even thornier, could be the questions of how or, indeed, whether Danny is invited. Does he require an advocate? And what about his parents? This raises further issues of accessibility and transport. All meetings have their own dynamics and this is where professional territorial disputes can emerge. This makes it all the more important to establish an agreed set of ground rules and to make sure that everybody observes them. Sending out a rationale and proposed agenda in advance to all parties should help settle the meeting down quicker than if the meeting is convened with a completely open agenda.

These are some of the issues that practitioners must be aware of when thinking about calling case meetings. The last point to make is that just having a meeting isn't necessarily a sign of working collaboratively. We have all been to meetings that have descended into a free-for-all or have merely been an excuse to let off steam. Some people are expert at sabotaging or hijacking meetings. Therefore, for a case meeting to be an effective collaborative working tool we need to think clearly about what we are hoping to achieve from it, how it will improve care, in short, what the meeting's aims and objectives are. People don't like their time being wasted by attending meetings that aren't relevant or useful to them. We cannot simply call a meeting in the hope that answers to difficult questions will spontaneously appear. We need to express our views and ideas and be prepared to amend them if needs be.

Liaison meetings

Liaison meetings differ from case meetings in that they are not called to discuss a specific case but are regular meetings between workers from different agencies. The purpose of such meetings can vary but usually the overall aim is to improve links between agencies. There could be some case discussion but there might be other items on the agenda such as one group explaining about a new service or procedure to the other. Key features of liaison meetings are information sharing, breaking down professional barriers and ensuring that the agencies work collaboratively to promote better care.

Think it over

1 Where you work are there any liaison meetings with other agencies or other workers?

  If there are, explain how they are arranged, venues, timing and so on. How effective are they in promoting collaborative working? How would you like to see them improved?

2 Which other agencies or workers don't you have liaison meetings with? What would it take to set them up?

As with case meetings, participants have to have a sense that attending the meeting is worth their while. Liaison meetings can sometimes become 'ritualistic' in that people meet just because they have the date in their diary. Signs that liaison meetings are not working effectively are usually when absenteeism increases, when meetings are often cancelled or postponed or when participants merely go through the motions covering old themes and topics. The shame is that when these meetings are originally set up it is probably with a great sense of purpose and commitment. Workers often cite work pressures or lack of time for withdrawing from liaison meetings but this is often because they no longer see the value of meeting.

If you see the signs that liaison meetings are flagging they shouldn't be allowed to simply whither away. Every section of this chapter has provided arguments for working collaboratively. To retreat into isolation, however tempting, raises the chances of client care suffering.

How to revive the flagging liaison meeting

- ⊃ Acknowledge the problem and renegotiate the terms for meeting – change the interval, venue, anything to bring a fresher feel to the meeting.
- ⊃ Invite 'new blood' to the meetings. This can either be new members from the agencies or another agency altogether.
- ⊃ Consider guest speakers for joint training purposes.
- ⊃ Introduce treats such as cake or even more exotic fare.
- ⊃ Invite senior managers from time to time. Let them see the initiatives you are undertaking; they can also hear first hand your joint concerns.
- ⊃ Set yourself a project, e.g. develop a new joint system in some area of working. You could even write it up and get it published!

Joint visits

The joint visiting of clients is a very obvious sign of working collaboratively and can have benefits. However, it can also create problems, so this all needs a fuller discussion. The benefits of visiting a client together with another worker are many. For the client it means that they avoid the duplication of two separate visits and have the benefit of two sources of knowledge being available at the same time. Joint visiting improves the likelihood that everything the client says will be better remembered and recorded. One worker can also observe whilst the other conducts the interview. Workers are less likely to take shortcuts in the company of workers from other agencies, and they are also less likely to slip into a narrow service-led approach. When it comes to broaching difficult or sensitive matters workers can be emboldened by the presence of a fellow worker. Consequently, important but difficult issues which may normally be minimised by the lone worker can get a fuller airing. During the visit, if one worker wants the other's opinion from their specialist perspective it can be offered straight away rather than waiting for a referral to take place and all the time that this may take. After the visit both workers will be in a position to compare their impressions and bounce ideas off each other because they will have both been there. The assessment will be all the more rounded as a consequence.

On the negative side two people visiting can be overwhelming for somebody. They can be inhibited in participating fully if they are confronted by two strangers in their house. We should always seek permission to visit jointly because it can increase the feeling of invasion into someone's home, however well-meaning the 'invaders' are. Joint visiting obviously takes up twice as much worker time, so the addition of another worker needs to actually add something to the visit to make it cost-effective, they can't simply be there for the ride. Joint visiting also won't be successful if the workers act out any differences of opinion in front of the client. Sometimes people deliberately try to play one worker off against the other often in an attempt to equalise the power difference. However, on occasions joint workers can be drawn into a competitive game with each other about who is the most helpful or who gets on best with the client. Never underestimate the powerful dynamics of the three-way meeting. Making joint visiting a success needs to ensure the visits are

- ⊃ well planned
- ⊃ on the basis of a shared philosophy of care
- ⊃ consensual
- ⊃ an effective use of two workers' time.

Think it over

Identify a recent example from your practice where it would have been useful to have made a joint visit. Explain clearly what the advantages would be and explain any possible disadvantages.

Joint training

Joint training can mean different things. It can mean workers from different agencies attending a course together on a particular topic, for example 'Managing Risk with Frail Elderly People'. In this type of event it could be that issues are being raised and messages being given to a range of people from different professional backgrounds. In other words, the audience is a 'joint' audience. However, the trainers might be coming from a single perspective, for example physiotherapy. Alternatively, the trainers themselves could be from different perspectives (joint trainers) and the audience from one professional background. It could be that the training is both jointly organised and jointly attended. In colleges and universities there are often modules which can be shared between students on different professional pathways. For example, health professionals and social work students may come together for a module entitled 'Policies and Practices for Community Care', but go their separate ways for other parts of their qualification. Joint training opportunities have been institutionalised in areas like child protection – all events are multi-disciplinary – but this is less the case in adult social care. Joint training can be a positive step towards effective collaborative working not only because of the knowledge and skills gained from the training, but also because of the opportunities for different workers from different backgrounds to meet informally, share experiences and generally get to know each other as people. Such opportunities ought be approached with an open mind, because professional rivalries and mistrust can easily be brought into the training situation. This diminishes the whole experience if joint training only serves to reinforce stereotypes and confirm prejudices.

Further Research

Find an opportunity to participate in joint training relevant to your job. Look on staff notice boards, newsletters, the internet, ask your training officer, but basically identify a training event that will enable you to mix with workers from different backgrounds. Use the opportunity in a positive way to understand others' roles and responsibilities, how they work and make contacts for further reference. Be positive about what your agency contributes.

Work shadowing

Figure 5.12 *Work shadowing is one way of learning to do a job*

In many people's minds, work shadowing tends be associated with new and inexperienced workers accompanying a more experienced worker in order to learn the job. It is indeed a useful technique to help inexperienced workers to learn, but there are other possibilities for work shadowing that contribute towards working collaboratively.

Work shadowing is, in many respects, similar to ethnography, an approach to social research where techniques, such as participant and non-participant observation, are used.

This is what sociologists Townroe and Yates (1999) say about participant observation:

> Participant observation means that the researcher actually joins the social world of those whom he or she wishes to study.

Participant observation may be the only way to collect information about a particular group.

Joining a group of people and experiencing how they live may offer the opportunity to gain a deep and accurate understanding of their lives. Other methods might not have this potential to provide detailed and valid data.

The participant observer just observes and records. The participant observer does not impose hypotheses and ideas on to the social reality of those under study. Researchers using interviews and questionnaires have already decided what they want to know and, as a consequence, social reality is shaped to fit their questions.

Whereas a survey may offer a snapshot picture of people's lives, participant observation may provide a changing picture of how their lives develop. (page 352)

Work shadowing is also a form of ethnographic observation, and it need not simply be seen as an activity for new workers. It is an excellent way of learning about other job roles, organisational cultures and how other agencies operate. All of this information is valuable in taking forward collaborative working. Therefore, we should seek to work shadow others and be receptive to others' request to work shadow us. To be done properly it needs to be set up with attention to detail. You need to be work shadowing someone over enough time to get a representative and valid picture of their work. You also need to consider the issue of permissions and the perennial social researcher's problem – what effect will your presence have on the person being shadowed? Finding sufficient time is always going to be an issue but it can genuinely be treated as staff development and will make the chances of collaborative working much more likely to happen and be effective when it does.

Think it over

Identify a worker who you would like to shadow. Explain why you chose that particular worker. Think about what you expect to learn from that person and explain what steps you need to take to put into practice what you learn.

⊃ Check your understanding

1 Make a list of *four* skills or ways of behaving that will facilitate collaborative working.
2 In your own words, explain what it is to be assertive.
3 Explain why it helps to be assertive if working collaboratively.
4 Have you got a clear sense of your job role? Briefly explain what it is. What are your specialisms?
5 Give examples of negative effects if we possess poor negotiating skills.
6 Identify *six* pointers from the successful negotiation checklist.
7 Describe some of the activities which could be placed under the umbrella of 'networking'.

8   Give *three* reasons why networking helps promote collaborative working.
9   Explain *two* methods that promote collaborative working.
10 What questions does a worker need to consider when deciding to call a case conference?
11 What is the difference between a case meeting and a liaison meeting?
12 Describe *two* advantages and *two* disadvantages of joint visiting.
13 What factors will ensure that joint visits are successful?
14 Explain how work shadowing can help with collaborative working.

References and further reading

Barclay Report (1982) *Social Workers, their Role and Tasks*, London, NISW

Burns T and Stalker G M (1961) *The Management of Innovation*, London, Tavistock

Department of Health (1995) *Child Protection: Messages from Research*, London, HMSO

Department of Health (1997) *Better Services for Vulnerable People*, London, HMSO

Department of Health (1998) *Modernising Social Services* , London, HMSO

Department of Health (2001) *Valuing People*, London, HMSO

Department of Health (2001) *National Service Framework for Older People*, London, HMSO

Hudson B (1987) 'Collaboration in social welfare: a framework for analysis' in *Policy and Politics*, vol 15, no. 3, pages 175–82

Hudson B (2000) 'Inter-agency collaboration – a sceptical view' in Brechin A *et al*, *Critical Practice in Health and Social Care*, London, Sage

Leathard A (1994) *Going Inter-Professional, Working Together for Health and Welfare*, London, Routledge

Loxley A (1997) *Collaboration in Health and Welfare*, London, JKP

Means R and Smith R (1998) *Community Care Policy and Practice*, 2nd edition, Basingstoke, Macmillan

Townroe C and Yates G (1999), *Sociology*, Harlow, Longman

Van Eyk H and Baum F (2002) 'Learning about interagency collaboration' in *Health and Social Care in the Community*, 10 (4) pp 262–9

Webb A (1991) in Means R and Smith R (1998) *Community Care Policy and Practice*, Basingstoke, Macmillan

6

assessment

his chapter focuses on the knowledge and skills required to assess competently. We begin by reflecting on the various meanings and take for granted assumptions attached to the key concept of 'assessment'. This raises interesting issues and questions that will help inform subsequent discussions in the chapter. From there, we consider the reasons why assessment has become so important in all forms of care work. In short, we ask the question, Why assess? We then aim to provoke both thought and discussion around the equally key but often difficult concepts of need and risk. Practitioners need to reflect on how the ambiguities and complexities of these concepts can affect practice – particularly in power relations.

All assessments take place within different contexts and we consider how the various contexts in which assessment takes place can influence, guide or constrain practice.

There are different views on how to assess and we discuss the strengths and weaknesses of different models of assessment. We address issues of empowerment and anti-discriminatory practice and relate these to assessment practices. Finally, we conclude by pulling together the various issues we have discussed as we aim to identify the elements of a competent assessment.

This chapter addresses the following areas:
- ⊃ What is assessment?
- ⊃ Why assess?
- ⊃ Assessment of need
- ⊃ Assessment of risk
- ⊃ The context of assessment
- ⊃ Models of assessment and assessment tools
- ⊃ Assessment, empowerment and anti-discriminatory practice
- ⊃ Elements of a competent assessment

After reading this chapter it is hoped that you will be able to
1 appreciate the importance of clarifying the scope and purpose of the assessment you are undertaking with all those involved.
2 understand the concepts of intersubjectivity and reflective practice and their relevance to assessment
3 be aware of the importance of the way language is used throughout the assessment process
4 have a clearer understanding of the key but ambiguous concepts of need and risk

5 locate a particular assessment in its various contexts and understand how the context(s) of assessment influence assessment

6 recognise the importance of how power operates in the assessment relationship

7 identify and evaluate different models of assessment

8 be aware of what assessment tools are and how they can be used to improve practice

9 make links between assessment, empowerment and anti-discriminatory practice

10 identify the elements of a competent assessment.

What is assessment?

Assessment is an important activity and core concept within all areas of social work and care practice. The requirement to assess can be found in a range of key documents.

The following extracts are all from either legislation or official guidance on social work and social care. As you read through them, reflect on whether it is clear what the activity of assessment actually is.

Competence in social work practice is the product of knowledge, skills and values. Qualified social workers must demonstrate their competence in practice to **assess** needs, strengths, situations, risks. [CCETSW Paper 30 Rules and Requirements for the Diploma in Social work (1991)]

… local authorities, in accordance with directions by the Secretary of State, will **assess** the care needs of any person who appears to them to need community care and decide in the light of the **assessment** whether they should provide any services. (S. 47 National Health Service and Community Care Act 1990)

A domiciliary care needs **assessment** regarding new service users is undertaken, prior to the provision of a domiciliary care service by people who are trained to do so, using appropriate methods of communication so that the service user and their representatives, are fully involved. (Standard 2, Domiciliary care – National Minimum Standards, Care Standards Act 2000)

In any case where the individual ('the carer') provides or intends to provide a substantial amount of care on a regular basis for the relevant person, the carer may request the local authority, before they make their decision as to whether the needs of the relevant person call for the provision of any services, to carry out an **assessment** of his ability to provide and to continue to provide care for the relevant person; and if he makes such a request, the local authority shall carry out such an **assessment** and shall take into account the results of that assessment in making that decision. [Carers (Recognition and Services) Act 1995 1 (1)]

As the extracts above indicate the concept of assessment lies at the heart of much of the writing and thinking about social work and social care. The frequency and location of where we find the term signals that it is an important activity. This raises important questions for us to consider at the outset:

1 What does it mean?

2 Does it have one clear, single meaning?

Consider the following extract from Smale and Tuson

> Imagine turning up at the supermarket to be met by an 'assessor', or 'gatekeeper of resources', perhaps called a 'shopping manager'. On entering the shop to acquire your package of goods, or perhaps the shopping manager visits you because somebody has told them you need some groceries but cannot go out, this person explains that their job is to work with you to identify your needs, and to form an opinion of what kind of package of goods you need and what resources can be called upon to obtain them. The shopping manager also explains that this particular supermarket no longer provides many 'goods' themselves but the manager will contract with a supplier who does. [Smale and Tuson (1993), page 4]

What meanings do the authors attach to assessment? Would you share their views? Smale and Tuson interchange assessor with gatekeeper, they create the image of the assessor as an opinion former, someone who will sort things out for you. Where else do we encounter the concept of assessment? NVQ candidates require assessors. Are these 'gatekeepers', 'opinion formers', or whatever you call them, people who you have to please in some way perhaps or present a certain side of yourself to?

Think it over

Brainstorm as many meanings as you can of the word assessment. Explain how the meaning might change depending on the context. In your mind what image does the word 'assessor' bring to mind?

Figure 6.1 *What assessment means depends on the context*

If you are now saying to yourself, 'Isn't it obvious what a care assessor does and what a care assessment is?', we would suggest not, not even amongst people working in the same office space. In any event, what happens when you make an appointment to 'assess' somebody – do they necessarily share your set of meanings?

Assessment is an 'intersubjective' activity

Because each assessment is about two or more human beings coming together, no two assessments are ever the same. Both the assessor and the person they are assessing bring their own individual ideas, interpretations and meanings to that particular social interaction. 'Intersubjectivity' is a difficult word but it sums up well what happens in the assessment situation. Assessments are about people meeting and getting to know each other. Each brings their own individual views, thoughts and perceptions to the meeting and, by the end, what emerges is unique. It is a coming together of each person's way of looking at things. Two different realties have collided producing a new reality. Even if there is a sharp disagreement, we are still changed through the experience.

The concept of intersubjectivity was introduced by a sociologist called Alfred Schütz. According to Schütz, when two or more individual people meet and share time and space with each other they become engaged in a process of communication and negotiation whereby they begin to discover and understand each other's thoughts and feelings. Intersubjectivity describes how people begin to inhabit each other's worlds. Social care is about trying to establish other people's wants and needs, their views, in short what their situation in the world is. It is also about those people understanding what we are about. This cannot happen in a mechanical way, it involves joining with each other in order to see the world through each other's eyes.

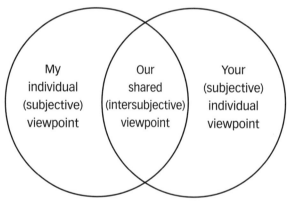

Figure 6.2 *Assessment is intersubjective*

Intersubjectivity and reflective practice

If we accept Schütz's view, assessment is more than a simple question and answer session. It is a complex social interaction where the meanings given to it are the product of an often unacknowledged negotiation between the two or more people involved. These meanings *cannot be automatically assumed*. The 'reality' of the assessment will be informed by each participant's taken for granted assumptions and preconceptions about what they believe 'goes on' in an assessment, what it is for and so on. As practitioners, we should always acknowledge the ambiguous and fluid nature of assessment. Those we are involved with will not necessarily share our viewpoint or our meanings. If we accept this then we should adopt an approach to assessment that is both self-aware and reflective.

Reflective practice means that assessors should be looking at themselves and asking themselves questions such as

⊃ What values and assumptions am I taking to this interaction?

⊃ What part am I playing in constructing this particular assessment the way it is?

⊃ Is the purpose of the assessment clearly understood by both parties?

⊃ What effect am I having on this person – and what effect are they having on me?

Reflective practice means assessors putting themselves in the picture by thinking and acting with the people they are serving, so that their understandings and actions are changed by the experiences with others. At the same time as this is going on, assessors are influencing and changing others and their social worlds. It's a two-way process.

Figure 6.3 *Assessment is a two-way process*

Think it over

1 Think about occasions when you have assessed someone and when you yourself have been assessed. What was happening in those assessments?

2 Write a list of all the activities that went on – put them under the headings of behaviours, thoughts, and feelings.

3 Compare your list with another person's, if it's possible. How does it differ? Does it make any difference whether you are the assessor or the 'assessed'?

The activity of assessment itself can bring about change

As practitioners it is likely that, from the beginning of the initial process of gathering information, we are instrumental in bringing about change. This is by the nature of the questions asked, by the fact we are listening to the person concerned and, sometimes, the members of their family. It is by paying attention to and therefore validating that person and/or their family's difficulties or concerns, and also by the fact of providing information and advice. This underlines both the dynamic and interactive relationship between those assessing and those being assessed.

Think it over

Reflect on a recent assessment in which you were involved.

⟳ What messages do you think you gave by the questions you asked, your response to what the individuals said, any advice or information that you gave – even the fact of turning up when you did?

⟳ From the beginning of the assessment to its finish, what do you think changed for them? What changed for you?

The importance of language in assessment

So far we have suggested that far from being a straightforward, clear-cut, bureaucratic or clinical process, assessments are always dynamic, 'intersubjective', complex social interactions. This is because assessments are about human beings coming together within a particular social context and constructing something unique. Each of the actors involved in an assessment brings their own set of meanings and assumptions based, to some extent, on past experiences. What they are there for, what is going on, the language used by each participant, in other words the 'reality' of each assessment is open to different interpretations. In *Getting the Message Across* the Social Services Inspectorate stated:

> Assessment is a participative process. It necessarily involves establishing mutual trust and understanding if meaningful information is to be obtained. The most effective way of achieving understanding may be to enable people to describe their situation in their own words, using their preferred language and at their own pace. Assessment should be a process of working alongside people. [Department of Health/Social Services Inspectorate (1991), page14]

In the same set of guidelines the SSI provided revealing evidence of how the language frequently used by professionals led those they were assessing to misinterpret what was going on.

The following are some examples of what users thought words meant:

⟳ *Voluntary agencies*	people with no experience, volunteers
⟳ *Sensitive*	tender and sore
⟳ *Agencies*	second-hand clothes shops
⟳ *Eligibility*	a good marriage catch
⟳ *Allocation process*	being offered re-housing
⟳ *Function*	wedding (party), funeral
⟳ *Gender*	most did not know this word
⟳ *Criteria*	most did not know this word
⟳ *Networks*	no-one knew this word
⟳ *Advocacy*	some users thought this word meant that if they did not agree with the assessment they would have to go to court. They wondered who would pay the bill.

[Department of Health/Social Services Inspectorate (1991), page 20]

This point is underlined by Smale and Tuson (1993) who stress that the assessor should possess the ability to 'join with people' and 'create a collaborative working relationship'. In other words, the assessor needs to enter the world of the assessed and ensure that the person being assessed understands the world of the assessor. Being aware of the problems of language is an important part of this.

The core of assessment is about understanding. This requires the assessor to listen, observe and relate both to what is being said and to the feeling with which this information is given. Whatever forms or templates we may need to fill in at some later stage it is always better to enable a person to tell their own story about their situation in their own way, in their own words, at their own pace. This approach allows somebody to convey what issues, events and questions they think is important.

Assessment as a form of story telling?

Carrying out an assessment could be regarded as establishing someone's story. As a story requires at least one author, this raises questions such as 'If *you* were being assessed who would *you* want to be the author of *your* story, bringing *you* to life and constructing *your* identity?' We continue this theme on page 323 in the section on assessment models.

Some of these ideas about the negotiated and dynamic nature of the assessor/client relationship might appear to be overly 'philosophical' at first. But we must recognise that assessment in social care or social work is a complex human activity and not simply a completed form or a checklist of questions. The importance of acknowledging the 'constructed' nature of assessment from the beginning will help inform discussions on all aspects of the assessment process and particularly those issues surrounding anti-discriminatory practices and 'power relationships' covered later in the chapter and elsewhere in the book.

⊃ **Check your understanding**

1 Identify three pieces of legislation or official guidelines where assessment is specifically mentioned.

2 In your own words explain what the term intersubjectivity means and how it applies to assessments in the care context.

3 Explain why it is important to think carefully about the language used in assessments.

Why assess?

We have established that assessment is a complex process and that what people understand is going on when an assessment is carried out should therefore not be taken for granted. We have also seen that, whatever the service user group, assessment is a key part of social care practice. Whilst the extracts set out above indicate that the requirement to carry out an assessment is embedded in several pieces of legislation and official guidance, we should also recognise that assessments take place in a variety of settings for a variety of reasons. Service providers, whether they be in residential, day or domiciliary settings, also carry out assessments. This raises questions of why assessing people is so central to social care work.

To some extent your answer will be determined by the setting in which you work. If you work in a statutory organisation then there will be a legal duty to assess and it should be your responsibility to ensure what the precise legal situation is as far as your agency is concerned. The main piece of legislation which guides the work of local authority social services departments for adults is the NHS and Community Care Act 1990. This Act and accompanying guidance should be available in all local authority offices.

Other key legislation that guides social care work includes:

- Chronically Sick and Disabled Act 1970
- Mental Health Act 1983
- Disabled Persons (Services, Consultation and Representation) Act 1986
- Children Act 1989
- Carers (Recognition and Services) Act 1995
- Crime and Disorder Act 1998
- Carers and Disabled Children Act 2000
- Children (Leaving Care) Act 2000
- Health and Social Care Act 2001

Which pieces of legislation apply depend on which branch of the service you work in. If you have never read the official guidelines for yourself you should make the effort to read those sections (for example Section 47 of the NHS and Community Care Act 1990) that apply to your job role.

That assessment is required by law is one obvious reason to assess, but this itself raises the further question of why assessment is made a legal requirement in the first place. The extract from *Caring for People* provides one very clear answer:

> The aim of assessment should be to arrive at a decision on whether services should be provided and in what form. Assessments will therefore have to be made against a background of stated objectives and priorities determined by the local authority. [Department of Health (1989)]

Tensions and pressures

For statutory organisations, a key function of assessment is without doubt a gatekeeping one. For assessors this inevitably creates tensions. On the one hand they are pulled by the idea of the full 'needs-led' assessment with its underlying values of holism and humanism, and on the other hand they are constrained by the (often tightly drawn) criteria for eligibility and priorities laid down by their agency. Research has shown that care managers experience stress when trying to reconcile the competing demands placed upon them by the sort of contradictions in their role highlighted above (Postle 2002).

Legal requirements

Bureaucratic procedures

Managerial control

Eligibility

Criteria

Budgets

Service availability

Needs-led

Person-centred

Humanism

Holistic approach

'Consumer' expectations

Figure 6.4 *Care managers are under pressure from both sides*

The working out of these tensions in a way that doesn't leave the assessor or the subject of the assessment negatively affected by the experience is difficult. We will address the issue of what skills, values and knowledge are required in more detail later.

Assessing because the law requires it is a key reason but is obviously not the only one, particularly for those people who work in non-statutory settings. Other reasons to assess include

- ➲ ensuring the suitability of provision – Will the person actually benefit from using or having it? Will they fit in? Is it the right match?
- ➲ exchanging information – Is it really what the person needs or wants? Could some more appropriate course of action be taken?
- ➲ establishing the level of need, thus helping to prioritise response
- ➲ fine-tuning – establishing which particular provision will be most effective; how much of the service is needed and when
- ➲ profiling – does the person being assessed fit the profile for which a particular service was designed, for example are they the 'right' age, gender, category of need etc.
- ➲ analysing what the situation is so that planning can take place
- ➲ finding out what the person is like as an individual.

Who knows best – the client or the assessor?

To go back to the supermarket scenario provided by Smale and Tuson, we might ask why people cannot make their own decisions about whether they have care and what form these services should take, after all the principle of client choice is at the heart of much social care literature. Those with sufficient funds can buy what they like. However, even if you purchased all your own care it wouldn't necessarily mean you were getting the most appropriate services. For example, some people, either because they have an exaggerated perception of risk or are simply unaware of how the care system can work, might choose to employ a 24-hour, live-in carer when they could almost certainly be helped to maintain their independence by having carers come in to attend them at several critical stages during the day with no greater risk and a lot less expenditure and intrusion into their lives. This raises difficult questions of when is choice *informed* choice? Whose 'solution' is the best?

Assessment can help address these issues, as long as potential ambiguities, complexities and conflicts are acknowledged at the outset. Assessment can be effective in determining

- someone's ability to exercise informed freedom of choice
- whether a particular service provision is likely to be adequate and effective
- that all aspects of a client' s situation are identified, their strengths as well as their problems. It helps us 'round' a person rather than just identify them with a minus.

The knowledge gained from assessment – fact or opinion?

You might have suggested that one reason to assess is to collect knowledge about somebody, their needs and their circumstances. In other words, to get at the 'true facts of the matter' – the unadorned truth. Quite a lot has been discussed already that would suggest this is not as simple as it may seem.

During an assessment some of the information gathered will certainly be factual: the person's name, address and age for example. Other items of knowledge about the person that assessors usually seek, such as someone's ethnic group or religion, can give the impression that this is factual as well. A lot of assessment paperwork reflects this view because a series of pre-coded options are given and it involves the 'straightforward' completion of boxes.

These coded categories are often based on official administrative categories such as 'white British' or 'black African' and it's not too difficult to see how a certain approach to assessment can 'create' rather than 'reflect' the person being assessed. Skellington cautions:

'Race', racial groups and categories…are not things that are given – objective facts waiting to be used – but concepts that have to be *constructed*. This construction involves a number of stages: differences of a certain kind between people have to be discerned; these differences have to be considered consequential; and these perceived shared attributes, such as skin colour, nationality, or regional or ethnic origins, have to become the basis for defining groups or categories of people. [Skellington (1992), pages 18–19]

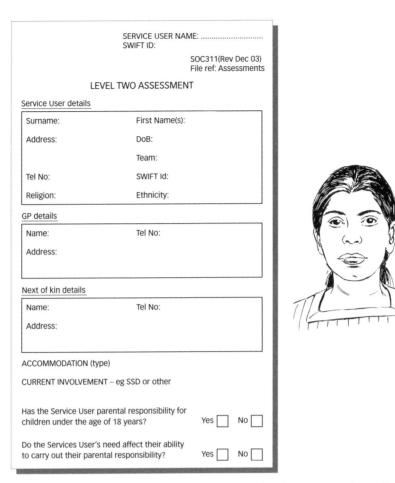

Figure 6.5 *You may need to be careful how you deal with matters such as religion and ethnicity in completing assessments*

Most of the data gathered in assessment is *qualitative* – it is information which describes what the person is like, their preferences, how they are feeling, how they are coping, their degree of mental capability and so on. Here, once again, it becomes apparent that assessment is not so much about 'discovering the facts' about someone's circumstances but 'creating a picture' based on the participation of those involved. Assessment places the assessor in the position of 'agent of knowledge'. The assessor has the power to construct someone's identity on paper and thereafter for the purposes of official business.

This raises more questions for assessors, for example:

➲ Who should be involved in assessment?

➲ Should the views and opinions of each participant in an assessment carry equal weight?

➲ How do we ensure that the picture is a valid and authentic one?

➲ What kinds of language and terminology do we use to record the findings?

➲ Is there always going to be a power imbalance between assessor and assessee because it is actually embedded in the structure of the relationship between the two parties?

○ How do we ensure that the assessor – 'the agent of knowledge' – doesn't either consciously or unconsciously abuse their power?

We will return to these issues later in the chapter but you might want to reflect on what your response would be and maybe raise further questions for yourself.

> ### ○ Check your understanding
> 1 Identify the main pieces of legislation that guide the work of your agency. Make sure you are aware of the main powers and duties as far as assessment is concerned.
>
> 2 List *four* reasons why assessment in care is an important activity.
>
> 3 What does it mean to say that data gathered in an assessment is *qualitative*?
>
> 4 What do we mean when we say that an assessor is an 'agent of knowledge'?

Assessment of need

Definitions and categories of need

We know from our look at the policy guidance earlier in the chapter that a major purpose of assessment is to establish what someone's 'needs' are. The problem is that there is no overall agreement on what the concept of need means – different people use 'need' in different ways. Consequently, in academic circles 'need' is described as a 'contested' concept. Middleton (1997) observed:

It is a pity that 'needs-led' has been set at the heart of community care, since it is fraught with the possibilities of misunderstanding. Hopes, wishes, aspirations, dreams and the barriers that prevent their realisation would have been so much easier to work with.

Figure 6.6 *You need to understand what the various terms used in care mean*

We have discussed how assessment is a complex, and far from straightforward concept. 'Need' is just as culturally situated and probably that much more complex again. As with assessment it is open to interpretation. This is acknowledged in official guidance:

Need is a complex concept which has been analysed in a variety of different ways. In this guidance, the term is used as shorthand for *the requirements of individuals to enable them to achieve, maintain or restore an acceptable level of social independence or quality of life, as defined by the care agency or authority.* [Department of Health/Social Services Inspectorate (1991), page 10]

However, need is also a personal concept. No two individuals will perceive or define their needs in the same way.

Those advocating a holistic approach to assessment sometimes place needs under a range of headings such as:

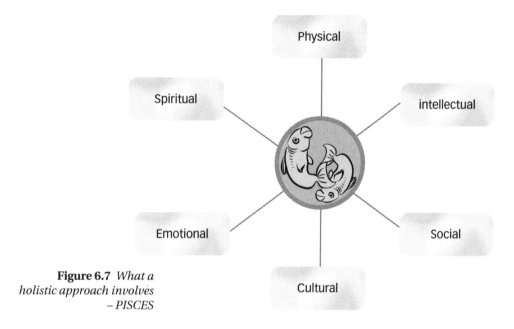

Figure 6.7 *What a holistic approach involves – PISCES*

Other typologies categorise needs in terms of the services or resources available, for example

⊃ medical   ⊃ nursing

⊃ social care   ⊃ home care

⊃ mobility.

Texts on human growth and development frequently utilise the humanist psychologist Abraham Maslow's 'hierarchy' of needs.

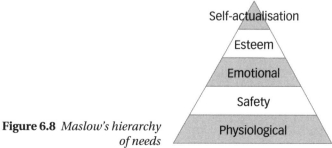

Figure 6.8 *Maslow's hierarchy of needs*

The basic point of Maslow's idea was that people have an in-built tendency to develop themselves or 'self-actualise' as they progress through life. However, the more basic needs at the bottom of the triangle need to be met before we can move up the 'hierarchy of needs' and start meeting other requirements for a fulfilling life. Whilst this view has been criticised for being an oversimplified account of human development it does serve as a useful way of distinguishing between different types of needs nevertheless.

Needs/wants

It is often said that care practitioners should be careful to distinguish between 'needs' and 'wants' as if this was a clear-cut exercise – the separation of the essential 'needs' from the 'less than necessary' wants. In day-to-day situations, people commonly interchange the two words. They do not necessarily adopt the language of PISCES or Maslow. This can make it difficult for assessors not to create an artificial picture by reinterpreting the comments of those they assess.

In academic circles, needs are often seen in terms of being 'relative' or 'comparative'. In deciding about what we need we compare ourselves to what others have. What this means is that material things like televisions, CD players, telephones, certain types of clothing and shoes and so on have symbolic values that are often more important than their material value. Deborah Stone cites the philosopher Michael Walzer, who says:

> People don't just have needs, they have ideas about their needs. [Walzer (1983) in Stone (1997)]

For example, food is not just nutrition – it has cultural and ritual aspects to it. Eating the same food as others can be a mark of belonging or membership. Think about why so many children come back from school with most of the contents of their lunch boxes untouched. You are in need if you cannot partake in the day-to-day activities of the culture in which you live. People from different cultures, histories, social groups will have different needs. So when we say need is relational or comparative we mean that need is specific to both place and time. If we accept that the symbolic aspect of need is important, then meeting people's needs means protecting their identities as well as keeping them alive.

Think it over

1 How would you define need?

2 What types of needs do you believe human beings have?

3 Look at the case study below, what needs would you identify Mr Robins as having?

4 Which of those needs would you say are the responsibility of health and social care agencies?

5 Once a need is identified, does the assessor have a responsibility to meet it?

Needs

Charles Robins is 67 years old. He lives alone in his own house. He used to live with his mother until she died 18 months ago. He has a son and a daughter who barely contact him. The house is very dirty and smelly, in fact it is squalid. Mr Robins has a state and a civil service pension. He usually lives off snacks and other convenience foods. Mr Robins hardly ever washes or changes his clothes. He uses a bucket to urinate in and empties it out of the front door. There is rubbish throughout the house and piled up in the garden. Recently he tripped and sprained his ankle which meant he could hardly get around. He is unable to climb the stairs to bed or go out shopping.

Questions

Think about this dialogue.

Assessor: You seem very isolated. Do you get lonely on your own?

Mr Robins: I need to get a new TV. The old one died on me.

Assessor: So you need social contact, would you like the company of others?

Mr Robins: No, I'm not saying that.

1 Do you keep going until Mr Robins admits that he wants to get out and meet people?

2 Do you record that Mr Robins 'needs a new TV'? If not, why not?

Bradshaw's 'taxonomy of need'

In 1972, a researcher, Jonathan Bradshaw, argued that there were four different ways of defining social need. Briefly they are:

➲ *Normative need* This is what the professional or the agency defines as a 'need' in any given situation.

➲ *Felt need* This is equated with 'want'.

➲ *Expressed need* This represents a further stage and is 'felt need turned into action'. Therefore, this is more of a demand.

➲ *Comparative need* This is where planners or researchers look at the characteristics of those already receiving a service and 'if people with similar characteristics are not in receipt of a service then they are in need.' For example, if there are elderly, lonely depressed people in one area able to access a day care service and others in another who aren't, then they would have 'comparative need'.

Need – living with ambiguity

You will have probably found that the activities will have raised many points about a wide range of issues, such as personal standards, choice, risk, how much you listen to what the other person wants, maybe even issues about mental health.

We need to have some sort of rules or framework to guide us through the conflicts and dilemmas which situations like the case study above raise. Of course, we need to be aware of the relevant legislation which guides our work, but that will not always help us with the kinds of issues raised above. It should be clear from the discussion so far that there can be no single text or authoritative set of guidelines which can answer all the questions raised in an unambiguous and straightforward way. We have to accept that 'need' is a contested concept. Parton and O'Byrne (2000) on the subject of assessment in general state 'that to pretend that there is certainty where there is little, is not good practice' (page 135).

Nevertheless, as we shall discuss in more depth later on in the chapter, assessment always takes place within a particular set of contexts. Assessors work within an agency or institutional context. Having a clear idea of their agency's function, the purpose of assessment within that agency and how that particular agency defines need, will at least ensure that ambiguities and differences of interpretation are brought out in the open, discussed and even recorded. Ironically, to be up front and honest about areas of uncertainty, possible misinterpretations and clashes of opinion – in other words acknowledging that you aren't sure and don't know everything – is a more professional approach than ploughing on, trying to convince yourself and others that all is crystal clear. Assessors can sometimes believe that it is a sign of their 'professionalism' that they can walk in and establish someone's needs single-handedly. In fact, usually the reverse is true. Letting go of this idea can only be beneficial for all concerned. By being honest about what you are uncertain about and what needs to be clarified, should either trigger a more specialist assessment, further discussion with the person themselves, or their carer. If you are not specifically trained in, say, mental health, sensory impairments or physiotherapy, then you won't properly be able to establish someone's needs in those areas. We discuss the need for collaborative working more fully in Chapter 5.

Further Research

Using material such as operational instructions, manuals, leaflets etc., collected from your workplace, make sure you can answer the following questions.

1 How does your agency define 'need' for the purposes of assessment?

2 What categories or types of need are specified? What language and terminology are these needs couched in?

3 What types of need are considered by your agency as their responsibility to meet?

4 What happens when other needs are identified that aren't considered the responsibility of your agency?

In 1991, anticipating the introduction of the NHS and Community Care Act, the Department of Health produced the following guidelines for staff involved in assessing need.

In order to undertake an assessment of need, staff have to know

⊃ the needs for which the agency accepts responsibility

⊃ the needs for which other care agencies accept responsibility

⊃ the needs of carers which qualify for assistance

⊃ the agency's priorities in responding to needs

⊃ the financial assessment criteria for determining users' contributions

⊃ the agency's policy on risk to the user and to community

⊃ the legal requirements.

[Department of Health (1991), page 46]

Think it over

Using the guidance above, how clear are you on each of the points outlined as far as your agency is concerned? Which ones require further investigation and clarity?

Barriers to a 'needs-led' assessment

Finally, we look at the research of Allison Worth. In 2002, she published her research into how both district nurses and care managers carried out assessments. Her observations showed that

Practitioners had considerable difficulty in conducting client-led assessments. Clients are unaware of what is available, therefore practitioners have to suggest services ….

One difficulty in incorporating the client's views was very apparent …. Many clients were unable to define their needs due to mental impairment, and others wanted to pursue their expressed needs (for example not to have help at home) in circumstances which practitioners, family and neighbours felt would mean an unacceptable level of risk. Another factor for some clients was an inability to express their views due to severe hearing loss or speech problems following a stroke. [Worth (2002) in Bytheway *et al* (eds), page 326]

Worth's research underlines the sheer range of issues practitioners have to grapple with when trying to adopt a needs-led approach to assessment. The key point is that despite the difficulties, it is a principle worth adopting. It would be easy to become cynical. However, being aware and honest about the possible pitfalls and complexities is a sign of professionalism. The worst thing would be for assessors to delude themselves and others that they are taking a needs-led approach when they are not.

> ⊃ **Check your understanding**
>
> 1 How does the Department of Health define need in its policy guidance?
>
> 2 What categories of need does PISCES stand for? Give an example of each.
>
> 3 What is the basic idea in Maslow's hierarchy of needs?
>
> 4 What are Bradshaw's four ways of defining need?
>
> 5 According to Department of Health guidance, what do staff need to know in order to undertake an assessment of need?
>
> 6 What barriers did Worth identify in her research into needs-led assessment?

Assessment of risk

It is very common in care work to talk about the need to do 'a risk assessment' on somebody. This can be for a multitude of reasons. For example, a person may be considered to be dangerous or aggressive, there might be moving and handling issues, there might be other health and safety issues, a person may be perceived at risk from falling, wandering, dehydrating, burglary or being abused by a stressed carer. It could be a combination of several or all of these factors, or something else completely.

Risk assessment is a term that, to many, has a reassuringly clinical, professional, clear-cut, even scientific feel about it. Whether such feelings are justified is another matter.

Several writers on social policy relating to social care and social work have commented that 'risk' is gradually replacing 'need' as the guiding principle

Figure 6.9 *What does risk mean?*

behind the assessment and delivery of services. Different reasons are offered for this shift. Kemshall (2002) argues that

> risk has become the dominant *raison d'être* of the personal social services, central to priority setting and rationing, and exhibited in the activities of staff and managerial systems used to hold them to account. (page 24)

Think it over

Think about your own job.

1 Do you regard your assessments as 'assessments of need' or 'risk assessments'? Maybe it's both, in which case what would you consider to be the difference between the two?

2 Would you agree with Kemshall that managers are more concerned with risk? If so, why do you think this is?

Meanings of risk

Just as with 'need' we find that 'risk' can be every bit as slippery and ambiguous a concept. People attach different meanings to it, often depending on the context in which it arises. For example, the doctor may use the term risk differently from the statistician.

Case Study

Mrs Prince and risk (1)

Mrs Prince is 71 years old and lives alone in a three bedroomed semi. She has Parkinson's disease which has impaired her mobility and creates difficulty in looking after herself. She falls occasionally – often when trying to get up and down stairs or transferring from her bed or chair to her walking frame.

Mrs Prince's daughter is very keen for her to move to a sheltered housing scheme and to accept carers to come and assist her with the activities of daily living.

Mrs Prince is determined that she is going to stay put and manage on her own. She likes her house and her neighbours and says that she can cope with the odd fall as long as she's near enough to a piece of stout furniture where she can haul herself up. An occupational therapist has fitted grab rails and other aids in the past. Mrs Prince is an intelligent woman and prides herself in not being a bother to others. She claims that she's a great fatalist and her attitude to life is 'what will be will be'.

Questions

1 Do you consider Mrs Prince to be 'at risk' – if so what are the risks?

2 Do you consider the risk of Mrs Prince staying at home without care an acceptable one? What would your preferred course of action be? Give reasons.

3 Has considering these points led you to formulate a working definition of risk? What is it?

Your discussion probably led you to question what 'at risk' means. Much of the time it is seen negatively and used interchangeably with 'danger'. Alaszewski (1998) observed that

> Like many concepts used in everyday language and in more technical settings, 'risk' has a variety of different meanings and can be used in different ways. (page 9)

Alaszewski talks about 'a narrow commonsense definition of risk' where risk is equated with danger and negative outcomes. He also says there are broader definitions in which 'negative outcomes are balanced against positive outcomes'. This might well describe the gambler's attitude to risk.

He goes on:

> Risk forms the tip of an iceberg of related words and terms. Some of these words tend to amplify the restricted meaning of risk in terms of the negative consequences of events; for example, hazard or harm. Other terms are linked to specific aspects of risk and tend to take the form of risk plus a qualifying term, relating to either a more specialist or technical use, such as risk assessment, or to an everyday use, such as risk taking. (page 10)

The risk iceberg illustrates the different associations and meanings attached to risk.

Two of the associated issues highlighted in the iceberg are risk perception and risk taking. It is clear that two people, when confronted by the same set of conditions, can often have completely different perceptions of whether there is any risk and what it might be. In addition, the behaviour of smokers, for example, shows us that even when 'experts' spell out a risk and back it up with evidence (in this case the greater chance of developing lung cancer, heart disease and so on) people choose to take the 'risk'. Both of these points are important to understand for those involved in assessment.

Figure 6.10 *The risk iceberg*

Whose risk?

An expert on the subject of risk, Deborah Lupton (1999) observed that 'lay' people often hold perspectives on risk that differ from those put forward by 'experts' (page 106). One reason, she continues, is

> That people may feel particularly safe in places in which they have chosen to live and bring up their families, with which they have an everyday familiarity, in sharp contrast to the assessment of experts.

Assessors need to recognise that differences in opinion over risk are not simply a question of who is right or wrong, or who is seeing things most clearly. If we return to the theme of intersubjectivity, that is to say the whole business of two or more people trying to put themselves into each other's position, it becomes evident that a key part of risk assessment is establishing both the other person's perception of risk and their attitude towards it. It shouldn't be the imposition of one's own 'expert' interpretation. This is important because as Lupton observes:

> People's perceptions and understandings of risk are established over a lifetime of personal experiences. (page 112)

She goes on to make the point that the risk position someone takes may also be important to his or her sense of self-identity. For example, it may be an important part of someone's self-concept that they see themselves as a 'survivor', a 'battler' or simply 'no trouble to anyone'. Worth (2002) found that in her research a woman with a serious visual impairment had to be strongly persuaded to accept a home help and a community alarm against her will. The woman is quoted as saying 'I'm not the sort of person of person to have a home help.' Worth concludes that

> ... by accepting help, an older person has to face that they have become a different sort of person, the sort of person who needs help to manage. Such situations occurred in half of the observed assessments and were all associated with practitioners' perceptions of risks not being acknowledged by clients. (page 327)

Case Study

Mrs Prince and risk (2)

Mrs Prince had another fall and suffered some grazing on her leg. She managed to get herself to her feet after about 20 minutes. The daughter was most concerned to learn about this and called the family GP. Mrs Prince was embarrassed to be the centre of such attention and said that it might be an idea to get a portable alarm system. The daughter explained to the GP that the risks were becoming more and more worrying and persuaded both her mother and the GP to refer to the social services. The talk, once again, is of a home care package and a possible move to sheltered accommodation.

Research carried out in this area by Lindow and Morris (1995) concluded that:

> Community care workers face pressures to minimise risks to those with whom they work …. Such pressures can get in the way of the person's own preferences being acted upon and may lead to action being taken which inhibits their ability to make choices.(pages 31–2)

We have argued that, in recent years, risk has moved to the foreground of care practice. We have also argued that it is a complex, subjective and 'slippery' concept. The sources of risk are many and varied. It is not always easy to establish in a clear, unambiguous way. Having identified risk, what to do next is not always straightforward either. This doesn't mean to say that risk shouldn't be uppermost in the assessor's mind. However, careful consideration needs to be given to certain questions. These are:

- What is the nature of the risk(s) being assessed?
- Who is saying it's a risk?
- Who is it a risk for?
- What tools, methods or other specialist opinion is available for the assessor to analyse or quantify the risk?
- If a risk is established what do official guidance or agency operational instructions say about what steps should be taken? Is there, for example, a legal power or duty to act?
- Whose responsibility is it to manage the risk?
- Should someone with mental capacity be free to live with any risks they choose to, however harmful or dangerous this may seem to those around them?
- How should the risks identified in the case of someone without mental capacity be managed?
- If there is no overall consensus about either the extent or nature of a risk or the best way of managing it, what legal, practice or moral framework will inform decision-making?

The way forward

A realistic approach to this complex area can best be summed up by Alaszewski (2002). He is referring to an article that Hazel Kemshall published in 2000 when he concludes:

> There is great merit in Kemshall's approach. She both recognises differences in assessment of risk and argues that effective risk management requires mutual respect and negotiation. While public and service users have become cynical about expert assessment of risk and are less willing to take them 'for granted', they are still willing to accept and trust these assessments if their own perceptions are acknowledged, and if they are involved in the process of decision-making and risk management. [Alaszewski (2002) in Bytheway *et al* (eds)]

⊃ Check your understanding

1 Explain why it is hard to come to one, agreed definition of risk.

2 Give an example where an assessor and a client might not share the same perception of risk.

3 How does your agency define risk?

4 What guidelines do you have for managing risk?

The context of assessment

We discussed earlier that assessment always takes place within a context of some kind or another. In reality, there are several interrelated contexts. We know that assessments don't happen 'spontaneously' or in 'a vacuum'. There is always a history, a reason and a purpose. The assessor themselves operates within a variety of different contexts. Apart from the legal context, the activity of assessment can be 'situated' in several overlapping contexts. The assessor needs to have a clear idea of how they are situated in order to make proper sense of what they are doing and to perform their role as professionally as they can.

Understanding the context as fully as possible helps promote assessment practices that are

- ⊃ meaningful
- ⊃ purposeful
- ⊃ holistic.
- ⊃ valid
- ⊃ effective

It prevents assessment becoming

- ⊃ superficial
- ⊃ partial
- ⊃ over-bureaucratic.
- ⊃ vague
- ⊃ ritualistic

The historical context: how does a person become a 'client'?

Usually, either the person themselves or someone professionally or personally close to them makes their situation known to a responsible agency. This can be through a variety of ways and methods.

We need to consider how, on occasions, the method and circumstances of referral 'set up' or at least colour certain aspects of the assessment to follow.

Figure 6.11 *Different contexts of making assessments*

An agency makes a decision whether to assess following someone else's decision to 'make a referral for an assessment'. Except that not everyone is familiar enough with the system to put it in those terms. Often the starting point is a situation being described with some course of action implied. A story starts to be told. What happens thereafter is a matter of interpretation, judgement and decision-making. The course of an assessment is never pre-ordained. It is difficult to say when an assessment actually starts but it would be fair to say by the time the assessor and 'assessee' first meet it's already started.

It might have become apparent that assessments are not of an individual but of a situation. What is going on 'around' the person – the context – is all relevant in some way. We would suggest that it is seldom the case that an assessor embarks on an assessment with a completely open mind. Smale and Tuson (1993) advocate developing a 'neutral perspective', one 'outside the network' under assessment. Whilst it is easy to understand the rationale behind this point of view we would argue that complete neutrality is unattainable. The assessor, like the person referred, is also situated in a context. They are not a free agent, neither are they insulated from a range of contextual factors – some of their own and some of the person being assessed.

Other contexts

It will have become apparent that it is important to be able to situate an assessment in its rightful context. Learning more about the different background factors allows you to learn how the events have unfolded, what decisions have led to referral, who the interested parties are, whose agenda is being pursued and so on. There are, however, other important contextual factors that we want to highlight here.

This is because there are features about each assessment that can create tensions, problems and dilemmas for assessors. Being aware of them helps you prevent them from distorting or invalidating both the process and outcome of an assessment.

Personal context

In many official texts on assessment the assessor is largely anonymous or invisible. It is the person on whom the assessment is carried out who is the focus of interest and the object of analysis. An assessor is more than a robotic 'putter into practice' of guidelines, they are a human being and a social actor with their

Figure 6.12 *An assessment has to be set in the right context*

own unique identity, values, views and feelings. It is neither possible nor desirable to completely divorce the 'professional' self from the 'personal' self. Too much 'role playing' by the assessor can lead to a lack of authenticity and genuineness.

> If those carrying out assessments and subsequent care management are to relate to their fellow citizens as 'partners' rather than as 'clients' then it is important that care managers do not fall into the trap of 'role-playing' their part in the relationship. It is essential that workers do not approach these relationships as a faceless representative of their agency but as a genuine human being. [Smale and Tuson (1993), page 48]

Each assessor inevitably brings something of themselves to assessments they are involved in. Exactly what that is cannot be stated simply here. It is for each individual to reflect on. The primary role of this section is to raise awareness rather than give instruction.

In Chapter 3 we discussed the values that inform policy and practice. There are a myriad of interrelated factors that shape us and make us who we are. Our perspective on life – work included – is influenced by a complex interplay of factors such as our background, our gender, our age, our ethnicity, sexual orientation, religious beliefs and life events such as death and divorce.

If we return to the idea of intersubjectivity then we are back to assessment as a negotiated process, a coming together of different perspectives. A story is told, heard, interpreted, retold again, reformulated, written down. The assessor can never be neutral in this process. One's own personal context is important for a variety of reasons. It will affect how we feel about the assessment, for example

⟳ whether we are confident, anxious, fearful, complacent, distracted or over-involved

- how patient we are

- how tolerant we are

- how focused on the other person as an individual we are

- what we are 'projecting' on to their situation

- what judgements we are making about the person and their situation based on things that we have personal experience of.

Figure 6.13 *A personal context of assessment*

Think it over

Write down brief notes on what your reaction (feelings and thoughts) would be were you to be required to assess a situation which involves

- dementia
- domestic violence
- a Moslem female
- a Jehovah's Witness female
- a personality disorder
- two older gay men.

- cancer
- deafness
- a Hindu man
- alcohol abuse
- a former prisoner

If possible exchange your comments with another. It would be surprising if your reactions were exactly the same. We are bound to be more relaxed and comfortable about some issues and more anxious and apprehensive about others. The important thing is to be aware that our 'personal' context is as important as the other contexts we work within, knowing the case history, the agency setting we work in and so on.

Agency context

As we discussed earlier one's role and responsibilities as an assessor are determined by the particular agency you work for. We can only emphasise again the importance of workers having as clear as possible an idea of what the roles and responsibilities of their particular agency are. Be clear *why* you are assessing, *what* the agency policies are, and on *what basis* the agency operates. For example, is it statutory, private or voluntary? You need to be aware of the framework of official and legislative guidance that you're working within.

Being clear on these points can make you aware that legislative and other policy directives can create their own conflicts and tensions. These need to be looked at and worked out professionally.

Dilemmas and conflicts

An example of this is the emergence since the mid-1990s of a range of policies that stress the need for social care agencies to take the needs of carers into account. 'Caring for the carer' has found expression in several ways: the National Carers Strategy, carer's assessments, Direct Payments for carers and so on. Workers have discovered that carers and the people they care for are not 'an item' whose needs, views and opinions are identical, in fact it is more likely that the opposite is the case. This can present problems for agencies. For example, if a worker carrying out an assessment with someone offers their carer a carer's assessment, should it be the same assessor who carries out both assessments? Clearly, this could easily place the assessor in an uncomfortable and confusing position.

Another potential conflict for workers can be in situations where some form of 'abuse' could be said to be taking place. Official guidance on protecting vulnerable adults is covered by the Department of Health publication *No Secrets*. This is covered more fully in the chapter on adult protection (Chapter 7). These guidelines identify six main forms of abuse. Two are defined as follows:

- ↄ *Psychological abuse*, including emotional abuse, threats of harm or abandonment, deprivation of contact, humiliation, blaming, controlling, intimidation, coercion, harassment, verbal abuse, isolation or withdrawal from services or supportive networks.
- ↄ *Neglect and acts of omission*, including ignoring medical or physical care needs, failure to provide access to appropriate health, social care or educational services, the withholding of the necessities of life, such as medication, adequate nutrition and heating.

Sometimes the 'abuser' is themselves vulnerable and in need of care. The case study below raises some of these difficult issues.

Case Study

A dilemma

Roger Macintosh is a 76-year-old man with Parkinson's disease. He lives with his 75-year-old wife Dawn. Mr Macintosh's condition has progressed to the point where he now needs help with all of the activities of daily living. His wife is his only carer. Mr Macintosh falls frequently and the latest fall led to the Macintoshes being referred for assessment by their GP. As an assessor you establish that Mr Macintosh doesn't want any services. He describes himself as a 'private man' and says that he is happy for his wife to continue looking after his care needs at home. Mrs Macintosh is clearly stressed and bitter about having to devote so much time and energy to her husband. She says 'I have no life of my own now.' However, she too is reluctant to have 'strangers in the house'. She wonders whether her husband might have to go into a home but clearly is in two minds about this saying 'When you marry them it is for better *and* for worse.' She describes her situation as 'Whereas before I was a wife, now I am just a skivvy.' She finds it hard to help her husband up after his falls. She already had a heart problem and now has persistent backache. Mrs Macintosh is also on tranquillisers prescribed for her 'bad nerves'.

She takes you to one side and tells you that now she routinely leaves her husband on the floor – sometimes for days when he falls. She only referred to the GP on this occasion because her daughter strongly urged her to. His bedroom floor reeks of urine. She knows it's wrong but can't see why she should 'bust a gut hauling him up all the time'. It is clear that there is an obvious punitive side to her behaviour.

Questions

1 As the assessor, who is your client in this situation?

2 Do you take the comments of Mr and Mrs Macintosh at face value?

3 Do you believe there is abuse going on and what, if anything, should you do about it?

4 What guidance would you refer to, to help you make progress with this situation?

The multi-disciplinary context

Chapter 5 deals in more depth with the whole issue of collaborative working. As we have seen, much of the focus of recent policy on health and social care has emphasised the need for the 'professionals' involved to work in partnership. A great deal of evidence has been generated to show the benefits of joint working, but much less discussion has been devoted to why such partnerships aren't always successful. Simply instructing people to 'work together' won't necessarily make it happen effectively. Problems can occur at either a personal or institutional level. If we concentrate on the personal level, there are several ways in which 'professional partners' can both regard and relate to one another. Importantly, each 'partner' is not a 'professional' in exactly the same way, with all that this means in terms of their professional autonomy, status, knowledge and training. Few GPs, for instance, see social care workers as their professional peers. Partnerships can be weakened or distorted by lack of trust, lack of respect, jealousy, rivalry, deference, and a lack of clarity about the other's role, powers and responsibilities. Some of the difficulties with partnership working come about from the confusion within the field of social work and social care itself, about such basic questions as what the core tasks are, who should carry out the tasks, how the tasks should be carried out and several others. This is not the time to go deeply into this long-running issue but it is relevant to the discussion on assessment. Historically, the low emphasis on training in social care, shorter qualification periods, and lower pay have led to the professional self-concept of social care workers being generally less clearly defined and 'weaker' than those in health care.

Think it over

1   Think about and identify the other main health and social care professionals who you might involve in your assessment of clients?

2   Write down in no more than two or three sentences what their particular skills expertise are. Do the same for your job role.

Cultural differences when health and social care work together

We focus more on the whole issue of different agencies working together in Chapter 5. But it is also worth talking about it briefly here. The work of each 'profession' is founded on its own body of knowledge, value base and discourses (language and practices). Traditionally, the medical model of care has informed the approach of health workers whereas social work has adopted the social model.

The *medical model* involves the understanding of a person's problem, behaviour or condition in terms of illness, diagnosis and treatment.

Social workers use the term 'medical model', often critically, to summarise what they consider to be the narrow, even oppressive, interpretation that medical practitioners and other health professionals sometimes apply to a client's condition. To put it simply, in the medical model the man in bed three with a ruptured spleen becomes just that, a ruptured spleen. His feelings, his opinions, what the effect is of his illness on his job and family are all ignored. The medical model concentrates on repairing that spleen.

Think it over

We have briefly summarised the medical and social models.

1   What for you are the chief differences? Write down the differences under the following headings.

	Medical model	Social model
Attitude to the person		
Type of language used		
Factors that cause disability		
Issues that the professional should attend to		

2   Which model more informs the work of your agency? Give examples.

The *social model* of care not only situates people in their social context but it also emphasises the importance of social factors in preventing people with physical impairments participating in normal, everyday activities rather than simply focusing on the illness or disability to the exclusion of all else.

It is therefore important to recognise that while the argument for multi-disciplinary working is a strong one – not least on the grounds of client-centredness – there are potential difficulties and conflicts within multi-disciplinary working that can, at times, seep into and affect the assessment process. The assessor needs to be aware of these in order that they are not allowed to affect their assessment negatively. See Chapter 5 for a fuller discussion of these issues and many more that are relevant to the whole issue of collaborative working.

⊃ Check your understanding

1 Identify *five* different contexts in which an assessment can take place.
2 Explain why an assessor should make themselves aware of the historical context of an assessment they are involved in.
3 Why should assessors be aware of falling into the trap of 'role-playing' their part in the relationship?
4 Give *two* ways in which our personal context can influence our assessment.
5 Discuss an example of how an assessor might find themselves facing 'role conflict'.
6 Explain how there may be cultural differences between a social care worker and a health professional.

Models of assessment and assessment tools

Deficit model

Throughout most of the history of social care the approach taken by workers to assessment (either implicitly or explicitly) has been to concentrate on what the individual being assessed could not do, the abilities they lacked, their moral and practical failings, in short – people's deficits.

The casework approach dominant throughout the 20th century had its origins in the 19th century philanthropic tradition, whereby voluntary visitors would visit poor families and dispense aid based on the principle of their being 'deserving' or 'non-deserving'. The visitor would make careful investigation into the habits and lifestyle of those seeking help. If the individual was considered to be of bad character, e.g. a drunkard, lazy or immoral, then they would be deemed 'undeserving' and denied charitable aid. If the individual accepted the error of their ways and was prepared to be reformed, then they would be considered 'deserving' and help would be offered. This approach essentially regarded the problem as constituted in the defective make-up of the individual (individual pathology) and took little account of wider cultural, social and economic factors. Moral judgements about people's lifestyles were at the heart of early social work assessment. For example, to 'allow' oneself to become a single parent and slip into poverty was regarded as sinful, immoral and, basically, undeserving. It was the source of much social condemnation and stigma.

Attitudes have changed since those times. Whilst it is possible to argue that social work is still essentially a 'practical-moral' activity [Parton and O'Byrne (2000)], a different value base has emerged organised around a different set of guiding principles. Social work in the latter decades of the 20th century, has consciously adopted a 'non-judgemental' stance towards most lifestyle issues. Nevertheless, the traditional casework assessment continued to focus almost exclusively on an individual's deficits or 'lacks'. The tradition of much assessment in social work has been 'hunting out the negative'.

Milner and O'Byrne (2002) writing about the influence of clinical psychology on social work with children and families observe:

> ... the identification of deficit of one sort or another became a central thrust of assessments, which set out to study problems in great depth, seeking explanations and remedies. Much of the discussion with service users was/is problem focused and service users came to learn to talk knowledgeably about problems and identify with them, such as 'I am an alcoholic'. The main engagement was with the problem rather than the person and often the pictures that emerged were unbalanced, failing to bring to life the strengths and coping abilities of people.

> Guidelines and formats for assessments were also biased towards the negatives and may have strengthened the pathologising tendency further. (page 263)

As social care and social work has developed and moved on, this 'pathologising tendency' has been acknowledged and conscious attempts have been made to correct the tendency to focus on the individual's weaknesses, faults and failings to the exclusion of all else. However, we have to accept that our cultural heritage in this respect is hard to throw off completely and we can easily slip into an unconscious deficit model.

Figure 6.14 *The deficit model assesses people according to what they can't do*

Think it over

1 What problems can you see with the model of assessment above?

2 How might your approach differ?

Further Research

This next section draws extensively on the research and writing of Gerald Smale and Graham Tuson. In 1993, at the point where the NHS and Community Care Act 1990 ushered in a whole new way of working with vulnerable adults, Smale and Tuson published, with the government's approval, a book titled *Empowerment, Assessment, Care Management and the Skilled Worker.* In it they distinguished between three broad approaches to assessment. We will summarise relevant parts here but it is recommended that you use research skills and track down a copy of this book and read through it. It will have relevance whatever context you undertake assessments in.

Where might be the best place to find this text? It was published by HMSO in 1993. Smale and Tuson's three models of assessment are:

➲ Questioning

➲ Procedural

➲ Exchange

The questioning model

Broadly speaking, the questioning model assumes that the worker is 'an expert in people, or both' (page16). The skilled worker working within this approach adopts an orientation towards their 'subject' which is attentive, respectful and aims to be empathetic. The worker forms an assessment on the information provided, using their professional knowledge and expertise. The assessor's role in this model has been likened to that of Sherlock Holmes, meaning that the expertise is all with the 'skilled professional' in forming an accurate assessment and taking the appropriate action.

The questioning model is a traditional approach in that it places the assessor in the expert role and concentrates on the 'dependency needs of the individual' (page 17).

Apart from the assumption of expert knowledge about somebody else's life, there are other problems with this approach. One obvious source of difficulty can be a technical one – with the very questions used.

➲ Questions may be limited to the worker's agenda

➲ The language in which the questions are couched may not be fully understandable to the people being interviewed.

Figure 6.15 *The questioning model sees the assessor as the expert*

➲ Too much closed questioning can limit the information received.

➲ Questions may be inappropriately eurocentric or ethnocentric

➲ Questions can too easily predetermine a way of looking at things. For example, 'What is wrong with you that prevents you going upstairs to the toilet?' creates a bias towards a medical model whereas, 'What change/adaptation to your property is required in order for you to get to the toilet?' implies a social model.

➲ It is not always easy for all those involved to establish which questions are the really important ones and others less so.

The procedural model

The questioning model assumes a degree of professional expertise and autonomy on behalf of the assessor. That is to say, the questions asked can largely be of the assessor's own choosing. In the procedural model, the assessor is very much seen as an agency functionary. As Smale and Tuson say

> … many workers will operate within given agency guidelines and criteria for the allocation of scarce resources and will be expected to gather specific information as a basis for judgements …. In this the goal of the assessment is to gather information to see if the client 'fits', or meets, certain criteria that will 'make them eligible for services'. Those defining the criteria for eligibility, in effect pre-allocating services for generally identified need, make the judgement as to what sort of person should get which resources. The worker's task is to identify the specific people who match the appropriate degree of need defined within the categories of service available and to exclude those not eligible. (page 19)

Many assessors working in statutory agencies have observed that the 'care management process' can tend easily towards the procedural model. They would argue that it has 'deskilled' the assessment process with its pre-coded forms, checklists, eligibility criteria and narrow scope. In its defence, if conducted properly, assessment within this model can be

- more cost effective
- a more equitable allocation of resources – everything is standardised
- a more efficient use of worker time – it asks the minimum number of questions necessary to determine eligibility
- relatively unobtrusive into people's lives – the obvious bureaucratic nature of the assessment can mean that people feel less threatened by it. There is no 'unnecessary' probing.

Other advocates of the procedural model claim that it is more 'honest' and doesn't raise false hopes. Basically, they ask why 'talk the talk' of a full 'needs-led' assessment if the assessment will, in reality, not only lead to one or two of those needs being seriously considered but also a limited service response.

What tends to make the procedural model unsatisfactory for many practitioners is that the emphasis on bureaucratic procedures is at odds with notions of person-centredness, holism, choice, and user participation. It is too agency centred. People at the point of needing any kind of social care assessment are generally vulnerable for some reason or another, their lives have become disrupted, but they are not given any freedom in the procedural model to express themselves or tell their story. If they try to, it is likely to be regarded as 'irrelevant information'.

Figure 6.16 *This model of assessment leans more towards a bureaucratic approach*

What the models described so far also seem to have in common is that they all assume it is possible, by using the correct form of questioning, to get to the 'facts of the situation' and that there is an underlying 'truth' to be uncovered. Milner and O'Byrne (2002) make this observation:

> In line with the medical model, these assessments are usually made before any intervention takes place, are based on past performance and past reports, and perhaps presented as once-and-for-all judgements, lacking an appropriate uncertainty.

> A further worrying aspect of such assessments is the suggestion that people are fixed in their problem identities, with a resultant lack of self-determination, and people are often categorised and denied the individualisation with which earlier social workers credited them. (page 53)

The exchange model

This model assumes that services users

⊃ are expert in themselves

and assumes that the care worker

⊃ has expertise in the process of problem solving with others

⊃ understands and shares perceptions of problems and their management

⊃ gets agreement about who will do what to support whom

⊃ takes responsibility for arriving at the optimum resolution of problems within the constraints of available resources and the willingness of participants to contribute. [Smale and Tuson (1993), page 18]

This approach 'typically includes more people and takes longer'. It recognises professional expertise in the assessor but sees an important part of that expertise in 'establishing partnerships' and facilitating participation. The agenda is neither strictly prescribed by the assessor nor an agency's guidelines. Others' views are taken into account and this widening out of participation can help in mobilising all potential resources.

If pursued properly, the exchange model of assessment is more likely to lead to attainment of key goals laid down in official guidance [Department of Health (1989)]. They are goals that see people

⊃ living as normal a life as possible

⊃ achieving maximum possible independence

⊃ having a greater say in how they live their lives and the services they need to help them do so.

The exchange does have its negative aspects. As mentioned, it is likely to be more time-consuming than the other models discussed so far. It is also argued by critics that the notions of mutual respect and equal status between assessor and client embodied in this model are illusory – a myth cherished by workers who are uncomfortable with the authority invested in them. Critics say that a model that puts so much emphasis on listening to others' views can blur issues of accountability. They argue that vulnerable people and their carers want and *expect* professionals to take a lead. If people could sort their own problems out then they

Figure 6.17 *You need to be careful not to assume that because a person doesn't say what they think that they are satisfied with things as they are*

wouldn't need a professional assessment in the first place. These are the potential difficulties and complexities with the exchange model. Dependency, leadership and power issues are clearly part of that. For this reason, it is important not to take too simplistic a view of this model of assessment, especially around issues of participation and self-determination. Because someone doesn't clearly articulate their views or express their needs in a conventional way, this doesn't necessarily mean that they are perfectly satisfied and at no risk to themselves or others.

The constructive model of assessment – more 'Colombo than Sherlock Holmes'

Oh and sir, just one more question. There's something I can't quite figure out.

In their book *Constructive Social Work*, Parton and O'Byrne outlined what they called 'constructive' assessment. It links to several of the themes discussed earlier in this chapter. That is to say, that assessment is essentially seen as an *intersubjective* exercise. It acknowledges that even the most 'basic' assessment is a potentially complex and ambiguous process. 'Facts' may be slippery, what is said one day may be different the next. The assessor is not some kind of all-knowing expert scientifically completing his or her 'diagnosis' before drawing up his or her 'treatment' plan. Rather (and this is the Colombo connection), the assessor is helping the client to tell their story. There is a conversational, 'two-way' feel to the experience. Parton and O'Byrne claim that the quality of assessments would actually improve if those doing the assessing gave up searching for 'false certainty' and instead, gave an honest account of how they were struggling for understanding (page 135). The assessor should try to shed the idea that they are some kind of expert analyst – putting their client in a 'box' – instead they should aim to be experts in drawing people out and gaining their trust. Nothing should be 'closed down'; all parties' perceptions of the problem should be sought in an on-going process.

It would be a gross misunderstanding of this approach to believe that it virtually leaves the practitioner out of the process and simply lets the client get on with it. Such a misunderstanding – deliberate or otherwise – deskills and deprofessionalises assessment.

The assessor's skills lie more in their ability to develop solutions *with* the person they are assessing. It is not claiming that the practitioner isn't any kind of expert. It is saying that the worker is not the *only* expert. Clients and their families are often more expert than us in the problem. However, we may be more expert in thinking about solution-development. We use our skills to draw people out, get them to look at the problems in different ways, offer some possibilities and then build solutions with people.

We can see then that the constructive approach to assessment seeks for a 'balance of strengths and deficits'. It also wants to get more closely to the particular meanings people attach to their situations.

You are your dominant story – 'resistance is futile'

For any individual's situation in life, there will not only be different strands to their story; there will be different stories. The assessor must not be content with taking the dominant story about someone as the 'narrative truth'. The Department of Health emphasises this very point:

> A weakness of many assessments was that they failed to present an overall, holistic picture of users and their needs. [Department of Health/Social Services Inspectorate (2000), page 30]

In health and social care, an individual's 'narrative' can too easily become reduced to a set of well-established and oft repeated 'facts'. Individual service users inevitably become situated in different discourses; particularly those of their informal networks and those of the professionals. 'Facts' about people inevitably become bandied about and shared by those who are involved around them. Sometimes these 'facts' are written in official files, but often they remain at the level of what people say and think about that person. Often, the individual will come to accept – even 'author' – his or her own dominant narrative. This can be for a range of reasons. It may be for a 'quiet life', or because they genuinely feel that others know best; it may be even that they have come to believe that that is all there is to their lives. All too often, people become summed up in a few well-polished and often repeated phrases. A typical example might be

> Mr Paterson, who is 86, a charming man, mildly confused, fiercely independent, never really got over the death of his wife, likes the occasional drink. Never been one to be overly concerned about personal hygiene. Daughter does all his housework and shopping. Yes, that's Mr Paterson.

We often slip into this mode of thinking about clients and it can make them seem very one-dimensional.

Think it over

Think about a family member. Write about them in a maximum of ten sentences. How does your writing reflect them as a person, their personality, background, likes, dislikes and so on?

It is salutary to think that for many clients to have a ten-sentence story circulating about them would be an indulgence. For much of the time people are often reduced to the kind of three-sentence characters like Mr Paterson in our 'case study'.

Parton and O'Byrne argue that

> …the dominant story always has important 'lived experiences' missing. A sense of 'persons engaged in action' may be missing and exceptional behaviours that contradict the dominant story are unnoticed if we listen only to the dominant story. Without a belief in exceptions and a search for exceptions, data will be misleading. (page 141)

This approach aims to challenge the dominant story. It is suggested that a broader, rounded, picture of our client will emerge if we

⊃ come from a position of 'not knowing'

⊃ are able to listen, and

⊃ as part of our discussion, engage them in 'problem-free' talk.

A useful way of taking this approach further is for assessors to use 'scale sheets' to enable people to tell their story in such a way that it picks up on the nuances, contradictions and complexities that might be missed. We discuss the use of scale sheets in more detail in the next section on assessment tools.

Finally, to return to the 'Colombo' connection. Those of us over a certain age will remember this TV detective and his unique style, others will wonder what is so distinctive about his approach. Colombo had the confidence in his skills and ability to appear diffident and unsure. He didn't cover up his confusion or ignorance. His skilled use of questions and his informal manner prompted others to talk. Rather than appearing as a superior know it all, he wondered out loud, scratched his head and gradually nudged his interviewees along. Obviously we mustn't take the analogy too far, after all social care workers are not out to convict their clients! Rather, we are advocating an assessment style that actually gives the client their voice and allows them to tell their own story in their own words.

Assessment tools

Ask most people to say what a tool is and the chances are they will bring implements such as hammers, saws and drills to mind. The common meaning of the term 'tool' is associated with manual or mechanical work.

It is worth acknowledging this because many workers in health and social care don't always regard themselves as 'tool users'. They struggle with the idea of using a tool because it appears to be transplanted from another type of work. However, we have to accept that nowadays the term 'tool' has taken on a broader meaning, and in this context refers to a range of devices designed to improve the assessment process. It shouldn't be regarded as just another example of unnecessary paperwork. Appropriate use of assessment tools can be very helpful for the person being assessed by getting a more accurate picture of their overall situation. They can be of use in assisting with risk analysis for example.

In guidance issued by the Department of Health in 2002 an assessment tool is defined as

a collection of scales, questions and other information, to provide a rounded picture of an individual's needs and related circumstances.

The Social Care Institute of Excellence Best Practice Guide (www.elsc.org.uk) explained that

Assessment tools are standardised systems that help to provide an equitable and fair approach. They can be the means whereby individual and particular assessments contribute to the overall picture ….

Tools include scales, checklists and interview schedules. They must be culturally sensitive, reliable and valid if they are to inform professional judgement.

Further Research

Think about your own agency. What 'tools' do you use to help complete assessments? Are there checklists, scales and interview schedules? Do you use other systems?

If possible, compare your findings with someone with another agency. Are there any differences?

It is highly probable that you would have identified that your agency uses a particular form in order to record its assessments. In some people's minds, the assessment begins and ends with the form. This reflects a very narrow and limited approach to the assessment process. As the Social Care Institute of Excellence Best Practice Guide states

> The standardised systems used within social work departments are usually not tools in the accepted sense, that are tested in terms of the quality or effectiveness of the information they provide about an individual's state. They are more often an administrative record, more likely to measure output and workload than outcome for an individual service user.

Scales

Department of Health (2002) guidance on the single assessment process describes an assessment scale as

> a means of identifying, and possibly gauging the extent of, a specific health or care condition such as ability for personal care, mobility, tissue viability, depression, and cognitive impairment.

Scales can have application across all service user groups. Parton and O'Byrne (2000) include several in their book. An example is set out on page 333.

They acknowledge that

> many service users say that the scale questions are the most encouraging part of the process; yet, they feel odd and mechanical to workers when they start to use them. (page 105)

Think it over

What do you think? Do you feel comfortable with the use of tools and scales as part of the assessment process?

CITY COLLEGE
LEARNING RESOURCE SERVICE

Please answer with a tick	Not at all	Just a little	Pretty much	Very much
1 Talks about his/her situation				
2 Talks about other things				
3 Likes him/herself				
4 Expresses anger about the past				
5 Makes decisions				
6 Interested in the future				
7 Sleeps OK				
8 Shakes hands with confidence				
9 Takes safety measures				
10 Chooses supportive relationships				
11 Relaxes				
12 Accepts criticism				
13 Accepts praise				
14 Feels part of a family				
15 Stands up for herself				
16 Keeps smart				
17 Goes to work or school				
18 Goes to social events				
19 Cares for relatives				
20 Eats well				
21 Copes with situations				
22 Meets new friends				
23 Laughs				
24 Has his/her own thoughts				
25 Feels in control				

NAME: _____ DATE: _____

Figure 6.18 *Scale for reclaiming life after drugs*

If a scale is valid, reliable and culturally sensitive, it can ensure that all parties involved can be more confident about the assessment having a beneficial outcome. It also acknowledges that people's situations are seldom 'black or white' but are often subtle and complex 'shades of grey'. It is important to see the use of scales as something that can enrich the assessment process and not simply the sum total of the assessment. The Department of Health cautions that a literal and narrow interpretation of scales should be avoided. Assessors should see the use of scales that broaden the discussion rather than narrow it.

Government initiatives

The Labour government set out its 'modernisation agenda' for social services in 1998. This applied across all service user groups. Good assessment practices feature in all official guidance. The Framework for the Assessment of Children in Need and their Families was launched in April 2000. This guidance emphasised, amongst other things, that good assessment was at the heart of the work. It stresses the importance of collaborative working and the importance of inter-agency, inter-disciplinary assessment practice. It also wants to make assessment more systematic and evidence based. The Framework for the Assessment of Children in Need and their Families sets out a range of important principles underpinning the assessment framework. In total, they

- are child centred
- are rooted in child development
- are ecological in their approach
- ensure equality of opportunity
- involve working with children and families
- build on strengths as well identify difficulties
- are inter-agency in their approach to assessment and the provision of services
- are a continuing, not a single event
- are carried out in parallel with other action and providing services
- are grounded in evidence-based knowledge.

[Department of Health (2000), page 10]

The training pack that accompanies the guidance incorporates a range of questionnaires and scales which practitioners are encouraged to use in their assessments. Assessors working with children and families should make a point of familiarising themselves with the framework, Working Together to Safeguard Children (1999), and any recent updating of either of these documents. This guidance clearly sets out the kinds of tools that practitioners should incorporate into their assessments as well as the processes that should be followed.

Single assessment process

Those working with older people need to be aware of the single assessment process. This major initiative was outlined in the National Service Framework for Older People. Anticipating its introduction in 2002, the Department of Health explains that

The single assessment process applies to health and social services…It recognises that many older people have health and social care needs, and that agencies need to work together so that assessment and subsequent care planning are person-centred, effective and co-ordinated.

It is claimed that the implementation will ensure that

- the scale and depth of assessment is kept in proportion to older person's needs
- agencies do not duplicate each other's assessments
- professionals contribute to assessments in the most effective way.

Local authorities are encouraged to 'explore and adopt' different assessment tools in producing their own overall single assessment process. However, guidance stresses that 'older people's views, strengths and abilities should be to the fore throughout assessment and that the contribution older people make to their assessment should be made explicit by the tool'.

Further Research

To see the full range of assessment tools and scales, access the relevant Department of Health web pages www.doh.gov.uk./scg/sap/. This will give you a better idea of what has already been developed.

Fair access to care

This is another important initiative originating from *Modernising Social Services* (1998). It has changed how assessments are carried out in statutory agencies. Fair Access to Care was implemented with effect from April 2003. The purpose of this change was to ensure that local authorities showed

- ⊃ consistency in the way people's needs are assessed
- ⊃ clear objectives, based on the overriding need to promote independence, which should apply to all stages in the process
- ⊃ a common understanding of risk assessment on which to base decisions about services
- ⊃ regular reviews to make sure the services continue to meet objectives.

The framework is based on individuals' needs and associated risks to independence, and includes four eligibility bands – critical, substantial, moderate and low. When placing individuals in these bands, the guidance stresses that councils should not only identify immediate needs but also needs that would worsen for the lack of timely help.

The guidance stresses that:

Assessment should be carried out in such a way, and be sufficiently transparent, for individuals to

- ⊃ gain a better understanding of their situation
- ⊃ identify the options that are available for managing their own lives
- ⊃ understand the basis on which decisions are reached.

The 'modernising agenda' launched by the government in 1998 is based around certain key principles: person-centredness, fair access, national consistency, promoting independence being some of the most important. Workers in statutory organisations will have had the national guidelines interpreted for them and placed into operational guidelines by their employing organisations. Forms may have changed and practices revised. Hopefully, training will have been given to ensure that practitioners understand the principles underlying changes in policy and practice. In any event, workers should always try to understand the policy context in which changes take place. For one thing, it helps when explaining the process to people being assessed. Lastly, it is worth restating an important point.

This is that whatever the policy context, whatever new framework for assessment is introduced, whatever assessment tools and scales are incorporated in the assessment process, the key part of the process is two (or more) human beings coming together attempting to communicate with each other and to gain a common understanding of what the issues are.

⊃ Check your understanding

1 Give a brief summary of the deficit model.

2 Write a few notes which outline the main points of the questioning and procedural exchange models. Write down advantages and disadvantages of each.

3 Why is it important not simply to accept the 'dominant story' about somebody?

4 Identify *three* key aspects of the 'constructive approach' to assessment.

5 How do both the Department of Health and SCIE define an assessment tool?

6 What, according to the DoH, is an assessment scale?

7 What is the rationale behind the single assessment process?

8 What is the official purpose behind Fair Access to Care?

Assessment, empowerment and anti-discriminatory practice

In Chapter 3 we looked at the value base of care work. As we have seen, the 'values climate' in which care takes place today emphasises several important principles. These would include person-centredness, respect, user-involvement, and promoting independence. In more recent years much has been spoken of the 'empowerment' of the service user. At the same time, the principle of anti-discriminatory practice has both been promoted by successive governments and embraced by organisations and agencies within the social work and care fields. It is tempting to assume that because these principles are much talked and written about in social care that it can be taken for granted that they now occur 'naturally' and that we can take such practices for granted.

Figure 6.19 *Don't take it for granted that carers are committed to the principles of anti-discrimination and empowerment*

It is not possible to do full justice to the large body of literature that has been written on these two important concepts. Suffice to say that there has been much argument and debate about the true meaning of these terms and, more importantly, what the implications are for practitioners. In this section, we first discuss whether ideas of empowerment can realistically be related to assessment. Then we discuss how the process of assessment can promote anti-discriminatory practice.

Empowerment

Empowerment has become a fashionable 'buzz word' in many areas of life over the last decade or so. It has certainly become a term that is frequently used in the field of care. For example, the guidance by Smale and Tuson discussed earlier and commissioned by the Department of Health was called *Empowerment, Assessment, Care Management and the Skilled Worker*.

Think it over

1 What is your understanding of the term empowerment?

2 Give examples of what you consider to be empowering practice.

3 If possible, compare your ideas with another.

Empowerment is very much a 'contested' term. That is to say, what it means exactly is the subject of debate and disagreement. As such, it has to be acknowledged that there is no single agreement on what empowering practice is exactly. Some writers regard the word 'empower' to be a much overused term, arguing that it is often used when we actually mean to 'help' or 'enable' someone to do something. Others would even argue that it is wrong to think that social care practitioners can actually 'empower' anyone in any meaningful sense. Sometimes we use the term 'empower' when all we are doing is providing a limited choice of options to someone to enable them to make up their own mind.

Despite these reservations, the goal of empowerment is considered to be a stated objective for many care organisations and therefore we need to reflect on how assessment practices may or may not impact on this goal.

In *Empowerment in Community Care*, Ray Jack (1995) argues that power cannot simply be given by social workers to powerless members of the community – it is they who have to *take* it. This is a theme taken up by Milner and O'Byrne (1998) who state that

> Social workers are not in a position to *give* people power, and their aim to *help reduce* the powerlessness that individuals and groups experience is likely to be limited by other individuals' and groups' investment in power positions *and* in the complex nature of power. (page 62)

Taking a slightly more optimistic view, Thompson (1993) states that empowerment

Involves seeking to maximise the power of clients and give them as much control as possible over their circumstances. It is the opposite of creating dependency and subjecting clients to agency power. (page 83)

It is clear the issues of empowerment and disempowerment are complex and go far beyond the field of social care. There are wider structural issues such as poverty, age, gender, race and so on that need to be taken into consideration when understanding how power operates in society. Milner and O'Byrne (1998) claim, 'it is naïve to underestimate the difficulties in operationalising empowering strategies'. Nevertheless, however simplistic and naïve it may be to believe that a worker in a care setting can easily 'empower' someone through their practice, this doesn't mean that we should completely ignore the issue of power imbalance in our relationships with those we assess.

Whilst it might be difficult to genuinely 'empower' someone through our practice in the broader sense of the term, that's not to say we shouldn't be aware of the likelihood that bad practices can actually further *disempower* already vulnerable people.

Avoidance of disempowering practices is as important as the adoption of empowering practices.

In his description of the 'disabling relationship', Jack (1995) cautions that in this form of professional relationship

> Professionals use their power to protect their own interests by exaggerating the value of their skills and knowledge and restricting access to them. Their power is founded on expertise in assessing and defining problems – offering solutions which require the skills only they possess. (page 14)

Talking about those on the 'receiving end' of assessment Jack claims that

> …it is simply right and proper that their views be given an airing and then taken seriously. No romantic view that clients and patients 'know best' is offered, but we do share the belief that the insights of the least powerful actors in social behaviour are as important as those of the most powerful. And if left unchecked, the voices of managers and professionals soon drown those of their clients. (page 52)

Significantly, Jack argues that 'participation is a better term than empowerment or partnership'. Maybe aiming for participation is more realistic and therefore achievable than striving for the more grand and lofty goal of 'empowerment'.

Like a supermarket marking all its products as 'new', 'improved', or 'farm fresh', indiscriminate use of the term 'empowerment' can easily mean the whole idea becomes 'debased currency' and loses all meaning. This can provoke cynicism in practitioner and client alike, and in doing so obscure the very real issue that assessors, as we have argued earlier, do have more power. They have the power to set the agenda, to define, to limit choice, to restrict access to resources and so on. This power can easily be abused without realising it.

Critically reflect on one or two of your recent assessments.

1 What factors, if any, made the person you were assessing relatively powerless?

2 Identify the points of the process where you used power.

3 What opportunities were given for the people involved in the assessment to do things another way, in a way of their choosing?

4 To what extent do you think they had 'control' over the situation?

5 How did you handle the imbalance in power between you, if there was one?

6 Would you agree that it is more realistic to aim for participation rather empowerment? If so, where do you see the difference?

The ladder of participation

Jack (1995) adapts Arnstein's concept of a 'ladder of participation' to represent the different levels of participation and involvement that a client can have in the assessor/client relationship.

Rung 8	Citizen control
Rung 7	Delegated power
Rung 6	Partnership
Rung 5	Consultation
Rung 4	Involvement
Rung 3	Keeping fully informed
Rung 2	Placation
Rung 1	Manipulation

Arnstein (1969)

Arnstein's 'ladder' was originally about local community politics. However, it provides a useful way of representing the differing degrees of power exercised by people in matters that concern them. We can adapt this idea to reflect the various types of power relationship that a social care worker can have with those they assess.

The following is an example.

Rung 1 – Manipulation This is where the assessor ensures that their agenda is followed and their interpretation of the situation is the one recorded. However, the client is nevertheless invited to sign the necessary paperwork and give their consent as if they had a say in the process.

Rung 2 – Placation This is essentially the same process as outlined above but the client is given the time to 'read through' their assessment and told they are free to raise any queries or make any amendments they want to. It is then signed. →

Rung 3 – Keeping fully informed The client is given a full written and verbal explanation of what the assessment and care planning process consists of, including the right to state their preferences and to complain if not happy at any stage.

Rung 4 – Involvement At each stage of the process the client is given information about what is involved, their rights, and what the various options are on what can be done. Their views (and the views of those around them) are actively encouraged and recorded using their own words.

Rung 5 – What comes next? Can the 'client' ever be fully in control of the process? At this level the limits to and tensions around 'empowerment' become more evident. To some extent, how much more control a person has over the process at this stage depends on the purpose and the context of the assessment. Some agencies promote varying degrees of self-assessment. However, the question remains whether this still has to conform to a format and set of criteria laid down by the assessing organisation.

Figure 6.20 *Clients need to actively participate in the relationship with the assessor*

We have argued throughout, that the assessment relationship is both a complex and dynamic one. We have also argued that for a variety of reasons, the assessor is always the more powerful person in the assessment process. The question remains, can assessment 'empower'? The answer must, to a great extent, be that it depends on what we mean by 'empower'. It could be argued that an assessment that enables a vulnerable person to live at home with a high degree of independence was an example of empowerment. However, this would omit the important issue of *how* that assessment was carried out. If decisions were made *for* and *about* that person with little or no participation by them along the way, then, in a sense, this only confirms and reinforces their powerlessness. Someone else has 'sorted them out' – however favourably.

Assessors should always be aware of power issues and, wherever possible, ensure that their practices don't disable those they assess. This requires a certain amount of openness and honesty with oneself. A starting point in the 'empowering' assessment is that the client should have as much control over the process as possible. There should be full sharing of information and a commitment to involvement and participation. Without these the person would almost certainly be disempowered. Whether with them they are positively empowered, is a matter for debate.

Anti-discriminatory practice

> Anti-discriminatory practice has … been featuring as a regular and high priority item on the social work agenda for some time now, although there sadly continues to be a great deal of misunderstanding and oversimplification of the issues. [Thompson (2001), pages 1–2]

This statement by Neil Thompson sounds a necessary note of caution to begin with. It would be impossible to do full justice to this key area in such a limited space. However, at the same time it would be wrong to conclude a chapter on assessment and not make some attempt to 'flag up' some key issues in this area, if only to give pointers for further development. Whereas the discussion around empowerment is sometimes ambiguous on such matters, there is no doubt that anti-discriminatory practice acknowledges political, cultural, social, and economic dimensions.

Anti-discriminatory practice (ADP) is an approach to social work which emphasises the various ways in which particular individuals and groups tend to be discriminated against and the need for professional practice to counter such discrimination.

The basis of discrimination

Discrimination can occur on the basis of differences arising from

- ⊃ ethnicity (racism)
- ⊃ gender (sexism)
- ⊃ class (classism)
- ⊃ age (ageism)
- ⊃ disability (disablism)
- ⊃ sexual identity (heterosexism)
- ⊃ mental health (mentalism)
- ⊃ language (linguistic oppression)

and various other less formally codified or documented forms of unfair or oppressive differentiation.

All such forms of discrimination can be seen to occur

- ⊃ at a personal level, in terms of individual attitudes and actions
- ⊃ at a cultural level, in terms of shared meanings, assumptions, values and stereotypes
- ⊃ at a structural level, in relation to the way society is organised vis-à-vis the distribution of power and life-chances.

[Thompson (1997) adapted from Davies (ed) (2000)].

As the box above indicates, anti-discriminatory practice aims to combat the various 'isms'. Milner and O'Byrne (1998) observe that

> The very real difficulties in operating anti-oppressive practice are most clearly seen when we examine the inter-relatedness and complexities of the various 'isms'. (page 63)

The trouble with ADP

There are many potential difficulties and complexities for workers getting to grips with ADP. This is partly because it involves looking at oneself critically on a personal, professional and political level. One must be prepared to both reflect on and challenge what might often be long-held views and feelings – part of what makes us 'us'! ADP training is probably most effectively carried out by experienced trainers, with other work colleagues and in a safe environment. Quite often, the mere mention of ADP can induce feelings of defensiveness, cynicism or hostility in workers. This is because people feel they are either being lectured, 'got at', blamed or made to feel guilty. All of this is counterproductive and the result can often be what Thompson (2001) calls 'colluding with the rhetoric'.

> What this means is that some people may use the right language and may make the right gestures but without any underlying commitment to the values and principles of anti-discriminatory practice. They are just going through the motions', perhaps through confusion, ignorance, or insecurity about how to practise in a genuinely anti-discriminatory way. [Thompson (2001), page 168]

The way forward

Our aim in this section is both modest and realistic. ADP cannot be covered in a few paragraphs. However, we can say that practitioners involved in assessment should, at the very least, aim to

⊃ be open-minded – the purpose of ADP is to make others' lives easier not yours harder

⊃ think seriously whether those they are assessing fall into a group that faces discrimination. There can be more than one form of discrimination obviously, and those different forms of discrimination can overlay and interact with each other

⊃ take responsibility for raising your own awareness of ADP matters. Use opportunities to go on proper ADP training, attend workshops, keep up with current debates on the subject

⊃ avoid stereotyping. Stereotyping is the process by which people lose their individuality. Someone who has been stereotyped will have a range of feelings, behaviours, impulses and other characteristics attributed to them because they happen to belong to a particular group. Stereotypes are simplifications and distortions. Stereotyped thinking leads to pre-judgements and assumptions being made about someone on the basis of a label or category rather than what they are really like as an individual.

Thompson (2001) claims that

> Ageist stereotypes can easily seduce us into making negative assumptions about older people and thus establishing a framework for discrimination and oppression. (page 107)

Practitioners can stereotype on the basis of medical categories, whether age is a factor or not. Descriptions such as 'dementia sufferer', 'wheelchair user', 'Parkinson's sufferer' can often lead to inaccurate but powerful assumptions about an individual's abilities. The stereotype of the 'dementia sufferer' is someone who is confused, wanders and cannot safely be left on his or her own. If a practitioner takes this mindset into an assessment then this almost predetermines the outcomes. Misconceptions often persist even once the person has been met and the assessment underway – such is the power of the label!

Ahmed (1990) argues that black people are especially prone to stereotyping. They tend to be more readily 'pathologised' and constructed as having 'special' rather than individual needs. According to Ahmed

> Consequently … Black clients' 'special needs' can only be effectively catered for by 'special' provision, which was outside the general or mainstream social work policy and practice. (page 7)

Any discrimination black people experience in wider society is compounded because workers become preoccupied with the 'difference' and 'otherness' of the black person. Imagine the difficulties with stereotyping a black person with dementia might experience!

Watch your language

We return to this key theme. Thompson (2001) writes that

> … it is not simply a matter of distinguishing between 'taboo' words and 'OK' words, as in the sense of political correctness. What is needed is not a simple list of proscribed words but, rather, an awareness of, and sensitivity to, the oppressive and discriminatory potential of language. (page 31)

In recent years, we have become sensitive to the depersonalising and dehumanising effect of words such as 'handicapped', 'crippled', or 'the elderly'. Nevertheless, to take up Thompson's point, if we write in an assessment that a young woman with severe mobility problems 'needs to be toileted after each meal', then the language used not only shows a lack of respect but constructs that woman less as a human being and more as an object of care or, at best, someone in an infantile state. Language actively constructs and changes reality.

Think it over

The box above (page 341) outlines the various bases for discrimination.

1 Take each basis in turn. Think about your own organisation or agency. Where might there be potential for discrimination in the assessment process?

2 Rate your agency on a scale of 0 to 10 (0 = no discriminatory practices at all, 10 = very discriminatory practice).

3 Assuming you have not given your agency a 0, identify ways in which ADP could be improved.

4 If possible, compare with another colleague.

We have emphasised the need for assessors to embrace ADP although we acknowledge that we have done no more than 'skimmed the surface' of the changing and contested field of ADP in this section.

Although it may not always feel like it, as an assessor one is a powerful person in the life of another. If your client is experiencing any form of discrimination then your intervention can either add to it, maintain it, or help to reduce it in some way. There is really no choice on what basis to proceed.

> ## ⊃ Check your understanding
> 1 What does it mean to say the empowerment is a 'contested' concept?
> 2 What is Thompson's definition of empowerment?
> 3 How does Jack describe the 'disempowering' relationship?
> 4 Explain how stereotyping people can lead to discriminatory practice.
> 5 Give examples of how the language we use can depersonalise or dehumanise the people we work with.

The elements of a competent assessment

This chapter has covered many different aspects of assessment and highlighted several factors for practitioners to consider when they assess. There is no such thing as the perfect assessment. Nevertheless, if we try to put it all together, what should the competent assessor be aiming for? In reading the list below, you will see that inevitably many of the elements overlap and combine with each other.

Elements of assessment

⊃ *Person-centred* Practically all official guidance makes this a priority. Start from where the person is at. Make them the prime focus of your assessment. Be guided by that person's particular situation, don't be governed by a set format.

⊃ *Ensure participation* A competent assessment should always aim to seek the active participation of those involved.

⊃ *Establish trust* You will establish trust by being clear, open and genuine.

⊃ *Valid* An assessment should be 'true to life' and present a genuine and authentic account of that individual's situation.

⊃ *Reliable* No two practitioners work in exactly the same way. However, a reliable assessment would be one where different assessors would produce a broadly similar set of findings whichever style or format they used. The assessor should therefore not be too idiosyncratic in the way they work.

⊃ *Culturally sensitive* The assessor should acknowledge and respect cultural difference and not impose their own cultural values. Be aware of cultural stereotyping.

⊃ *Clarify the purpose and scope* Don't assume that the various parties involved in an assessment understand what the point, purpose and scope of it is. The word 'assessment' can have different meanings to ⟶

---

different people, so can 'social worker', as can 'care manager'. Ensure that you clarify what the other parties' understanding of what your role is, what is expected of them, what the assessment is about and, just as pertinently, what it is not about. Are you assessing an individual, household, a risk situation? To clarify these points for others you must have a clear idea yourself first.

⮌ *Assessment is not a one-off, static event* Situations are dynamic, fluid and changing all the time. An assessment should reflect this.

⮌ *Your assessment will change the situation whatever else happens* The very fact of assessing somebody will change the situation. How you are, what questions you ask and how you ask them will produce change in itself.

⮌ *Be sensitive to the language you use* This is important at each stage of the process. How does the language used construct that person, that situation, tell that person's story? Would the person recognise himself or herself, would they use the same words, are you using jargon or somehow medicalising the problem?

⮌ *Complexities, contradictions and tensions are acknowledged* They're bound to be there – don't gloss over them. This would particularly apply to issues around 'need' and 'risk', they're easy to take for granted when, in reality, they are difficult concepts.

⮌ *Don't assume that any one person has to be the expert* It would be a rare occasion if the assessor had all the answers and unlikely that the person themselves knew everything they needed know.

⮌ *Aim to be inclusive* Seek the views of others – especially carers. However, no single view should predominate to the exclusion and detriment of others.

⮌ *Holistic* An individual needs to be assessed 'as a whole'. People are more than the sum of their parts.

⮌ *Distinguish between needs, wants and preferences* Easy to say but a lot harder to do in reality – at least be aware of the differences though.

⮌ *Be consistent with agency function and ensure your assessment conforms to any national and local guidelines and any relevant legislation* If you are tempted to play the 'maverick' and do your own thing, it could well be your client who pays the price either by having unfairly raised expectations, services withdrawn or having the inconvenience of a reassessment by somebody else.

⮌ *Draw on best practice by using properly tried and tested assessment scales and tools* This is particularly useful in respect of risk assessment. A good assessment tool can help with risk analysis. However, we must recognise that not everybody shares the same perception of risk. We must also remember that a form – whatever headings or boxes it may contain – is not an assessment. A care assessment is a dynamic human process, drawing on interpersonal skills, judgement and interpretation. ⟶

> ⊃ *Avoid repetition, duplication and ritualistic behaviour* Research consistently shows that this is high on people's lists of hates. Amongst other things, this means spending time doing some research before the assessment.
>
> ⊃ *The assessor should, as far as possible, free themselves from unnecessary baggage, preconceptions and presumptions*
>
> ⊃ *Avoid a narrow, medical, pathologising or medical model* See 'holistic'.
>
> ⊃ *Power aspects are acknowledged whether they be for the good or bad* This is most important. An assessment can be manipulated the assessor's way – even without them realising it.
>
> ⊃ *Anti-discriminatory practice* This is of paramount importance. Be aware of how discrimination can be present in many forms and extend beyond the main areas of race and gender to include many other areas – age, disability, sexual orientation and so on.

⊃ Check your understanding

The last section set out 22 points that could be said to be characteristics of a competent assessment.

1 From memory, write down as many as you can.

2 What points do you think are missing?

References and further reading

Ahmed B (1990) *Black Perspectives in Social Work*, Birmingham, Venture Press

Alaszewski A *et al* (eds) (1998) *Risk Health and Welfare Policies, Strategies and Practice*, Buckingham, Open University Press

Alaszewski A (2002) 'Risk and dangerous' in Bytheway (eds) *Understanding Care, Welfare and Community*, London, Routledge

Department of Health (1989) *Caring for People: Community Care in the Next Decade and Beyond*, London, HMSO

Department of Health (1991) *Care Management and Assessment: Manager's Guide* London, HMSO

Department of Health/SSI (1991) *Getting the Message Across*, London, HMSO

Department of Health (1998) *Modernising Social Services*, London, HMSO

Department of Health (1999) *Working Together to Safeguard Children*, London, HMSO

Department of Health/SSI (2000) *New Directions for Independent Living*, London, HMSO

Department of Health (2000) *The Framework for the Assessment of Children in Need and their Families*, London, HMSO

Jack R (ed) (1995) *Empowerment in Community Care*, London, Chapman and Hall

Kemshall H (2002) *Risk, Social Policy and Practice*, Buckingham, Open Univerisity Press

Lindow V and Morris J (1995) *Service User Involvement*, York, JRF

Lupton D (1999) *Risk*, New York, Routledge

Middleton L (1997) *The Art of Assessment*, Birmingham, Venture Press

Milner J and O'Byrne P (1998) *Assessment in Social Work*, Basingstoke, Macmillan

Milner J and O'Byrne P (2002) *Assessment in Social Work Practice*, Basingstoke, Macmillan

Parton N and O'Byrne P (2000) *Constructive Social Work Towards a New Practice*, Basingstoke, Macmillan

Postle K (2002) 'Between the idea and the reality: ambiguities and tensions in care managers', in *British Journal of Social Work*, vol 32, issue 3, Oxford, Oxford University Press

Skellington R (1996) *Race in Britain Today*, London, Sage

Smale G and Tuson G (1993) *Empowerment, Assessment, Care Management and the Skilled Worker*, London, HMSO

Thompson N (1997) in Davies M (ed) (2000), *Blackwell Encyclopaedia of Social Work* (2000), Oxford, Blackwell

Thompson, N. (2001) *Anti-Discriminatory Practice*, Basingstoke, Macmillan

Walzer M (1983) in Stone D (1997) *Policy Paradox: The Art of Political Decision Making*, London, Norton

Worth A (2002) 'Health and social care assessment in action' in Bytheway B *et al* (eds) (2002) *Understanding Care, Welfare and Community*, London, Routledge

adult protection

This chapter explores adult protection. It covers the subject of abuse and the general good practice in the protection of adults from poor standards of care. Its aim is to increase your awareness of what abuse is in the context of care work, and to be aware of how to respond to such situations if they arise.

The chapter starts by looking at definitions of abuse and explores how abuse can affect individuals. We explore theories that attempt to provide an explanation of why abuse occurs, and how the anticipation of this may enable adults to be more protected from vulnerable situations. We will also look at the policy context of adult protection and what you can do as a care worker to protect the people that you work with. It identifies good practice with adults as a means of managing adult protection.

This chapter addresses the following areas:

- ➲ Definitions of abuse
- ➲ Forms of abuse
- ➲ The context of abuse
- ➲ Signs and symptoms of abuse
- ➲ The experience of abuse
- ➲ Explanations of abuse
- ➲ The policy context of adult protection
- ➲ Protection from other service users
- ➲ Procedures and good practice
- ➲ Support as a care worker

After reading this chapter it is hoped that you will be able to

1 understand definitions of abuse
2 be able to recognise indicators of abuse
3 know the relevant policy framework
4 be aware of theories of abuse
5 understand how abuse can affect individuals
6 be able to apply principles of adult protection practice to your own care work.

In your own care practice you may have experienced a case of abuse following the discovery or disclosure of a particular incident. Adult protection is of course about these incidents. However adult protection should inform everyday care practice and not just be about these isolated events. It is important to become skilled in your awareness of vulnerability so that you can adopt good practice with all service users and work towards the prevention or early identification of abuse.

It is useful to think about your current role and the responsibilities you have in relation to abuse. If you are a care manager you may include assessment of risk, if you are a care worker in a care home you will have an ongoing remit to ensure that everyday practice does not expose service users to risk, and that the needs of service users are not overlooked or neglected.

In this chapter you will be reading about theories and perspectives on adult protection. Check these out in the glossary if you need a reminder of what they are. Before we can look at what adult protection involves we need to understand what makes individuals vulnerable to abuse. Firstly, let us explore what is meant by the word 'abuse'.

Definitions of abuse

If we were to mention the word abuse to a room of people there would be various feelings, thoughts and reactions from the individuals in the group. Abuse is not an objective area of study in which facts and figures tell us what experiences people have, and exactly what we should do in such situations. Each of us come to this area of study with different experiences and views.

Think it over

Think about the service user group that you work with and write down a definition of abuse relating to this group of people. Then compare it to the following descriptions.

Abuse is a violation of an individual's human and civil rights by any other person or persons. [Department of Health, *No Secrets* (2000)]

Abuse in any situation is a misuse of power. It can happen when people do something that they ought not to have done. This is sometimes referred to as committing abuse. Abuse can also occur when people fail to do something that they ought to have done. This is referred to as abuse by omission. [Bradley (2001), page 35]

There are different definitions of abuse and these can change over time. What is clear is that abuse is a serious and complex area of care work involving adults, and one that has been previously neglected. The protection of adults is a concern for all care providers, and therefore all individual care workers.

Think it over

Let us explore what your views on abuse might be. Order the following examples of abuse according to how severe you think they are.

1 A client being left in soiled clothing for an hour because the care worker got involved with another task.

Abuse can be viewed from different perspectives. A starting point may be to look at it focusing on the actions of the abuser.

What is going on in all the examples in the Think it over above?

The first case was not an intentional act of abuse, the care worker was distracted by another task.

In the second case the care worker thinks they understand what the person needs and what is being communicated to them.

In the third the abuse is a premeditated and calculated act with the intention of causing harm.

In the fourth the well-being of other service users has been considered and this is seen as a sensible solution.

In the last case the carer may be struggling with their ability to continue coping emotionally.

As we said at the beginning of this chapter, abuse can be viewed either as just those isolated premeditated actions, or as being on a continuum of care practice:

Careless neglect ⟶ Deliberate abuse

Neglect means that actions are not being carried out, which then has a detrimental effect on the person being cared for. Abuse here refers to the actions that are carried out and which have a negative effect on the person. This views the situation from the perspective of the abuser, what their motives are and how they have behaved.

Neglect may occur as a result of lack of attention to what the care task should involve and general poor care practice. An example of this may be a care worker holding a person's arms too tight because they don't know how to assist the individual with their physical mobility. It also refers to deliberate and premeditated actions that cause harm, for example a carer denying a service user their meal because that person has annoyed them.

As you will see in the section on good practice, it can be useful to consider abuse from the perspective of the abuser. It may help you to form a deeper understanding of situations where protection needs to be a particular focus. However it must be remembered that the intention is not to provide excuses for the abuser and overlook the victim's experience of the abuse. The aim in this chapter is for you to develop a better understanding of all the issues relating to abuse so that you are able to become more effective in your role in adult protection; this should then provide a more positive outcome for all the individuals you support who are vulnerable to abuse.

Let us return to the list of abusive situations that you were asked to put in order of severity. Having considered what might be going on with the abuser in each situation let's look at what the experience of the individual victims might be.

1 *A client being left in soiled clothing for an hour* This person may feel physical discomfort, embarrassment at the smell and a loss in their sense of dignity. They may also experience infections and ill-health.

2 *A person being given a smaller portion of dinner because they are slow at eating* This person may experience gradual weight loss and lack of nutrition. They may also sense the inconvenience that they are causing and feel anxious when eating, thereby developing low self-esteem.

3 *An individual being punched by a stranger* They may be fearful of going out again, and therefore become socially isolated and depressed.

4 *A person being given sedatives to keep them quiet* This person may not realise that the medication is having that effect on them and be unaware of the changes to their disposition.

5 *A person being told every day that they are worthless, a waste of space and a burden to the carer* This person may believe what is being said to them and feel guilty about the trouble they are causing. They may think that everyone has this opinion of them.

It is impossible to predict the actual effect that abuse will have on individuals, as people are different. Careless neglect can be as damaging an experience for the victim as an act of deliberate abuse. We may not be helping to address abuse if we just focus on deliberate actions; we need to also look at neglect as a significant area of adult protection.

Another way of looking at abuse is its duration. Was it a one-off incident, or is it ongoing treatment?

An isolated incident ⟶ Persistent and ongoing treatment

For instance, in the above example of neglect the long-term effects of mishandling the service user could be bruising, damage to joints, or in the short-term the person falling to the floor; the person may also experience a sense of being unworthy of better treatment. The denying of one meal as an isolated incident may not have long-term damage to the individual, but ongoing lack of nutrition or drinks can cause dehydration and ill-health.

Again, our perception of this may be what we think of the abuser's reasons for the abuse. The following is what a son says about hitting his older mother, a one-off incident:

'I just flipped, I didn't mean to hit her, I feel terrible about it. I just can't listen to that moaning anymore. I love her though.'

A one-off incident can affect individuals in a variety of ways. One person may be able to understand that a situation got out of hand and may want things to carry on as they did before. They may feel that the initial physical or emotional pain will go away, and there will be no long-term damage.

Another person who has experienced a one-off incident may feel very unsafe in that environment and wonder when the next hit is coming. They may also have had their sense of worth affected, wondering what they did to cause it. They may have physical damage, such as broken ribs, which are very painful and are going to take a long time to heal. The person may have had to spend a very traumatic time in hospital feeling very vulnerable and anxious about whether they should report the incident.

So, if abuse relates to such a diverse range of experiences how are we meant to identify whether abuse is taking place, and if so what our role is in responding to it?

The following table provides a useful way of looking at criteria for deciding if an action constitutes abuse. It separates out what the intentions of the person carrying out the actions are (potential abuser), and what the experience is of the person on the receiving end of the actions (potential victim of abuse).

Categories of intent and experience	Intended as abusive	Not intended as abusive	Impossible to ascertain intent
Experienced as abusive	Clearly abuse	Probably abuse	Should be initially treated as abuse
Not experienced as abusive	Probably abuse	Clearly not abuse	Probably not abuse
Impossible to ascertain how experienced	Should be initially treated as abuse	Probably not abuse	Impossible to tell whether or not abuse

[McCarthy and Thompson (1994) in Carnaby (ed) (2002), page 59]

Some of these categories are more straightforward than others. If someone intends to abuse another person, and then that individual experiences this as abuse, then it is easy to determine that abuse has taken place. Some of the other categories illustrate how complex this dimension of care work is. We could even question the category of the box 'Not experienced as abusive' and 'Not intended as abusive' being 'Clearly not abuse', as stated in the table.

When we think about the status of individuals in society and the power relationships that people have, we may need to recognise that abuse can take place even if it is not intended as abuse, and not experienced as abuse.

	Not intended as abuse
Not experienced as abuse	**Clearly not abuse?**

Let us look at the following scenario to explore this idea.

A case of abuse?

As a refugee from Algeria, Tahir Said-Guerni has low expectations of the treatment he will receive by those supporting him in Britain; he is just grateful that he is no longer in a situation where he was facing physical torture.

Josephine works with Tahir at the Resource Centre. His low expectations are confirmed by the care he is provided with by Josephine, who unintentionally lowers her standards when working with him.

Examples of her practice with him include

- ignoring statements he makes which she is unable to understand
- not accessing interpretation services for him
- not encouraging him to engage in social contact outside of the Resource centre, and therefore limiting his development
- accepting his poor health as something attributable to the fact that he is a refugee and not accessing health care services for him.

Tahir seems content with the support that he receives (not experienced as abuse) and Josephine is just working in the same way as other care workers (not intended as abuse).

Question

What do you think? Is abuse taking place?

Let us look at the facts:

Tahir gets

- ignored
- denied access to appropriate services to which he is entitled
- limited and inaccurate assessment of his needs.

Josephine

- ignores Tahir
- fails to access appropriate care services for him
- provides inadequate support compared to how she supports others at the Centre.

So how can it be that an abusive situation is not recognised as being abusive by both the victim (Tahir) and the perpetrator (Josephine)?

We now need to look at the dynamics of this situation.

Tahir has low self-esteem, partly due to degrading treatment he has previously received. This has lowered his expectations of how he should be treated; he doesn't feel as though he is deserving of a good quality experience. Therefore, Tahir does not recognise that he is being neglected.

Josephine has picked up on the low expectations that Tahir has, and is working in a way that reinforces these. She feels that Tahir would let her know or complain if he wanted to. She doesn't understand the complex nature of his situation and how she needs to be more aware of working in an anti-discriminatory way. Therefore, Josephine does not see that she is neglecting Tahir and certainly would not think of herself as an abuser.

As onlookers we can be more objective and identify that Josephine's poor practice does constitute neglect towards Tahir. She is not fulfilling her responsibilities to him and she is colluding with her colleagues in adopting a very poor practice when working with him. Abuse seems to be taking place.

Just as the context of the relationship influenced Tahir and Josephine's perception of whether abuse was taking place, there are various factors that influence our understanding of what abuse is.

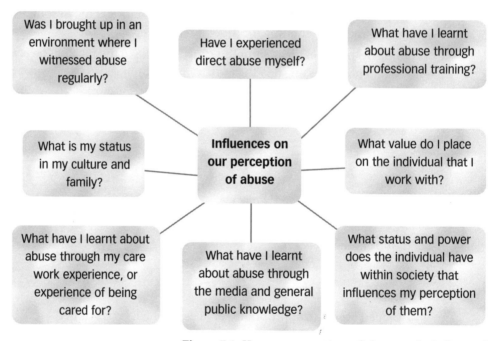

Figure 7.1 *How our perceptions of abuse can be influenced*

Eastman (1994) has researched the issue of dependency and how this influences a person's perception of whether a situation is abusive. He also explores the role of culture in setting expectations of behaviour, which may or may not be defined as abuse. People's perception of whether an individual incident is abusive is affected by further factors, including what they think of the individual abuser or the victim.

It is important for us to spend some time on why people have different perceptions of what abuse is as this has a big impact on our responsibilities to individuals. An illustration of this is from research by Brown and Thompson (Mental Health Foundation 1995). This found that the physical behaviour of a service user was interpreted in different ways by female staff. The learning disabled man was regularly touching women on the cheek; some felt that this was a form of communication, whereas others thought this behaviour to be inappropriate and it needed to be stopped. There is a big difference between touch as a form of communication and inappropriate touch, and yet professional care workers differed in their interpretation of this behaviour.

Identifying whether abuse is taking place is therefore made more complex by the subjective nature of it. In this next section we shall be focusing on the different forms of abuse that can be prevalent in the context of care work.

Forms of abuse

Just as there are a number of definitions of abuse, there are also different ways of categorising abusive behaviour. Some of these actions are not specific to the context of care; abuse takes place in society amongst people who are not involved in care services, either as professionals or as individuals using services. For example, anyone can be punched, kicked or shouted at. Some individuals may experience some of these actions because they are vulnerable due to their age, mental capacity or physical mobility. Sometimes an incidence of abuse may be the reason for the individual to access the support of care services. Other forms of abuse are specific to the care task, such as a woman with limited physical mobility being left in soiled clothing or a person with mental health problems being befriended and supported in order to access their money.

Abuse may be categorised into the following forms:

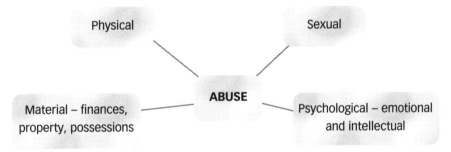

Figure 7.2 *Categories of abuse*

For each of the following forms of abuse we will look at

- ⊃ examples of deliberate abuse
- ⊃ examples of neglect
- ⊃ examples of how this form of abuse relates to the care task
- ⊃ a case study.

Physical abuse

Examples of physical abuse are

- ⊃ hitting
- ⊃ slapping
- ⊃ pinching.

Such abuse relates to care tasks in cases of

- handling a person roughly
- placing them in a bath that is too hot
- leaving a person in soiled clothing
- not taking a person to the toilet to change their continence aids regularly.

Examples of *deliberate* physical abuse include tying someone to a chair to stop them from wandering around, and physical *neglect* includes failing to monitor a person's medication, or not ensuring that someone has sufficient drinks and allowing them to become dehydrated.

Individuals usually decide the type and amount of physical contact they have with people but not everyone has the luxury of such control over their lives. Physical contact can be more commonplace in the lives of people who need support than is usual with others. Manual dexterity and general mobility affects the amount and nature of physical contact that some people have with others, including care workers. Some abuse may happen to anyone, such as kicking or other kinds of physical assault. Other abuse originates from the care task and involves deliberate abuse of power or neglecting the responsibility to provide appropriate care. Individuals in care may have little control over the physical contact that they have with people or little control over their physical needs, which increases their dependency on people.

Case Study

Physical abuse

Colin has cerebral palsy and uses a wheelchair for mobility. He has limited control over his gross motor skills and little manual dexterity; he requires physical support with all aspects of his personal care. Colin hates it when Sharon looks after him as she is very rough with him physically and he feels as though he is being yanked around. She never checks the bath temperature and he dreads being lowered in on the hoist as he has been scalded before.

Sexual abuse

Examples of sexual abuse are

- inappropriate touching
- rape
- teasing of a sexual nature
- unwanted physical contact of a sexual nature
- taking lewd photos.

Examples of such abuse as it relate to the care task include

- unnecessary exposure of the person's body
- denying a person the freedom of expression in relation to their sexuality

- ⊃ deliberately dressing someone provocatively
- ⊃ not allowing someone choice in the expression of their sexuality.

Deliberate sexual abuse may involve an abuser getting an individual to touch their genitals. A case of *neglect* would be a care worker not responding to an obvious sexual risk with a person they are caring for.

Sexual abuse is not just a form of physical abuse; it also has a psychological dimension. People in care can be more vulnerable to sexual abuse when they have carers touching them as part of their personal care needs. The danger is that the boundary between care and sexual abuse may become less obvious and the person being cared for may at first be unclear about what is happening.

The people we care for may have a different sexual status in society than what is considered the norm. For example, older people are assumed to not have a sexual identity at all, let alone want to engage in healthy sexual relationships. This may prevent sexual abuse from being identified or acknowledged. Historically, society has felt the need to protect people with learning disabilities from their own promiscuity; women have been sterilised, and lives have been segregated according to gender to avoid the risk of sexual contact. This has been due to professional labelling. Today, people who form meaningful relationships may have them undermined as being meaningless and insignificant. If a person is not seen as a sexual being, the care provided may just focus on the physical actions, and any other aspects of their physicality are overlooked; this can then expose someone to sexual abuse.

An important area to consider in this respect is that of consent. The issues involve a person's

- ⊃ ability to consent
- ⊃ ability to articulate not consenting
- ⊃ willingness to consent
- ⊃ understanding of what is being consented to
- ⊃ awareness of the implications of consenting.

Working with individuals at risk should not mean that they are denied opportunities for exploring or expressing their own sexuality.

Psychological abuse

Examples of psychological abuse are

- ⊃ shouting at the person being cared for
- ⊃ frightening them
- ⊃ threatening them
- ⊃ humiliating them
- ⊃ ignoring them.

Examples of such abuse relating to care work include

- ⊃ limiting a person's opportunity to develop their life skills
- ⊃ not providing appropriate stimulation, causing a disruption in a person's development through the lifestages

⊃ talking at a pace that the individual cannot understand

⊃ making the person feel inadequate by emphasising what they cannot do.

Deliberate psychological abuse could be a case of telling someone how useless they are because of the time it's taking them to get dressed. *Neglect* may be leaving someone alone for periods of time that are detrimental to them.

A person may experience abuse in terms of not being supported in their development appropriately. This may not be evident at first, and delay in development may be assumed as being part of the person's characteristics. Not reaching recognised milestones can provide a useful indicator of abuse in children, but these are less apparent in some adults. For example, a learning disabled individual may not be able to make themselves a hot drink and this may not be identified as being a feature of neglect. It could be because they have not developed such life skills even though they have the ability to learn these if they had been supported.

Some carers may generate fear in a service user if their approach to working with that person is abrupt, rushed, anxiety-provoking. If the care worker is always in a hurry and gets annoyed when the service user takes a long time to eat their meal/put their clothes on/get up the steps, then this may communicate to the service user and it could cause pressure and distress.

Material abuse – possessions and finances

Examples of this kind of abuse are

⊃ theft of personal property

⊃ persuading the individual to sign over property rights in the will.

Examples of this that relate to the care task are

⊃ lending personal items to another service user without the permission of the person who owns the items

⊃ using an individual's personal finances to pay for a purchase that will be used by everyone in the care home.

Deliberate material abuse may involve a person encouraging an older person to buy them gifts when they go out shopping. *Neglect* may be allowing a person with learning disabilities to spend all their money on buying other people drinks etc. on the first day of a holiday when they needed support to make sure it lasted a week.

There are several reasons why a care user may need carers to be involved in looking after their possessions. They may depend on support for making purchases or in dealing with financial issues because of their cognitive understanding of these matters. Abuse may arise from situations created by the abuser, for example the behaviour of a stranger towards the service user may appear very friendly and beneficial, but then the stranger starts to steal money from that person. Older people are more vulnerable, particularly to strangers, because they live on their own, have set patterns of social contact etc. and are socially isolated.

A care user with reduced physical mobility may require support from others, such as relatives, to handle and manage their possessions. However, you shouldn't assume that such a care user can make sound judgements about their relatives' motives and abilities for taking responsibility for them.

There are two further forms of abuse that are identified in the government guidance *No Secrets*, which we look at in the section on policy, namely discrimination and neglect. We look at these separately as they can be discrete areas of abuse, even though they are also forms of physical, social, psychological and material abuse. The process and effects of discrimination on individuals is discussed in more depth in the chapter on values in care practice (Chapter 3).

Discrimination

Examples of discrimination are

- being excluded from activities
- being shouted at, called names
- being denied the opportunity to observe religious practices.

Discrimination may be the motive for abuse. An abuser may be motivated by racial hatred and intend to abuse individuals who are of a particular racial background. An example is a carer discriminating against a Muslim service user by not observing their wish not to eat during Ramadan. There are various reasons why people abuse others, and it is not always easy to discern if discrimination is behind some of this. Discrimination is not just about a person being treated differently; it also occurs when an individual is treated the same as other people, but has a negative experience of it. For example, a group of people being told certain information, but a person who is deaf not being provided with an interpreter so that they can also share the information.

An example of *deliberate* abuse in this sense may be teasing someone about their use of English, or the clothes they choose to wear to reflect their culture. *Neglect* may be not supporting a person to access services because they are thought to be too old. Ageism may lead carers to make assumptions about an older person's needs, which could mean that some of that person's needs are not met.

Discrimination represents a violation of a person's identity. The actual method of discrimination may reflect any of the other forms of abuse. We will not be focusing on this a great deal in this chapter as it is dealt with substantially in the chapter on values in care practice.

There may be tensions over what constitutes abuse. Genital mutilation or female circumcision is widely practised in some countries, and highly valued by some cultures. In 2003 the government banned individuals in this country from taking children abroad in order to have this practice performed, as it is viewed as being an abuse of the child.

Neglect and acts of omission

Examples of neglect are

- 'accidents' happening regularly
- leaving someone alone for long periods without any stimulation.

Examples related to the care task are

- ⊃ leaving someone in the bath too long
- ⊃ not providing basic care
- ⊃ not ensuring an older person has regular visits to the toilet and leaving them in soiled clothing
- ⊃ being careless and giving medication at the wrong time or in the wrong amounts
- ⊃ letting someone have accidents regularly without obtaining professional support or advice, accepting that falls are inevitable.

Neglect is a significant issue of abuse as it acknowledges that abuse is broader than just deliberate, premeditated actions that are intended to harm. Abuse can take place because of what has not been done, and are described as acts of omission. This also acknowledges that abuse can take place even if the perpetrator does not intend to do harm. They may not be motivated to abuse but what is important is that the individual victim has experienced a detrimental level of care. Pritchard distinguishes between active and passive neglect, and identifies the problems of defining, identifying and proving neglect as well as the issue of what to do about it once it has been identified [Pritchard (2001), page 226].

> **Active neglect** is deliberately not carrying out appropriate care tasks, e.g. withholding items that are necessary for healthy daily living.
>
> **Passive neglect** is overlooking, not knowing what care a person needs, e.g. being careless, being left alone for too long.

Think it over

Think about the potential for the different forms of abuse that the individuals you support may experience. Why are they more vulnerable to some forms of abuse?

- ⊃ Physical
- ⊃ Social
- ⊃ Discrimination
- ⊃ Psychological
- ⊃ Material
- ⊃ Neglect

The context of abuse

Having looked at what abuse is and the different forms it may take, we will now explore how abuse happens and why.

The government has specified the following dynamics of abuse in the *No Secrets* guidelines. These illustrate the range of situations in which abuse might happen, and why those we work with are more vulnerable to abuse.

Dynamics of abuse

Scenarios of abuse

Serial abusing	The perpetrator seeks out and grooms vulnerable adults in preparation for abuse. There have been well reported situations where children have been led into a relationship with another 'child' on the internet, and a relationship formed which then takes the form of sexual abuse when the two meet.
Long-term abuse	Ongoing abuse, sometimes in the context of a carer or relative relationship. Many people live in isolated circumstances without anyone being able to identify that abuse is taking place, let alone to free someone from the situation.
Opportunistic abuse	This happens as situations are presented to the perpetrator. A shopkeeper may not give a learning disabled person their change and tell them there isn't any.
Situational abuse	This is due to pressures building up or difficult and challenging behaviour.
Neglect of needs	This is due to a carer not being able to support the individual appropriately.
Institutional abuse	The poor care standards and routines that do not suit the needs of the service users.
Unacceptable treatments	Intervention which may be seen as part of a programme but is actually abusing the individual, such as sanctions or punishment, restraining people or withholding food.
Staff not observing ADP	The lack of responsiveness of staff to the needs of individuals due to their culture, religion, sexuality. Individuals discriminating against some groups.
Failure to access services	This involves not securing support or guidance for an individual from other agencies. Not accessing services for people perhaps because they are not valued enough and not seen as worth it.
Misappropriation of a person's money	This is misuse of benefits, usually by a family member. An individual claiming money for the person and then not spending it on their care needs.
Fraud or intimidation, as in the case of wills and property	This is altering a person's financial situation without them knowing or through coercion.

Adapted from Department of Health (2000) *No Secrets*

The following scenarios illustrate the different contexts in which abuse can occur, to show just how broad is the range of situations that can illicit abuse, and that there is not one set of characteristics of abusers that will enable you to recognise them as they walk through the door!

Contexts of abuse

Victim of abuse	Cleo is a 86-year-old woman who lives in her own home	Daniel is 44, he lives with his older brother since his mum died
Abuser	Sophie is a home care worker who visits Cleo in the morning	Victim's brother
Form of abuse	Physical	Psychological Financial
What the abuser thinks	'I admit I might be a bit rough with her but its nothing more than that – she's difficult to work with.'	'He was given more attention when we were children, and now he's a burden to me. Its his fault that Mum died, caring for him all the time. I only agreed to him moving in with me because that is what Mum wanted.'
What the person being abused thinks	'She scares me, I feel exhausted when she's gone and I ache all over.'	Daniel is not aware that he is being abused, he just doesn't like his brother, and knows his brother doesn't really like him.
Consequences of abuse	Physical pain Fear	Daniel is restricted in his social contact and does not develop skills which could facilitate independent living
Location of abuse	The victim's own home	Daniel's home
Duration of abuse	Regularly each week for years	Just started, since Daniel's mum died
Reasons why abuse may occur	Isolation of the care–victim relationship	Family values in society mean that the motivations of the abuser, carer stress, are seen as being OK.

Risk and responsibility

One of the difficult aspects of supporting individuals who may be experiencing abuse is that of risk and responsibility. An adult may decide that they want to remain in the situation where abuse is taking place and it is not within the powers or responsibilities of the care worker to remove them from that situation without their consent.

Think it over

With the service user group that you work with, what forms of abuse are they most vulnerable to?

'Harm' should be taken to include not only ill-treatment (including sexual abuse and forms of ill-treatment which are not physical), but also the impairment of, or an avoidable deterioration in, physical, intellectual, emotional, social or behavioural development. [Law Commission (1995)]

Institutional abuse

Part of what we have discussed so far relates to the fact that abuse needs to be located in the same dialogue as that of care practice in order for it not to be sidelined as a rare issue, or abusers to be thought of as instantly recognisable. Institutional abuse is an example of where the care practice of individuals can go undetected and unreported for years as a culture of abuse prevents individuals, care workers or service users, from identifying it. It is called institutional abuse because the abuse is related to the organisation, the culture and practices of the institution, whether this is a care home, day centre, home care agency etc.

Institutional abuse may be a consequence of the following activities:

Figure 7.3 *Causes of institutional abuse*

In care settings abuse may be a symptom of a poorly run establishment. It appears that it is most likely to occur when staff are inadequately trained, poorly supervised, have little support from management or work in isolation. [Action on Elder Abuse]

Think it over

1 Why do you think institutional abuse can develop?
2 Why do individual care workers not identify, tackle or report abuse that takes place at work?

The local policy of an organisation can constitute abuse. In the early part of the 1900s the Mount School for the Deaf and the Blind near Stoke-on-Trent made use of the following practices as part of general discipline.

> There was one side of the building for us blind boys and the other side was for deaf boys. One of the worst punishments was to go and live on the deaf side for a couple of days .... Now the thing was, of course, that the deaf couldn't hear, and we couldn't lip read. [Humphries and Gordon (1992), page 91]

This was an environment set up for children with specific needs, and yet it was felt appropriate to adopt abusive practices.

Punishments and sanctions have in the past been seen as a necessary feature of the development of individuals, but many previously lauded behaviour modification programmes with learning disabled people would be interpreted as abusive today. This illustrates how important it is that organisations do not become closed environments, so that those within or external to an organisation are allowed to comment on the practices of that organisation.

Some environments may develop practices that are not recognised as abusive because they are commonplace and sanctioned by management or colleagues. Organisational constraints or requirements may perpetuate incidences of abuse or promote a culture where abuse is not tackled effectively.

Signs and symptoms of abuse

So far we have been looking at what abuse is and its context in different situations. We will now look at how abuse can affect individuals and, importantly, at the signs of abuse we can all look out for. As mentioned earlier, it is not possible to state how abuse will affect an individual. It is however important to have a knowledge about the range of effects so that care workers

➲ know how to recognise that someone is being abused

➲ know how to support an individual who has been abused.

Symptoms of abuse

A symptom of abuse is what happens to the person as a consequence of them being abused. Some types of abuse will harm a person in particular way, whilst other abuses will produce more general effects.

The effects of abuse may be

- immediate or delayed
- short-term or long-term
- noticeable or undetectable
- physical
- emotional
- intellectual
- social
- financial.

To illustrate how one form of abuse can produce a range of effects, let's look at the examples of physical and psychological abuse.

	Physical abuse (e.g being punched)
Physical effects	- Causes bruising and internal damage - Temporary or more permanent loss of mobility depending on injuries
Psychological effects – emotions	- Loss of ability to undertake daily living tasks will affect an individual's sense of independence and self-esteem - Fear of abuse may preoccupy the person
Psychological effects – intellect	- The pain experienced may affect an individual's ability to concentrate
Social effects	- Withdrawal due to physical mobility - Lack of motivation to socialise due to loss of self-esteem

	Psychological abuse (e.g. being ignored and isolated for long periods of time)
Physical effects	- May affect a person's mobility or physical development. Withdrawal from social situations, affects communication
Psychological effects – emotions	- Will affect the individual's self-esteem - Anxiety about what is going on - Depression
Psychological effects – intellect	- Lack of stimulation means that the person is not engaging in activities that will stimulate them intellectually
Social effects	- Lack of contact with others - No opportunity for communication and development of relationships - Lack of opportunity to develop social skills

Indicators of abuse

Signs	Indicators
Physical	⊃ Bruises ⊃ Incontinence ⊃ Broken limbs ⊃ Scars
Emotional	⊃ Being distracted ⊃ Anxiety ⊃ Depression ⊃ Lack of confidence
Intellectual	⊃ Delay in development ⊃ Confusion ⊃ Inability to concentrate
Social	⊃ Withdrawal from usual pattern of social interaction ⊃ Difficulty in relating to other people or in general communication ⊃ Not wanting to be in the company of the abuser or behaving in a particular way with the abuser (i.e. flinching when they approach)

The presence of these signs does not mean that abuse is necessarily taking place. There can be legitimate reasons for all the above. A person with dementia may experience confusion about what they are doing on a daily basis and who other people are in their lives. A person who has recently experienced bereavement may become withdrawn and depressed. A person with changes to their physical mobility who has not had a review or reassessment may fall frequently and have bruising. (If an assessment is not made this may fall into the category of neglect.)

Concern should be raised if changes are

⊃ sudden

⊃ unexplained

⊃ inconsistent with explanations provided by the person or others.

Adult protection is about being more aware and alert to potential situations of abuse. Having a good knowledge of the signs of abuse can enable you to think about whether a situation of abuse may be occurring.

The experience of abuse

The Care Standards Act 2000 means that there are national expectations of what good quality care should involve, and service users should be aware of the requirements of those who support them. They do not have to be accepting of poor quality care that can result in neglect or abuse. This is important because people who are experiencing abuse may not be in a good position, either physically or psychologically, to actually challenge the abuse and be instrumental in protecting themselves.

The following are the sort of feelings the service user might have about being abused:

'I deserve it.'
'It was an accident.'
'They didn't mean it.'
'It must be a strain for them looking after me.'

or

'I don't deserve this, I should be treated better.'
'That wasn't an accident, she deliberately let me fall.'
'They did that on purpose.'
'They should be more professional.'

Think it over

In what ways are the following individuals vulnerable to abuse?

- ⊃ Keith has learning disabilities; he has limited verbal communication. He lives with his older parents who are experiencing changes in their own physical mobility.

- ⊃ Dave is currently homeless and has been living in a hostel for a couple of weeks. He has been experiencing mental health problems.

Lack of expectation about Keith's life may lead to him being neglected socially and intellectually. His parents may not realise that they are neglecting him and others around the family may be very aware of the love that Keith's parents have for him, so do not want to comment on or intrude into the situation. It is more difficult to ascertain developmental neglect where the usual patterns of development may be less clear.

The low status that homeless people have may make Dave more accepting of abusive behaviour towards him. He has got used to people swearing or spitting at him. His lack of esteem may expose him to further abusive behaviour, as he will not have the motivation to challenge it. He may feel that society is against him and therefore not feel that there is much point in complaining.

Some explanations of abuse tend to place a certain level of responsibility for the abuse onto the victim of it. For example, they regard the individual service user as somehow contributing to the cause of the abuse. As care professionals it is important to identify what your understanding of abuse is, and how this affects your practice. This can call for tough reflection and honesty about the way care is delivered.

Figure 7.4 *Examples of abuse*

Fear of abuse

Fear of abuse can be debilitating to an individual. How does it potentially affect people? Most of us worry about things at times and on occasions this can preoccupy us and affect our daily living. We may not eat, or we may eat excessively. We may not want to talk to anyone, not want to go out, or not want to be at home alone etc. Why might a person fear being abused? Might it be

⊃ because they are being abused regularly

⊃ they have been abused previously

⊃ they have been threatened with abuse

⊃ they feel vulnerable because of the attitude someone has towards them?

Fear can affect people in a number of ways, as the diagram shows.

Figure 7.5 *The effects of abuse*

You will notice that some of the effects of the *fear* of abuse are the same as the effects of actual abuse. This reinforces what we discussed earlier about focusing on the experience of the person being abused, rather than the intentions of the abuser.

A particular group of people who experience abuse are lesbians and gay men. As discussed in the chapter on values in care practice (Chapter 3), prejudice against individuals can result in discrimination, which may take the form of abuse. Negative feelings about a person or groups may make someone feel justified in the abusive behaviour they display towards them. Individuals who are lesbian, gay men, bisexual, transsexual or a transvestite may feel exposed to potential abuse due to prejudiced ideas about them.

The conclusions of over two decades of research are, sadly, unambiguous. Lesbians and gay men who use health and social care services are accustomed to being treated with contempt, hostility and neglect. [Wilton (2000), page 178]

Explanations of abuse

We mentioned earlier that it is important for care workers to always focus on the needs of the vulnerable adult. It can, however, be useful for us to gain an insight into the reasons why abuse takes place. In this section we will be looking at possible explanations.

Case Study

Vulnerable to abuse

Mrs Petrokov is a 72-year-old Kosovan. She has difficulty in her physical mobility; she was attacked in her home town and did not receive appropriate medical care which has now left her with difficulty in walking. She moved here as a refugee with her son and his family. Her English is limited and she is not confident about learning a new language and new culture.

> Mrs Petrokov experiences incontinence. This is explained away by reference to her age and the physical effects of her mobility. Her communication difficulties and confusion in her environment are attributed to dementia.
>
> *Question*
>
> Why is Mrs Petrokov vulnerable to abuse?

Negative images of refugees by the media create a low status of Mrs Petrokov. An abuser may think that she deserves it, or that it is not as serious as abusing someone who is English. Only having limited English means that an abuser may think that she will be unable to tell anyone what they are doing.

Relationship between oppression and abuse

An understanding of what service users need develops over time, and subsequent changes in practice mean that some previous care practices are now considered to be abusive whereas previously they were not. This is an important consideration for care workers and reinforces the need to reflect on our own practices and the work practices of the organisations that we work for in order to ensure that potentially abusive practices are not condoned. Care workers do need to be aware of the potential for extreme examples of abuse, but it is equally important that we are conscious of the more subtle forms of abuse. Focusing on the experience of the service user enables care workers to consider whether any areas of our practice may be experienced in a negative way by service users.

> There is evidence that people with learning difficulties are seriously disadvantaged by the justice system. [Sharkey (2000), page 135]

Any limitations of the process that is implemented once abuse has been identified has an impact on the view of abuse for that group in the future. This highlights the relationship between individual abuse and the oppression of groups in, and by, society.

Theories of abuse

Theories can provide a framework for understanding why abuse might take place. They can be useful to care professionals when attempting to make sense of situations, when we are trying to understand what has happened, or for being aware of potential risks to individuals.

Phillips (1986) in Bytheway (1995) identified the following approaches.

1 The situational model

This explanation considers the situation surrounding the perpetrator–abused relationship. It explores whether the relationship is based on dependency. If one person is very reliant on the other for support then the person doing the caring may experience exceptional stress. This stress may develop into an inability to cope or a need to manage the caring relationship in a way that leads to abusive behaviour.

'Carer stress' has provided an interpretation of abuse but it has also been criticised for making abuse sound simplistic. There are many family carers and care workers who are regularly placed under incredible physical and emotional strain when supporting people, who do not abuse and would not be able to comprehend any reason to abuse. There are also people who have no direct responsibility in supporting people and therefore are not subject to great strain who do nonetheless abuse individuals that they know.

2 Exchange theory

This theory identifies the importance of power in relationships. It looks at the dynamics of relationships and the importance of rewards and punishments as a feature of relationships. Relationships may be viewed as give and take, with a sharing in terms of needs. If a relationship changes and is no longer reciprocal this can create a change in the attitude of one person and create circumstances where abuse is more likely. Situations where spouses no longer feel important in a relationship, or the relationship has changed significantly and one person does not fulfil the role that they once did, could be explained by this theory.

There are some relationships where from the onset there is an apparent imbalance in what individuals gain from the relationship, and yet both parties are very content with the relationship. Some people feel very fulfilled from providing a caring role to others and would not perceive that they are gaining nothing from the relationship.

3 Symbolic interactionism

This idea places more emphasis on the expectations of certain groups than individual rewards and punishments. Assumptions as to how certain groups will respond with no understanding of the individual's history can set up circumstances for abuse.

Older people living in a care home may as a group be more predisposed to abuse than individual adults in their own homes as they have a different status in society, and the expectation that society has of how this group are treated may be lower than that of adults in their own homes.

Biggs and Phillipson (1992) in Bytheway (1995) added a further approach.

4 Social construction

Whilst this theory was developed in relation to older people it can be applied to other groups. Society creates an understanding of groups and their expected behaviour by creating beliefs about individuals. People are then encouraged to conform in their behaviour that confirm those beliefs.

Case Study

Applying theory to abuse

Robert

Robert has multiple sclerosis and is now using a wheelchair for his mobility. He requires support with all his care tasks. His communication skills are changing so that he has reduced speech, but has not yet acquired another form of visual communication. Robert is being abused by his wife; they still live together. She shouts at him when he can't do things and constantly tells him how useless he is and he is making her a prisoner because she has to care for him all the time and can't do other things.

Joni

Joni is the care worker for a home care agency. She visits the same individuals on a regular basis, some of them each morning; she works on her own. She rushes when she is with people, moving individuals in a very rough way. She once tied a woman to a chair with her own belt so that she couldn't keep moving around.

Questions

1 Apply the theories of why people abuse to the situations of Robert and Joni.

2 What could be done to improve the situations? Think of how the situations could change in order to either

- ⊃ prevent the abuse from happening in the first place, or
- ⊃ stop the abuse happening now and ensure it doesn't start again.

There are other dimensions to the theories on why individuals abuse:

- ⊃ *Attachments in early life* The ability of individuals to make emotional connections to people can be influenced by the attachments that they had in their own life, including those in early childhood.

- ⊃ *Own experience of abuse* When we looked at what influences our own perception of whether abuse is taking place, one of the factors was whether we had experienced abuse ourselves. This could be as witnesses to regular abuse between parents or to other siblings, or it might be ourselves as the victims.

- ⊃ *Social interaction* The place of individuals within society has an impact on how they are treated. The oppression of groups can reinforce any negative behaviour by an individual to a member of that group, or make a person think that it is acceptable.

Who are the perpetrators of abuse?

You will find that abusers can be

- ⊃ family members – mothers, fathers, aunts, uncles, brothers, sisters
- ⊃ relatives by birth or marriage
- ⊃ other family relationships
- ⊃ individual care workers
- ⊃ groups of care workers
- ⊃ neighbours
- ⊃ friends
- ⊃ strangers.

The policy context of adult protection

As we discuss in the chapter on reflective practice (Chapter 2), the way we work is influenced by our knowledge, understanding and experience. Part of this knowledge is provided by legislation and guidance from government, from organisational policies and procedures.

The history of the caring professions provides some startling examples where good practice of care delivery at one time is then viewed as poor or even abusive practice at a later date. One reason why this happens is due to changes in values and how these are reflected in policies that are introduced at different times. Adult protection has not featured strongly in policy historically, and some would say it has been completely neglected. Child protection is a large area of the work of local authorities, and has been since the 1989 Children Act. Spouse and partner violence and violence from strangers in the context of discrimination are current concerns of government. Research into abuse has also been limited, partly due to it not being on the mainstream political agenda, and therefore not receiving funding.

All care workers have a responsibility to protect their service users from abuse. This is however a complex area due to the relationship of the state with the adult, which is significantly different to the framework that supports professionals in child protection. A Law Commission report in 1995 recommended that the government produce legislation to place the onus of responsibility with the local authority to investigate when they suspected abuse, but this legislation has not materialised. Local authorities are however now required to work with NHS organisations, trusts and primary care trusts, the police service and independent care providers in order to develop local joint strategies, policies and procedures for practice in relation to the protection of vulnerable adults (POVA), as the result of the government's *No Secrets* document published in 2000.

There is no specific legislation that provides a comprehensive framework for the care professional to work to, in relation to adult protection. A range of policies need to be considered depending on the vulnerable group that you work with, the care setting, and what your role is with individuals.

Policies that are historically linked to adult protection include:

The National Assistance Act 1948	Allows for local authorities to remove individuals with their consent from their homes to protect them for up to three months
National Assistance (Amendment) Act 1951	This allows for immediate removal with consent from the home
Court of Protection Rules 1948	The management of an individual's financial affairs
Domestic Violence and Matrimonial Proceedings Act 1976	Provides for injunctions against individuals

Domestic Proceedings and Magistrates Courts Act 1978	Introduced the idea of protecting the spouse from their partner
Mental Health Act 1983	Introduced the idea of capacity and ability of local authorities to remove an individual to safety
Matrimonial Homes Act 1983	This allowed for restricting, or reinforcing, the the right of a spouse to live at home
NHS and Community Care Act 1990	Provides for the assessment of individual need
Enduring Powers of Attorney Act 1995	Allows for an individual to act on behalf of the vulnerable adult
Human Rights Act 1998	Ensures that the articles in the European Convention are not contravened in England
Disclosure of Public Interest Act 1998	Rights of (care) workers when reporting incidents
Care Standards Act 2000	Creation of National Minimum Standards Registration of the care workforce

Powers of attorney

This is the process whereby someone is afforded responsibility for the management of an individual's finances. An individual, usually the next of kin, has to contact all other close relatives in the application of the power of attorney. There is of course the potential for this process to be abused. If a person is provided with powers of attorney and they start to abuse the power that they possess in making decisions about the individual's finances, then these can be reversed. An individual may require someone to be appointed with enduring power of attorney if they need the responsibility for decision-making to be taken on by someone else in the long term.

The 1998 Human Rights Act

This came into force on 2 October 2000.

> The HRA 1998 redresses the balance between the powers of the state and the citizen. It provides a framework of rights that can be used as a benchmark for reviewing the actions of social services and other public authorities. [Williams (2001)]

This legislation, which is discussed in more detail in the chapter on values in care practice (Chapter 3), allows individuals to consider whether an organisation is acting appropriately in the way that it sets up care. Individuals can challenge situations, those most relevant to care and potential situations of abuse may be the Articles relating to privacy and right to family life.

Care Standards Act 2000

This comprehensive piece of legislation set up the current framework for the regulation of care services. One of the strategies that this legislation introduced was the National Minimum Standards for particular areas of care. These provide a benchmark of quality that can be referred to about how care should be provided.

An illustration of their role in relation to addressing abuse is that if you provide home care for an adult with a physical disability there are now standards of service provision relating to domiciliary care.

> Standard 14 National Minimum Standards Domiciliary Care
>
> Robust procedures for responding to suspicion or evidence of abuse or neglect (including whistle-blowing) ensure the safety and protection of service users

The translation of this policy into working practices involves the development of procedures within an organisation, staff training and education about vulnerability, and also the inclusion of service users in identifying issues of abuse and ensuring they are aware of their rights and the responsibility of the service.

Further Research

1 Locate the relevant National Minimum Standards for the sector that you work in. Think about how your organisation has responded to these standards, by finding and reading all the documents – policies and procedures – that mention abuse and adult protection.
2 What message does the current Mental Health Bill give to society in relation to the status of individuals with mental health problems, and what protection do those individuals require from abuse?
3 Find out who is responsible for coordinating PoVA investigations, and what role you might have.

No Secrets

The most recent policy statement relating to adult protection is the *No Secrets* document [Department of Health (2000)]. This paper provided a detailed discussion of issues relating to the protection of adults from abuse and established expectations of how care services would work with other agencies.

Some key features of this document are that

- ⊃ it provides definitions of abuse (as stated earlier in this chapter)
- ⊃ it is not service specific and relates to all adults who experience vulnerability
- ⊃ it recognises that abuse can take a number of forms and is prevalent in a range of situations with people
- ⊃ it provides guidance and information about how agencies should work together.

No Secrets requires that agencies follow the principles of

- ⊃ working together
- ⊃ actively promoting the empowerment of individuals
- ⊃ supporting the rights of individuals
- ⊃ recognising people who are unable to take their own decisions
- ⊃ recognising that self-determination can involve risk
- ⊃ ensuring the safety of vulnerable adults
- ⊃ ensuring that when independence and choice is at risk that the individual is supported
- ⊃ ensuring that people know the law and access the judicial process appropriately.

[Department of Health (2000), page 21]

Other features are that

- ⊃ within organisations there should be one person responsible for managing responses to allegations of abuse
- ⊃ the National Care Standards Commission should be informed of abuse in care settings
- ⊃ the police should be involved more, and organisations should not attempt to deal with abuse as simply an issue of organisational discipline
- ⊃ sexual relationships between staff members and service users are illegal.

The above policies relate very specifically to adult protection. There are other types of policy that may have an impact on the experience of abuse, or provide an opportunity for preventing situations of abuse from arising.

Carers (Recognition and Services) Act 1995

1-(1)

The carer may request a local authority … to carry out an assessment of his ability to provide and to continue to provide care for the relevant person; and if he makes such a request, the local authority shall carry out such an assessment and shall take into account the result of that assessment when making their decision.

Think it over

Think about the section on theoretical explanations of abuse and consider how the Carers (Recognition and Services) Act 1995 might contribute to the prevention of abuse.

Your response may include the comments that

- ⊃ a carer's stress can create a change in the relationship between individuals
- ⊃ the government's recognition of the important role that carers play in supporting individuals can enable them to feel more valued
- ⊃ a carer can receive support to reduce their stress and isolation.

Community Care (Direct Payments) Act 1995

Your response may include:

- ⟳ being in control of the finances and organisation of his own care may empower him
- ⟳ feeling more valued as someone who is not just a recipient of care
- ⟳ having the power to stop a carer from providing his care.

The relationship between policy and abuse is not a clear one. It could be said that looking at the social construction theory as an explanation of abuse, Direct Payments could enable people with disabilities and older people to maintain a different status in society and have more power. It is felt by some commentators that the reason for abuse being neglected as an area of study is the low value attributed to groups who are the most vulnerable [Kingston and Penhale (1995)].

Further Research

When you have identified all the policies and procedures that are relevant to adult protection in your area of work, think about your awareness of each policy and identify where you can obtain more information about these.

Protection from other service users

We identified earlier that perpetrators of abuse come in many forms and are not restricted to one type of person. It is therefore necessary to spend some time thinking about service users who are perpetrators of abuse themselves.

It is important not to dismiss the inappropriate or abusive behaviour of a service user as just being a part of the person's learning disability, mental health or age. This is not respectful of either the victim or the capacity of the individual who is abusing. Abuse from other service users has been acknowledged more recently due to the impact of the Human Rights Act 1998. Historically, much abuse has been ignored as a consequence of group care or dealt with within the confines of the organisation.

In the chapter on values in care practice (Chapter 3) we discuss the idea of labelling and grouping individuals together within false categories. Just because four people share the label of 'learning disabled' doesn't mean that they are best suited to live together. The needs or personalities of these four individuals may not necessarily match up. Trying to meet everybody's needs may result in compromises being made; individuals may be unable to exercise full choice or liberty when sharing an environment with others.

Even if usual daily living is fine, due to resource constraints, care provision often has to be prioritised; if an emergency situation arises with one service user, the provision of care to others is affected.

The above examples illustrate that group care has the potential to reduce the quality in the experience of individuals. The immediate effect may be small, and not even noted in a care plan, but the ongoing persistent nature of it may prove very detrimental to an individual.

Case Study

A source of abuse

Cliff is keyworker to both Lisa and Suzanne, who are both learning disabled. Cliff had planned a trip with Suzanne as part of her care plan to develop her independence in using public transport travelling to college. On the morning of the day, Lisa has been destructive in the home and damaged some of Suzanne's personal possessions. She is aggressive, and although she has never physically harmed anyone her behaviour has created an unpleasant atmosphere. The team decide that Lisa needs some one-to-one input to both distract her from her current actions and to explore why she is feeling and behaving in the way that she is. This means that Suzanne's one-to-one trip is postponed to another day.

Whilst the team may feel that they have managed the situation well and prevented further disruption, what do you think Suzanne's experience of that day is? Her trip was cancelled and her potential for developing independence skills put on hold.

Another issue is where the actions of one person are directed at another service user and cause them harm. Individuals should not be exposed to more abuse by others because they share the same care needs. An experience of abuse is not lessened because that person has mental health needs themselves, or is physically or learning disabled. The importance of addressing the abuse is not reduced because the abuser is also a service user. This is where identification of risk in care plans is so important and the significance of individuals being supported in advocacy or provided with advocates is important.

Self-injury

It is not possible in this chapter to explore all the issues relating to self-injury, but brief mention will be made of some points here.

Self-injury ranges from scalding a hand to overdosing and suicide. Cutting is considered to be the most common form of self-harm. The key feature is that the victim is also the abuser. This does not mean that others do not hold any responsibility. The injuries may be self-inflicted, but this does not mean that the cause of it is down to the individual.

Research has led to current thinking that self-injury is associated with deep emotional pain. An individual engages in self-injury as a way of responding to that emotional pain. It helps because cutting oneself or burning oneself releases feelings of self-hatred, anger, anxiety. This is a complex process and one that requires specialist support. As a care worker it would be important not to respond to an individual inappropriately and to acknowledge that you might not have the knowledge or skills to support this person without any guidance from others. The individual is entitled to the knowledge and skills of a professional trained in this area of work, and you would benefit from appropriate support.

An outcome of self-injury for the person is that of punishment or taking control of their own feelings.

It is easy to dismiss self-harm as just attention-seeking behaviour. This simplifies what psychological processes are involved in the behaviour and limits the potential for an appropriate response. There is a strong association between attempted suicide, deliberate self-harm and successful suicide.

It is important to know when the experience and expertise of other professionals is required to support you as a care worker in an area of care that you may feel inadequately trained or prepared for. Accessing other support is a right of the individual and demonstrates your awareness of your responsibilities.

Procedures and good practice

This section now identifies some other areas of good practice involved in the protection of adults.

In following good practice you should

- ⮌ always make reference to national or local standards and procedures that state good practice
- ⮌ keep up to date with new policies and procedures
- ⮌ access advice from voluntary organisations who support the service user group that you work with.
- ⮌ ensure that service users are empowered and in control of the care that they are provided with, and not just passive recipients of care.
- ⮌ ensure that individuals do not have a different or watered down language used to explain their experience of abuse. For example, don't report that 'John was just being teased…', if John was being tormented verbally.

Cambridge in Carnaby (2001) exposes the use of the word 'sedation' instead of poisoning in relation to medication and people with learning disabilities.

Good practice starts with acknowledging that abuse does take place in care work, and sometimes the abusers are care workers, friends or relatives of the service user; abusers will not stand out from the crowd, they may look the same as you or I.

Good practice and procedures need to respond to the following dimensions of abuse:

- ➲ The vulnerability of the individual
- ➲ The nature and extent of the abuse
- ➲ The length of time it has been occurring
- ➲ The impact on the individual
- ➲ The risk of repeated or increasingly serious acts.

[Department of Health (2000)]

We investigated why abuse can take place in care settings when we looked at institutional abuse. Let us look at the dynamics of relationships with colleagues in order to anticipate possible scenarios, and for you to explore how you might handle situations if they arise.

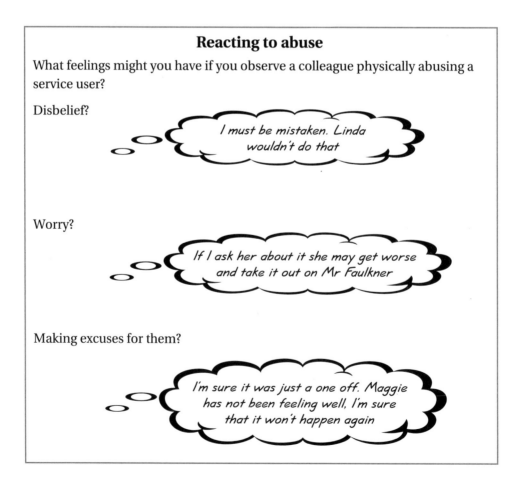

Reacting to abuse

What feelings might you have if you observe a colleague physically abusing a service user?

Disbelief?

I must be mistaken. Linda wouldn't do that

Worry?

If I ask her about it she may get worse and take it out on Mr Faulkner

Making excuses for them?

I'm sure it was just a one off. Maggie has not been feeling well, I'm sure that it won't happen again

Doing nothing is NOT an option, even if

➲ *you are worried about the consequences*
Think about the consequences of the abuse continuing.

➲ *you are friends/close colleagues with the abuser*
How long are you going to ignore the abuse – will you leave it too late?

➲ *you dislike the person being abused*
We cannot like everyone who we meet in our lives. As professional carers we do not have to like everyone to be an effective source of support for care users, and to have professional responsibility for them.

➲ *it is a senior person or your manager doing the abusing*
Your loyalty and responsibilities lie clearly with the service user being abused. There is legal protection for you in disclosing abuse through the Public Interest Disclosure Act.

Doing nothing is NOT an option
even if you don't know what to do

Sometimes care workers can be guilty of interpreting situations and explaining away abuse as we saw in the thought bubbles earlier. This is our way of having to deal with situations.

If you do nothing then you are

➲ colluding with the abuser

➲ supporting the abuser

➲ allowing the person to be abused

➲ contributing to the abuse of the person.

Care workers need to review their own practice and to expose situations for what they are, when they have identified an issue of abuse. We learn in the chapter on working with service users (Chapter 4) the importance of not always relying on a professional's interpretation of the relationship. This is true also of perceptions of abuse; it would not be right to only acknowledge abuse when a professional had deemed it to be so.

You may think that

➲ no one else has said anything

➲ the client hasn't said anything.

None of these mean that abuse is not taking place.

If you are in doubt

➲ ask the care worker – let them know that you saw what happened and that you thought it was unacceptable

➲ ask the service user – their account of what is happening is important.

You may be in a position to manage the risk through the care plan.

Good practice also involves prompt and accurate recording procedures.

> Verbal accounts of incidents were not supported by written notes in case files. This exacerbated the risks to the men's reputations without leading to appropriate safeguards for others. [MHF (1995)]

In making an accurate record of what happened you need to

- ⊃ make a written note of what happens in the appropriate document
- ⊃ make this written record immediately after the event
- ⊃ make sure your written record in the organisation's documentation is an accurate description of what you witnessed, not your opinions or thoughts
- ⊃ make a written record of your thoughts and opinions separately, in case you need to refer to these at a later date
- ⊃ inform your manager verbally as well
- ⊃ follow up your reporting of an incident. If no one responds to let you know that they are managing the situation, ask why?

Good practice with regard to a person's material possessions would include

- ⊃ handing someone their handbag for them to get out their purse rather than getting it out for them
- ⊃ handling personal possessions in full view of the person so that they have a sense of you doing it for and with, rather than instead of, them
- ⊃ not allowing common access to people's possessions. For some people they may need encouragement to retain their sense of personal space. Just because someone says 'Don't worry about me', doesn't mean it would be good practice to always accept this. Consider how to empower people to assert themselves in situations that could lead to abuse.
- ⊃ encouraging the person to be proactive in their own protection by
  - discussing his or her experience of care with people, so that it makes it easier to raise concerns and not wait for more serious issues and complaints
  - not always being accepting and trusting of people, to be discerning and retain their control over situations.

Consider what the service user's experience of any changes to their care might be.

Challenge the care practice of yourself and those around you. Make sure that abuse is not just seen as isolated events and that it is discussed in relation to a continuum of good/bad practice. Good practice in relation to values and empowerment, for example, can limit the potential for abuse happening.

This allows care workers to discuss neglect and abuse in a practical way that does

Figure 7.6 *Poor practice can lead to abuse*

not make it a taboo area of discussion. It can be an emotive area of practice to discuss and whilst you do not want to develop a culture of blame and accusations, you also do not want to work in a culture of secrecy and fear. It also will help you as an individual to review your own professional practice in an open way that challenges preconceptions of abuse as being something that only happens in highly public tabloid-headline ways.

Case Study

Organisational abuse

Fleetwood Lodge is a care home for older people. There is only one waking night staff on duty after 10 pm so clients have to be in bed by this time. Service users are sometimes rushed in their preparation for bed and 'encouraged' to put bed clothes on straight after dinner, as it makes things easier for the care staff. One service user who needs much support goes to bed at 6.30 pm and doesn't have company in the evening.

Questions

1 What do you think of the practices of the care staff in this organisation?

2 Write a list of what could be done to address the situation at Fleetwood Lodge.

The organisational constraints on good practice include

- ➲ routines of the service users being dictated by the staff rota
- ➲ service users not valued and given choice
- ➲ the needs of individuals not set out in care plans for the staff to follow.

What to do if you …

In this section we offer some more opportunities to reflect on how you might handle situations that arise, and then offer some practical advice about what might be appropriate good practice.

What would you do in the following situations?

1 You suspect a person is being abused

'I'd pretend its not happening and wait for it to stop.'

'I'd leave the job – I can't be dealing with issues like that.'

This is NOT how to respond.

Good practice would be to

- ➲ ensure that the service user is supported and reassured
- ➲ report the reasons you suspect someone is being abused to a senior manager
- ➲ start by believing the service user, even though after investigation it is shown to be a false allegation.

2 You witness abuse

'I'd walk away and pretend it didn't happen.'
'I'd ask to move to a different work environment.'

This is NOT how to respond.

Good practice would involve

- ⊃ telling the service user what you have seen and that you are required to report it to your manager
- ⊃ reporting what you observe
- ⊃ reassuring the service user that your manager will support them and try to ensure their safety.

3 Someone tells you that they are being abused by a colleague

'I'd think that they were exaggerating or misinterpreting something that had happened.'
'I'd tell them that it was probably just a one-off and I'm sure the person didn't mean it to be harmful.'

This is NOT how to respond.

Good practice would involve

- ⊃ telling the service user that they have done the right thing in reporting the abuse
- ⊃ asking the service user what they would like to happen in terms of reporting the abuse
- ⊃ asking the service user what support they feel that they would need in overcoming the abuse
- ⊃ being clear with the service user about your responsibilities and issues of disclosure/confidentiality.

Support as a care worker

What do you need as a care worker when supporting an individual who is being abused? Being a care worker does not make you immune to the emotional experience of situations, or give you automatic skills to cope with new events. Your ability to handle situations of abuse may be affected by

- ⊃ your own experience of abuse
- ⊃ the support you have or expect to be given by colleagues and/or manager
- ⊃ who the abuser is. It can be distressing to have to challenge the actions of respected colleagues or managers.

What can help is to focus on the needs of the service user and to access support early on. Focusing on the fact that you have contributed to the abuse stopping may provide you with a means of handling any emotions that arise. This can be important, especially where the service user may have not been aware of the abuse and they liked the abuser.

Depending on the role you have and the nature of the organisation, you may be able to access support through formal supervision, team meetings, a mentor. Your manager should be able to support you, but you may need to ask for their support if it is not offered to you.

If a situation at work raises issues you have not previously dealt with then you may need the support of professional help outside of the organisation. This does not mean you are not fit to be a care worker, it is simply that you need appropriate support.

References and further reading

Bradley (2001) *Understanding Abuse*, Worcestershire, British Institute of Learning Disabilities

Bytheway B, Bacigalupo V, Bornat J, Johnson J, Spurr S (1995) *Ageism*, Buckingham, Open University Press

Carnaby S (ed) (2002) *Learning Disability Today: Key Issues for Providers, Managers, Practitioners and Users*, Brighton, Pavilion

Department of Health (2000) *No Secrets*, London, HMSO

Department of Health (2000) *Care Standards Act*, London, HMSO

Department of Health (Date?) *National Minimum Standards for Care Homes*, London, HMSO

Eastman M (1994) *Old Age Abuse: A New Perspective*, London, Chapman and Hall/ Age Concern

Humphries S and Gordon P (1992) *Out of Sight*, Plymouth, Northcote House

Law Commission (1995) *Mental Incapacity*, London, HMSO

Pritchard J (ed) (2001) *Good Practice with Vulnerable Adults*, London, Jessica Kingsley

Sharkey P (2000) *The Essentials of Community Care*, Basingstoke, Macmillan

Williams J (2001) *British Journal of Social Work* 31

Wilton T (2000) *Sexualities in Health and Social Care: A Textbook* , Buckingham, Open University Press

If you work with a particular service user group it will be worthwhile looking at any text books on good practice with that group.

Become very familiar with the *No Secrets* document and keep up to date with your local policies of your own organisation.

Websites

Some websites of voluntary organisations have detailed information on abuse relating to individual service user groups.

Action on Elder Abuse, www.elderabuse.org.uk

Mental Health Foundation, www.mentalhealth.org.uk

planning and reviewing services

This chapter takes an in-depth look at all aspects of care planning. We start with a discussion on definitions and meanings. This is to ensure that, as usual, we do not take understanding for granted, and that we check with others that they fully know what is going on and what to expect. From there, we look at what legislation and official guidance has to say about the purpose and practices of care planning. In particular, we discuss in more detail the series of linked care planning activities that are outlined in guidance on care management. The chapter then takes a long look at how practitioners can create choice in their care planning, with particular reference to the use of Direct Payments.

An important recent development is the use of care outcomes. In this chapter, guidance is given on drawing up different types of care outcome. One theme of this whole book has been the need for practitioners to ensure that care practice is person centred and culturally sensitive. This theme is discussed in relation to care planning based on findings from research. In the latter sections of the chapter, we turn the focus on two very important but sometimes undervalued elements of care planning: monitoring and review. We explain why these activities are important, offering suggestions on good practice and again look at evidence from research.

This chapter addresses the following areas:

- ⊃ Definitions and meanings
- ⊃ Where care planning features in legislation and official guidance
- ⊃ Features of effective care planning
- ⊃ Care planning, care outcomes and care objectives
- ⊃ Care planning as a holistic and culturally sensitive activity
- ⊃ Monitoring care plans
- ⊃ Reviewing

After reading this chapter it is hoped you will be able to

1 explain what care planning means and why it is a key activity in all areas of social care work

2 identify key features of effective care planning

3 understand and apply the concept of care outcomes in care planning

4 explain the importance of monitoring care plans as well as methods of carrying them out

5 understand what purpose a review serves in the care planning process.

Definitions and meanings

As was evident when we looked at assessment, it is often useful to give consideration to the various possible meanings and interpretations that people can attach to a particular term. That way, we can anticipate and, hopefully, deal with any possible misunderstandings, ambiguities and uncertainties that may occur. Even though professionals might have a clear idea about what they're talking about (and this cannot be taken for granted!), this doesn't mean that those they work with share that understanding.

Think it over

Do a quick brainstorm. What comes to mind when the term care plan or care planning come to mind?

The term 'care plan' crops up in different contexts and has different meanings in each. Hospitals have care plans for their patients; health insurance companies also offer care plans. Outside of the care world, car salesmen, electrical retailers and a host of other firms, sometimes talk about having 'customer care plans'. In many of these contexts, the customer signs up to a scheme or a service which has been formulated, worded and arranged by the company. The terms and conditions naturally vary depending on the situation. Often the customer's input is minimal – it is something they get given.

It's clear that in the situations we have outlined, meanings differ and, as a result, it is unreasonable to expect someone who is a stranger to the care system to know exactly what care planning and a 'care plan' is. In the absence of any detailed explanation, people are likely to construct what for them is a plausible explanation. In many spheres of life, plans are seen as courses of action or documents drawn up by 'experts'. Often people take this assumption into social care situations as well.

Figure 8.1 *It's important to understand what a care plan is and what it involves*

In social care, it is worth noting that people interested in services hardly ever request a care plan. They might ask for a particular service, 'some help' or even an assessment but seldom will somebody specifically ask for a 'care plan'. Most people's tacit expectations are that once a need has been identified or a problem highlighted, the route to meeting that need or solving that problem will be left in the hands of you, the 'professional'. Expectations about being involved in the planning of care are often very low or even non-existent. Traditionally, social care workers also have left such assumptions unchallenged.

Clearly, these are generalisations but it is always a good idea never to take for granted knowledge of what care planning is. It is also worth reflecting on the forms of language we use and the different shades of meaning that can emerge often without us realising it. *What* a care plan is, *What* it is for, *What* it should include, *Who* should be involved, even *What* a care plan should look like, are all possible areas where interpretations can diverge. As we observed with the chapter on assessment (Chapter 6), it would be easy to assume that everybody automatically had the same meaning of what was going on, what processes were being followed – basically what should be happening. To help put this discussion into a context, we shall see how official guidelines explain what care planning means.

Where care planning features in legislation and official guidance

The following two extracts adapted from Mandelstam (1999) set out the legal basis of care plans within the sphere of community care.

> [1] Provision of services: care plans
> Care plans are not demanded by legislation, but are referred to in both policy guidance [*Community Care in the Next Decade and Beyond*, Department of Health (1990)] and practice guidance [*Care Management and Assessment: Practitioners' Guide*, Department of Health (1991)]. Failure, in respect of care plans and their content, to follow the former type of guidance without good reason, and to have regard to the latter, is unlawful. (page 63)

> [2] Care plans: scrutiny by the law courts
> When scrutinising closely the actions and decisions of local authorities, the courts have been prepared to examine how closely authorities follow the guidance about care plans – and to declare that substantial divergence from it without good reasons is unlawful .... The court in the Rixon case also pointed out that 'a care plan is the means by which the local authority assembles the relevant information and applies it to the statutory ends, and hence affords good evidence to any inquirer of the due discharge of its statutory duties'.

> In practice, reports have continued to suggest that service users do not receive care plans as envisaged by guidance. [Mandelstam (1999), pages 151–2]

Whilst there is no specified duty in law for local authorities to produce care plans, there is an official expectation that such plans will be not only be drawn up but also shared with those for whom the care is intended. The requirement for care plans is also emphasised in official guidance resulting from Care Standards legislation such as the regulations for National Minimum Standards in Residential Care and Domiciliary Care. In the *Care Management and Assessment* guidance issued to practitioners by the Department of Health in 1991, it is stated:

> A copy of the assessment of needs should normally be shared with the potential user, any representative of that user and all the people who have agreed to provide a service. Except where no intervention is deemed necessary, this record will normally be combined with a written care plan setting out how the needs are to be addressed. Where other agencies are involved, they should also have a copy of these plans. [Department of Health (1991), page 56]

This is emphasised again later.

Recording the care plan

Care plans should be set out in concise written form, linked with the assessment of need. The document should be accessible to the user, for example in braille or translated into the user's own language. A copy should be given to the user but it should also, subject to constraints of confidentiality, be shared with other contributors to the plan. The compilation and distribution of such records has implications for the necessary levels of administrative support.

A care plan should contain

- the overall objectives
- the specific objectives of
    - users
    - carers
    - service providers
- the criteria for measuring the achievement of these objectives
- the services to be provided by which personnel/agency
- the cost to the user and the contributing agencies
- the other options considered
- any point of difference between the user, carer, care planning practitioner or other agency
- any unmet needs with reasons – to be separately notified to the service planning system
- the named person(s) responsible for implementing, monitoring and reviewing the care plan
- the date of the first planned review.

[Department of Health (1991), page 67]

Below is a typical care plan produced in the late 1990s for an elderly man on the point of being discharged from hospital.

South London Social Services Community Care Division

Care Plan for:

Name: William Rees

Address: 17 Addison Road, London SW

DOB: 09.08.1921

Age: 78

Objectives of care plan (How are identified needs to be met?)

Mr Rees has a history of Parkinson's disease, which has now impaired all aspects of his life. Mr Rees will require a nursing home placement on discharge from hospital to meet both his physical and mental health care needs.

Planned start date:	As soon as possible.
Services to be provided:	
Service:	The provision of all nursing care needs
Frequency/Manner of provision:	Everyday
Provided by:	The Grove Nursing Home
Financial arrangement:	Client, and when Mr Rees's finances fall below the threshold, Social Services Department
Service:	To monitor and treat appropriately all pressure points, to prevent sacral pressure sores
Frequency/Manner of provision:	Everyday
Provided by:	The Grove Nursing Home
Service:	Assistance with all transfers
Frequency/Manner of provision:	As and when required
Provided by:	Nursing care staff
Service:	Assistance with nutrition, i.e. feeding and drinking
Frequency/Manner of provision:	As and when required
Provided by:	Nursing care staff
Service:	Assistance with toileting
Frequency/Manner of provision:	As and when required
Provided by:	Nursing care staff
Service:	Administering of medication
Frequency/Manner of provision:	As per discharge instructions
Provided by:	Nursing care staff
Service:	Assistance with all personal care tasks, i.e. washing, dressing, chiropody, fingernail care and any other personal care tasks required
Frequency/Manner of provision:	7 days per week
Provided by:	Nursing care staff
Service:	Finance/Personal allowance
Frequency/Manner of provision:	On a monthly basis
Provided by:	Private, Mrs Rees and her daughter Mrs Dawes
Financial arrangement:	Client and family

Monitoring and review

Who is responsible for putting the Care Plan into effect?

Name: Sarah Horne – Care Manager

Discharge Planning Team: South London Hospital, Candlewick Grove, London SE

Telephone: 020 7 777 7777

Who is responsible for monitoring the Care Plan?

Name: Sarah Horne

Address: As above.

Arrangements for review:

When? 6 weeks after placement

Where? The Grove Nursing Home

How? To be arranged by allocated care manager

What would trigger an early review? Home failing to keep to conditions of Care Plan

(*Assessor*) **Sarah Horne**   (*Manager*) **Tom Shore**

(12 July 1999)   (12 July 1999)

Think it over

1   The care plan above is based on a real life example but with the names changed. Evaluate the format. What do you think of the headings? Do they conform to the official guidance? What do you think of the language used? Comment on the style. What picture do you get of Mr Rees? What changes, if any, would you make?

2   Think about the care plans produced in your own agency. How far do they follow the points outlined in the official guidance? If possible, compare your findings with another.

In most texts, assessment and care planning go 'hand in hand'. In the care management guidance the seven stages involved in arranging care for someone in need are

- publication of information
- determining the level of assessment
- assessing need
- care planning
- implementing the care plan
- monitoring
- reviewing.

Stages 3–7 are regarded as part of the care planning cycle and this raises an important question. Are assessment and care planning two discrete and separate activities or are they two stages of what is fundamentally the same activity? To some extent, this depends on what we define as care planning. On the question of the care planning process, the guidance cited says that

Wherever possible, the practitioner responsible for assessing needs should carry on to relate those needs to the available resources. This will help to ensure that assessment does not become a theoretical exercise but is firmly rooted in practical reality. As with the assessment of need, it is helpful if practitioners approach care planning as a series of linked activities:

- ⊃ determine the type of plan
- ⊃ set priorities
- ⊃ complete definition of service requirements
- ⊃ explore the resources of users and carers
- ⊃ review existing services
- ⊃ consider alternatives
- ⊃ discuss options
- ⊃ establish preferences
- ⊃ cost care plan
- ⊃ assess financial means
- ⊃ reconcile preferences and resources
- ⊃ agree service objectives
- ⊃ co-ordinate plan
- ⊃ fix review
- ⊃ identify unmet need
- ⊃ record the care plan.

[Department of Health (1991), page 61]

We will return to discuss how many of these linked activities work out in practice later on.

Further Research

For a fuller official explanation of what is suggested for each of the linked activities listed it would be best to go to the source text: *Care Management and Assessment: Practitioners' Guide*. All statutory departments should have one. If not, a good academic library will have one in stock. In any event, locate the guidelines in question and ensure that you have a clear picture of what the Department of Health's own guidelines envisaged the care planning process to involve.

If your role in social care is more working for a domiciliary or residential service provider you should find and acquaint yourself with:

Department of Health (2002), *Care Homes For Older People National Minimum Standards Care Homes Regulations*, London, HMSO

Department of Health (2003), *Domiciliary Care National Minimum Standards Regulations*, available from Department of Health, PO Box 777, London SE1 6XH or website
http://www.doh.gov.uk/domiciliarycare/index.htm

Different agency approaches to the care planning cycle

We have seen what the guidelines say. Different agencies have evolved their own practices depending on their interpretation of how the assessment and care planning process should be undertaken. In some it is expected that the same practitioner will carry out all of the assessment, care planning and review activities in respect of their client. In others, one practitioner might do the assessment, another draw up the care plan and yet another the review. It is therefore important that practitioners are aware of their own agency's operating instructions and how the different activities relate to each other.

Think it over

Take the two different approaches outlined above. In the former, one person sees the whole process through. In the latter, tasks are divided up.

1 What system is in operation in your organisation? Discuss this with someone else from another agency.

2 What are the advantages and disadvantages of each approach?

⊃ Check your understanding

1 Is the need to produce a care plan specified in law? Explain.

2 According to the 1991 practitioners' guide (a) what should a care plan contain and (b) what are the 'series of linked activities'?

Features of effective care planning

Creating choice

As we discussed in the chapter on values (Chapter 3) offering choice to clients is a key value underpinning care activity. Good care practice is built around the important values of user participation, the rights of the individual to take risks and the individual's right to exercise choice and state their preferences about the way they are cared for. The spirit of the NHS and Community Care Act 1990 was that there should be a shift away from 'off the peg' service-led care planning and a move towards a more 'needs-led' individualised care planning process. This required a considerable shift in culture.

It's debatable as to what extent the service-led model has been abandoned. Critics argue that the fact that most local authorities block purchase much of their domiciliary, day and residential care from a small number of providers makes the possibility of a fully 'tailor-made' care system unrealistic. Budgetary constraints also tend to limit the choice of options available. Practitioner, client and carers therefore have to make choices within a framework of constraints.

We will cover many of the issues and difficulties in ensuring choice. We begin our discussion by looking at one of the most significant steps forward in this respect.

In an attempt to give more control over options to 'the consumer', in recent years governments have introduced and steadily expanded the concept of Direct Payments. This means that instead of having care services arranged for them, people considered eligible will be offered a sum of money with which they can purchase their own services.

The rationale for Direct Payments

The passing of the Community Care (Direct Payments) Act 1996 represents a significant change in the way local authorities provide for those deemed eligible for care services. The National Assistance Act 1948 which largely mapped out the post-war social care landscape, actually forbade local authorities from giving out money – it was for the bureau-professionals to arrange welfare services in kind for their clients. The 1996 Act enabled local authorities to make cash payments in lieu of services. Direct Payments represent a shift from the 'welfarist' tradition to 'consumerism'. Glasby and Littlechild (2002) argued that one of the barriers to Direct Payments being fully implemented was the following:

> By involving social workers in cash payments to individual services users, direct payments will have to overturn more than fifty years of social work practice if they are to become a mainstream feature of social service provision. [Glasby and Littlechild (2002), page 63]

Glasby and Littlechild felt that a lot of social workers' uneasiness in promoting Direct Payments could be explained by their reluctance to return to something that had echoes of social work's previous function as reliever of poverty in the days of the Poor Law. This might assume a stronger grasp of social work history than perhaps many of today's care managers actually possess, but it is another attempt to explain the less than full backing they seem to have received from many workers within the caring services.

In the first instance, only physically disabled people under the age of 65 were eligible. This has subsequently been extended.

In their key document *Modernising Social Services.* which was published in 1998, the New Labour government stated:

> One way to give control people over their lives is to give them the money and make them make their decisions about how their care is delivered.

> Direct Payments are giving service users new freedom and independence in running their own lives and we want more people to benefit from them.

It is now possible for people over 65, people with learning disabilities, and the parents of disabled children to receive Direct Payments.

The process

People still need to be assessed and meet the eligibility criteria at the level set by the local authority. If the eligibility criteria are met and the person is willing and able to use the money to buy services themselves, then payments will be made to an equivalent value of the level of care decided in the assessment.

Usually the person on Direct Payments effectively becomes an employer of their own staff or 'personal assistants'. The money must be used to buy support which meets their identified needs. This can also include financing short breaks away from the home, or services out of the home such as educational and recreational activities.

Most authorities have developed means by which independent agencies can give advice, assistance and support to people who need help with the employment and financial management aspects.

Obstacles to successful implementation

Although it is relatively early to judge, studies reveal that whilst increasing the take up of Direct Payments has been made a social services performance indicator, they aren't yet proving to be the 'revolution' in choice and control that was intended.

Hasler (2003) cites a study which revealed that a major concern amongst potential older applicants was the difficulty in being able to find a suitable person as a personal assistant. Other barriers that older people were facing in gaining access to a direct payment included

- a lack of knowledge about what a personal assistant is or can do
- no designated Direct Payments support worker to help them
- some care managers' uncertainty or confusion about the 'willing and able' criteria for eligibility to Direct Payments
- lack of time for care managers to explain the scheme properly
- concerns over protecting users from risk
- confusion over the role of informal carers

[Hasler (2003)]

A major issue which has been found from many different studies is that people could not employ their own relatives as personal assistants. Although new regulations issued by the Department of Health in 2003 decreed that, in appropriate cases, local authorities could approve the use of relatives [*Community Care, Services for Carers and Children's Services (Direct Payments) Guidance*, England (2003)].

Think it over

1 How much do you know about Direct Payments in your area?

2 What is the level of take up?

3 Do you know any service users on Direct Payments?

4 What are the advantages and disadvantages as far as care planning and choice are concerned?

5 How can the take up of Direct Payments be improved?

Hasler (2003) produces evidence that points to the fact that more people would consider Direct Payments if they could be assured of ongoing support, advice and back up. In the same article, she warns against practitioners making blanket assumptions about who could use Direct Payments and who couldn't. For example, given enough time and support, people with dementia have been able to benefit from Direct Payments but workers often presume that they won't be either willing or able.

Other ways of ensuring choice

Direct Payments are a way of creating more choice for service users but they are not the only way. The practitioner guidance (1991) contains the following statements about creating choice in care planning:

(1) Consider alternatives
However, in taking a fresh look at users' needs practitioners should not be constrained by the existing set of services. They should be equipped with the knowledge, or access to the knowledge, about the full range of services, not only in the statutory sector but also the independent sector.

Care planning should not be seen as matching needs with services 'off the shelf' but as an opportunity to rethink service provision for a particular individual. Within resource constraints, practitioners should give full rein to their creativity in devising new ways of meeting needs, picking up clues from users and carers about what might be most relevant and effective. Clearly, those who have some or all of the budget delegated to them, will have greater scope to create alternatives or to press service providers into arranging different forms of service.

(2) Discuss options
Once identified, these options should be fully discussed with the user and any relevant carers. This may involve service providers being invited to discuss the detail of their services directly with users, or users being taken on observation visits. For those users who have limited knowledge of what services provide or have difficulty with the concept of choice, for example those with learning disabilities, this exploration of options has to be as practical as possible so that they can begin to understand what it will mean for them personally.

(3) Establish preferences
Wherever possible, users should be offered a genuine choice of service options, appropriate to their ethnic and cultural background. This enables them to feel that they have some control over what is happening to them and reinforces their sense of independence.
[Department of Health (1991), page 63]

Choice, alternatives, options, preferences

The message from government guidance could not have been clearer. The Department of Health emphasise what they considered to be the key phrase in bold type. 'Wherever possible, users should be offered a genuine choice of service options'. In reality, the key phrase has probably turned out to be 'wherever possible' because despite practitioners' best efforts, there are many constraints around providing genuine choice.

In the days of stagecoaches the Cambridge liveryman Thomas Hobson became famous for offering his customers a choice of any of his horses – as long as they took the one nearest the door. This is the kind of choice that many practitioners have reluctantly become used to offering to service users.

Clearly, it is an exaggeration to claim that no genuine choice is being offered. There are many examples of innovative and creative practice up and down the country. However, as we saw with the implementation of Direct Payments, there can often be a gap between what is meant to be happening and what happens in reality. We need to look at reasons why.

Think it over

Reflect on your practice and the practice within your agency in general. Do you think that service users have a 'genuine choice of service options'? If they don't, what reasons are there for this?

The mixed economy of care

The whole basis of the community care system introduced in the early 1990s was that it would operate within a 'mixed economy of care'. This was a deliberate shift away from relying mainly on social services provision. The White Paper, *Caring For People* [Department of Health (1989)] laid out the vision. It expected local authorities to take all reasonable steps to secure a diversity of care provision. Local authorities were urged to ensure that new providers could enter the 'market' with ease. Money was deliberately channelled towards the independent sector to ensure that this sector would be stimulated. This policy was designed to create more competition in the care market (thus achieving more efficiency and effectiveness) and more choice for the 'consumer'.

When community was first introduced, various models of care management were discussed as being appropriate for local authorities to adopt (Clark and Lapsley, 1996). One model sees the practitioner holding a 'devolved budget', dealing with providers on an individual basis, negotiating service specification, agreeing contracts and so on. Here, an individual care manager has a relatively large amount of autonomy in how they dip into the mixed economy of care. In reality, the most common model adopted is one where the business of negotiating care provision and making contracts takes place centrally within a local authority. The individual practitioner in this case has much less autonomy because they mostly 'commission' from what has already been contracted. Most authorities operate a list of approved, contracted care providers who, in the first instance, their care managers are expected to use. Therefore, to a large degree, the amount of choice a service user has is bound to be linked to the range of provision their care manager is expected to commission from. In some areas, there will be more diversity than in others.

The degree of choice and diversity of provision will be shaped by wider social and economic factors such as budgets, the geography of the area – for example, rural or urban – the local labour market, the size and characteristics of the local voluntary sector and so on. This is why the phrase 'wherever possible' is such an important one. This is also why it is important for practitioners to make sure that unmet needs are fed back to those responsible for planning service provision. It is no good for staff on the front line to complain about lack of options if they don't pass on to those higher up their specific comments about what should be available and what needs are not being met.

Costs

The issue of choice of provision cannot be raised without consideration of costs. All social care takes place within a financial context and care planning is bound to be constrained by budgetary factors. Practitioners are expected to produce care plans that are cost effective and good value for money.

The tradition of means testing in adult social care means that before a care plan is implemented the service user has to undergo a financial assessment. There is also the separate point that the cost of a care plan usually has to fall within certain 'bench mark figures' or else the practitioner is required to argue a special case with those who control the budgets. Several pieces of research indicate that practitioners are not always comfortable with the financial aspects of care planning. For some, this 'preoccupation' with costs and charging cuts across 'social work' principles such as need.

> Sorry to ask all these questions, but I need to assess and also if you've got any savings as well I need to know. We should have been accountants not social workers. [Worth (2002), page 324]

However, anyone responsible for producing a care plan is not doing anyone any favours (least of all the service user) by trying to ignore the financial dimension to care planning. It would be easy to produce an attractive, costly, but ultimately unauthorisable care plan. All this is likely to do is unfairly raise expectations only to dash them later. It can also create unnecessary equity issues within the agency. The budget constraints are usually there to ensure a fair allocation of resources as much as anything else. Skilful care planning exploits the system rather than simply fights or denies it. Issues of cost can be tackled in various ways.

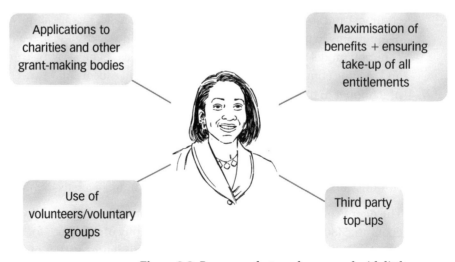

Applications to charities and other grant-making bodies

Maximisation of benefits + ensuring take-up of all entitlements

Use of volunteers/voluntary groups

Third party top-ups

Figure 8.2 *Resources that can be accessed with little or no cost*

Case Study

Care planning

Graham Deakin is 52. He is a wheelchair user and has some cognitive impairment affecting memory and communication due to a motor vehicle accident about 16 years ago. He is on benefits and lives in a flat in a sheltered scheme. He receives domiciliary care every day. However, he gets bored and lonely, often complaining that he is 'fed up with the same four walls'. This can often lead him to get drunk as a way of dealing with his loneliness. This tendency has made it even more difficult for him to make relationships with other people. He has two sons but they both live quite a distance away. In fact one has been in and out of prison several times which upsets Graham. He blames himself and slips into self pity.

You suspect that Graham is quite depressed but he won't accept help in this respect. For the last five years, his only annual holiday has been a week in a Welsh seaside resort. This is part of a scheme run by a charity for people with disabilities. This holiday is classified as 'respite' by the social services and is subsidised out of their younger person's physical disability respite budget. Pressures on this budget mean that only one week a year can be afforded.

Questions

Having discussed it with Graham, you want to produce a care plan that enables him to have not only more holiday opportunities but also more chances to get out and meet people in general.

1 What ideas can you generate to enable him to meet this care objective?

2 Using a format suggested by official guidance, put together a care plan which addresses Graham's needs.

Information

A major way of ensuring genuine choice is by the provision of information so that basically people know what is available and they can then make an informed choice. In its guidelines issued to social services departments in 1991, the Social Service Inspectorate outlined the following set of instructions:

> Your information system should
>
> ⊃ ensure that people have information that is straightforward, relevant, accurate and sufficient so that they can make informed choices
>
> ⊃ ensure that everyone has access to this information in a variety of forms appropriate to their needs
>
> ⊃ be regularly reviewed and up-dated →

and take special account of those people who

- have different cultures and languages
- are sensorily impaired
- have restricted mobility
- are isolated within their communities
- have difficulty with reading or writing
- are not motivated to seek or use information.

You can do this by

- consulting users, their carers, community groups and those who provide services about the content and style of the information
- giving better information to callers. You should consider the role of receptionists in relation to this
- building information networks on existing patterns of community life, e.g. libraries, religious and community centres, post offices and surgeries. Include key community leaders and spokespeople
- being open about what people can and cannot have and the constraints on their choices
- using the expertise and experience of others to define the content and presentation of information.

Information in your guide about users whose needs make them eligible for services and the types of services available should be brief and clear.

It should say

- for whom the service is intended
- what it does
- how available it is
- what it costs
- how to apply for it.

[Department of Health/Special Services Inspectorate (1991), pages 11–12]

The bulk of this message is applicable to any care agency. It is clearly not just about the quantity of information given out but also the quality. Information has to be communicated in a meaningful format. Morris (1997) makes the following point:

> The need for information is on-going. Services change, personnel change, and people's conditions/impairments may change – all of this means that it is unlikely that someone's entitlement to information will be met once and for all at a particular time. And information must be in a form which makes sense to, and in a format which is accessible to, the person concerned. (page 47)

Further Research

Figure 8.3 *Agencies need to make clients aware of the options so that they can make informed choices*

Time and effort

What we have seen so far indicates that if care planning is to properly involve service users and offer them genuine choice this means that the practitioner has to be prepared to put in time and effort.

Firstly, they have to ensure that they, themselves, are up to date with as much relevant information as they can be. Strategies for this are the following:

➲ Collecting, reading and storing relevant leaflets, brochures etc. on services – build up your own database. Ensure that you are familiar with the information stored in your office – or at least where to find it!

⊃ Network both within your own organisation and in the wider community – locate and learn how to access the knowledge of others – other people's databases. There is more on working collaboratively in Chapter 5.

⊃ Look out for open days, professional lunches, conferences etc.

⊃ Get your name on mailing and emailing lists of relevant information, e.g. Help the Aged, Mencap

⊃ Internet – explore what's on the web and bookmark relevant sites.

The important thing with this is not to attempt to walk around with every last detail in your head but to know where to access information and to have a general idea of the range of information that's 'out there'.

The second important point in this respect, is for time and effort to be spent passing the correct information onto your client in a meaningful and helpful way. It is possible to run through various options relatively quickly on a verbal basis. However, have they all been heard, remembered and understood?

It is important to be aware of the language we use, and to check understanding.

An equally challenging task is enabling people to sample or try out different services so that they actually experience them before giving their agreement to a care plan.

For example, it is good practice to give an older person the opportunity to see a choice of facilities (this could be day centres or residential homes), in order to help them find the provision that most suits their needs and preferences. However, this does raise some pertinent questions. Apart from the logistical questions of arranging transport and availability, an obvious one is how many should they see – all the ones on the list or just those with vacancies at the present time? Then there's the question of whether you should accompany them. Can they take a friend or relative? How long should they stay? Is it possible to get a realistic feel of a place anyway just by visiting?

This throws up fundamental issues for the practitioner, particularly about their power to create or limit choice. It is very easy to manipulate choice. If someone never hears of an option how are they able to choose it?

It's impossible to provide the perfect formula on exactly how to resolve all these issues. For one reason, if a practitioner is trying to manage a full caseload, there are limits to how much time and effort they can devote to one client at the expense of others. This can easily run into discriminatory practice. Clearly, practitioners need to work within their own agency's practice guidance, but the most effective way of promoting choice takes us back to the principle of user involvement. Much has been discussed on this topic in various sections of this book. As far as care planning is concerned, it is helpful to consider the four types of interaction set by Morris [(1997), pages 52–53]. These are:

1 **Consultation** This means literally asking someone about what they want to happen in their lives and is the minimum form of involvement. Morris cautions that 'it can be all too easy to limit consultation to a friend/relative/neighbour identified as a "carer" who is probably easier to communicate with'.

2 **Participation** This is a more active involvement in the decisions to be made about how to meet someone's needs. It requires professionals to recognise the expertise and experience of the person who needs support in their daily lives. This doesn't mean diminishing the expertise and experience of the practitioner but rather putting this at the disposal of the service user. Morris states that this 'requires a shift in culture'.

3 **Veto** Giving someone a veto means giving them the right to say no. A care manager or a personal support worker could, for example, say to a service user, 'Let's try out this way of meeting your need but if you're not happy you can say no and we'll try something else.' Veto according to Morris 'is an important way of shifting the balance of power and a key method of enabling people to make choices'.

4 **Delegated control** This means passing over responsibility for making decisions about how assessed needs are met to the person who needs the support. Direct Payments could be seen as a form of delegated control, but in practice some argue that local authorities attach too many strings to Direct Payments for them to be regarded as a pure example.

In choosing which type of interaction to pursue, Morris [(1997), page 57] argues that 'It is not a question of picking just one form of user involvement but often using a combination, or using different forms at different times.'

As far as the question of offering choice in care planning is concerned, we have seen that there is a range of issues and constraints that practitioners and their agencies need to be aware of. These need to be confronted if the rhetoric of genuine choice is to become a meaningful reality for service users. Issues of cost need to be fully recognised. Good quality information needs to be communicated and, finally, achieving 'genuine choice' for service users will inevitably involve time and effort for practitioners as they do their research, gather information and enable meaningful decision-making to take place. This requires that service users and carers have properly understood what's available.

⊃ Check your understanding

1 What is the rationale for Direct Payments?

2 How is the procedure for Direct Payments supposed to work and what can sometimes prevent the smooth running of the procedure?

3 What are the three statements in practitioner guidance that refer to choice?

4 Why is it important to consider costs when care planning?

5 How can practitioners help with costs?

6 Identify *six* points that an agency needs to take note of in the way it provides information.

7 Explain *three* ways in which practitioners can gather the information they need to care plan effectively.

8 What are Morris' four types of interaction to ensure user involvement?

Care planning, care outcomes and care objectives

We saw that the Department of Health practitioner guidance talked about care planners setting objectives as well as the criteria for measuring how and whether they had been met. In recent years, there has been considerable discussion on how to successfully tighten up and focus this aspect of care planning by utilising a 'care outcomes' approach [Qureshi and Nicholas (2001)]. This can be related to key messages from government. Much New Labour policy has been based on the concept of the 'Third Way'. This means that they are not committed to total public sector control of social care, neither are they committed to total privatisation. Instead they are happy to combine elements of each as long as certain key objectives are met. The government would say it is operating on the basis of 'what works'. We see evidence of this approach in *Modernising Social Services*:

> Our third way for social care moves the focus away from who provides the care, and places it firmly on the quality of services experienced by, and the outcomes achieved for, individuals and their carers and families.
> (Cm 4169, Para 1.7)

> At the individual level care planning needs to be thorough and outcome focused. [Social Care Group (1998), para 3.4]

> It is rare to see the desired outcome of any service in the care plan or written in the case file. [Audit Commission/SSI (2000), page 5]

The idea of using care outcomes in all areas of social work and social care is endorsed by recent shifts towards 'evidence-based practice'. It is an approach to care planning that emphasises transparency, accountability and, importantly, interventions based again on the principle of 'what works'. Risk assessment and risk management tools are examples of where evidence-based practice has become more established. Nevertheless, Qureshi and Nicholas argue that this shift towards focusing more on outcomes requires a 'culture change' in social services. Arguments for using an outcomes approach are that it helps clarify the rationale and purpose of any intervention and, if the desired outcomes are written in clear achievable objectives, not only are all parties clear about what's happening and why, the effectiveness of any intervention should be easier to measure – as the desired outcomes will be there as a clear point of reference together with the steps taken to achieve them. Evaluation of the effectiveness of social work interventions is another major, related theme of the late 1990s onwards.

What is an 'outcome'?

An 'outcome' is interpreted as the impact or effect on the lives of service users or carers [Qureshi and Nicholas (2001)]. Specifically designed to inform the practice of those working with older people, the authors introduce three different types of outcome. Those concerned with: maintenance, change and process. The following extracts explain more about what is meant by these three outcomes.

Maintenance outcomes

These outcomes have to be maintained in a continuing way although the level of service required to achieve this may vary over time. They may be maintained in the short term, during recovery or rehabilitation for example, or in the long term, perhaps where deterioration in a person's condition is expected.

An example of a maintenance outcome for the older person would be for that person to be

Personally clean and comfortable.

An older person who is not able to carry out their own personal care is personally clean and comfortable, presentable in appearance, has a nutritious and varied diet, and is in bed or up at appropriate times of day.

A maintenance outcome for the carer would be to

Maintain health and well-being (physical, mental, emotional, spiritual).

Negative impacts of caring on health and well-being minimised; able to have sufficient sleep, exercise and some fulfilment/satisfaction within their life.

Change outcomes

Change outcomes are changes which result from tackling barriers to achieving quality of life, or reducing risks.

An end point to the intervention can be defined, at which the intended improvement can be said to have been achieved, or partly achieved, and the level of services required can be reduced, or the focus of continuing services becomes maintenance.

Qureshi and Nicholas (2001) give 'recovery or rehabilitation' as a general area for a change outcome. A specific example of such an outcome is

Regaining skills and capacities (for independent living).
Only an outcome of services if social care staff are explicitly working on specific activities which are designed to help people to re-acquire skills and capacities.

Another example of a change outcome is

Reducing or eliminating risk of harm.

Modifying the environment, averting homelessness, dealing with possible physical abuse or injury (if risks are being reduced and kept at lower levels by continuing service input then maintaining personal safety is perhaps more appropriate than this category).

An example of a family and carer related change outcome would be

Improving significant /close relationships.

Enabling people to see each other's point of view, reducing tensions within relationships; mediating between conflicting interests.

Process outcomes

Process outcomes are the results or impacts of the way in which the package of services is provided.

A general area for a process outcome is that

Services 'fit' with (or support) other sources of assistance and life choices.

A specific example of a 'process outcome' is

'Good fit' with cultural and religious preferences.

The person feels that services take account of preferences about relevant issues, such as the way in which domestic tasks are performed, expectations of family members, staff characteristics, language skills and the nature of appropriate food and activities.

Yet another general process outcome area would be that the older person has

Influence over services, and impact of interactions with staff.

With the following being a specific process outcome:

Having a say over personal and domestic assistance.

The user or carer can, if they wish, influence tasks performed, timing or personnel involved, in order to achieve their desired outcomes

Case Study

Care outcomes

Sidney Skinner is 58 years old. He has two grown-up children – Roy 30 and Maureen 28 – who live nearby with their own families. Sidney is a foreman in a French polishing company. He has worked for the company for over 30 years. His main leisure activities are the occasional trip to the pub and going to football with his son Roy most weekends. His wife, Elsie, does a part-time job three mornings a week in the local newsagent. Sidney is a smoker, but despite having a bit of a cough in the mornings, has never had a day off work sick.

Three weeks ago Sidney had a bad stroke and was taken to hospital. The signs are that, whilst he may regain some functioning, he will remain mainly paralysed down his left side. The doctors are saying that his ability to speak will remain affected, as will his ability to eat the way he used to. His mobility is also likely to remain impaired and he will need physiotherapy. Incontinence will also be a factor in his life.

Sidney's employers are being understanding but it is clear that unless his recovery exceeds expectations, he will not be able to return to his job. Sidney says he will be at a complete loss just being at home all day. Elsie has indicated that she will attend to Sidney's personal care needs as far as possible. She is in a dilemma about working. She could extend her hours at the newsagent's but that would mean leaving Sidney longer on his own at home.

Task

Imagine you need to draw up a care plan for Sidney. Using the outcomes described, try to write your care plan in terms of care objectives.

How outcomes are useful

There is clearly a skill in being able to draw up meaningful, clear and measurable outcomes for care plans. It is easy to lapse into identifying a service and making this the outcome instead of specifying an outcome and then identifying a particular service or strategy as a means of attaining that outcome. Many agencies are using the kinds of headings and examples given above, others are drawing up their own. However generally applicable some of the outcomes might seem they shouldn't just be used in an 'off-the-peg' fashion, they still need to be individualised around a particular client. The 'outcomes' approach is meant to improve and clarify the links between the assessment stage and the care planning stage, particularly the activities of

- ⊃ setting priorities
- ⊃ discussing options
- ⊃ establishing preferences
- ⊃ reconciling preferences and resources
- ⊃ agreeing service objectives.

For most people you could say that the intended outcome was for them 'to remain living as independently as possible'. Whilst completely understandable as an aim, it is nonetheless very vague and wouldn't tell anyone what to do next. It needs to be broken down. The care planning work between worker and client is about turning that broad aim into more specific outcomes. Importantly, the first task is gathering an understanding of what independence means for that person and then, in order for it to be realisable, looking at what should stay the same, what should change and how care should be arranged so that the broad aim is realised.

Subjective and objective dimensions to outcomes

A strength of using outcomes together with agreed indicators of how you know when that outcome is being met, is that it helps the process of monitoring the effectiveness of the care plan. Care planning becomes more focused. However, a possible weakness of this approach is that, if applied simplistically, it might over-emphasise what can be seen from 'the outside', concentrating simply on externally observable life conditions because they are the easiest to measure. As far as possible, both objective and subjective aspects should be considered. If, for example, we take the desired outcome for someone 'to be secure' then we should recognise that security is a subjective feeling as much as it is a set of objective circumstances, such as locks on doors and windows, safety systems fitted and so on. This underlines the prime importance of negotiating with the client themselves, establishing what 'feeling secure' actually means for them. Their own indicators might be the knowledge that someone was on the end of a phone, or that someone was going to call round at a particular time of day. These kinds of activities can then be built into a care plan and linked to that particular outcome.

Time objectives

Lastly, it is good practice to set a timescale for care planning. There are several good reasons for this, such as

- ⊃ so that needs can be met in a timely fashion and so prevent a situation deteriorating
- ⊃ so that unnecessary risks are not allowed to develop
- ⊃ all parties have some way of checking the progress of the implementation process. This enables people to have realistic expectations of what will happen and when
- ⊃ relieving pressure on others – either informal networks or other services
- ⊃ avoidance of drift.

The time scale one sets will be influenced by a range of factors, including

- ⊃ the complexity and seriousness of the case
- ⊃ known availability of resources
- ⊃ agency and government guidelines – for example over discharges from hospital
- ⊃ time available to the practitioner.

It is pointless and counterproductive to promise immediate results, if, in reality, the plan is going to take time to come together. Similarly, to give no indication of timing leaves people anxious, uncertain, devalued and powerless.

Figure 8.4 *There is no point in making promises that can't be kept*

User-defined outcomes

Most of what we have discussed so far has been about care outcomes that have been largely drawn up by professionals. In the spirit of 'user-involvement', there is no reason why service users shouldn't be able to participate in drawing up their own outcomes. This practice is in its infancy but has been tried in various locations. The 'Shaping Our Lives' project has been working in this area since 1996. Together with other groups, it has conducted research into what a variety of service users (older people, mental health users, minority ethnic communities and disabled people) made of this idea and how it worked in practice.

The study found that

- it was impossible to separate ideas of user-defined outcomes from action to define and achieve them
- involvement to support user-defined outcomes takes more time and resources than usually envisaged
- users felt that services continued to show a lack of respect. The value of their own outcomes was not acknowledged nor valued
- users valued the ordinary things in life – cleaning, shopping, support at home; they found it very difficult to get services to prioritise support in these areas
- other services were very important to people beyond ideas of social care, in particular, housing and information
- although the initial research had highlighted the value of direct payments, the development projects showed that users were still not aware of this option
- it was important for users to meet together to strengthen their own voice in achieving the outcomes they valued.

There are several significant messages in these findings. One in particular showed that 'people in receipt of Direct Payments had very clear ideas about the outcomes that they had from the support that they arranged. This clearly showed the effectiveness and importance of Direct Payments in this regard – and pointed to possible lessons for other services to provide a similar level of choice and empowerment.' Another important finding was that once service users grasped the idea of looking at services in terms of outcomes, they tended to view the outcomes they wanted for themselves from a 'holistic perspective'. This meant that they didn't confine themselves to outcomes which could only be met by social care services; they included housing, transport, employment, income and benefits, and broader issues around discrimination and equality. This means that these broader outcomes – if they are to be met – imply at the very least, multi-disciplinary working and, more likely, new ways of working which require a degree of linking up and collaboration hitherto unprecedented in social care.

Case Study

User-defined outcomes

Lucy Garner is 83 years old. She has very restricted mobility and cannot walk unaided. This is because of rheumatoid arthritis, osteoporosis and an ulcerated leg. Her husband, Harry, is physically fit but suffers from dementia. Together, the couple have coped reasonably independently. There is a daughter who lives locally and keeps an eye on them. She works full-time. Because of a recent fall, Mr Garner is now in hospital for a least a month, maybe longer.

Task

You have visited to assess and make a care plan for Mrs Garner. She has expressed a wish to stay in her own home.

➲ Reread the section on care outcomes (pages 405–406). How might your planning be expressed in terms of maintenance, change and process outcomes?

➲ Give your views on how the time objectives for this care plan might be realistically assessed and set.

➲ How might you ensure that at least some of your outcomes are 'user-defined'?

➲ Check your understanding

1 Explain why the use of care outcomes has become more popular.

2 What is an 'outcome' and what three kinds of outcome are outlined by Qureshi and Nicholas? Give examples of each.

3 Explain the difference between subjective and objective aspects of outcomes.

4 Give five reasons to set time-scale objectives.

5 Give a brief summary of what research into 'user-defined' outcomes has found.

Care planning as a holistic and culturally sensitive activity

We argued in Chapter 6 that a good assessment takes the whole person into consideration, their strengths and weaknesses, their existing networks, in short, their total situation. Care planning should be informed by exactly the same values. Terms like care plan and care package can often convey meanings that are clinical, businesslike, treating care as if it is a commodity, something 'cut and dried'. The person for whom the care plan has been drawn up runs the risk of being dehumanised or objectified by this way of thinking about care planning.

To achieve a care plan that is holistic and culturally sensitive we must take a person-centred approach. As we have already observed, many agencies and practitioners take it for granted that their practice is person-centred. Often we believe this without stopping to think whether this is actually the case.

Think it over

Brainstorm responses to the following two questions:

1 In care, what does 'person-centred' actually mean?

2 How would a 'person-centred care plan' differ from a 'non-person-centred care plan'?

Below is an example of a format developed and used by a team for people with learning disabilities. It has been put together in a way which keeps everything linked to that particular person's life. What are your thoughts?

who am I?
* Sociable
* Able
* Nice smile   ☺ ☺ ☺
* Tidy
* Organised
* Routine
* Kind
* Friendly
* Likeable
* Smart
* Helpful
* Sense of humour
* Warm
* He hugs

The message from research

Research carried out by the Social Services Inspectorate found that:

> ... often care managers moved too readily to suggesting the use of an existing service. Across the inspected councils, many of the care plans which we examined were really service plans. They lacked a focus on intended outcomes against which the contribution of particular services could be assessed. Such service plans made it difficult to determine what the service provided was intended to achieve. The haste to identify services limited opportunities to explore other ways of achieving desired outcomes or goals which did not rely on existing services. [Department of Health/Social Services Inspectorate (2000), page 31]

Think it over

From your own experience how far would you say that the care plans produced by your agency are actually *service plans*? If they are, what are the reasons behind this? How can things change?

The SSI report flags up the value of focusing on intended outcomes rather than fitting the person into an existing service. If, as a practitioner, you work for an agency that uses a lot of block contracted provision, the temptation is to 'take the provision' to the client and the care plan boils down to basically linking the person to the services in the most appropriate way with very little other discussion. This probably happens quite frequently and probably most people make the most of it in a kind of 'fits where it touches' way – such are the low levels of many service users' expectations. However, this approach is unsatisfactory for all concerned and can be improved by at least starting with the person and not with the service.

Cultural sensitivity

As we have seen elsewhere, all aspects of social care should be underpinned by anti-discriminatory practice. Most workers are aware of this but can interpret it in a way that is superficially well-intentioned but lacks culturally sensitivity. The quotation below illustrates this well-meaning but misguided approach.

> It doesn't matter to me what colour their skin is. I've been working with older people for 23 years and I treat them all the same. [A white social worker, Department of Health/Social Services Inspectorate (1998), page 40]

That report found that 'there were some good examples of practice and service delivery'. However, it was also found that the variety of services available which actually offered choice to older black people was limited and the ethnocentric (mainly white-orientated) nature of service provision meant that many black elders had difficulty in having their needs met.

Cultural issues that can cause problems

Language difficulties

If someone doesn't have English as their first language this raises many important issues about communication. For example, how do we ensure that we fully understand someone's situation? There are risks associated with using a relative as a translator because they may well give their own slant to what is being said – even without realising it. We need to seek the person's own views – unmediated. Serious consideration therefore needs to be given to finding a proper, trained interpreter.

An important point about language is that it is an essential part of what makes us who we are – our identity in other words. Care services given in a language that is not our own is the same as living in a silent world. It cuts us off from social contact and an opportunity to express ourselves. Through language we establish who we are and what we're like. To take the opportunity to communicate away from somebody is to take away much of that person's individuality.

Case Study

A cultural issue

Pavel Szymczyk is a 78-year-old man who came from Poland after the Second World War. He is a widower with no children locally. He learned to speak English pretty well. However, a few years ago he began to develop dementia. The effect of the dementia has been to make it more or less impossible for him to understand and communicate in English. Polish seems to be the only language he uses. The

GP feels that Mr Szymczyk is in need of a care assessment because he is at risk of loneliness, he is forgetting to feed himself and failing to attend properly to his personal care.

Questions

1 What cultural issues does this case study raise?
2 What approach would you take to ensure that your care planning was culturally sensitive?

Diet

Diet is important in many religions and cultures. It is one of many cultural issues that can be problematic and can easily lend itself to stereotyping. The case study will illustrate one such difficulty.

Case Study

An issue of diet

Ai Heng is an elderly Chinese woman who came to the attention of the social services. She had come to Britain about 10 years ago when she joined her family. She has been in a sheltered scheme for the last three years. Her English is not particularly strong. The family are quite busy with their work and searched for help when Ai Heng became rather restricted in her mobility and quite low in mood. She was found a place in a day centre. The manager, in an attempt to be culturally sensitive, decided that they would order food especially for her from the local Chinese takeaway. They had great pleasure in serving up a meal of sweet and sour pork on a bed of rice. However, they were taken aback by Ai Heng's outraged response. Only with further investigation did it emerge that Ai Heng was Muslim and had never eaten pork in her life.

There are many religious restrictions on diet. But religion need not be the only factor – vegetarians often feel that their lifestyle is ignored when care services are planned.

Religious practices

Residential homes or day centres that are predominantly geared up for white, Christian service users need to be sensitive to the desire of people from other cultures and religions to participate in religious worship. One home's response when they were told that a Muslim resident wanted to have a place where he could worship was to partially clear the laundry. In Islam Friday is the Sabbath. It just so happened that Friday was the home's main laundry day. This rather added insult to injury. The resident was given the feeling that he was creating a fuss and disrupting the running of the home. This important part of his care plan had not been thought through, possibly because the care manager who placed him was not religiously minded. In certain religions, there are particular ways of washing and dressing that need to be understood. There are also other issues to consider, such as whether it is permissible for a male member of staff to care for a female service user and vice versa. Helping a Muslim to eat using your left hand would cause offence. Different religions also take different stances on illness, dying and bereavement.

> ### Think it over
>
> Given that few of us are expert on all the religions of the world, how can we ensure that we don't cause offence without realising it or formulate care plans that result in someone's basic needs not being met?

Culturally sensitive care planning requires that, as practitioners, we need to ensure maximum user involvement and participation. This requires an approach to care planning that is based on openness, good communication and creative thinking. Good practice encourages both the involvement of ethnic minority older people in their assessment and the development of their care plans. Such procedures should include ensuring that, where relevant, the service user and carer receive a copy of the care plan. In their report the SSI found that

> The majority of care plans only provided a minimum of information about the arrangements for a service. The facility was available in most SSDs for care plans to be translated on request, but assessors were of the view that because the care plan contained limited information, it was therefore not worthwhile to be translated. After the assessment interview (sometimes assisted with an interpreter), the service user was given a copy of the care plan. This was usually in English regardless of the language spoken or literacy. Most of the black elders seen could not recall receiving a care plan and those who had did not understand it.   [Department of Health/Social Services Inspectorate (1998), page 47]

> ### Think it over
>
> Having read through the different extracts from the SSI report on community care services for black and ethnic minority older people, write down five points that practitioners must try to do when they are care planning with people from another culture or ethnic group.

Having written your five points it would be interesting to compare your notes with another. Once you've done that, look through the following guidance from the Commission for Racial Equality see how your comments compare with theirs. You could write an action plan for your agency if you feel certain points need to be addressed.

Care planning

Developing care plans or hospital discharge plans for ethnic minority service users may involve some additional work for the key worker in

- ➲ researching the performance of existing providers (whether mainstream or ethnic minority) in attracting and keeping ethnic minority patients or users
- ➲ exploring other potential options which make use of the resources, including voluntary groups and informal care networks, of the relevant ethnic minority community
- ➲ introducing potential users to other existing ethnic minority users and support groups
- ➲ providing 'taster' experiences for users unfamiliar with the services available
- ➲ offering advocacy support for gaining access to other services or service providers
- ➲ facilitating complaints or concerns from users and carers about the racial or cultural appropriateness, or otherwise, of services.

For some users, care services tailored to their own cultural and linguistic backgrounds will be important, others may prefer referral to mainstream services. The key worker should seek to accommodate their wishes as much as available resources allow. However, users should not be expected to accept services in which the cultural dimension is a tokenistic 'bolt-on' extra (e.g. providing Asian meals in a mainstream day centre, with the remainder of the service unaltered). Cultural awareness must be integral to the service as a whole. Users and, where appropriate, their carers should be given copies of their care plan or discharge plan. For those unable to read English, it should be translated into a form they can understand.

There are aspects of implementing care or discharge plans for ethnic minority patients or users that call for particular attention, such as

- ➲ checking the race equality policies and practices of possible providers
- ➲ influencing changes in provision, such as methods used to publicise provision, or the time and place of service delivery
- ➲ ensuring that interpreting and translation support services are available
- ➲ providing feedback to providers whose services are not found acceptable by potential ethnic minority patients or users
- ➲ initiating action through planning and service development sections to secure alternative services.

[Commission for Racial Equality (1997), pages 60–1]

The need for a culturally sensitive care plan

Mohamed Al Haq is a Pakistani. He is 81 years old and lives with his son's family. He is a Muslim and has very limited English. He has severe shortness of breath and other problems related to heart disease. He is very immobile and needs a lot of help with personal care. There are incontinence problems, and he is also prone to ulcerated legs. Reluctantly the family have had to seriously consider residential care because the family set-up and the fairly crowded living conditions mean that caring for Mr Al Haq safely in the home is proving very difficult.

You have used a proper interpreter and establish that Mr Al Haq is willing to accept residential care for the good of the family, but he wants to go to a home where there are other Pakistani men. The problem is your locality is mainly white and all of the homes in the immediate area don't have any other male Pakistani elders in them. The nearest home that would suit Mr Al Haq's wishes is a more multi-ethnic town in a different county some forty miles away. Not only is the family not too happy about the distance they would have to travel, you also learn that the fees are above your local authority's benchmark figure.

Questions

1 Do you see any dilemmas for the practitioner in this scenario? What are they?

2 From the guidance you have read in this section, what approach would be constructive in achieving a culturally sensitive care plan?

Achieving culturally sensitive care plans can be difficult. It can pose dilemmas to practitioners. Research shows that families from minority ethnic-cultural communities do not necessarily want separate services. They would be happy with mainstream provision if their needs were being met and if they didn't feel that they were being patronised. Agencies need staff with a detailed knowledge of the communities they serve. Ethnic minority communities also need to know about the services that are available. Services need to meet the needs of different communities because a one-size-fits-all approach doesn't work.

Monitoring care plans

Guidance tells us that the final task of the implementation phase consists in the establishment of monitoring arrangements to ensure that the care plan remains on course. Monitoring is one of the most important aspects of care planning but is also one of the most 'taken for granted' parts of the process. For many practitioners, the key activity of care planning is actually putting the package together, whilst for some care workers their role would be to implement the care plan. What happens in the period between implementation and review is often likely to be quite 'ad hoc' and reactive, as practitioners' attention necessarily switches to the more formal aspects of their job role – carrying out assessments, producing care plans and conducting reviews. To some extent, the feeling that monitoring is a kind of 'Cinderella' activity is reinforced both by a relative lack of coverage in official guidance and text books and by institutional practices which tend to mainly focus on the quantifiable, e.g. number of assessments, care plans and reviews undertaken. Monitoring is harder to quantify. One of the factors that makes monitoring harder to quantify is that practitioners aren't always clear what monitoring actually is. It can feel like quite a nebulous activity that somehow 'happens' in a variety of ways that are hard to pin down. In some cases, the assumption seems to be that the main responsibility for monitoring lies with service users and the care providers. This is a 'no news is good news' approach.

> **Think it over**
>
> Note down the ways that you can monitor a care plan. Compare your list with another. Which is your most common method? Does it change depending on the type of care? Does it change depending on job role, e.g. whether a care manager, or a care worker in a day or residential setting? Explain your answers.

The official practitioner guidance (1991) states:

> The type and level of monitoring should relate to the scale of intervention and the complexity of the needs that are being addressed. Monitoring may be performed in a number of ways:
>
> ⊃ Home visits
>
> ⊃ Telephone calls
>
> ⊃ Letters
>
> ⊃ Questionnaires
>
> ⊃ Inter-staff/agency consultation
>
> ⊃ Observation.
>
> All users who are in receipt of continuing services should have the benefit of some form of monitoring to ensure the appropriateness of that provision. However, the form of monitoring should be designed to cause as little disruption as possible to the users' daily pattern of living. [Department of Health (1991), page 78]

Case Study

Monitoring care plans

Liam

Liam Atkins is a 40-year-old former sergeant in the army. An accident 10 years ago has left him paraplegic. He opted for Direct Payments three years ago mainly out of exasperation. The domiciliary package that had been put together by social services was not going to his liking. He didn't like the attitude of some of his carers and thought they hadn't always been properly briefed. There was also a problem with the timings of the calls. He has made three official complaints to the highest level. He used his connections to hire a small team of personal assistants. He has said that social services have now effectively 'washed their hands' of him.

Beatrice

Beatrice Godden is 84. She lives on her own despite having advanced vascular dementia. She is adamant she wants to stay in her home of the last 40 years. Her GP thinks residential care would be a safer option, as she is often having to attend to Mrs Godden, but respects Mrs Godden's wishes in staying where she is. Mrs Godden is also known to CPNs and other mental health specialists. The neighbours in her street quite often find her wandering or distressed because she has locked herself out. They usually either contact one of Mrs Godden's two daughters or the social services. Mrs Godden has four domiciliary calls a day and attends a day centre for people with mental infirmity three times a week.

Task

From these two situations explain which methods you would use to monitor these two care plans.

➲ Would you use the same methods for both cases? Give reasons.

➲ Explain how you would agree and then record your monitoring arrangements.

➲ Would you make any arrangements in either case for when you are absent from work for whatever reason, if so, what?

An important point to acknowledge is that monitoring arrangements must, as far as possible, be agreed with the service user and their carer(s). Over-monitoring is as intrusive as under-monitoring is neglectful. Many people would find being under constant surveillance oppressive however well intentioned it was. Lightness of touch and subtlety are likely to be appreciated by all parties.

Why monitor?

The activities should have provoked you to reflect more on the purpose of monitoring a care plan. As we saw at the start of this section, it is 'to ensure that the care plan remains on course'. This becomes easier the more clear and specific the care outcomes are. Monitoring can also lead to care objectives being modified and the care plan either 'tweaked' or even altered extensively. As we have stated before, not only can some situations change rapidly, but you cannot always get it right first time. For example, someone who has attended a day centre once or twice might find that joining with a group of strangers is 'not their cup of tea' after all. Having tried the experience, they might express a wish to stay at home. This in turn, might lead to a discussion about how a solution might be found that lies somewhere between staying in all the time and going out to a day centre. It could possibly mean that the need is redefined. Instead of seeing it as a need for social contact, it could be that it is more about mental stimulation. Acquiring a computer and learning how to use it might meet this need, alternatively so might buying a tortoise and looking after it! It all depends on the individual concerned. Effective monitoring recognises the fluid and dynamic quality of care planning.

Monitoring then, is a key part of the quality control process and as such is also about ensuring that the care provision is delivered as per service specifications. One of the reasons for creating the purchaser/provider split was to allow care planners to shop around more, and implicit in this was the desire to keep providers 'on their toes'. In reality, this has only partially happened. In areas where there are care shortages the providers are in a greater position of strength than was originally foreseen. For all kinds of reasons, an unhealthy collusion between purchaser and providers can sometimes exist. In such instances, the care planner has to ensure that meaningful monitoring actually does take place even when there is a feeling that providers need to be kept on good terms.

Figure 8.5 *Part of monitoring is to make sure the care provision meets the client's needs*

Lastly, the official guidance (1991) states that an important purpose of monitoring is to 'support users, carers and service providers'. It continues:

> Support may take different forms:
> - ⊃ Counselling
> - ⊃ Progress-chasing
> - ⊃ Resolving conflicts or difficulties.
>
> (Department of Health, page 79)

To carry out these important activities properly, clearly requires a full range of interpersonal, communication and caring skills on behalf of the practitioner. They often go unacknowledged by management or else are considered commonplace, straightforward activities. These are the 'behind the scenes' aspects of the care planning role that don't usually get quantified and recognised but without which care planning could not take place. They are in many ways the 'bread and butter' of the job.

Think it over

How much of your care planning role is spent in the kinds of activities outlined above? How much training and guidance have you had in developing these skills? Compare your answer with someone from another agency.

Who should monitor?

Monitoring is the responsibility of the practitioner responsible for implementing the care plan. In many instances this is the care manager but it might be a key worker. However, this doesn't mean that monitoring should be their sole responsibility. In the spirit of user-involvement, the service user should be encouraged to monitor their own care plan. Often the day-to-day monitoring will be carried out by a key worker employed by the care providers. There is nothing wrong with providers monitoring care plans, they after all are very close to the service user, have expertise, and on many matters are able to comment knowledgeably about how things are going. A report on services for older people with dementia published in 1997 however found that

> Monitoring was generally a well managed activity although there was some anxiety that it was sometimes more about contract compliance than quality or continuing appropriateness of service. There was also concern that in some cases monitoring was carried out only by service providers and whilst this may be appropriate in some circumstances there must also be room for questioning whether service providers monitoring their own activities is the surest way to proceed with checking on quality of service. [Department of Health/Social Services Inspectorate (1997), page 19]

A certain amount of caution also needs to be exercised when relying solely on carers for monitoring purposes. This is because the informal carer's agenda is not necessarily that of the service user. Service users who, for whatever reason, are unable to communicate their own views might end up with their carer expressing their views for them. There are, for example, cases where much needed home care provision has been cancelled by carers because they feel the arrangements are having a negative impact on their own lives. Domiciliary care assistants can be seen as an intrusion, or somehow competitors, and the carer can also feel under surveillance in such situations. Giving and receiving care is a complex human activity and whilst carers are rightly seen as an essential component of community care this doesn't mean that their views about what is best for the one they care for should be left unchallenged.

Some reasons why effective monitoring doesn't always happen

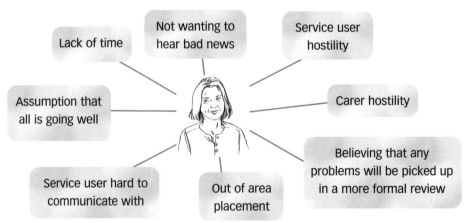

Figure 8.6 *Factors that prevent effective monitoring*

The last word

The monitoring of care should be taken seriously and therefore should have the appropriate amount of time allocated to it. To use an old adage 'a stitch in time saves nine', i.e. learning about and reacting quickly to care plan difficulties early on can prevent even bigger problems emerging later. The practitioner has to take a lead in this. It cannot simply be left on a 'let me know if there are any problems' basis.

It is also apparent that to monitor what is after all a complex set of human activities, there needs to be a variety of methods used. Monitoring should usually be undertaken in a flexible, unobtrusive but focused fashion. It requires a range of different skills. If a 360° view is to be achieved then more than one perspective needs to be sought. The ways the care plan is going to be monitored should be discussed with the relevant parties, especially the service user. Covert surveillance is usually best left to MI5.

⊃ Check your understanding

1 Give reasons why monitoring does not always get the emphasis it should.
2 Should the type and level of monitoring always be the same for each case? Explain.
3 Describe *five* methods of monitoring a care plan.
4 Explain *three* reasons for monitoring a care plan.
5 Who should be involved in monitoring?
6 Explain the difficulties that might occur from simply using one source of information.
7 Identify *six* reasons why monitoring doesn't always happen.

Reviewing

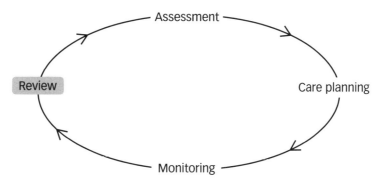

Figure 8.7 *Reviewing is the final phase in the assessment and care cycle*

Reviewing completes the assessment and care planning cycle. It is undertaken as a more formal activity than monitoring. As with other activities we have discussed, it should never be assumed that service users expect a review or even know what one is.

What is a review?

This is a good question. In some agencies, a distinction is made between a review and a reassessment, but it is questionable whether there is a clear difference. The practice guidance (1991) regards one of the purposes of a review as being to 'reassess current needs' (page 84).

> A review of people's community care needs and services is not a concept to be found in legislation, except for a fleeting and general reference in relation to residential accommodation. Arguably, 'review', as the term is commonly used, amounts to reassessment. Policy guidance states that the review process should look at whether services need to be increased, revised or withdrawn. [Mandelstam (1998), page 172]

Different agencies tackle reviews differently. Care providers carry out reviews, and they would be guided by the National Minimum Standards Regulations. In community care, arranged through statutory agencies, it is common for the review function to be separated out and given to dedicated 'Review Officers'. This has been for a variety of reasons – increasing the number of reviews to meet government targets is probably a key one. 'Clients receiving a review' is a Performance Assessment Framework Indicator for social services departments. The effects of this separation are hard to generalise. On the one hand, it could be regarded as elevating the importance of this activity by giving reviews a special status. On the other hand, especially where the status and pay of review officers is lower than that of other frontline workers, it is likely to somehow downgrade the activity. Reviews also take place in residential and day care settings where the manager or another representative of the care provider conducts them. Reviews have specific meanings in specific contexts.

Think it over

Consider these questions, carrying out research where necessary.

1 What is the purpose of a review in your setting?

2 How are reviews carried out? For example, who is invited? Who runs it? How often do they take place?

3 Is there a distinction made between a review and a reassessment? If so, what is it?

4 Is it clearly explained to service users what a review is?

The following points are taken from the *Care Management and Assessment: Practitioner's Guide.*

➲ (A review is)…the mechanism by which changing needs are identified and services adapted accordingly.

⊃ Like assessment, reviewing should be needs-based.

⊃ The **scope** of the review will depend upon the complexity of need and the level of invested resources. The **frequency** will be governed by how much the needs are subject to change.

⊃ The form and venue of the review should be substantially governed by what is judged to be the most effective way of involving users and carers.
[Department of Health (1991), page 83]

This guidance can be applied to any adult care review whatever the setting. Bearing in mind that the guidance is directed more specifically at care managers in statutory organisations, it goes on to state:

A review fulfils a number of different purposes which are to

⊃ review the achievement of care plan objectives

⊃ examine the reasons for success or failure

⊃ evaluate the quality and cost of the care provided

⊃ reassess current needs

⊃ reappraise eligibility for assistance

⊃ revise the care plan objectives

⊃ redefine the service requirements

⊃ recalculate the cost

⊃ notify quality assurance/service planning of any service deficiencies or unmet needs

⊃ set the date for the next review

⊃ record the findings of the review.

Discussion of the case study will have highlighted several issues. An important one is that in such cases a review needs to be based on a multi-disciplinary approach. This needn't mean that each of the professionals involved should attend a review in person. Any attempt to do this would not only be difficult to arrange in practical terms – and therefore likely to cause unnecessary delay – but it would also be potentially overwhelming for the service user and their carer(s). Therefore, the reviewer needs to ensure that other professional opinion is sought by other means: reports, letters or pre-set review forms. Only with a full range of information from other disciplines, together with the service user's own input, can a meaningful interpretation be made of how effective the existing care plan is in meeting need and managing risk.

Confidentiality and recording issues

Reviews, like assessments, should be recorded in line with agency guidance, which in turn should reflect good practice principles. Reviews are an opportunity to exchange case information between all relevant parties: service users, carers, providers and so on. Sometimes this can slip into a kind of competition about who knows the most about the service user. If the information is relevant to the

Case Study

Reviewing a care plan

Ahmed Rahman (58) was admitted to hospital after a stroke. This left him with right-side hemiplegia. After two weeks of medical investigation, treatment and rehabilitation, he was considered ready for discharge. He lives with his wife, an anxious and frail woman, and two teenage children aged 14 and 17.

The discharge care plan was based on medical opinion that he would gradually regain some use on his right side but that he would continue to experience spells of giddiness and dizziness. The family were advised that he shouldn't be left alone for long periods. Mr Rahman was offered physiotherapy as a day patient. He was also referred for an occupational therapy assessment. Mr Rahman's care assessment found that he could not wash, dress or get to the toilet without assistance, neither could he prepare and eat food. He agreed to have a care package of two domiciliary calls, one to help him get up and get dressed in the morning and the other to help with getting to bed.

The family were keen for him to return home and assured the assessor that they would take care of everything else. He was also issued a care call alarm in case of accidents.

After four weeks, the OT has assessed and issued on loan to Mr Rahman certain items of assistive technology, e.g. equipment for the bathroom. Information was given about where to purchase other smaller items. Suggestions were also made about how to adapt the house. These suggestions have not yet been taken up.

Several recent calls from the 17-year-old daughter make it clear that the family are under great stress. Mrs Rahman was said to have what appears like nervous exhaustion. The situation is not going well. Mr Rahman has not attended any physiotherapy, possibly because he is not ready in time for the hospital transport. The 14-year-old is now missing school to help out.

Questions

1 Refer back to the section on monitoring. How do you think this care plan should have been monitored? Give reasons.

2 You decide to call a review of the care plan. Explain how you would organise it. Who would you involve? Where would it take place? What would be its scope?

3 What ideas might you have at this stage about how the care plan could be altered?

care plan then this is obviously useful and can help the fine-tuning process. However, information about service users should remain confidential if there is no need for other parties to have it. Reviewers need to be clear with service users what the rules of confidentiality are. In addition, their consent should be sought for what comments and details are to be passed to others, and in what form. For example, just because during a review a service user speaks of difficulties with their family, this shouldn't mean that this information needs to go any further, or even be recorded. The service user should have some control over what is written.

Pitfalls

As mentioned before in drawing a distinction between a review and a reassessment some agencies imply that somehow a review is the lesser activity. Some authorities have allowed this distinction between assessments, reassessments and reviews to develop into a two-tier system. In their inspection of community care services for black and ethnic minority older people, the SSI (1998) found:

> It was not clear that black elders and their carers understood the review process. The reviewing of care plans across SSDs, from those which adhered to procedural guidelines and were done at regular frequencies or were dictated by a change in the service user's circumstances, to those which were more on an *ad hoc* basis if done at all. In some cases, the assessors involved the service users and carers and where necessary, an interpreter. However, the review was sometimes a paper exercise with some pressure on the worker and the service user as well to avoid change.

[Department of Health/Social Services Inspectorate (1998), page 44]

It would be fair to say that many of those points made could be more generally applied. People don't always understand the point of reviews because sometimes review officers indicate that if anything major needs changing the case will have to be 'reassessed'. This is not only a waste of time, it is a very confusing message to give. We make these points to underline the fact that a review is just that – a review. The reviewer should expect to reassess need and redefine care provision if appropriate. A review should not be a rubber-stamping exercise that enables agencies to meet performance targets. It is usually the only formal opportunity the service user has to raise any problems or highlight inadequacies they may be experiencing with their care provision.

Because of this, the use of advocates should be considered when reviewing the care of those without the ability to communicate meaningfully. In most areas voluntary agencies run advocacy services for different service user groups. If an appropriate independent advocate can be found, they will aim to ensure that the views of the service user are properly represented. Of course, advocates are not miracle workers or mind readers, so to function properly they need to have a chance to get to know the person on whose behalf they are advocating. When an advocate is simply brought in at the last minute, apart from them being an independent presence, there is usually no way they can gain any familiarity with the person's situation. However, even if an advocate is limited because of lack of personal knowledge, this is better than relying on carers. This is not good enough for the reasons we have explained before.

Tips for ensuring reviews go smoothly

Preparation for the review:

⊃ Look at the case file, in particular the initial assessment, subsequent assessments, care plans, records of past reviews and recent correspondence.

⊃ Note down what the original issues were. What additional issues have emerged?

⊃ Are there any recurrent themes, unmet needs or past issues unactioned?

⊃ Who has been involved?

⊃ Speak to staff in your agency who are familiar with the case. Is there anything in particular that needs to be raised? Any difficult or sensitive issues?

⊃ Decide who the 'core group' should be – typically this is the client, relatives, care providers, any other regular worker such as a district nurse

⊃ Contact them and agree a convenient time, date and venue

⊃ Ask whether anyone else should be invited

⊃ Is an advocate or interpreter required? Has the advocate got enough time to ensure they are effective?

⊃ Send out invitations to all relevant parties. Include the purpose of the review and what the review will cover – this will also need to conform to agency format.

⊃ Ask to confirm attendance or not.

⊃ For key parties not able to attend send out paperwork/questionnaire seeking their input where appropriate. Enclose SAE and give timescale.

⊃ Establish arrangements for chairing the meeting – normally the care manager, but it could be somebody else such as a key worker or home manager if in a residential setting.

⊃ Establish an arrangement for recording the review. Think about whether the person chairing it should record it or whether it would be better if somebody else did this.

During the review:

⊃ Ensure privacy and confidentiality.

⊃ Give an idea of the time it will take.

⊃ Clarify who is there, who they are – do people know each other?

⊃ Repeat the purpose of the review.

⊃ Explain the procedures for recording, disseminating the notes and so on.

⊃ However limited their powers of comprehension and communication always respect the service user by addressing them. Do not talk over or talk about them as if they weren't there. This is very important.

⊃ Don't use jargon.   →

> ⊃ Try to ensure that the overall atmosphere of the review is relaxed but businesslike.
>
> ⊃ Make sure that everyone has the opportunity to speak.
>
> ⊃ Refer back to previous review.
>
> ⊃ Use the prescribed format but not too mechanistically.
>
> ⊃ Agree plan of action if necessary, assign responsibilities, set timescales, agree date of next review if possible or at least agree a timescale, e.g. in six months time.
>
> *After the review:*
>
> ⊃ Send all relevant parties a written record.
>
> ⊃ Follow up any recommendations or other actions.

Workers in different agencies will all have their own particular procedures but the watchwords are user and carer involvement, good recording, and to make the review purposeful it should not be simply a rubber-stamping ritual.

Power imbalances

Many service users are vulnerable and dependent people. They often worry that anything construed as dissatisfaction on their part may either cause their care provider to take offence or lead to the provision being taken away altogether. In such situations, service users will not 'rock the boat' for fear of being placed in a worse situation. It is a consequence of their powerlessness. The reviewer needs to be sensitive to this and do their best to empower their client.

Collusion between reviewer and care provider is easy to slip into for several reasons. In residential and day care settings, when the provider is on 'home territory', effort needs to be made by the reviewer to avoid becoming institutionalised. A service user's behaviour can easily be labelled 'awkward' or 'difficult' without challenge. Having two powerful figures ranged against them at 'their' review gives the service user little or no chance to express their opinion fully – particularly if it is critical. They are left with no 'voice' and no 'exit'. They must go along with what's decided for them.

Reviewers and providers can also easily lapse into jargon without realising it – this too excludes service users. As we stated earlier, service users often have little or no idea what a review is. Some people, especially those in institutions, believe that it is actually their behaviour under review. This creates unnecessary anxiety. Confusion about reviews can also emerge when a service user faces several different types of review from different workers. Research has shown that some service providers conduct reviews within the setting in which they provide the services. This happens a lot in residential homes, day centres and day hospitals, even domiciliary care providers do this. These 'partial reviews' focus primarily, but not entirely, on the service user in that particular setting or as a receiver or that particular service. They mean that people can go through several reviews by different workers, in different settings, and addressing different circumstances. Any changes arising from these 'partial reviews' will obviously impact on the remainder of the care plan. Therefore, the outcomes of these 'partial reviews' need to be carefully co-ordinated if the care plan is to remain viable and remain in line with the original objectives. Multiple small-scale 'partial' reviews can easily lead to the overall care plan unravelling as different service providers tinker with their bit of it.

Think it over

You need to review the care of a woman who has been in residential care for over a year. She is mentally fine but hard of hearing. There is a range of health problems including diabetes, emphysema and heart problems. Mobility is very impaired.

How would you arrange things so that (a) they could express their views as freely and frankly as possible and (b) you get a full picture of whether their needs are being met?

How regularly should reviews be held?

There is no 'correct' answer to this to cover all care situations. It depends on the case in question and the context. Official guidance does not determine what 'regular' means as far as statutorily arranged community care is concerned. However, National Minimum Standards regulations are more specific. The policy initiative Fair Access to Care Services stresses the need for local authorities to carry out regular reviews to ensure that services continue to meet objectives. Department of Health guidance (2001) stated:

Reviews
Councils should review the circumstances of all individuals in receipt of social care services. Reviews should

- establish how far the services provided have achieved the outcomes, set out in the care plan
- re-assess the problems and issues of individual service users
- help determine users' continued eligibility for support, and
- comment on how individuals are managing direct payments, where appropriate.

To pick up on the last point, as we know the government wants to increase the take up of Direct Payments for reasons explained elsewhere. With this is mind, it should be remembered that someone on Direct Payments is still a service user but with more freedom to arrange their own services. As such, the approach to reviewing people on Direct Payments should be the same as that for those in receipt of care. Sometimes the feeling exists within practitioner groups that to be on Direct Payments is to want to be left completely alone, and this is what being 'independent' means. However, the situation still needs to be sensitively monitored and reviewed to ensure that the level of direct payment is correct for the level of need.

With respect to older people with dementia, the SSI (1997) argued:

> ...the particular vulnerability of older people with dementia, the potentiality
> for rapid changes in their circumstances and needs, and the likelihood that few
> will be able to report changes effectively or quickly, indicates the wisdom of
> more frequent reviews than for other, perhaps more articulate, service users.
> [Department of Health/Social Services Inspectorate (1997), page 19]

This guidance suggests that agencies and reviewers should avoid being
bureaucratic in their approach to the timing of reviews. Just because
operational guidelines might say that a review must take place within three
weeks, six months or one year, this doesn't mean that it is a sign of efficiency
to make sure that they take place on the exact day three weeks or six months
later. The timing should be governed by factors such as need, risk and
complexity. Some research by the SSI into how carers' needs were managed
made this point:

> Only a small number of cases will be actively care managed. Authorities need to
> be thinking about when and how to review the majority of cases. Evidence
> from this study indicates the need for a regular review
>
> ⊃ where the person care being cared for has needs arising from a condition
>   which is fluctuating or deteriorating
>
> ⊃ where care packages rely heavily on the provision of informal care
>
> ⊃ where there are no available alternatives to informal care
>
> ⊃ where there is conflict between users and carers, or a history of poor family
>   relationships
>
> ⊃ where the health of the carer is uncertain.
> [Department of Health/Social Services Inspectorate (1995), page 25]

Reviews as part of the rationing process

In recent years reviews have become a means by which local authorities have
been able (not without considerable challenge) to cut back on or withdraw
services. Local authorities are not allowed under community care legislation
to cut or withdraw services to a service user unless they change their criteria
for service *and* review (or reassess) the case against these changed criteria.
The Gloucestershire case in the 1990s was one of many which established
that local authorities could respond to diminished resources by cutting back
care, even if previous assessments had identified a need for that care.

Therefore before care can be reduced, an individual's care must be
reassessed against changed criteria. These need to be applied to all service
users in the cause of fairness. In effect, this has meant that, faced with
budgetary pressures, some local authorities have asked reviewers to
participate in what is basically a cost-cutting exercise. This is generally a
demoralising process for all concerned. What is described as a review

Gloucestershire case

Gloucestershire County Council had reduced services to users on the basis that it had insufficient resources to continue service provision at pre-existing levels. This was challenged by some users by way of judicial review. In 1995 the High Court determined in favour of Gloucestershire County Council, stating that a local authority was able to take into account the availability of its resources when assessing needs and when deciding what arrangements to make to meet those needs.

The High Court found that a reduction in services could not be made unless the local authority had first reassessed the needs of the user. In that reassessment, if the changed level of resources available to the authority was a factor, it could then be properly taken into account in deciding what service provision should be made in response to the assessment. It was also stated that even allowing for resource constraints, it would be unreasonable for an authority to reduce services to such an extent that an individual would be exposed to severe physical risk.

The High Court's decision was then reversed by the Court of Appeal in1996. Here it was held that the availability of resources was irrelevant, and that the local authority's duty was to provide services to meet basic needs.

In March 1997 the final decision on the matter was given by the House of Lords. By a majority of 3–2, the Lords found in favour of the local authority and restored the original decision of the High Court.

actually means the reviewer is going out and raising the threshold for services, almost inevitably meaning that for many, they lose provision. Reviewers can react to this situation in many ways; for example, resistance, cynicism or sometimes with a 'neutral'/bureaucratic 'just doing my job' approach. Some reviewers even become over-zealous in their role as money savers. In such cases, it is all the more important for reviewers to act in a professional manner. Fair distribution of resources is an important principle, so simply to falsify the review so that 'your' client doesn't lose out is not good practice. Neither is it good practice to go with the intention of cutting the service 'come what may'. It is always good practice to explain the context and purpose of the review as fully as possible, explain what rights of redress service users have, and then to conduct the review in the normal way – that is to say on a needs-led basis.

The review process can also be invoked when an agency decides to change care provider, for example from 'in house' to a private agency. Again, the practitioner needs to be frank about what's going on, the review should not be about 'rubber stamping' a *fait accompli*, service users need to be given opportunities to state their preference and they should also be properly informed of what complaints procedures are in place, should their preference not be met.

⊃ Check your understanding

1 Why does the meaning, nature and scope of a review need to be clarified with those involved?

2 Identify at least six different purposes a review can serve.

3 Explain the benefits of taking a multi-disciplinary approach to reviews.

4 Explain ways in which a reviewer can avoid a review becoming either a rubber-stamping exercise or one in which powerful professionals take over.

5 Explain factors that need to be taken into consideration when determining the timing of a review.

6 Identify possible circumstances when to call a particular process a 'review' is probably misleading because there is an ulterior motive.

References and further reading

Commission for Racial Equality (1997) *Race, Culture and Community Care*, London

Department of Health (1991) *Care Management and Assessment: Practitioner's Guide*, London, HMSO

Department of Health/Social Services Inspectorate (1991) *Getting the Message Across*, London, HMSO

Department of Health/Social Services Inspectorate (1995) *What Next for Carers?*, London, HMSO

Department of Health/Social Services Inspectorate (1997) *At Home with Dementia*, London, HMSO

Department of Health/Social Services Inspectorate (1998) *They Look After Their Own, Don't They?*, London, HMSO

Department of Health/Social Services Inspectorate (2000) *New Directions for Independent Living*, London, HMSO

Department of Health (2001) *Fair Access to Care Services*, London, HMSO

Glasby, J. and Littlechild J (2002) 'Independence pays? – barriers to the progress of direct payments', in *Practice*, vol 14 no 1

Hasler, F (2003) 'Making choice a reality' in *Care and Health*, issue 34,

23 April–6 May

Mandelstam, M (1998) *A–Z of Community Care Law*, London, JKP

Mandelstam, M (1999) *Community Care Practice and the Law*, London, JKP

Morris J (1997) *Community Care: Working in Partnership with Service Users*, Birmingham, Venture Press

appendix Mapping of care qualifications

Qualification	Context of Care	Reflective Practice	Values in Care Practice	Working with Service Users	Collaborative Working	Assessment	Adult Protection
NVQ Level 4 Care (current)	This chapter is useful in relation to the legislation, policy and funding aspects of all the units	*CU7* Develop one's own knowledge and practice *CU8* Contribute to the development of the knowledge and practice of others *MC1/D4* Provide information to support decision-making	*O2* Promote people's equality, diversity and rights *O3* Develop, maintain and evaluate systems and structures to promote the rights, responsibilities and diversity of people *SNH4U4* Promote the interests of client groups within the community	*SC14* Establish, sustain and disengage from relationships with clients *SC20* Contribute to the provision of effective physical, social and emotional environments for group care	*SC15* Develop and sustain arrangements for joint working between workers and agencies	*SC16* Assess individual's needs and circumstances	*SC17* Evaluate risk of abuse, failure to protect and harm to self and others

Qualification	Context of Care	Reflective Practice	Values in Care Practice	Working with Service Users	Collaborative Working	Assessment	Adult Protection
NVQ Level 4 Care (current)	This chapter is useful in relation to the legislation, policy and funding aspects of all the units	*HSC/E3.2* Take responsibility for the continuing professional development of self and others *HSC/E3.1* Contribute to the development of the knowledge and practice of others	*HSC/A1.8* Promote the individual's choice, ability and right to care for and protect themselves *HSC/D1.5* Develop, maintain and evaluate systems and structures that enable individuals to exercise their rights and responsibilities and promote their equality and diversities	*HSC/A1.5* Improve communication systems, structures and methods	*HSC/C2.1* Develop joint working agreements and practice	*HSC/A2.7* Carry out assessment to identify and prioritise needs *HSC/A2.9* Assess individual's mental health and related needs *HSC/A8.21* Assess the needs of carers and families of individuals with mental health needs	*HSC/B1.4* Protect individuals who are at risk

glossary

Activities of daily living (ADLs) ADLs are physical functions that a person would normally perform independently every day, including washing, dressing, using the toilet, moving about, eating and grooming.

Advocate A person who 'speaks for' for another person or helps them to present their point of view. Advocates are used in social care particularly when someone's ill-health or disability means that they have trouble communicating their own views clearly. Some argue that the inappropriate use of advocates can actually disempower people by speaking on their behalf rather than letting them speak for themselves – they would argue for self-advocacy instead.

Anti-discriminatory practice (ADP) ADP became established in social work and social care from the early 1990s. This is an approach to working which seeks to combat all forms of direct and indirect discrimination. Use of language is an important part of ADP.

Anti-oppressive practice This is an approach to practice which seeks to combat all forms of oppression, for example racism, sexism, heterosexism, ageism and disablism. Anti-oppressive practice emerged from the recognition that all minority groups face forms of discrimination and harassment. Anti-oppressive practice assumes that all examples of oppression arise in unequal power relationships.

Approved social worker (ASW) An ASW is a qualified social worker who has been trained and assessed for approval to fulfil a range of statutory duties in the field of mental health. This applies particularly to carrying out mental health assessments (sectioning) under mental health legislation.

Care management This refers to the whole process by which a care package is organised for one or more individuals. The term was introduced as part of the implementation of the NHS and Community Care Act 1990. The care management process involves assessment, planning, implementation, monitoring and review.

Care package A range of services put together to achieve one or more objectives of a care plan.

Care plan This is a plan designed and drawn up to meet an individual's needs. The plan should be made following an assessment and involve users, carers and their families as well as other workers who may be contributing to the plan. The plan aims to match services to needs.

Care trusts A care trust is an NHS organisation to which local authorities can delegate health-related functions, in order to provide integrated health and social care to their local communities. Care trusts were announced in the NHS Plan in July 2000.

Carer's assessment A carer for the purposes of a carer's assessment is 'A carer is someone of any age whose life is restricted because they are looking after a relative, friend, partner or child who cannot manage without help because of illness, age, or a disability of any kind'. The carer's assessment should look at the carer's ability and willingness to continue caring.

From the assessment, services can be put in place to assist with the job of caring. This also extended Direct Payments to disabled 16 and 17 year olds – see below.

Carers and Disabled Children Act 2000 The Carers and Disabled Children Act 2000 gives a right to an assessment for carers of adults and people with parental responsibility for disabled children. This right to an assessment gives local councils the opportunity to provide carers with services to meet their own assessed needs.

Chronically Sick and Disabled Persons Act 1970 This Act laid down a duty on local authorities in England and Wales to identify the number of people with physical disabilities in their area and empowered them to make certain provisions and services to enhance their quality of life.

Commission for Social Care Inspection (CSCI) CSCI came into being in 2004. It combines the functions of the Social Services Inspectorate, the social care functions of the National Care Standards Commission, and the functions of the SSI/Audit Commission Joint Review team. It is intended that CSCI works in tandem with the proposed Commission for Healthcare Audit and Inspection (CHAI) and will have comparable and compatible duties.

Community Care (Direct Payments) Act 1996 This Act empowers local authorities to make direct payments to people with disabilities to employ their own carers rather than rely on services commissioned and provided by the local authority. Subsequently the offering of direct payments to all adult service users has been made obligatory.

Community psychiatric nurse (CPN) A CPN is a nurse specially trained in psychiatry in order to help people with mental health problems in their own homes. CPNs usually work in a multi-disciplinary setting.

Data Protection Act 1998 This Act sets out the rules for the collection, storage and use of personal data by individuals and organisations. The Act replaced the Data Protection Act 1984 which only covered data stored electronically. The Act gives the right to individuals to see data relating to themselves and to have corrected and/or claim damages for incorrect data in all but a small number of situations wherever the data is held. It thus applies to most social care records.

Department of Health (DoH) The Department of Health has overall responsibility for the National Health Service and for oversight of the personal social services and social care generally in England.

Direct payments see Community Care (Direct Payments) Act 1996.

Eligibility criteria These are criteria used by local authorities to establish who qualifies for a service.

Fair Access to Care Services This is a new eligibility framework introduced in April 2003 for local authorities to use. It is graded into four bands, which describe the seriousness of the risk to independence or other consequences if needs are not addressed. The four bands are as follows: Critical, Substantial, Moderate and Low. It is designed to bring a fairer system of assessment across the whole of England.

General Social Care Council The General Social Care Council (GSCC) was established in October 2001 under the Care Standards Act 2000. It acts as the guardian of standards for the social care workforce in England. The function of the GSCC is to increase the protection of service users, their carers and the general public by regulating the social care workforce and by ensuring that work standards within the social care sector are of the highest quality.

Keyworker A worker whose job role is to be responsible for coordinating the care of one person.

National Service Frameworks (NSFs) Launched in 1998, NSFs set national standards and identify key interventions for a defined service or care group. They put in place strategies to support implementation, establish ways to ensure progress within an agreed time scale and form one of a range of measures to raise quality and decrease variations in service.

Needs-led assessment This was officially introduced by the NHS and Community Care Act 1990. It is an assessment whose starting point is looking at a person's needs and working from there rather than assessing with a particular service in mind.

Normalisation This is the principle that, whatever a person's disability, their daily life should follow the rhythms and patterns of the daily lives of the majority of people in their society. This was first introduced by Nirje in the 1970s and developed by Wolfensberger in the 1980s. See social role valorisation.

Purchaser/provider split A system of organising the delivery of social care services in which a purchaser unit assesses the need for services and purchases (or commissions) them from a provider unit. This arrangement was introduced into the UK in the early 1990s with the implementation of the NHS and Community Care Act.

Respite care This is a form of care which is usually provided for the benefit of carers as much as for the service user. It helps to give both the service user and the carer a break from a situation which may be proving tiring or stressful.

Risk assessment A procedure for assessing the risks involved in a particular situation. Such an assessment implies that actions will then follow to help reduce or control any risks identified. It assumes that risks can be sufficiently well assessed to enable them to be managed. Perception of risk though is subjective. Everyone accepts some degree of risk in their lives – some people have higher thresholds than others. So the chance that a general agreement can be reached on an acceptable level of risk is low.

Role conflict A situation, often at work, where there is potential conflict between the ways in which we should and could behave. This can lead to emotional and psychological tension.

Self-advocacy This is advocating on behalf of oneself, possibly with support of an independent group. This form of advocacy developed out of the experiences of people with learning disabilities who didn't always feel that their carers, families or advocates always represented their views adequately.

Social Care Institute for Excellence (SCIE) SCIE is an independent organisation created in response to the government's drive to raise standards and to promote evidence-based practice. SCIE was set up in 2001 and is funded by the Department of Health and the Welsh Assembly. The role of the Social Care Institute for Excellence is to gather and publicise knowledge about how to make social care services better.

Social model of disability A view that challenges traditional so called 'medical' models of disability which focus on what is wrong or 'defective' with an individual. Such models are overly preoccupied with someone's diagnosis or medical label. The social model argues that the way society is organised is the problem. A disabling society is one that is constructed both for and by able-bodied people to the exclusion of others who don't fall into that category. Societies therefore disable rather than produce any particular condition.

Social role valorisation This is the principle that, whatever a person's disability, the roles they play should be clearly valued by those around them and by the rest of society. The principle represents a step on from the perceived limitation of normalisation. Often normalisation has been conceived in a superficial or stereotyped way and hasn't always positively impacted on the most important ways in which a person is treated by others.

Valuing People Published by the DoH in March 2001 *Valuing People* was the first White Paper on learning disability services for thirty years. It is a major document which has the aim of improving services and opportunities for people with a learning disability.

index

Page numbers in italics refer to illustrations and diagrams

Kolb model/cycle 80–3, 101
  and learning theories 85–8
  not a solitary activity 96–9, 102, 103
  strategies 81
  when to reflect 101–2
reflective practice 58–63, 93–4. 296–7
  aims 62–3
  and learning 74–5
regional planning 3
regulation 45–53
rehabilitation 6, 31, 225
relationships between carers 220, 384–5
  see also collaborative working
relationships with service users 184–9
  support 185–7
    through conflict and difficulties 187–9
    through life changes 190–4
religion 137–8, 301, 302, 413–14
research 86–8, 95–6, 411, 428
residential care 4, 5, 29, 240, 402, 413, 422–3,
  427–8
resources and core provision 8–9, 27, 40, 392,
  393, 398, 407, 415, 430–1
respect 115, 153, 165–6, 167, 195, 236
respite care 16–17, 437
responsibility 63, 64, 99, 115, 168, 169, 226, 363,
  367
reviewing care plans 421–31
  confidentiality 425, 427
  multi–disciplinary 424
  pitfalls 425–7
  power imbalances 427–8
  preparations for 426–7
  as rationing 430–1
  regularity 428–9
  scope and frequency 423
rights 1, 108, 115, 122, 123, 130, 151–2, 153,
  155–8, 167, 168, 376
risk assessment 231–2, 310–15, 363, 404, 437

scales used in assessment 332–3, 345
Scotland 1
Sector Skill Council for Social Care/TOPSS 115,
  122, 152
self-actualisation 233
self–development 57, 61, 62, 70, 93–4, 232
self–disclosure 202–3
self–empowering 212
self-evaluation 57
  and learning 74, 99
self-injury 378–9
serial abuse 361
service user control 44, 179
  see also empowerment
service users' prejudice 150–1
Sex Discrimination Act 1975 (SDA) 125, 151
  1986 125
sexual abuse 355, 356–7
sexual rights 231
sexuality 121–4, 137, 341
sheltered employment 6
sheltered housing 30
situational abuse 361, 370
skills in relationships 195–207

skills/psychomotor domain 58, 59, 60, 61, 70,
  71–2
  acquisition 71
small talk 202
social activities 230–1
Social Care Institute for Excellence (SCIE) 331–2,
  438
social control 169
social exclusion 7–8
social factors 1, 3
social model see health services and social care
social services departments 4, 10, 11, 240
Social Services Inspectorate (SSI) 27, 30, 46, 47,
  159, 298, 399, 411, 414, 425
social support 221, 230–2
Special Educational Needs and Disability Act
  (SENDA) 2001 10, 131
standards of care 167–9
statutory provision 11, 13
stereotyping 134, 143–4, 261–3, 342, 413
  negative 152
stress at work 237–8, 376
structural discrimination 142–3
structure of care services 10–13
substance abuse and care services 9
support and services provision 1, 175
supported living 29, 133, 179
SWOT analysis 95, 96

talking treatments 236
technical rationality/knowledge of facts 65, 66
tenancy arrangements 29
tensions and pressures of assessment 300–1
theory and practice 95
touch 205, 222
triangulation 90
trust 195, 344
understanding/attitude/affective domain 58, 59,
  60, 61, 62, 70, 73
user-led research 87

values 107, 151–2, 195
  acquisition of 110–12
  society's 112-13, 129
  see also care values
values and policy 24–5, 41–5, 113–15, 129–30, 147
values, personal awareness of 66, 72
verbal communication 198–201
veto 403
vocational training 240
voluntary organisations 5, 6, 11, 12, 263, 298,
  397, 415, 426
volunteers 13, 220

Wales 1, 438
welfare state 3, 10, 240
White Papers 7, 17-18, 28, 33, 218
  (1944) 3
  (1989) 398
  (1999) 117
  (2001) 5, 8, 10, 115, 130, 242, 438
work diary 93–4, 102
work houses 2
working directives 13, 18

Such Sweet Sorrow

Katie Flynn has lived for many years in the north-west.
A compulsive writer, she started with short stories and
articles and many of her early stories were broadcast
on Radio Merseyside. She decided to write her Liverpool
series after hearing the reminiscences of family members
about life in the city in the early years of the twentieth
century. She also writes as Judith Saxton. For several
years, she has had to cope with ME but has continued
to write.

Praise for Katie Flynn

'It is a tale full of the typical warmth and nostalgia
expected of Katie Flynn. A well-written,
comfortable read.'
Historical Novels Review

'If you pick up a Katie Flynn book it's going to be a
wrench to put it down again.'
Holyhead and Anglesey Mail

'Arrow's best and biggest saga author.
She's good.'
Bookseller

'An inspiration to other writers . . . What the reader
gets . . . is nostalgia, good-humoured historical detail,
a wide range of compelling characters and a big,
fascinating story . . . I admire Katie Flynn's grit. The
writer is like the heroes and heroines of her novel:
she gets on with it, and her work is
gripping until the end.'
Mslexia

For Barbara and Noel Hughes,
just in time for your Golden Wedding
(when the last thing you will be
doing is reading this book!).
Much love, Katie Flynn

Good night, good night!
Parting is such sweet sorrow,
That I shall say good night till it be morrow.

Spoken by Juliet in William Shakespeare's
Romeo and Juliet, Act 2, scene 2

Chapter One

1939

'Well I never, if it isn't our Miss Wainwright! Sorry, I should have said Mrs Sheridan, of course. Good gracious, it must be all of two years since you popped into Gowns to say hello. And this will be your little girl; why, she must be seven or eight and this is the first time I've set eyes on her . . . Libby, isn't it? She don't favour you, love. I suppose she must be like her da . . . though I can't see no resemblance meself. Christmas shopping, are you?'

Libby, who had been carefully licking the pink sugar off an iced bun and watching through Lewis's window the snowflakes whirling down from the threatening grey sky, jumped at the strident voice and turned to stare at the speaker. It was a tall, heavily built woman, wearing a pair of gold-rimmed glasses, and she was beaming at Marianne Sheridan as though they were old friends, though Libby was sure she had never set eyes on the woman before. However, being a well brought up child, she would have greeted her politely had the woman so much as glanced in her direction, but the stranger's attention was focused upon Marianne, the small brown eyes in the heavy face flicking over Libby's mother as though searching for something.

1

'Oh, Miss Harding, how you startled me!' Marianne said. 'I have visited Gowns several times, actually, but you haven't been around. Libby's come in with me a couple of times to meet the staff . . . but I'm forgetting my manners! Would you care to join us? As you say, we've been Christmas shopping, but when it started to snow we decided it was time for some elevenses, especially since Libby fancied some lemonade and a cake. It's really lovely to see you . . . do sit down and I'll order another pot of tea. Goodness, Miss H, fancy you remembering Neil. I'm sure you only saw him at our wedding, and that's getting on for eight years ago now.'

Libby crossed her fingers beneath the starched white tablecloth and willed Miss Harding to refuse the invitation. The cake stand in the middle of the table still held a chocolate eclair and a macaroon, as well as a couple of fairy cakes, and Libby had intended to go for the eclair if her mother suggested she might like a second cake. Of course it was possible that, if Miss Harding did join them, more cakes would be forthcoming, but it was equally possible that her mother might say there was a war on and offer the cakes to the newcomer.

Miss Harding, however, pulled out a chair and sat down heavily upon it, then pushed up the sleeve of her coat and peered short-sightedly at her wristwatch. 'We-ell, it won't hurt to take the weight off me feet for five minutes, only I don't want to be late. I dare say no one's told you, queen, but I retired a year or so back. Well, I had ever such a nice letter from Mr Eccles – he's the floor manager, new since your time – telling me that what with the young men joining the armed forces and the young girls queuin' to get into factories he were desperately short of staff, and wondered whether I'd consider comin' out of retirement. He's offerin' a full wage though the job's part time: ten in the mornin' till four in the afternoon, and no weekends.'

'Golly!' Marianne said. 'But I suppose he would have to offer a decent salary because the girls in the factories are really well paid, I believe. But what about your pension?'

'That's why I'm here today,' Miss Harding said. She was staring very hard at the plate of cakes. 'Chocolate eclairs! Ooh, I'd ha' done murder for a chocolate eclair when I were a kid. As for the pension, it's to sort out such details that Mr Eccles sent for me.'

Marianne stared at Libby and made a little jerk of her head which Libby understood all too well. She leaned forward and propelled the cake stand towards the newcomer. 'Would you like one, Miss Harding?' she said politely. 'I'm afraid we don't have a spare plate but you can use mine if you like; I've finished.'

'I don't mind if I do,' Miss Harding said. She extended a plump, very white hand and took the eclair without a second's hesitation, then turned to Marianne. 'You've not been approached, I

3

suppose? But of course it's so long since you worked here that I dare say you aren't even on the books any more.'

'No, I've heard nothing, but I'm sure you're right and they've forgotten me,' Marianne said cheerfully. 'But I don't think I would come back even if they asked me to. You see, it's not war work, and like everyone else I'd rather help the war effort if I could. If it wasn't for Libby here, I'd join one of the services. Neil's in the Navy so I rather favour the Wrens . . .'

'Someone told me Mr Sheridan's an officer, as I recall,' Miss Harding said, rather thickly. She had demolished the eclair whilst Marianne was speaking and Libby was forced to admire the speed at which she had gobbled it up and the fact that not one speck of cream had managed to escape to mar her bright pink lipstick, or her powdered cheeks and chin. 'I remember him at your weddin'; best-lookin' feller I ever set eyes on, apart from fillum stars of course.' She had been carrying a large handbag which she had pushed under her chair when she sat down, but now she hooked it out, opened it, and produced a tiny powder compact, flicking it open and peering anxiously at her reflection. She patted her hair, then replaced the compact in her bag and turned once more to Marianne. 'That reminds me. Didn't it say on the wireless that children were to be evacuated to the country as soon as war started? Surely little Libby should have gone with her classmates?'

Libby sighed. It was a remark she had heard all too often back in September and October, although it was voiced less frequently now that a great many parents had reclaimed their children from their foster families. Libby knew that everyone had expected bombs to start falling from the moment war had been declared, and when this had proved not to be the case a large number of children had returned to their own homes. Schools which had been shut down would open again in the New Year, but Libby knew that this phoney war, as they were calling it, could not last for ever. Her father was a first lieutenant on a corvette which protected the convoys bringing supplies from the United States of America. The merchant ships in his charge had been harassed and attacked by both U-boats and German warships, and he had told Libby the last time he was in port that she would have to leave the city as soon as things began to hot up.

But Marianne was answering her old colleague's question as patiently as though she had not done so over and over in the weeks that had elapsed since 3 September. 'Oh, Libby would have gone all right, but on the very day the children were told to assemble at Lime Street station she threw out a rash. It was measles, and she had a really bad attack followed by tonsillitis, and when that had cleared up the poor little soul got chicken pox. She wasn't out of quarantine until November, so Neil and I talked it over and decided that I would concentrate on building her up to

5

her former state of health before we let her go anywhere without us.'

'My goodness!' Miss Harding said, looking properly at Libby for the first time. 'Now you mention it, she does look a bit peaky. Still, it's best to get all the childish ailments over in one go. I don't suppose I ever told you,' she added, turning her gaze back to Marianne, 'but the reason I wear glasses were measles. I gorr'em when I were fifteen and though me mam told me to lie quiet in a darkened room I had me sister Edna smuggle me in copies of *Peg's Paper* and the like and read 'em by candlelight, or pulled back the curtain a little way so's some light could come in. I knew me eyes ached like anything, but I didn't stop, and by the time I were well enough to gerrup me sight were affected.' She turned back to Libby. 'I dare say your mam warned you as how measles could ruin your eyesight?'

Libby, who had indeed been nagged on the subject, said that she had been deprived of books from the moment the first spot appeared. At the time she had felt badly done by, but her mother had spent hours reading aloud to her and now, seeing how Miss Harding had had to peer at her wristwatch through her ugly little spectacles, Libby was grateful that reading had been impossible for her. 'And I don't have any brothers or sisters to smuggle anything up to my room,' she added.

'Well, I'm sure it's grand to be an only child,' Miss Harding said rather doubtfully. 'I were one

6

of nine kids so I wouldn't know. But you must let me pay you for that eclair, Miss Wain – I mean Mrs Sheridan,' she added, making a half-hearted attempt to open her handbag again.

'It's quite all right, Miss Harding,' Marianne said immediately. 'Goodness, look at that snow! It looks as though we shall be having another white Christmas, and they said 1938 was the first one for eleven years.'

'Oh, I do hope so,' Libby said, clasping her hands like the heroine in a fairy story. 'Daddy expects to be in port for Christmas and I've asked for a sledge because when Daddy was a little boy he went sledging in the hills, and he's promised to take me if the snow is right.'

'Me and me brother Sid – he were the nearest to me in age – used to take trays to Havelock Street. You had to station someone on Netherfield Road so's you could shout to whoever were comin' down on the tray if there were vehicles approachin'. Eh, it were grand whooshing down the hill with the wind tryin' to tear off your scarf and everyone screamin' wi' the excitement of it all.' Miss Harding got ponderously to her feet. 'Well, listen to me gabblin' on! It won't make a very good impression on Mr Eccles if I'm late, for though I've been tellin' meself it ain't an interview I reckon it is really. Fancy me bein' late for me first interview in twenty years! Bye-bye, Miss Wain – I mean Mrs Sheridan. Bye-bye, chuck. Wish me luck!'

Both Libby and her mother did so, though Libby

7

still felt a trifle resentful over the chocolate eclair. They watched the older woman disappear through the big glass doors, turning to wave as she headed for the lifts, then Libby picked up her glass of lemonade and drained the last mouthful. Her mother glanced at her wristwatch, then examined the cake stand. 'It's only twenty past eleven and we don't have to be at Gammy's till one.' She smiled at her daughter and hailed a passing wait-ress. 'Could you bring us another chocolate eclair, please? And a little more hot water.'

The waitress complied and presently Libby was finishing off the extra eclair whilst her mother ate the macaroon. 'You're a really good girl, Libby,' her mother said when Libby thanked her for the pastry. 'I knew you wanted it, of course, but you behaved just as you should and never even looked wistful when Miss Harding took it. And as soon as we've finished, queen, I think we ought to do a bit more shopping because if this weather keeps up we shan't want to come out more than we have to.'

'But I thought we'd nearly finished,' Libby said, struggling with the last button of her coat. 'Who haven't we bought for? Oh, Mummy, do you think I'll get that sledge?' The two of them had made their way out of the café and down the stairs and were now hovering just inside the big doors which led to the street. Libby, staring out at the huge snowflakes, wondered why they looked grey against the sky as they floated to earth, even though

8

everyone knew that snowflakes were just about as pure white as anything could be. 'You bought Daddy the book you said he wanted and the beautiful curly pipe and I bought him the packet of tobacco, and we're both giving Gammy the lovely blue cardigan you knitted . . . who's left?'

'Darling, you can't have forgotten your Aunt Fiona,' her mother said incredulously. 'She's your only aunt!'

'But you said the woolly hat and scarf were for Auntie Fee,' Libby said reproachfully. 'You said that not everyone could wear yellow, but it suited her perfectly.'

Libby had always loved shopping with her mother, but they had been at it since early morning, and it was a fair way to Gammy's little house in Crocus Street. What was more, the last time she had visited her grandmother she had left a half-finished storybook on the kitchen table, and she knew that if they went straight to Crocus Street she would be allowed to read whilst Gammy chipped potatoes and Mum laid the table.

'Ye-es, but Fiona's my only sister and she does love pretty things,' her mother said now. 'Daddy and I can give her the hat and scarf, and you can give her . . . some really nice earrings.' They were both carrying various packages, but at least earrings would not add much to the weight of their burdens, Libby thought, following obediently as her mother turned away from the doors and headed for a display of costume jewellery. 'Why,

9

you can choose earrings in a second and then we can scoot for the tram and be in Crocus Street before you can say knife.'

But in fact the display of earrings was so enticing that it was a good twenty minutes before the final selection was made. Libby had wanted to purchase a pair of large gold hoops studded with chips of artificial diamond, but her mother was in favour of two tiny gold hearts with a green leaf depending from each of them. 'But Mummy, Auntie Fee's got such masses of hair and it's so long that your little earrings won't show,' Libby pointed out. 'You'll be able to see those lovely big hoops even when she's just washed her hair and it's all puffed out round her face.'

Marianne laughed. 'The thing is, my love, that Fee has to tie her hair back for work and though I do agree that the gold hoops are very striking, I don't think she could wear them in an insurance office.'

'Oh, but they're so pretty,' Libby said mournfully. 'She could wear them when she goes to the Grafton, or one of the other dance halls. Still, I expect you're right. We'll buy the gold hearts.'

So presently they left the store with the little earrings in a tiny velvet box, wrapped around with tissue paper and pushed into her mother's smart leather handbag. Outside, the huge flakes were still falling and Libby wasted several moments, tongue extended and eyes crossing, trying to catch them as they whirled earthwards. She caught a couple, remarking to Marianne that they tasted exciting, but then she saw the tram they wanted to catch clattering along the road, and the pair of them hurriedly crossed over to the stop, dodging the traffic and clutching their various parcels.

In fact, they need not have hurried since there was a fairly lengthy queue. 'I don't believe we'll get on this one,' Libby grumbled, as people began to edge forward. 'If I was by meself, I'd squiggle past everyone else and get aboard first, but it's only kids that can do that. Folk would shove a grown-up back and tell them to keep to their bleedin' place.'

'Libby!' Marianne said on a gasp. 'I never thought to hear my little girl swear. And as for jumping the queue, don't you dare let me catch you doing such a thing.'

'I wasn't swearing, Mummy, I was repeating what I've heard people say when a grown-up shoves their way to the front,' Libby said placidly. She thought to herself that her mother did not know the half of it and perhaps it was a good thing. When her mother and father went off for a weekend, or to visit her paternal grandparents, they usually left her with Gammy, which meant of course that she played with the children living in Crocus Street. Libby was well aware that her mother would not have approved of a good many of the pastimes in which she indulged when staying there. She went with the other kids to the Saturday Rush, though she seldom had to relinquish her fourpence. One of the boys would go in through the foyer and make his way straight to the fire exit. The rest of them would squiggle down the outside of the cinema until they reached the double doors, which would be opened from the inside to let them in. Naturally, the boy would charge everyone a penny for his services, but even so this would leave Libby with threepence to spend on ice creams, popcorn or her favourite sweets, sherbet lemons.

There were other ploys, which Gammy took for granted but Libby knew her mother would not condone. Getting a free ride by hanging on to the back of a tram – skipping a lecky, the kids called it – or begging fades from the stallholders in St John's market, or carrying shopping or doing messages for the elderly of the court in return for a penny, or even a ha'penny. Libby, who got sixpence a week pocket money, never revealed to the other children that she had no need of the money and besides, it came in useful. Sometimes, when she had fetched water for old Mrs Bradshaw, she would accept the ha'penny the old lady gave her, but carefully conceal three or four pennies amongst the crocks on the draining board waiting to be dried up and put away. It made her feel like Robin Hood, but she would never have dreamed of admitting what she did to the other kids, let alone boasting about it. Mrs Bradshaw, notoriously vague, would assume that she herself must have dropped the money there when sorting though her purse, and would be a little better off as a result.

But right now, Marianne was saying, in a shocked voice, that the rules were the same for grown-ups as for children; one waited one's turn and never, never pushed ahead.

'No, Mummy, I never do. It's what I've seen other kids do,' Libby said virtuously, crossing her fingers in her white woollen gloves. 'Downstairs is full . . . well, almost; shall we go up?' She clattered up the stairs and, glancing behind her, saw her mother following. Then she looked down the aisle and saw to her dismay that almost all the seats were taken up here too. However, there was one right at the very front and another half a dozen rows back, so she hurried up the aisle whilst the tram was still stationary, took her place on the front seat, and saw her mother slide into the other vacant one.

Then she settled back to enjoy the ride, for the front of the tram was her very favourite place. She reflected that not even the tram driver had a better view, and hoped that the falling snow would not stick to the glass. Unfortunately, it did so, but the side window remained clear, and when the large and bewhiskered man seated next to it saw her trying to peer past him he grinned cheerfully at her. 'Hang on, queen. If you want to sit agin the window, then we'd best swap places,' he said. 'I'm gerrin' out in another half-mile or so, an' it takes me all me time to walk the length of the tram and geddown them 'orrible stairs wi'out fallin' flat on me face. If I'm on the outside seat I'll gerra head start.'

13

Changing places, Libby thanked him very prettily, dug in her pocket, and produced an Everton mint, which he accepted after an initial pretence of reluctance. Then she pressed her small nose against the glass and began to scan the shop windows and the scurrying crowds. For the first time she realised that there were a large number of men on the pavement below, many of them in naval uniform, and this made her think that probably a ship, or ships, had just docked. How lovely it would be if she spotted her father; after all, he had hoped to be home for Christmas so it was perfectly possible that his corvette, the *Marjoram*, might be in port right now. Naturally, the thought made Libby stare harder than ever, planning as she did so how, if she saw him, she would bang on the glass, then run as fast as she could towards the stairs, shouting the news to her mother, ringing the bell to warn the driver, and diving off at the very next stop. And how thrilled Daddy would be to find his little girl rushing towards him through the thickening snowflakes! She would make him get aboard the tram and join her mother on the top deck, chattering away to him as she did so, clutching his hand, helping him with his Gladstone bag and not asking him whether he had brought her a present for, though he always tried to do so, in wartime it was not always possible.

But of course all of this depended on her seeing her daddy and she realised, with a little dismay, that identifying someone when you could only see